CLYMER®

SUZUKI

LT-4WD, LT-4WDX & LT-F250 • 1987-1995

The world's finest publisher of mechanical how-to manuals

PRIMEDIA
Business Directories & Books

P.O. Box 12901, Overland Park, Kansas 66282-2901

Copyright ©1995 PRIMEDIA Business Magazines & Media Inc.

FIRST EDITION
First Printing September, 1995
Second Printing October, 1997
Third Printing November, 1998
Fourth Printing September, 1999
Fifth Printing December, 2000
Sixth Printing February, 2002

Printed in U.S.A.

CLYMER and colophon are registered trademarks of PRIMEDIA Business Magazines & Media Inc.

ISBN: 0-89287-643-3

Library of Congress: 94-79864

Technical photography by Ed Scott.

Technical and photographic assistance by Curt Jordan, Jordan Engineering, Santa Ana, California.

Technical illustrations by Mitzi McCarthy and Robert Caldwell.

COVER: Photographed by Mark Clifford, Mark Clifford Photography, Los Angeles, California.

PRODUCTION: Dylan Goodwin.

CONTENTS

QUICK REFERENCE DATA

TIRE INFLATION PRESSURE (COLD)*

| | Tire pressure | | | |
| | Front tires | | Rear tires | |
Load capacity	kPa	psi	kPa	psi
LT-F250 models				
All loads	25	3.6	25	3.6
LT-4WD models				
Up to 80 kg (175 lb.)	30	4.4	20	2.9
80-172 kg (175-380 lb.)	35	5.1	20	2.9
LT-4WDX models				
All loads up to 177 kg	30	4.4	27.5	4.0
(90 lb.) maximum				

* Tire inflation pressure for original equipment tires. Aftermarket tires may require different inflation pressure.

REFILL CAPACITIES AND SPECIFICATIONS

	Capacity	Type
Fuel tank		85-95 octane
Including reserve	12 liters (3.2 U.S gal.)	or higher
Reserve only	2.0 liters (2.1 U.S qt.)	
Engine oil		SAE 10W/40
Oil change	3,500 ml (3.7 U.S. qts.)	
Oil and filter change	3,600 ml (3.8 U.S. qts.)	
Engine overhaul	3,860 ml (4.1 U.S. qts.)	
Front differential	150 ml (5.1 U.S. oz)	Hypoid gear oil
(4-wheel drive)		SAE 90 (GL-5)

TUNE-UP AND MAINTENANCE TIGHTENING TORQUES

Item	N•m	ft.-lb.
Cylinder head 8 mm nuts		
250 cc	18-23	13-16.5
280 cc	21-25	15-18
Cylinder head-to-cylinder 6 mm nuts	7-11	5-8
Cylinder to-crankcase 6 mm nuts	7-11	5-8
Timing hole cap (17 mm)	20-25	14.5-18.0
Engine oil drain plug	18-23	13-16.5
Front differential		
Fill cap	20-30	14.5-21.5
Drain bolt	20-30	14.5-21.5
Exhaust system		
Exhaust pipe-to-cylinder head nuts	9-12	6.5-8.5
Muffler-to-exhaust pipe bolt	18-23	13-16.5
Muffler mounting bolts	18-28	13-20

TUNE-UP SPECIFICATIONS

Valve clearance	
Intake	0.03-0.08 mm (0.001-0.003 in.)
Exhaust	0.08-0.13 mm (0.003-0.005 in.)
Compression pressure (at sea level)	
Standard	1,000-1,400 kPa (142-199 psi)
Service limit (min.)	800 kPa (114 psi)
Spark plug standard type	
U.S. models	NGK D7EA, ND X22ES-U
Canadian models	NGK DR7EA, ND X22ESR-U
Spark plug gap	0.6-0.7 mm (0.024-0.028 in.)
Idle speed	
250 cc models	1,350-1,450 rpm
280 cc models	1,400-1,600 rpm
Pilot screw initial opening	
250 cc models	2 turns out
280 cc models 2 5/8 turns out	

REPLACEMENT BULBS

Item and Model	Voltage/Wattage
Headlight	
LT-250	12V 45/45W
LT-4WD, LT-4WDX	12V 30/30W
Taillight	12V 5W
Speedometer and odometer	12V 3.4W
Indicator light	
LT-250	12V 2W
LT-4WD, LT-4WDX	12V 3.4W

CLYMER®

SUZUKI

LT-4WD, LT-4WDX & LT-F250 • 1987-1995

INTRODUCTION

This detailed, comprehensive manual covers the Suzuki LT-F250, LT-4WD and LT-4WDX from 1987-on.

The expert text gives complete information on maintenance, tune-up, repair and overhaul. Hundreds of photos and drawings guide you through every step. The book includes all you will need to know to keep your Suzuki running right.

A shop manual is a reference. You want to be able to find information fast. As in all Clymer books, this one is designed with you in mind. All chapters are thumb tabbed. Important items are extensively indexed at the rear of the book. All procedures, tables, photos, etc., in this manual are for the reader who may be working on the vehicle for the first time or using this manual for the first time. All the most frequently used specifications and capacities are summarized in the *Quick Reference Data* pages at the front of the book.

Keep the book handy in your tool box. It will help you better understand how your vehicle runs, lower repair costs and generally improve your satisfaction with the vehicle.

CHAPTER ONE

GENERAL INFORMATION

This detailed, comprehensive manual covers the Suzuki LT-F250, LT-4WD and LT-4WDX from 1987-on.

Troubleshooting, tune-up, maintenance and repair are not difficult, if you know what tools and equipment to use and what to do. Step-by-step instructions guide you through jobs ranging from simple maintenance to complete engine and suspension overhaul.

This manual can be used by anyone from a first time do-it-yourselfer to a professional mechanic. Detailed drawings and clear photographs give you all the information you need to do the work right.

Some of the procedures in this manual require the use of special tools. The resourceful mechanic can, in many cases, think of acceptable substitutes for special tools—there is always another way. This can be as simple as using a few pieces of threaded rod, washers and nuts to remove or install a bearing or fabricating a tool from scrap material. However, using a substitute for a special tool is not recommended as it can be dangerous to you and may damage the part. If you find that a tool can be designed and safely made, but will require some type of machine work, you may want to search out a local community college or high school that has a machine shop curriculum. Shop teachers sometimes welcome outside work that can be used as practical shop applications for advanced students.

Table 1 lists the chassis serial numbers (VIN) for models covered in this manual.

Metric and U.S. standards are used throughout this manual. U.S. to metric conversion is given in **Table 2**.

Tables 1-5 are found at the end of the chapter.

MANUAL ORGANIZATION

This chapter provides general information and discusses equipment and tools useful both for preventive maintenance and troubleshooting.

Chapter Two provides methods and suggestions for quick and accurate diagnosis and repair of problems. Troubleshooting procedures discuss typical symptoms and logical methods to pinpoint the trouble.

Chapter Three explains all periodic lubrication and routine maintenance necessary to keep your Suzuki operating well. Chapter Three also includes recommended tune-up procedures, eliminating the need to consult other chapters on the various assemblies.

Subsequent chapters describe specific systems such as the engine top end, engine bottom end, clutch assemblies, transmission, sub-transmission, fuel, exhaust, electrical, suspension, 2-wheel and 4-wheel drive-trains, steering and brakes. Each chapter provides disassembly, repair, and assembly procedures in simple step-by-step form. If a repair is impractical for a home mechanic, it is so indicated. It is usually faster and less expensive to take such repairs to a Suzuki dealer or competent repair shop. Specifications concerning a particular system are included at the end of the appropriate chapter.

NOTES, CAUTIONS AND WARNINGS

The terms NOTE, CAUTION and WARNING have specific meanings in this manual. A NOTE provides additional information to make a step or procedure easier or clearer. Disregarding a NOTE could cause inconvenience, but would not cause damage or personal injury.

A CAUTION emphasizes areas where equipment damage could occur. Disregarding a CAUTION could cause permanent mechanical damage; however, personal injury is unlikely.

A WARNING emphasizes areas where personal injury or even death could result from negligence. Mechanical damage may also occur. WARNINGS *are to be taken seriously.* In some cases, serious injury and death has resulted from disregarding similar warnings.

SAFETY FIRST

Professional mechanics can work for years and never sustain a serious injury. If you observe a few rules of common sense and safety, you can enjoy many safe hours servicing your own machine. If you ignore these rules you can hurt yourself or damage the equipment.

1. *Never* use gasoline as a cleaning solvent.

> *WARNING*
> *Gasoline should only be stored in an approved safety gasoline storage container, properly labeled. Spilled gasoline should be wiped up immediately.*

2. Never smoke or use a torch in the vicinity of flammable liquids, such as cleaning solvent, in open containers.

3. If welding or brazing is required on the machine, remove the fuel tank and rear shock to a safe distance, at least 50 feet away.

4. Use the proper sized wrenches to avoid damage to fasteners and injury to yourself.

5. When loosening a tight or stuck nut, be guided by what would happen if the wrench should slip. Be careful; protect yourself accordingly.

6. When replacing a fastener, make sure to use one with the same measurements and strength as the old one. Incorrect or mismatched fasteners can result in damage to the vehicle and possible personal injury. Beware of fastener kits that are filled with cheap and poorly made nuts, bolts, washers and cotter pins. Refer to *Fasteners* in this chapter for additional information.

7. Keep all hand and power tools in good condition. Wipe greasy and oily tools after using them. They are difficult to hold and can cause injury. Replace or repair worn or damaged tools.

8. Keep your work area clean and uncluttered.

9. Wear safety goggles during all operations involving drilling, grinding, the use of a cold chisel or anytime you feel unsure about the safety of your

eyes. Safety goggles (**Figure 1**) should also be worn anytime solvent and compressed air are used to clean a part.

10. Keep an approved fire extinguisher (**Figure 2**) nearby. Be sure it is rated for gasoline (Class B) and electrical (Class C) fires.

11. When drying bearings or other rotating parts with compressed air, never allow the air jet to rotate the bearing or part. The air jet is capable of rotating them at speeds far in excess of those for which they were designed. The bearing or rotating part is very likely to disintegrate and cause serious injury and damage. To prevent bearing damage when using compressed air, hold the inner bearing race by hand (**Figure 3**).

SERVICE HINTS

Most of the service procedures covered are straightforward and can be performed by anyone

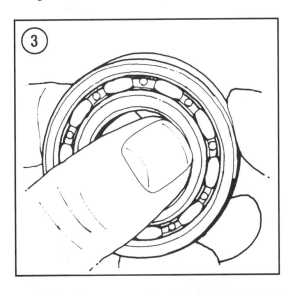

reasonably handy with tools. It is suggested, however, that you consider your own capabilities carefully before attempting any operation involving major disassembly of the engine or transmission.

Take your time and do the job right. Do not forget that a newly rebuilt engine must be broken in the same way as a new one. Keep the rpm's within the limits given in your Suzuki owner's manual when you get the vehicle back on the dirt.

NOTE
Some of the procedures or service specifications listed in this manual may not be applicable if your Suzuki has been modified or if it has been equipped with non-stock equipment. When modifying or installing non-stock equipment, file all printed instruction or technical information regarding the new equipment in a folder or notebook for future reference. If your Suzuki was purchased second hand, the previous owner may have installed non-stock parts. If necessary, consult with your dealer or the accessory manufacturer on components that may affect tuning or repair procedures.

1. "Front," as used in this manual, refers to the front of the vehicle; the front of any component is the end closest to the front of the vehicle. The "left-" and "right-hand" sides refer to the position of the parts as viewed by a rider sitting on the seat facing forward. For example, the throttle control is on the right-hand side. These rules are simple, but confusion can cause a major inconvenience during service.

2. Whenever servicing the engine or clutch, or when removing a suspension component, the vehicle should be secured in a safe manner and the parking brake applied.

WARNING
Never disconnect the positive (+) battery cable unless the negative (−) cable has first been disconnected. Disconnecting the positive cable while the negative cable is still connected may cause a spark. This could ignite hydrogen gas given off by the battery, causing an explosion.

3. Disconnect the negative battery cable (**Figure 4**) when working on or near the electrical, clutch or starter systems and before disconnecting any elec-

trical wires. On most batteries, the negative terminal will be marked with a minus (–) sign and the positive terminal with a plus (+) sign.

4. Tag all similar internal parts for location and mark all mating parts for position (A, **Figure 5**). Record number and thickness of any shims as they are removed. Small parts such as bolts can be identified by placing them in plastic sandwich bags (B, **Figure 5**). Seal and label them with masking tape.

5. Place parts from a specific area of the engine (e.g. cylinder head, cylinder, clutch, shift mechanism, etc.) into plastic boxes (C, **Figure 5**) to keep them separated.

6. When disassembling transmission shaft assemblies, use an egg flat (the type that restaurants get their eggs in) (D, **Figure 5**) and set the parts from the shaft in one of the depressions in the same order in which it is removed.

7. Wiring should be tagged with masking tape and marked as each wire is removed. Again, do not rely on memory alone.

8. Finished surfaces should be protected from physical damage or corrosion. Keep gasoline and brake fluid off painted surfaces.

9. Use penetrating oil on frozen or tight bolts, then strike the bolt head a few times with a hammer and punch (use a screwdriver on screws). Avoid the use of heat where possible, as it can warp, melt or affect the temper of parts. Heat also ruins finishes, especially paint and plastics.

10. No parts removed or installed (other than bushings and bearings) in the procedures given in this manual should require unusual force during disassembly or assembly. If a part is difficult to remove or install, find out why before proceeding.

11. Cover all openings after removing parts or components to prevent dirt, small tools, etc. from falling in.

12. Read each procedure *completely* while looking at the actual parts before starting a job. Make sure you *thoroughly* understand what is to be done and then carefully follow the procedure, step-by-step.

13. Recommendations are occasionally made to refer service or maintenance to a Suzuki dealer or a specialist in a particular field. In these cases, the work will be done more quickly and economically than if you performed the job yourself.

14. In procedural steps, the term "replace" means to discard a defective part and replace it with a new or exchange unit. "Overhaul" means to remove, disas-

semble, inspect, measure, repair or replace defective parts, reassemble and install major systems or parts.

15. Some transmission shaft operations require the use of a hydraulic press. It would be wiser to have these operations performed by a shop equipped for such work, rather than to try to do the job yourself with makeshift equipment that may damage your machine.

16. Repairs go much faster and easier if your machine is clean before you begin work. There are many special cleaners on the market, like Bel-Ray Degreaser, for washing the engine and related parts. Follow the manufacturer's directions on the container for the best results. Clean all oily or greasy parts with cleaning solvent as you remove them. See *Washing the Vehicle* in this chapter.

> *WARNING*
> *Never use gasoline as a cleaning agent. It presents an extreme fire hazard. Be sure to work in a well-ventilated area when using cleaning solvent. Keep a fire extinguisher, rated for gasoline fires, handy in any case.*

17. Much of the labor charge for repairs made by dealers are for the time involved during in the removal, disassembly, assembly and reinstallation of other parts in order to reach the defective part. It is frequently possible to perform the preliminary operations yourself and then take the defective unit to the dealer for repair at considerable savings.

18. If special tools are required, make arrangements to get them before you start. It is frustrating and

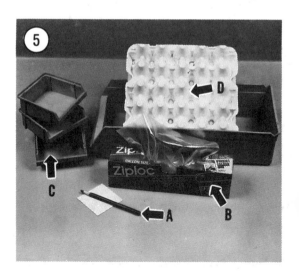

time-consuming to get partly into a job and then be unable to complete it.

19. Make diagrams (or take a Polaroid picture) wherever similar-appearing parts are found. For instance, crankcase bolts are often not the same length. You may think you can remember where everything came from—but mistakes are costly. There is also the possibility that you may be sidetracked and not return to work for days or even weeks—in which time the carefully laid out parts may have become disturbed.

20. When assembling parts, be sure all shims and washers are replaced exactly as they came out.

21. Whenever a rotating part butts against a stationary part, look for a shim or washer. Use new gaskets if there is any doubt about the condition of the old ones. A thin coat of oil on non-pressure type gaskets may help them seal more effectively.

22. High spots may be sanded off a piston with sandpaper, but fine emery cloth and oil will do a much more professional job.

23. Carbon can be removed from the head, the piston crowns and the exhaust ports with a dull screwdriver. Do *not* scratch machined surfaces. Wipe off the surface with a clean cloth when finished.

24. If it is necessary to make a clutch cover or ignition cover gasket and you do not have a suitable old gasket to use as a guide, you can use the outline of the cover and gasket material to make a new gasket. Apply engine oil to the cover gasket surface. Then place the cover on the new gasket material and apply pressure with your hands. The oil will leave a very accurate outline on the gasket material that can be cut around.

CAUTION
When purchasing gasket material to make a gasket, measure the thickness of the old gasket and purchase gasket material with the same approximate thickness.

25. Heavy grease can be used to hold small parts in place if they tend to fall out during assembly. However, keep grease and oil away from electrical and brake components.

26. The carburetor is best cleaned by disassembling it and soaking the parts in a commercial cleaning solvent. Never soak gaskets and rubber parts in these cleaners. Never use wire to clean out jets and air passages. They are easily damaged. Use compressed air to blow out the carburetor only if the float has been removed first.

27. There are many items available that can be used on your hands before and after working on your vehicle. A little preparation prior to getting "all greased up" will help when cleaning up later. Before starting out, work Vaseline, soap or a product such as Invisible Glove onto your forearms, into your hands and under your fingernails and cuticles. This will make cleanup a lot easier. For cleanup, use a waterless hand soap such as Sta-Lube and then finish up with powdered Boraxo and a fingernail brush.

WASHING THE VEHICLE

Since the vehicle is an off-road vehicle designed for use on construction sights, agricultural areas, etc., you will spend a lot of time cleaning the ATV if you want to maintain it properly. After riding it in extremely dirty areas, wash it down thoroughly. Doing this will make maintenance and service procedures quick and easy. More important, proper cleaning will prevent dirt from falling into critical areas undetected. Failing to clean the vehicle or cleaning it incorrectly will add to your maintenance costs and shop time because dirty parts wear out prematurely. It's unthinkable that your vehicle could break down because of improper cleaning, but it can happen.

When cleaning your Suzuki, you will need a few tools, shop rags, scrub brush, bucket, liquid cleaner and access to water. Many owners use a coin-operated car wash. Coin-operated car washes are convenient and quick, but with improper use, the high water pressures can do more damage than good to your vehicle.

CAUTION
If you use a car wash to clean your vehicle, don't direct the high pressure water hose at steering column bearings, carburetor hoses, suspension linkage components, brake back panels, wheel bearings and electrical components. The water will flush grease out of the bearings or damage the seals.

NOTE
A safe biodegradable, nontoxic and nonflammable liquid cleaner that works well for washing your vehicle as well as

for removing grease and oil from engine and suspension parts is Simple Green. Simple Green can be purchased through some supermarkets, hardware, garden and discount supply houses. Follow the directions on the container for recommended dilution ratios.

When cleaning your vehicle and especially when using a spray type degreaser, remember that what goes on the vehicle will rinse off and drip onto your driveway or into your yard. If you can, use a degreaser at a coin-operated car wash. If you are cleaning your vehicle at home, place thick cardboard or newspapers underneath the vehicle to catch the oil and grease deposits that are rinsed off.

1. Place the vehicle on level ground and set the parking brake.

2. Check the following before washing the vehicle:
   a. Make sure the gas filler cap is screwed on tightly.
   b. Make sure the engine oil, front differential, front gear case and final drive unit fill caps are tight.
   c. Plug the muffler opening with a large cork or rag.

3. Wash the vehicle from top to bottom with soapy water. Use the scrub brush to get excess dirt out of the wheel rims and engine crannies. Concentrate on the upper controls, engine, side panels and gas tank during this wash cycle. Don't forget to wash dirt and mud from underneath the fenders, suspension and engine crankcase.

4. Wrap a plastic bag around the ignition coil and CDI unit. Concentrate the second wash cycle on the frame tube members, outer airbox areas, suspension linkage and shock absorbers.

5. Direct the hose underneath the engine. Wash this area thoroughly. If this area is extremely dirty, you may want to tip the vehicle up on its rear wheels and rear carrier. Protect the finish when placing the vehicle in this position.

6. The final step is rinsing. Use cold water without soap and spray the entire vehicle again. Use as much time and care when rinsing the vehicle as when washing it. Built up soap deposits will quickly corrode electrical connections and remove the natural oils from tires, causing premature cracks and wear. Make sure you thoroughly rinse the vehicle off.

7. Tip the vehicle from side-to-side to allow any water that has collected on horizontal surfaces to drain off.

8. If you are washing the vehicle at home, start the engine. Idle the engine to burn off any residual moisture.

9. Before taking the vehicle into the garage, wipe it dry with a soft cloth or chamois. Inspect the machine as you dry it for further signs of dirt and grime. Make a quick visual inspection of the frame and other painted pieces. Spray any worn-down spots with WD-40 or Bel-Ray 6-in-1 to prevent rust from building on the bare metal. When the vehicle is back at your work area you can repaint the bare areas with touch-up paint after thoroughly cleaning off all WD-40 residue. A quick shot from a touch-up paint can each time you work on the vehicle will keep it looking sharp and stop rust from building and weakening parts.

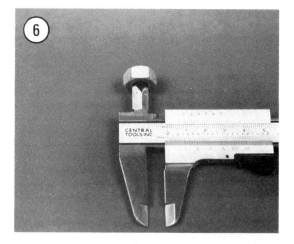

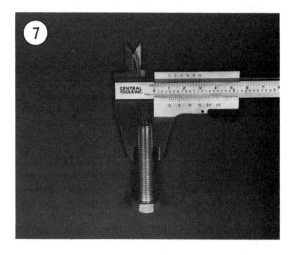

TORQUE SPECIFICATIONS

Torque specifications throughout this manual are given in Newton-meters (N•m) and foot-pounds (ft.-lb.).

Existing torque wrenches calibrated in meter kilograms can be used by performing a simple conversion. All you have to do is move the decimal point one place to the right—for example, 3.5 mkg = 35 N•m. This conversion is accurate enough for mechanical work even though the exact mathematical conversion is 3.5 mkg = 34.3 N•m.

Refer to **Table 3** for standard torque specifications for various size screws, bolts and nuts that may not be listed in the respective chapters. To use the table,

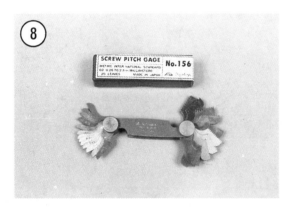

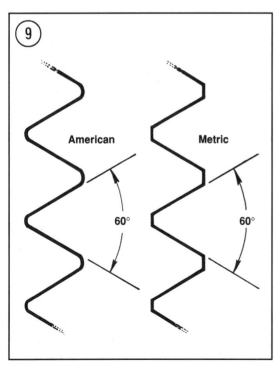

first determine the size of the bolt or nut. Use a vernier caliper and measure the inside dimension of the threads of the nut (**Figure 6**) and across the threads for a bolt (**Figure 7**).

FASTENERS

The materials and designs of the various fasteners used on your Suzuki are not arrived at by chance or accident. Fastener design determines the type of tool required to work the fastener. Fastener material is carefully selected to decrease the possibility of physical failure.

Nuts, bolts and screws are manufactured in a wide range of thread patterns. To join a nut and bolt, the diameter of the bolt and the diameter of the hole in the nut must be the same. It is just as important that the threads on both be properly matched.

The best way to tell if the threads on 2 fasteners are matched is to turn the nut on the bolt (or the bolt into the threaded hole in a piece of equipment) with fingers only. Be sure both pieces are clean. If much force is required, check the thread condition on each fastener. If the thread condition is good but the fasteners jam, the threads are not compatible. A thread pitch gauge (**Figure 8**) can also be used to determine pitch. Suzuki ATV's are manufactured with ISO (International Organization for Standardization) metric fasteners. The threads are cut differently than that of American fasteners (**Figure 9**).

Most threads are cut so that the fastener must be turned clockwise to tighten it. These are called right-hand threads. Some fasteners have left-hand threads; they must be turned counterclockwise to be tightened. Left-hand threads are used in locations where normal rotation of the equipment would tend to loosen a right-hand threaded fastener.

ISO Metric Screw Threads

ISO (International Organization for Standardization) metric threads come in 3 standard thread sizes: coarse, fine and constant pitch. The ISO coarse pitch is used for most all common fastener applications. The fine pitch thread is used on certain precision tools and instruments. The constant pitch thread is used mainly on machine parts and not for fasteners. The constant pitch thread, however, is used on all metric thread spark plugs.

ISO metric threads are specified by the capital letter M followed by the diameter in millimeters and the pitch (or the distance between each thread) in millimeters separated by the sign "—". For example a M8—1.25 bolt is one that has a diameter of 8 millimeters with a distance of 1.25 millimeters between each thread. The measurement across 2 flats on the head of the bolt (**Figure 10**) indicates the proper wrench size to be used. **Figure 11** shows how to determine bolt diameter.

> *NOTE*
> *When purchasing a bolt from a dealer or parts store, it is important to know how to specify bolt length. The correct way to measure bolt length is by measuring the length starting from underneath the bolt head to the end of the bolt (Figure 12). Always measure bolt length in this manner to avoid purchasing bolts that are too long.*

Machine Screws

There are many different types of machine screws. **Figure 13** shows a number of screw heads requiring different types of turning tools. Heads are also designed to protrude above the metal (round) or to be slightly recessed in the metal (flat). See **Figure 14**.

Bolts

Commonly called bolts, the technical name for these fasteners is cap screws. Metric bolts are described by the diameter and pitch (or the distance between each thread). For example a M8—1.25 bolt is one that has a diameter of 8 millimeters and a distance of 1.25 millimeters between each thread. The measurement across 2 flats on the head of the bolt (**Figure 10**) indicates the proper wrench size to be used. Use a vernier caliper and measure across the threads (**Figure 7**) to determine the bolt diameter and to measure the length (**Figure 12**).

Nuts

Nuts are manufactured in a variety of types and sizes. Most are hexagonal (6-sided) and fit on bolts, screws and studs with the same diameter and pitch.

Figure 15 shows several types of nuts. The common nut is generally used with a lockwasher. Self-

locking nuts have a nylon insert which prevents the nut from loosening; no lockwasher is required. Wing nuts are designed for fast removal by hand. Wing nuts are used for convenience in non-critical locations.

To indicate the size of a metric nut, manufacturers specify the diameter of the opening and the thread pitch. This is similar to bolt specifications, but without the length dimension. The measurement across 2 flats on the nut indicates the proper wrench size to be used (**Figure 16**).

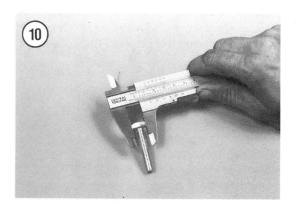

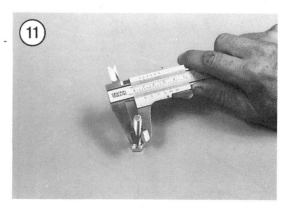

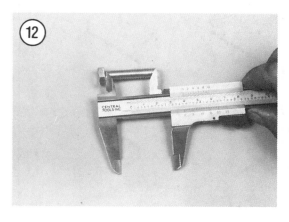

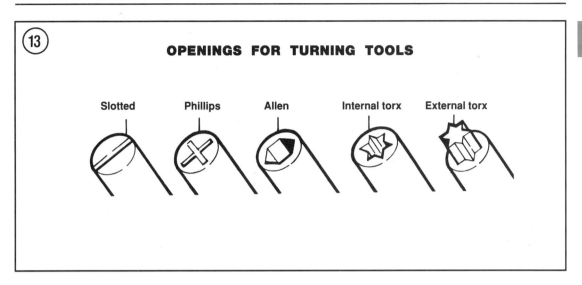

⑬ **OPENINGS FOR TURNING TOOLS**

Slotted   Phillips   Allen   Internal torx   External torx

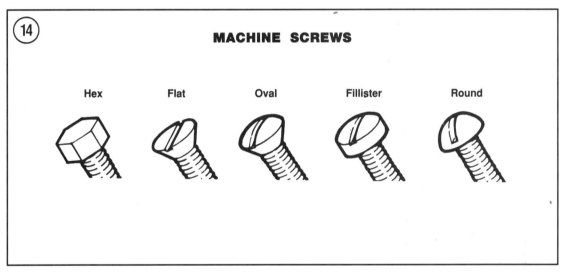

⑭ **MACHINE SCREWS**

Hex   Flat   Oval   Fillister   Round

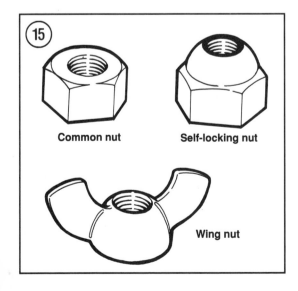

⑮

Common nut   Self-locking nut

Wing nut

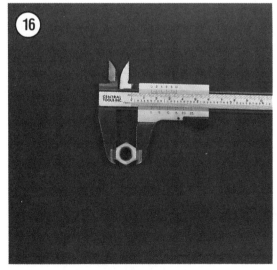

⑯

Self-Locking Fasteners

Several types of bolts, screws and nuts incorporate a system that develops an interference between the bolt, screw, nut or tapped hole threads. Interference is achieved in various ways: by distorting threads, coating threads with dry adhesive or nylon, distorting the top of an all-metal nut, using a nylon insert in the center or at the top of a nut, etc.

Prevailing torque fasteners offer greater holding strength and better vibration resistance. Some prevailing torque fasteners can be reused if in good condition. Others, like the nylon insert nut, form an initial locking condition when the nut is first installed; the nylon forms closely to the bolt thread pattern, thus reducing any tendency for the nut to loosen. When the nut is removed, the locking efficiency is greatly reduced. For greatest safety, it is recommended that you install new prevailing torque fasteners whenever they are removed.

Washers

There are 2 basic types of washers: flat washers and lockwashers. Flat washers are simple discs with a hole to fit a screw or bolt. Lockwashers are designed to prevent a fastener from working loose due to vibration, expansion and contraction. **Figure 17** shows several types of washers. Washers are also used in the following functions:

a. As spacers.

b. To prevent galling or damage of the equipment by the fastener.

c. To help distribute fastener load during torquing.

d. As seals.

Note that flat washers are often used between a lockwasher and a fastener to provide a smooth bearing surface. This allows the fastener to be turned easily with a tool.

Cotter Pins

Cotter pins (**Figure 18**) are used to secure special kinds of fasteners. The threaded stud must have a hole in it; the nut or nut lock piece has castellations around which the cotter pin ends wrap. Cotter pins should not be reused after removal.

Circlips

Circlips can be internal or external design. They are used to retain items on shafts (external type) or within tubes (internal type). In some applications, circlips of varying thicknesses are used to control the end play of parts assemblies. These are often called selective circlips. Circlips should be replaced during installation, as removal weakens and deforms them.

Two basic styles of circlips are available: machined and stamped circlips. Machined circlips

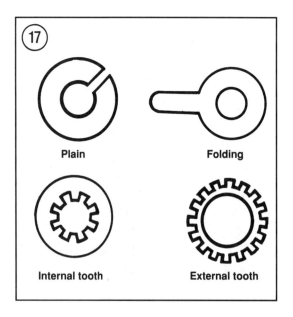

Plain   Folding

Internal tooth   External tooth

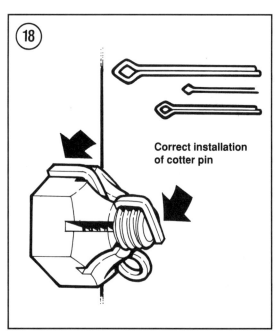

Correct installation of cotter pin

(**Figure 19**) can be installed in either direction (shaft or housing) because both faces are machined, thus creating two sharp edges. Stamped circlips (**Figure 20**) are manufactured with one sharp edge and one rounded edge. When installing stamped circlips in a thrust situation (transmission shafts, fork tubes, etc.), the sharp edge must face away from the part producing the thrust. When installing circlips, observe the following:

a. Compress or expand circlips only enough to install them.

b. After the circlip is installed, make sure it is completely seated in its groove.

Transmission circlips become worn with use and increase side play. For this reason, always use new circlips when ever a transmission is be reassembled.

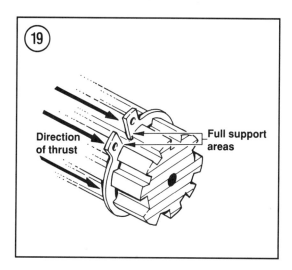

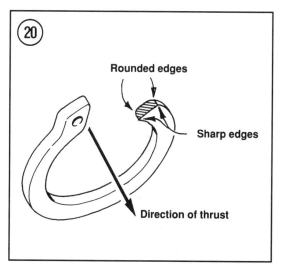

LUBRICANTS

Periodic lubrication assures long life for any type of equipment. The *type* of lubricant used is just as important as the lubrication service itself, although in an emergency the wrong type of lubricant is better than none at all. The following paragraphs describe the types of lubricants most often used on motorcycle equipment. Be sure to follow the manufacturer's recommendations for lubricant types.

Generally, all liquid lubricants are called "oil." They may be mineral-based (including petroleum bases), natural-based (vegetable and animal bases), synthetic-based or emulsions (mixtures). "Grease" is an oil to which a thickening base has been added so that the end product is semi-solid. Grease is often classified by the type of thickener added; lithium soap is commonly used.

Engine Oil

Four-cycle oil for motorcycle and automotive engines is classified by the American Petroleum Institute (API) and the Society of Automotive Engineers (SAE) in several categories. Oil containers display these classifications on the top or label.

API oil classification is indicated by letters; oils for gasoline engines are identified by an "S." Suzuki models described in this manual require SE or SF graded oil.

Viscosity is an indication of the oil's thickness. The SAE uses numbers to indicate viscosity; thin oils have low numbers while thick oils have high numbers. A "W" after the number indicates that the viscosity testing was done at low temperature to simulate cold-weather operation. Engine oils fall into the 5W-30 and 20W-50 range.

Multi-grade oils (for example 10W-40) are less viscous (thinner) at low temperatures and more viscous (thicker) at high temperatures. This allows the oil to perform efficiently across a wide range of engine operating conditions. The lower the number, the better the engine will start in cold climates. Higher numbers are usually recommended for engine running in hot weather conditions.

Grease

Greases are graded by the National Lubricating Grease Institute (NLGI). Greases are graded by number according to the consistency of the grease;

these range from No. 000 to No. 6, with No. 6 being the most solid. A typical multipurpose grease is NLGI No. 2. For specific applications, equipment manufacturers may require grease with an additive such as molybdenum disulfide (MOS2) (**Figure 21**).

RTV GASKET SEALANT

Room temperature vulcanizing (RTV) sealant is used on some pre-formed gaskets and to seal some components. RTV is a silicone gel supplied in tubes and can be purchased in a number of different colors (**Figure 22**).

Moisture in the air causes RTV to cure. Always place the cap on the tube as soon as possible when using RTV. RTV has a shelf life of one year and will not cure properly when the shelf life has expired. Check the expiration date on RTV tubes before using and keep partially used tubes tightly sealed.

Applying RTV Sealant

Clean all gasket residue from mating surfaces. Surfaces should be clean and free of oil and dirt. Remove all RTV gasket material from blind attaching holes, as it can cause a "hydraulic" effect and affect bolt torque.

Apply RTV sealant in a continuous bead. Circle all mounting holes unless otherwise specified. Torque mating parts within 10 minutes after application.

THREADLOCK

A chemical locking compound should be used on all bolts and nuts, even if they are secured with lockwashers. A locking compound will lock fasteners against vibration loosening and seal against leaks. Loctite 242 (blue) and 271 (red) are recommended for many threadlock requirements described in this manual (**Figure 23**).

Loctite 242 (blue) is a medium strength threadlock and component disassembly can be performed with normal hand tools. Loctite 271 (red) is a high strength threadlock and heat or special tools, such as a press or puller, may be required for component disassembly.

Applying Threadlock

Surfaces should be clean and free of oil, grease, dirt and other residue; clean threads with an aerosol electrical contact cleaner before applying the Loctite. When applying Loctite, use a small amount. If too much is used, it can work its way down the threads and stick parts together not meant to be stuck.

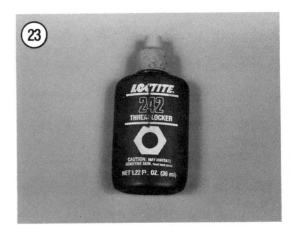

GASKET REMOVER

Stubborn gaskets can present a problem during engine service as they can take a long time to remove. Consequently, there is the added problem of secondary damage occurring to the gasket mating surfaces from the incorrect use of gasket scraping tools. To quickly and safely remove stubborn gaskets, use a spray gasket remover. Spray gasket remover can be purchased through automotive parts houses. Follow the manufacturer's directions for use.

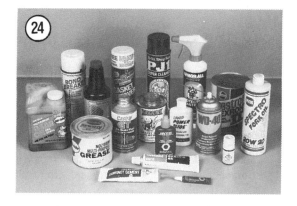

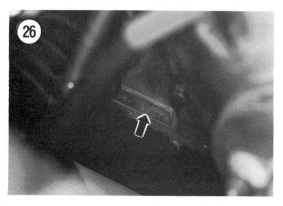

EXPENDABLE SUPPLIES

Certain expendable supplies are required during maintenance and repair work. These include grease, oil, gasket cement, wiping rags and cleaning solvent (**Figure 24**). Ask your dealer for the special locking compounds, silicone lubricants and other products which make ATV maintenance simpler and easier. Cleaning solvent or kerosene is available at some service stations, paint or hardware stores.

WARNING
Having a stack of clean shop rags on hand is important when performing engine and suspension service work. However, to prevent the possibility of fire damage from spontaneous combustion from a pile of solvent soaked rags, store them in a lid sealed metal container until they can be washed or discarded.

NOTE
To avoid absorbing solvent and other chemicals into your skin while cleaning parts, wear a pair of petroleum-resistant rubber gloves. These can be purchased through industrial supply houses or well-equipped hardware stores.

PARTS REPLACEMENT

Suzuki makes frequent changes during a model year, some minor, some relatively major. When you order parts from the dealer or other parts distributor, always order by frame and engine numbers. The frame number serial number is stamped on the rear frame vertical member (**Figure 25**). The engine number is stamped on a raised pad on the rear right-hand side of the crankcase (**Figure 26**) below the rear drive axle.

Write the numbers down and carry them with you. Compare new parts to old before purchasing them. If they are not alike, have the parts manager explain the difference to you. **Table 1** lists engine and frame serial numbers for the models covered in this manual.

NOTE
If your Suzuki was purchased second-hand and you are not sure of its model year, use the vehicle's chassis serial

number and the information listed in **Table 1**. *Read your vehicle's chassis serial number, then compare the number with the chassis serial numbers listed in* **Table 1**. *If your vehicle's serial number is listed in* **Table 1**, *cross-reference the number with the adjacent model number and year.*

BASIC HAND TOOLS

Many of the procedures in this manual can be carried out with simple hand tools and test equipment familiar to the average home mechanic. Keep your tools clean and in a tool box. Keep them organized with the sockets and related drives together, the open-end combination wrenches together, etc. After using a tool, wipe off dirt and grease with a clean cloth and return the tool to its correct place.

Top-quality tools are essential; they are also more economical in the long run. If you are now starting to build your tool collection, stay away from the "advertised specials" featured at some parts houses, discount stores and chain drug stores. These are usually a poor grade tool that can be sold cheaply and that is exactly what they are—*cheap*. They are usually made of inferior material and are thick, heavy and clumsy. Their rough finish makes them difficult to clean and they usually don't last very long. If it is ever your misfortune to use such tools, you will probably find out that the wrenches do not fit the heads of bolts and nuts correctly and damage the fastener.

Quality tools are made of alloy steel and are heat treated for greater strength. They are lighter and better balanced than cheap ones. Their surface is smooth, making them a pleasure to work with and easy to clean. The initial cost of good quality tools may be more but they are cheaper in the long run. Don't try to buy everything in all sizes in the beginning; do it a little at a time until you have the necessary tools.

The following tools are required to perform virtually any repair job on an ATV. Each tool is described and the recommended size given for starting a tool collection. **Table 4** includes the tools that should be on hand for simple home repairs and/or major overhaul as shown in **Figure 27**. Additional tools and some duplicates may be added as you become more familiar with the ATV. Almost all ATVs use metric

size bolts and nuts. If you are starting your collection now, buy metric sizes.

Screwdrivers

The screwdriver is a very basic tool, but if used improperly it will do more damage than good. The slot on a screw has a definite dimension and shape. A screwdriver must be selected to conform with that shape. Use a small screwdriver for small screws and a large one for large screws or the screw head will be damaged.

Two basic types of screwdrivers are required: common (flat- or slot-blade) screwdrivers (**Figure 28**) and Phillips screwdrivers (**Figure 29**).

Note the following when selecting and using screwdrivers:

a. The screwdriver must always fit the screw head. If the screwdriver blade is too small for the screw slot, damage may occur to the screw slot and screwdriver. If the blade is too large, it cannot engage the slot properly and will result in damage to the screw head.

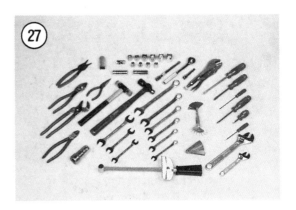

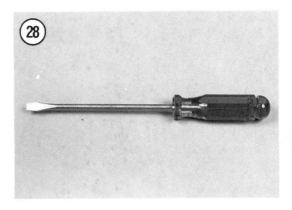

b. Standard screwdrivers are identified by the length of their blade. A 6-inch screwdriver has a blade six inches long. The width of the screwdriver blade will vary, so make sure that the blade engages the screw slot the complete width of the screw.

c. Phillips screwdrivers are sized according to their point size. They are numbered one, two, three and four. The degree of taper determines the point size; the No. 1 Phillips screwdriver will be the most pointed. The points become more blunt as their number increases.

NOTE
You should also be aware of another screwdriver similar to the Phillips, and that is the Reed and Prince tip. Like the Phillips, the Reed and Prince screwdriver tip forms an "X" but with one major exception, the Reed and Prince tip has a much more pointed tip. The Reed and Prince screwdriver should never be used on Phillips screws and vise versa. Intermixing these screwdrivers will cause damage to the screw and screwdriver. If you have both types in your tool box and they are similar in appearance, you may want to identify them by painting the screwdriver shank underneath the handle.

d. When selecting screwdrivers, note that you can apply more power with less effort with a longer screwdriver than with a short one. Of course, there will be situations where only a short handle screwdriver can be used. Keep this in mind though, when having to remove tight screws.

e. Because the working end of a screwdriver receives quite a bit of abuse, you should purchase screwdrivers with hardened tips. The extra money will be well spent.

Screwdrivers are available in sets which often include an assortment of common and Phillips blades. If you buy them individually, buy at least the following:

a. Common screwdriver—5/16 × 6 in. blade.

b. Common screwdriver—3/8 × 12 in. blade.

c. Phillips screwdriver—size 2 tip, 6 in. blade.

d. Phillips screwdriver—size 3 tip, 6 and 8 in. blade.

Use screwdrivers only for driving screws. Never use a screwdriver for prying or chiseling metal. Do not try to remove a Phillips, Torx or Allen head screw with a standard screwdriver (unless the screw has a combination head that will accept either type); you can damage the head so that the proper tool will be unable to remove it.

Keep screwdrivers in the proper condition and they will last longer and perform better. Always keep the tip of a standard screwdriver in good condition. **Figure 30** shows how to grind the tip to the proper shape if it becomes damaged. Note the symmetrical sides of the tip.

Pliers

Pliers come in a wide range of types and sizes. Pliers are useful for cutting, bending and crimping. They should never be used to cut hardened objects or to turn bolts or nuts. **Figure 31** shows several pliers useful in repairing your Suzuki.

Each type of pliers has a specialized function. Slip-joint pliers are general purpose pliers and are used mainly for holding things and for bending. Needlenose pliers are used to hold or bend small objects. Water pump pliers can be adjusted to hold various sizes of objects; the jaws remain parallel to grip around objects such as pipe or tubing. There are many more types of pliers.

CAUTION
Pliers should not be used for loosening or tightening nuts or bolts. The pliers' sharp teeth will grind off the nut or bolt corners and damage it.

CAUTION
If slip-joint or water pump pliers are going to be used to hold an object with

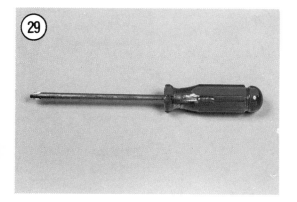

(29)

a finished surface, wrap the object with tape or cardboard for protection.

Vise-grip Pliers

Vise-grip pliers (**Figure 32**) are used to hold objects very tightly while another task is performed on the object. While vise-grip pliers work well, caution should be followed with their use. Because vise-grip pliers exert more force than regular pliers, their sharp jaws can permanently scar the object. In addition, when vise-grip pliers are locked into position, they can crush or deform thin wall material.

Vise-grip pliers are available in many types for more specific tasks.

Circlip Pliers

Circlip pliers (**Figure 33**) are special in that they are only used to remove circlips from shafts or

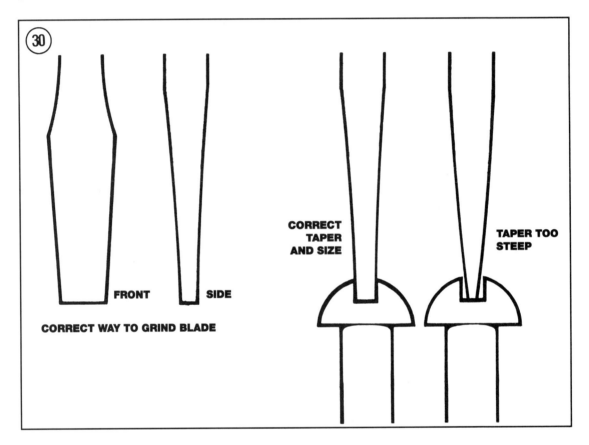

CORRECT TAPER AND SIZE

TAPER TOO STEEP

FRONT   SIDE

CORRECT WAY TO GRIND BLADE

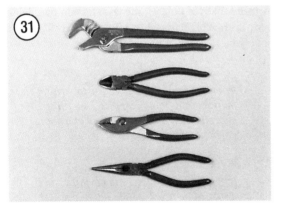

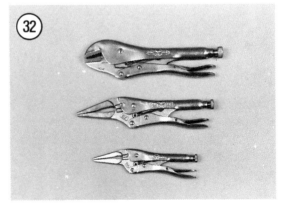

within engine or suspension housings. When purchasing circlip pliers, there are two kinds to distinguish from. External pliers (spreading) are used to remove circlips that fit on the outside of a shaft. Internal pliers (squeezing) are used to remove circlips which fit inside a gear or housing.

WARNING
Because circlips can sometimes slip and "fly off" during removal and installation, always wear safety glasses.

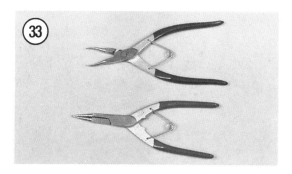

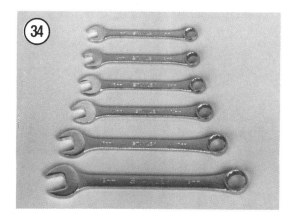

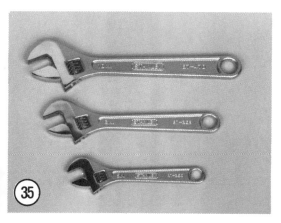

Box-end, Open-end and Combination Wrenches

Box-end, open-end and combination wrenches are available in sets or separately in a variety of sizes. On open- and box-end wrenches, the number stamped near the end refers to the distance between 2 parallel flats on the hex head bolt or nut. On combination wrenches, the number is stamped near the center.

Open-end wrenches are speedy and work best in areas with limited overhead access. Their wide flat jaws make them unstable for situations where the bolt or nut is sunken in a well or close to the edge of a casting. These wrenches grip only two flats of a fastener so if either the fastener head or the wrench jaws are worn, the wrench may slip off.

Box-end wrenches require clear overhead access to the fastener but can work well in situations where the fastener head is close to another part. They grip on all six edges of a fastener for a very secure grip. They are available in either 6-point or 12-point. The 6-point gives superior holding power and durability but requires a greater swinging radius. The 12-point works better in situations with limited swinging radius.

Combination wrenches (**Figure 34**) have open-end on one side and box-end on the other with both ends being the same size. These wrenches are favored by professionals because of their versatility.

Adjustable Wrenches

An adjustable wrench (sometimes called crescent wrench) can be adjusted to fit nearly any nut or bolt head which has clear access around its entire perimeter. Adjustable wrenches (**Figure 35**) are best used as a backup wrench to keep a large nut or bolt from turning while the other end is being loosened or tightened with a proper wrench.

Adjustable wrenches have only two gripping surfaces, which make them more subject to slipping off the fastener, damaging the part and possibly injuring your hand. The fact that one jaw is adjustable only aggravates this shortcoming.

These wrenches are directional; the solid jaw must be the one transmitting the force. If you use the adjustable jaw to transmit the force, it will loosen and possibly slip off.

Adjustable wrenches come in all sizes but something in the 6 to 8 in. range is recommended as an all-purpose wrench.

Socket Wrenches

This type is undoubtedly the fastest, safest and most convenient to use. Sockets which attach to a ratchet handle (**Figure 36**) are available with 6-point or 12-point openings and 1/4, 3/8, 1/2 and 3/4 in. drives. The drive size indicates the size of the square hole which mates with the ratchet handle.

Allen Wrenches

Allen wrenches are available in sets or separately in a variety of sizes. These sets come in U.S. standard and metric size, so be sure to buy a metric set. Allen bolts are sometimes called socket bolts. Some times the bolts are difficult to reach and it is suggested that a variety of Allen wrenches be purchased (e.g. socket driven, T-handle and extension type) as shown in **Figure 37**.

Torque Wrench

A torque wrench is used with a socket to measure how tightly a nut or bolt is installed. They come in a wide price range and with either 3/8 or 1/2 in. square drive (**Figure 38**). The drive size indicates the size of the square drive which mates with the socket. Purchase one that measures 0-280 N•m (0-200 ft.-lb.).

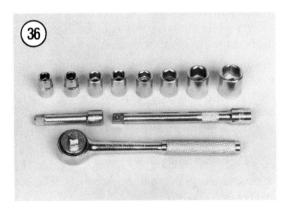

Impact Driver

This tool might have been designed with the ATV in mind. This tool makes removal of fasteners easy and minimizes damage to bolts and screw slots. Impact drivers and interchangeable bits (**Figure 39**) are available at most large hardware, motorcycle or auto parts stores. Don't purchase a cheap one as they do not work as well and require more force (the "use a larger hammer" syndrome) than a moderately priced one. Sockets and Allen wrenches can also be used with a hand impact driver. However, make sure

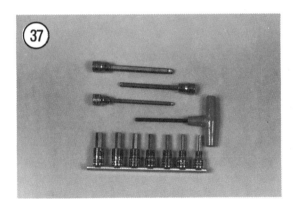

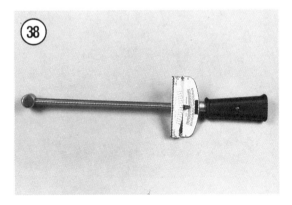

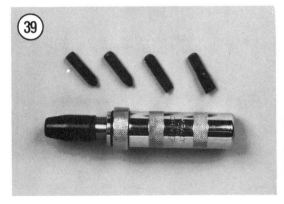

that the socket, or Allen wrench, is designed for use with an impact driver or air tool. Do not use regular hand sockets, as they may shatter during use.

Hammers

The correct hammer (**Figure 40**) is essential to perform certain repairs. A hammer with a face (or head) of rubber or plastic or the soft-faced type that is filled with lead shot are sometimes necessary in engine tear downs. Never use a metal-faced hammer on engine or suspension parts, as severe damage will result in most cases. Ball-peen or machinist's hammers are required when striking another tool, such as a punch or impact driver. When striking a hammer against a punch, cold chisel or similar tool, the face of the hammer should be at least 1/2 in. (12.7 mm) larger than the head of the tool. When it is necessary to strike hard against a steel part without damaging it, a brass hammer should be used. A brass hammer can be used because brass will give when striking a harder object.

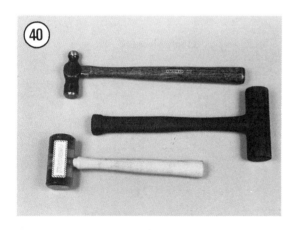

When using hammers, note the following:
a. Always wear safety glasses when using a hammer.
b. Inspect hammers for damaged or broken parts. Repair or replace the hammer as required. Do not use a hammer with a taped handle.
c. Always wipe oil or grease off of the hammer before using it.
d. The head of the hammer should always strike the object squarely. Do not use the side of the hammer or the handle to strike an object.
e. Always use the correct hammer for the job.

Tap and Die Set

A complete tap and die set (**Figure 41**) is a relatively expensive tool. However, when you need a tap or die to clean up a damaged thread, there is really no substitute. Be sure to purchase one for metric threads when working on your Suzuki.

Drivers and Pullers

These tools are used to remove and install oil seals, bushings, bearings and gears. These will be called out during service procedures in later chapters as required.

TEST EQUIPMENT

Multimeter or VOM

This instrument (**Figure 42**) is invaluable for electrical system troubleshooting. See *Electrical Troubleshooting* in Chapter Eight for its use.

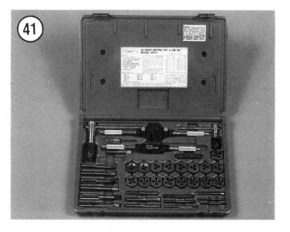

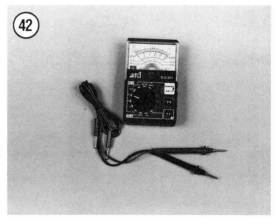

Compression Gauge

An engine with low compression cannot be properly tuned and will not develop full power. A compression gauge (**Figure 43**) measures engine compression. The one shown has a flexible stem with an extension that can allow you to hold it while cranking the engine. Open the throttle all the way when checking engine compression. See Chapter Three.

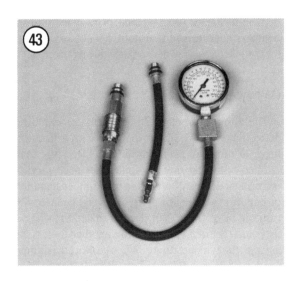

Cylinder Leak-Down Tester

Certain engine problems (leaking valve, broken, worn or stuck piston rings) can be isolated by per-

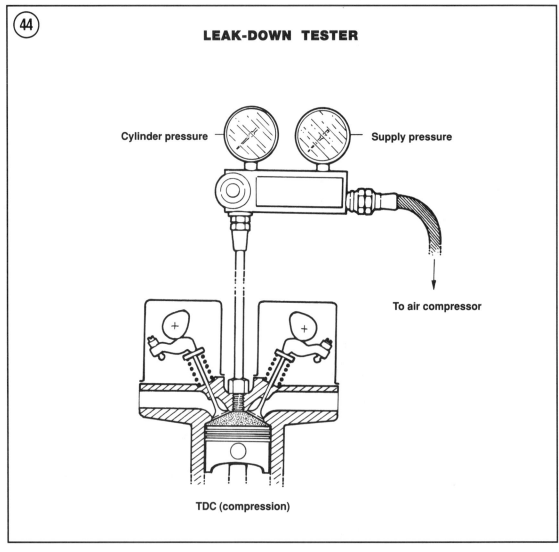

LEAK-DOWN TESTER

Cylinder pressure

Supply pressure

To air compressor

TDC (compression)

forming a cylinder leak-down test. An air compressor and a cylinder leak-down tester (Figure 44) are required to perform a leak-down test. To leak-down test a cylinder, position the piston on its compression stroke (both valves closed), then pressurize the cylinder and listen for escaping air through the carburetor(s), exhaust system or cylinder head mating surface. This procedure is fully explained in Chapter Three. A cylinder leak-down tester can be purchased through Suzuki dealers, tool manufacturers and automotive tool suppliers.

Battery Hydrometer

A hydrometer (**Figure 45**) is the best way to check a battery's state of charge. A hydrometer measures the weight or density of the sulfuric acid in the battery's electrolyte in specific gravity.

Portable Tachometer

A portable tachometer (**Figure 46**) is necessary for tuning. Ignition timing and carburetor adjustments must be performed at specified engine speeds. The best instrument for this purpose is one with a

low range of 0-1,000 or 0-2,000 rpm and a high range of 0-4,000 rpm. Extended range (0-6,000 or 0-8,000 rpm) instruments lack accuracy at lower speeds. This instrument should be capable of detecting 25 rpm on the low range.

Strobe Timing Light

This instrument is useful for checking ignition timing. By flashing a light at the precise instant the spark plug fires, the position of the timing mark can be seen. The flashing light makes a moving mark appear to stand still opposite a stationary mark.

Suitable lights range from inexpensive neon bulb types to powerful xenon strobe lights (**Figure 47**). A light with an inductive pickup is recommended to eliminate any possible damage to ignition wiring. Use according to manufacturer's instructions.

PRECISION MEASURING TOOLS

Measurement is an important part of motorcycle and ATV service. When performing many of the service procedures in this manual, you will be required to make a number of measurements. These include basic checks such as valve clearance, engine compression and spark plug gap. As you get deeper into engine disassembly and service, measurements will be required to determine the size and condition of the piston and cylinder bore, valve and guide wear, camshaft wear, crankshaft runout and so on. When making these measurements, the degree of accuracy will dictate which tool is required. Precision measuring tools are expensive. If this is your first experience at engine or suspension service, it may be more worthwhile to have the checks made at a Suzuki dealer or machine shop. However, as your

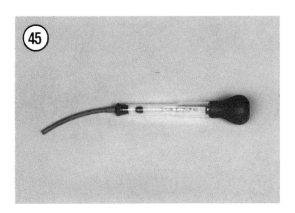

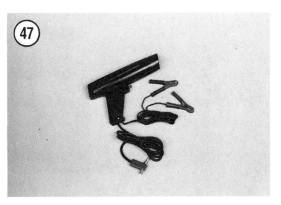

skills and enthusiasm increase for doing your own service work, you may want to begin purchasing some of these specialized tools. The following is a description of the measuring tools required during engine and suspension overhaul.

Feeler Gauge

Feeler gauges come in assorted sets and types (**Figure 48**). The feeler gauge is made of either a piece of a flat or round hardened steel of a specified thickness. Wire gauges are used to measure spark plug gap and valve clearance. Flat gauges are used for all other measurements. Feeler gauges are also designed for specialized uses, such as for measuring valve clearances. On these gauges, the gauge end is usually small enough and angled so as to make checking valve clearances easier.

Vernier Caliper

This tool (**Figure 49**) is invaluable when reading inside, outside and depth measurements. A vernier caliper is accurate to 0.001 in. (0.025 mm). It can be used to measure clutch spring length and the thickness of clutch plates, shims and thrust washers.

Outside Micrometers

One of the most reliable tools used for precision measurement is the outside micrometer (**Figure 50**). Outside micrometers are required to measure valve shim thickness, piston diameter and valve stem diameter. Outside micrometers are also used with other tools to measure the cylinder bore and the valve guide inside diameters. Micrometers can be purchased individually or as a set.

Dial Indicator

Dial indicators (**Figure 51**) are precision tools used to check dimension variations on machined

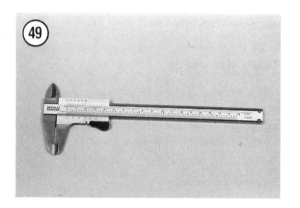

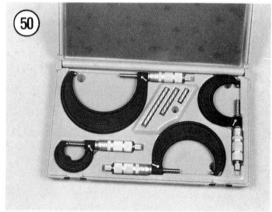

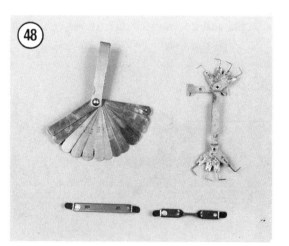

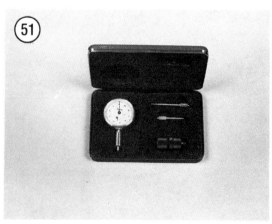

parts such as transmission shafts and axles and to check crankshaft and axle shaft end play. Dial indicators are available with various dial types; select a dial indicator with a continuous dial (**Figure 52**).

Cylinder Bore Gauge

The cylinder bore gauge is a very specialized precision tool. The gauge set shown in **Figure 53** is comprised of a dial indicator, handle and a number of length adapters to adapt the gauge to different bore sizes. The bore gauge can be used to make cylinder bore measurements such as bore size, taper and out-of-round. Depending on the bore gauge, it can sometimes be used to measure brake caliper and master cylinder bore sizes. An outside micrometer must be used together with the bore gauge to determine bore dimensions.

Small Hole Gauges

A set of small hole gauges (**Figure 54**) allow you to measure a hole, groove or slot ranging in size up to 13 mm (0.512 in.). A small hole gauge is required to measure valve guide, brake caliper and brake master cylinder bore diameters. An outside micrometer must be used together with the small hole gauge to determine bore dimensions.

Telescoping Gauges

Telescoping gauges (**Figure 55**) can be used to measure hole diameters from approximately 5/16-6 in. (8-150 mm). Like the small hole gauge, the

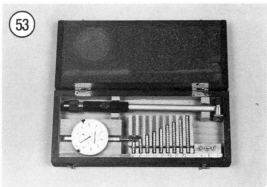

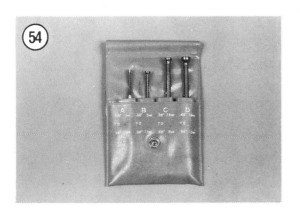

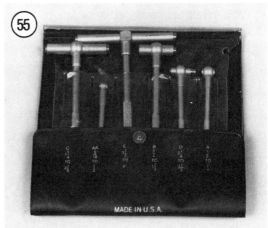

telescoping gauge does not have a scale gauge for direct readings. Thus, an outside micrometer is required to determine bore dimensions.

Screw Pitch Gauge

A screw pitch gauge (**Figure 56**) determines the thread pitch of bolts, screws, studs, etc. The gauge is made up of a number of thin plates. Each plate has a thread shape cut on one edge to match one thread pitch. When using a screw pitch gauge to determine a thread pitch size, try to fit different blade sizes onto the bolt thread until both threads match.

Magnetic Stand

A magnetic stand (**Figure 57**) is used to hold a dial indicator securely when checking the runout of a round object or when checking the end play of a shaft.

V-Blocks

V-blocks (**Figure 58**) are precision ground blocks used to hold a round object when checking its runout or condition. In ATV repair, V-blocks can be used when checking the runout of such items as valve stems, camshaft, balancer shaft, crankshaft, wheel axles and fork tubes.

Surface Plate

A surface plate is used to check the flatness of parts or to provide a perfectly flat surface for minor resurfacing of cylinder head or other critical gasket surfaces. While industrial quality surface plates are quite expensive, the home mechanic can improvise. A thick metal plate can be put to use as a surface plate. The metal surface plate shown in **Figure 59** has a piece of sandpaper or dry wall surface sanding sheets glued to its surface that can be used for cleaning and smoothing cylinder head and crankcase mating surfaces.

NOTE
Check with a local machine shop on the availability and cost of having a metal plate resurfaced for use as a surface plate.

SPECIAL TOOLS

A few special tools may be required for major service. These are described in the appropriate chapters and are available either from a Suzuki dealer or other manufacturers as indicated.

This section describes special tools unique to this type of ATV's service and repair.

The Grabbit (Clutch Holding Tool)

The Grabbit (**Figure 60**), or clutch holding tool, is a special tool used to hold the clutch boss when removing and tightening the clutch nut.

Other Special Tools

A few other special tools may be required for major service. These are described in the appropriate chapters and are available from Suzuki dealers or other manufacturers as indicated.

CLEANING SOLVENT

With the environmental concern that is prevalent today concerning the disposal of hazardous solvents, the home mechanic should select a water soluble, biodegradable solvent. These solvents can be purchased through dealers, automotive parts houses and large hardware stores.

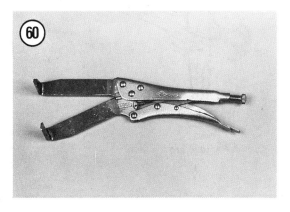

Selecting a solvent is only one of the problems facing the home mechanic when it comes to cleaning parts. You need some type of tank to clean parts as well as to store the solvent. There are a number of manufacturers offering different types and sizes of parts cleaning tanks. While a tank may seem a luxury to the home mechanic, you will find that it will quickly pay for itself through its efficiency and convenience. When selecting a parts washer, look for one that can recycle and store the solvent, as well as separate the sludge and contamination from the clean solvent. Most important, check the warranty, if any, as it pertains to the tank's pump. Like most tools, when purchasing a parts washer, you get what you pay for.

WARNING
Having a stack of clean shop rags on hand is important when performing engine work. However, to prevent the possibility of fire damage from spontaneous combustion from a pile of solvent-soaked rags, store them in a lid-sealed metal container until they can be washed or discarded.

NOTE
To avoid absorbing solvent and other chemicals into your skin while cleaning parts, wear a pair of petroleum-resistant rubber gloves. These can be purchased through industrial supply houses or well-equipped hardware stores.

MECHANIC'S TIPS

Removing Frozen Nuts and Screws

When a fastener rusts and cannot be removed, several methods may be used to loosen it. First, apply penetrating oil such as Liquid Wrench or WD-40 (available at hardware or auto supply stores). Apply it liberally and let it penetrate for 10-15 minutes. Rap the fastener several times with a small hammer; do not hit it hard enough to cause damage. Reapply the penetrating oil if necessary.

For frozen screws, apply penetrating oil as described, then insert a screwdriver in the slot and rap the top of the screwdriver with a hammer. This loosens the rust so the screw can be removed in the normal way. If the screw head is too chewed up to use this method, grip the head with vise-grip pliers and twist the screw out.

Avoid applying heat unless specifically instructed, as it may melt, warp or remove the temper from parts.

Removing Broken Screws or Bolts

When the head breaks off a screw or bolt, several methods are available for removing the remaining portion.

If a large portion of the remainder projects out, try gripping it with vise-grip pliers. If the projecting

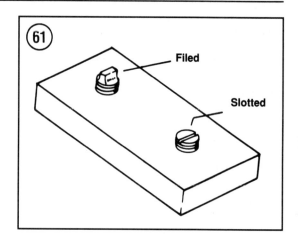

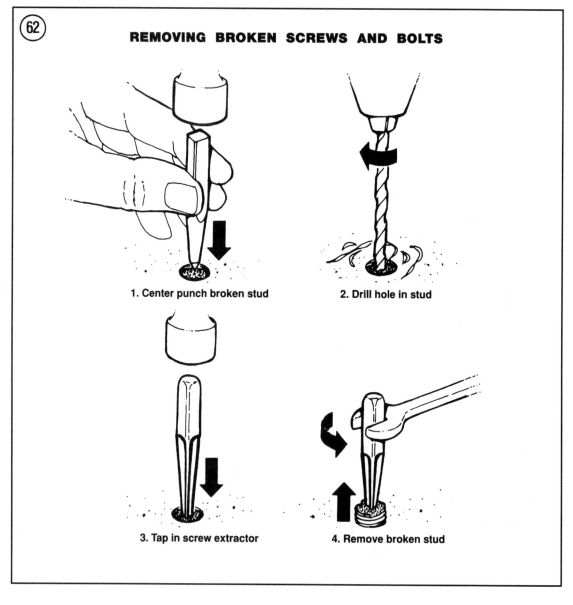

REMOVING BROKEN SCREWS AND BOLTS

1. Center punch broken stud

2. Drill hole in stud

3. Tap in screw extractor

4. Remove broken stud

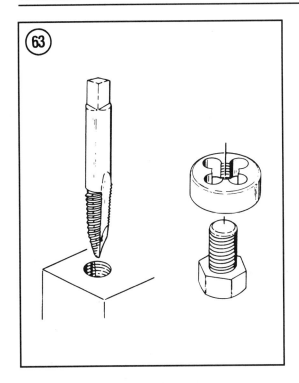

portion is too small, file it to fit a wrench or cut a slot in it to fit a screwdriver. See **Figure 61**.

If the head breaks off flush, use a screw extractor. To do this, center punch the exact center of the remaining portion of the screw or bolt. Drill a small hole in the screw and tap the extractor into the hole. Back the screw out with a wrench on the extractor. See **Figure 62**.

Remedying Stripped Threads

Occasionally, threads are stripped through carelessness or impact damage. Often the threads can be cleaned up by running a tap (for internal threads on nuts) or die (for external threads on bolts) through the threads. See **Figure 63**. To clean or repair spark plug threads, a spark plug tap can be used (**Figure 64**).

NOTE
Tap and dies can be purchased individually or in a set as shown in **Figure 41**.

If an internal thread is damaged, it may be necessary to install a Helicoil (**Figure 65**) or some other type of thread insert. Follow the manufacturer's instructions when installing their insert.

Removing Broken or Damaged Studs

If a stud is broken or the threads severely damaged, perform the following. A tube of red Loctite (No. 271), 2 nuts, 2 wrenches and a new stud will be required during this procedure (**Figure 66**). Studs that are stripped or damaged will require the use of a stud remover.

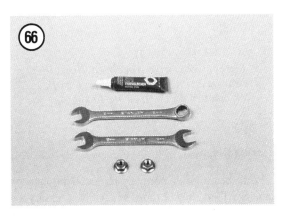

1. Thread two nuts onto the damaged stud. Then tighten the 2 nuts against each other so that they are locked.

> *NOTE*
> *If the threads on the damaged stud do not allow installation of the 2 nuts, you will have to remove the stud with a stud remover.*

2. Turn the bottom nut counterclockwise and unscrew the stud.

3. Threaded holes with a bottom surface should be blown out with compressed air as dirt buildup in the bottom of the hole may prevent the stud from being torqued properly. If necessary, use a bottoming tap to true up the threads and to remove any deposits.

4. Install 2 nuts on the top half of the new stud as in Step 1. Make sure they are locked securely.

5. Coat the bottom half of a new stud with red Loctite (No. 271).

6. Turn the top nut clockwise and thread the new stud securely.

7. Remove the nuts and repeat for each stud as required.

8. Follow Loctite's directions on cure time before assembling the component.

BALL BEARING REPLACEMENT

Ball bearings (**Figure 67**) are used throughout your Suzuki's engine and chassis to reduce power loss, heat and noise resulting from friction. Because ball bearings are precision made parts, they must be maintained by proper lubrication and maintenance. When a bearing is found to be damaged, it should be replaced immediately. However, when installing a new bearing, care should be taken to prevent damage to the new bearing. While bearing replacement is described in the individual chapters where applicable, the following can be used as a guideline.

> *NOTE*
> *Unless otherwise specified, install bearings with the manufacturer's mark or number on the bearing facing outward.*

Bearing Removal

While bearings are normally removed only when damaged, there may be times when it is necessary to remove a bearing that is in good condition. Depending on the situation, you may be able to remove the bearing without damaging it. However, bearing removal in some situations, no matter how careful you are, will cause bearing damage. Care should always be given to bearings during their removal to prevent secondary damage to the shaft or housing. Note the following when removing bearings.

1. When using a puller to remove a bearing on a shaft, care must be taken so that shaft damage does not occur. Always place a piece of metal between the end of the shaft and the puller screw. In addition, place the puller arms next to the inner bearing race. See **Figure 68**.

2. When using a hammer to remove a bearing on a shaft, do not strike the hammer directly against the

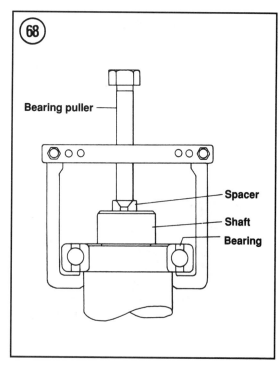

Bearing puller

Spacer

Shaft

Bearing

shaft. Instead, use a brass or aluminum spacer between the hammer and shaft (**Figure 69**). In addition, make sure to support both bearing races with wood blocks as shown in **Figure 69**.

3. The most ideal method of bearing removal is with a hydraulic press. However, certain procedures must be followed or damage may occur to the bearing, shaft or case half. Note the following when using a press:

a. Always support the inner and outer bearing races with a suitable size wood or aluminum spacer ring (**Figure 70**). If only the outer race is supported, the balls and/or the inner race will be damaged.

b. Always make sure the press ram (**Figure 69**) aligns with the center of the shaft. If the ram is not centered, it may damage the bearing and/or shaft.

c. The moment the shaft is free of the bearing, it will drop to the floor. Secure or hold the shaft to prevent it from falling.

Bearing Installation

1. When installing a bearing in a housing, pressure must be applied to the outer bearing race (**Figure 71**). When installing a bearing on a shaft, pressure must be applied to the *inner* bearing race (**Figure 72**).

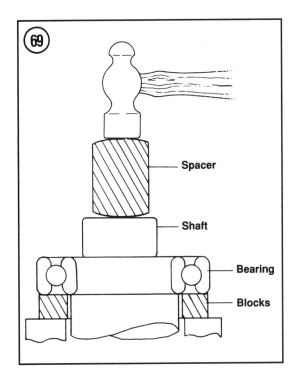

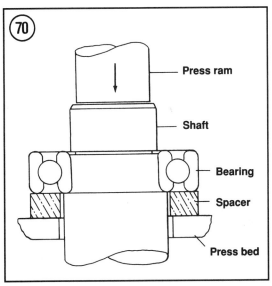

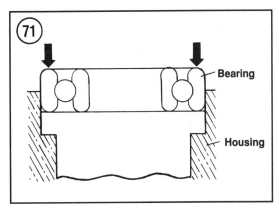

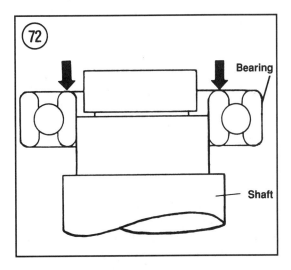

2. When installing a bearing as described in Step 1, some type of driver will be required. Never strike the bearing directly with a hammer or the bearing will be damaged. When installing a bearing, a piece of pipe or a socket with an outer diameter that matches the bearing race will be required. **Figure 73** shows the correct way to use a socket and hammer when installing a bearing over a shaft.

3. Step 1 describes how to install a bearing in a case half and over a shaft. However, when installing a bearing over a shaft and into a housing at the same time, a snug fit will be required for both outer and inner bearing races. In this situation, a spacer must be installed underneath the driver tool so that pressure is applied evenly across *both* races. See **Figure 74**. If the outer race is not supported as shown in **Figure 74**, the balls will push against the outer bearing track and damage it.

Shrink Fit

1. *Installing a bearing over a shaft:* When a tight fit is required, the bearing inside diameter will be smaller than the shaft. In this case, driving the bearing on the shaft using normal methods may cause bearing damage. Instead, the bearing should be heated before installation. Note the following:

   a. Secure the shaft so that it can be ready for bearing installation.

   b. Clean the bearing surface on the shaft of all residue. Remove burrs with a file or sandpaper.

   c. Fill a suitable pot or beaker with clean mineral oil. Place a thermometer (rated higher than 248° F [120° C]) in the oil. Support the thermometer so that it does not rest on the bottom or side of the pot.

   d. Remove the bearing from its wrapper and secure it with a piece of heavy wire bent to hold it in the pot. Hang the bearing in the pot so that it does not touch the bottom or sides of the pot.

   e. Turn the heat on and monitor the thermometer. When the oil temperature rises to approximately 248° F (120° C), remove the bearing from the pot and quickly install it. If necessary, place a socket on the inner bearing race and tap the bearing into place. As the bearing chills, it will tighten on the shaft so you must work quickly when installing it. Make sure the bearing is installed all the way.

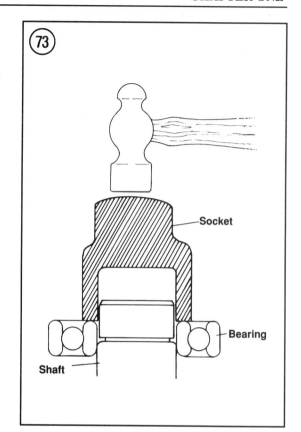

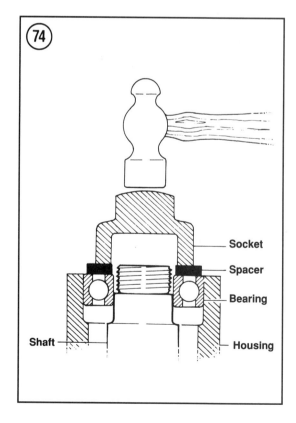

2. *Installing a bearing in a housing:* Bearings are generally installed in a housing with a slight interference fit. Driving the bearing into the housing using normal methods may damage the housing or cause bearing damage. Instead, the housing should be heated before the bearing is installed. Note the following:

> *CAUTION*
> *Before heating the crankcases in this procedure to remove the bearings, wash the cases thoroughly with detergent and water. Rinse and rewash the cases as required to remove all traces of oil and other chemical deposits.*

a. The housing must be heated to a temperature of about 212° F (100° C) in an oven or on a hot plate. An easy way to check to see that it is at the proper temperature is to drop tiny drops of water on the case as it heats up; if they sizzle and evaporate immediately, the temperature is correct. Heat only one housing at a time.

> *CAUTION*
> *Do not heat the housing with a torch (propane or acetylene) never bring a flame into contact with the bearing or housing. The direct heat will destroy the case hardening of the bearing and will likely warp the housing.*

b. Remove the housing from the oven or hot plate and hold onto the housing with a kitchen pot holder, heavy gloves or heavy shop cloths-it is hot.

> *NOTE*
> *A suitable size socket and extension works well for removing and installing bearings.*

c. Hold the housing with the bearing side down and tap the bearing out. Repeat for all bearings in the housing.

d. While heating up the housing halves, place the new bearings in a freezer if possible. Chilling them will slightly reduce their overall diameter while the hot housing assembly is slightly larger due to heat expansion. This will make installation much easier.

> *NOTE*
> *Always install bearings with the manufacturer's mark or number facing outward.*

e. While the housing is still hot, install the new bearing(s) into the housing. Install the bearings by hand, if possible. If necessary, lightly tap the bearing(s) into the housing with a socket placed on the outer bearing race. Do not install new bearings by driving on the inner bearing race. Install the bearing(s) until it seats completely.

OIL SEALS

Oil seals (**Figure 75**) are used to contain oil, water, grease or combustion gasses in a housing or shaft. Improper removal of a seal can damage the housing or shaft. Improper installation of the seal can damage the seal. Note the following:

a. Prying is generally the easiest and most effective method of removing a seal from a housing. However, always place a rag underneath the pry tool to prevent damage to the housing.

b. Grease should be packed in the seal lips before the seal is installed.

c. Oil seals should always be installed so that the manufacturer's numbers or marks face out.

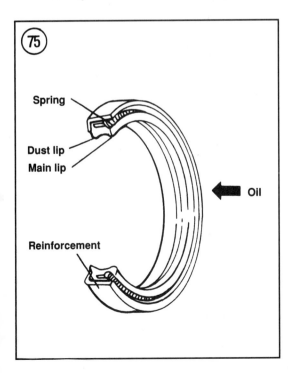

⑦⑤

Spring

Dust lip
Main lip

← Oil

Reinforcement

d. Oil seals should be installed with a socket placed on the outside of the seal as shown in **Figure 76**. Make sure the seal is driven squarely into the housing. Never install a seal by hitting against the top of the seal with a hammer.

RIDING SAFETY

General Tips

1. Read your owner's manual and know your machine.
2. Check the throttle and brake controls before starting the engine.
3. Know how to make an emergency stop.
4. Never add fuel while anyone is smoking in the area or when the engine is running.
5. Never wear loose scarves, belts or boot laces that could catch on moving parts.
6. Always wear eye and head protection and protective clothing to protect your *entire* body (**Figure 77**). Today's riding apparel is very stylish and you will be ready for action as will as being well protected.
7. Riding in the winter months requires a good set of clothes to keep your body dry and warm, otherwise your entire trip may be miserable. If you dress properly, moisture will evaporate from your body. If you become too hot and if your clothes trap the moisture, you will become cold. **Figure 78** shows some recommended inner and outer layers of cold weather clothing. Even mild temperatures can be very uncomfortable and dangerous when combined with a strong wind or traveling at high speed. See **Table 5** for wind chill factors. Always dress according to what the wind chill factor is, not the ambient temperature.
8. Never allow anyone to operate the vehicle without proper instruction. This is for their bodily protection and to keep your machine from damage or destruction.
9. Use the "buddy system" for long trips, just in case you have a problem or run out of gas.
10. Never attempt to repair your machine with the engine running except when necessary for certain tune-up procedures.
11. Check all of the machine components and hardware frequently, especially the wheels and the steering.

Operating Tips

1. Never operate the machine in crowed areas or steer toward persons.

2. Avoid dangerous terrain.

3. Cross highways (where permitted) at a 90° angle after looking in both directions. Post traffic guards if crossing in groups.

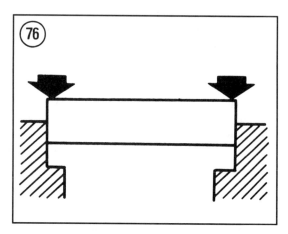

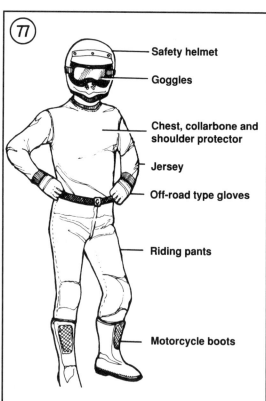

Safety helmet
Goggles
Chest, collarbone and shoulder protector
Jersey
Off-road type gloves
Riding pants
Motorcycle boots

4. Do not ride the vehicle on or near railroad tracks. The ATV's engine and exhaust noise can drown out the sound of an approaching train.

5. Keep the headlight and taillight free of dirt and never ride at night without the headlight and taillight ON.

6. Do not ride without the seat and fenders in place.

7. Always steer with both hands.

8. Be aware of the terrain and avoid operating the ATV at excessive speed.

9. Do not panic if the throttle sticks. Turn the engine stop switch (**Figure 79**) to the OFF position.

10. Do not speed through wooded areas. Hidden obstructions, hanging tree limbs, unseen ditches and even wild animals and hikers can cause injury and damage to the vehicle.

11. Do not tailgate. Rear end collisions can cause injury and machine damage.

12. Do not mix alcoholic beverages or drugs with riding—ride straight.

13. Keep both feet on the foot pegs. Do not permit your feet to hang out to stabilize the machine when making turns or in near spill situations; broken limbs could result.

14. Check your fuel supply regularly. Do not travel farther than your fuel supply will permit you to return.

15. Check to make sure that the parking brake is *completely released* while riding. If left on. the rear brake shoes will be damaged.

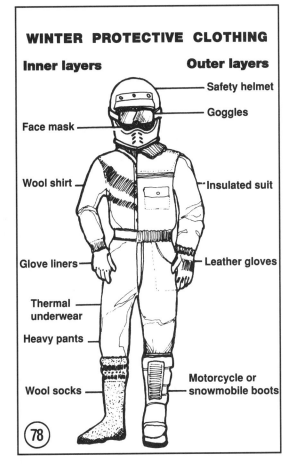

WINTER PROTECTIVE CLOTHING

Inner layers

Outer layers

- Safety helmet
- Goggles
- Face mask
- Wool shirt
- Insulated suit
- Glove liners
- Leather gloves
- Thermal underwear
- Heavy pants
- Wool socks
- Motorcycle or snowmobile boots

⑦⑧

⑦⑨

Table 1 FRAME SERIAL NUMBERS

Model numbers	Years	Frame number
2-Wheel Drive (250 cc) Models		
LT-F250J	1988	JSAAJ47A J2100001-on
LT-F250K	1989	JSAAJ47A K2100001-on
LT-F250L	1990	JSAAJ47A L2100001-on
LT-F250M	1991	JSAAJ47A M2100001-on
LT-F250N	1992	JSAAJ47A N2100001-on
LT-F250P	1993	JSAAJ47A P2100001-on
LT-F250R	1994	JSAAJ47A R2100001-on
LT-F250S	1995	JSAAJ47A S2100001-on
(continued)		

Table 1 FRAME SERIAL NUMBERS (continued)

Model numbers	Years	Frame number
4-Wheel Drive (250 cc) Models		
LT-4WDH	1987	JSAAJ45A H2100060-on
LT-4WDJ	1988	JSAAJ45A J2100001-on
LT-4WDK	1989	JSAAJ45A K2100001-on
LT-4WDL	1990	JSAAJ45A L2100001-on
LT-4WDM	1991	JSAAJ45A M2100001-on
LT-4WDN	1992	JSAAJ45A N2100001-on
LT-4WDP	1993	JSAAJ45A P2100001-on
LT-4WDR	1994	JSAAJ45A R2100001-on
LT-4WDS	1995	JSAAJ45A S2100001-on
4-Wheel Drive (280 cc) Models		
LT-4WDXM	1991	JSAAK42A M2100001-on
LT-4WDXN	1992	JSAAK42A N2100001-on
LT-4WDXP	1993	JSAAK42A P2100001-on
LT-4WDXR	1994	JSAAK42A R2100001-on
LT-4WDXS	1995	JSAAK42A S2100001-on

Table 2 DECIMAL AND METRIC EQUIVALENTS

Fractions	Decimal in.	Metric mm	Fractions	Decimal in.	Metric mm
1/64	0.015625	0.39688	33/64	0.515625	13.09687
1/32	0.03125	0.79375	17/32	0.53125	13.49375
3/64	0.046875	1.19062	35/64	0.546875	13.89062
1/16	0.0625	1.58750	9/16	0.5625	14.28750
5/64	0.078125	1.98437	37/64	0.578125	14.68437
3/32	0.09375	2.38125	19/32	0.59375	15.08125
7/64	0.109375	2.77812	39/64	0.609375	15.47812
1/8	0.125	3.1750	5/8	0.625	15.87500
9/64	0.140625	3.57187	41/64	0.640625	16.27187
5/32	0.15625	3.96875	21/32	0.65625	16.66875
11/64	0.171875	4.36562	43/64	0.671875	17.06562
3/16	0.1875	4.76250	11/16	0.6875	17.46250
13/64	0.203125	5.15937	45/64	0.703125	17.85937
7/32	0.21875	5.55625	23/32	0.71875	18.25625
15/64	0.234375	5.95312	47/64	0.734375	18.65312
1/4	0.250	6.35000	3/4	0.750	19.05000
17/64	0.265625	6.74687	49/64	0.765625	19.44687
9/32	0.28125	7.14375	25/32	0.78125	19.84375
19/64	0.296875	7.54062	51/64	0.796875	20.24062
5/16	0.3125	7.93750	13/16	0.8125	20.63750
21/64	0.328125	8.33437	53/64	0.828125	21.03437
11/32	0.34375	8.73125	27/32	0.84375	21.43125
23/64	0.359375	9.12812	55/64	0.859375	22.82812
3/8	0.375	9.52500	7/8	0.875	22.22500
25/64	0.390625	9.92187	57/64	0.890625	22.62187
13/32	0.40625	10.31875	29/32	0.90625	23.01875
27/64	0.421875	10.71562	59/64	0.921875	23.41562
7/16	0.4375	11.11250	15/16	0.9375	23.81250
29/64	0.453125	11.50937	61/64	0.953125	24.20937
15/32	0.46875	11.90625	31/32	0.96875	24.60625
31/64	0.484375	12.30312	63/64	0.984375	25.00312
1/2	0.500	12.70000	1	1.00	25.40000

Table 3 STANDARD TORQUE SPECIFICATIONS

Conventional or "4" Marked bolt*		
Bolt diameter (mm)	N·m	ft.-lb.
4	1-2	0.7-1.5
5	2-4	1.5-3.0
6	4-7	3-5
8	10-16	7-11.5
10	22-35	16-25.5
12	35-55	25.5-40
14	50-80	36-58
16	80-130	58-94
18	130-190	94-137.5

"7" Marked bolt*		
Bolt diameter (mm)	N·m	ft.-lb.
4	1.5-3	1-2
5	3-6	2-4.5
6	8-12	6-8.5
8	18-28	13-20
10	40-60	29-43.5
12	70-100	50.5-72.5
14	110-160	79.5-115.5
16	170-250	123-181
18	200-280	144-202

*Number is marked on top of Suzuki bolt head. These are Suzuki numbers and do not appear on aftermarket bolts.

Table 4 WORKSHOP TOOLS

Tool	Size or specificaton
Screwdriver	
Common	1/8 x 4 in. blade
Common	5/16 x 8 in. blade
Common	3/8 x 12 in. blade
Phillips	Size 2 tip, 6 in. overall
Pliers	
Slip joint	6 in. overall
Vise-grip	10 in. overall
Needlenose	6 in. overall
Adjustable	12 in. overall
Snap ring	Assorted
Wrenches	
Box-end set	Assorted
Open-end set	Assorted
Adjustable	6 in. and 12 in. overall
Socket set	1/2 in. drive ratchet with assorted metric sockets
Socket drive extensions	1/2 in. drive, 2 in., 4 in. and 6 in.
Socket universal joint	1/2 in. drive
Allen	Socket driven (long and short), T-handle driven and 90°
Hammers	
Soft-faced	–
Plastic-faced	–
Metal-faced	–
Other special tools	
Impact driver	3/8 in. drive with assorted bits
Torque wrench	1/2 in. drive (ft.-lb.)
Flat feeler gauge	Metric set

Table 5 WIND CHILL FACTOR

Estimated wind speed in mph	Actual thermometer reading (°F)											
	50	40	30	20	10	0	−10	−20	−30	−40	−50	−60
	Equivalent temperature (°F)											
Calm	50	40	30	20	10	0	−10	−20	−30	−40	−50	−60
5	48	37	27	16	6	−5	−15	−26	−36	−47	−57	−68
10	40	28	16	4	−9	−21	−33	−46	−58	−70	−83	−95
15	36	22	9	−5	−18	−36	−45	−58	−72	−85	−99	−112
20	32	18	4	−10	−25	−39	−53	−67	−82	−96	−110	−124
25	30	16	0	−15	−29	−44	−59	−74	−88	−104	−118	−133
30	28	13	−2	−18	−33	−48	−63	−79	−94	−109	−125	−140
35	27	11	−4	−20	−35	−49	−67	−82	−98	−113	−129	−145
40	26	10	−6	−21	−37	−53	−69	−85	−100	−116	−132	−148
*												

Little danger (for properly clothed person)

Increasing danger

Great danger

• Danger from freezing of exposed flesh •

*Wind speeds greater than 40 mph have little additional effect.

TROUBLESHOOTING

Every ATV engine requires an uninterrupted supply of fuel and air, proper ignition and adequate compression. If any of these are lacking, the engine will not run.

Diagnosing mechanical problems is relatively simple if you use orderly procedures and keep a few basic principles in mind.

The troubleshooting procedures in this chapter analyze typical symptoms and show logical methods of isolating causes. These are not the only methods. There may be several ways to solve a problem, but only a systematic approach can guarantee success.

Never assume anything. Do not overlook the obvious. If you are riding along and the vehicle suddenly quits, check the easiest, most accessible areas first.

If nothing obvious turns up in a quick check, look a little further. Learning to recognize and describe symptoms will make repairs easier for you or a mechanic at the shop. Describe problems accurately and fully. Saying that it won't run isn't the same thing as saying it quit at high speed and won't start, or that it sat in a garage for 3 months and then wouldn't start.

Gather as many symptoms as possible to aid in diagnosis. Note whether the engine lost power gradually or all at once. Remember that the more complicated a machine is, the easier it is to troubleshoot because symptoms point to specific problems.

After the symptoms are defined, areas which could cause problems are tested and analyzed. Guessing at the cause of a problem may provide the solution, but it can easily lead to frustration, wasted time and a series of expensive, unnecessary parts replacements.

You do not need fancy equipment or complicated test gear to determine whether repairs can be attempted at home. A few simple checks could save a large repair bill and lost time while the ATV sits in a dealer's service department. On the other hand, be realistic and don't attempt repairs beyond your abilities. Service departments tend to charge heavily for putting together a disassembled engine that may have been abused. Some won't even take on such a job, so use common sense and don't get in over your head.

OPERATING REQUIREMENTS

An engine needs 3 basics to run properly: correct fuel/air mixture, compression and a spark at the correct time (**Figure 1**). If one or more are missing, the engine will not run. Four-stroke engine operating principles are described under *Engine Principles* in Chapter Four.

If the machine has been sitting for any length of time and refuses to start, check and clean the spark plug and then look to the gasoline delivery system. This includes the fuel tank, fuel shutoff valve and fuel line to the carburetor. Gasoline deposits may have formed and gummed up the carburetor jets and air passages. Gasoline tends to lose its potency after standing for long periods. Condensation may contaminate the fuel with water. Drain the old fuel (fuel tank, fuel pump, fuel lines and the carburetor) and try starting with a fresh tankful.

TROUBLESHOOTING INSTRUMENTS

Refer to Chapter One for a list of the instruments needed.

STARTING THE ENGINE

When experiencing engine starting troubles, it is easy to work out of sequence and forget basic engine starting procedures. The following outline will guide you through basic starting procedures. In all cases, make sure there is an adequate supply of fuel in the tank.

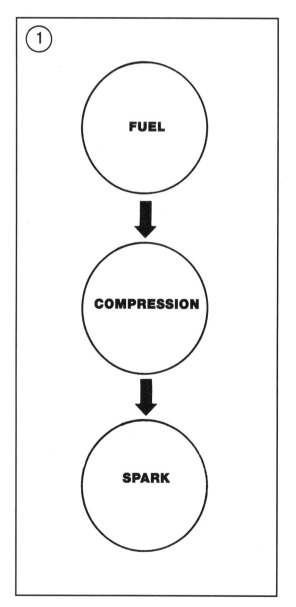

Starting a Cold Engine

1. Apply the parking brake.

2. Shift the transmission into NEUTRAL.

3. Move the engine stop switch (**Figure 2**) to the RUN position.

4. Turn the fuel shutoff valve to the ON position.

5. Install the ignition key and turn the ignition switch to ON.

6A. On 1987-1989 models, pull the choke knob out to the ON position.

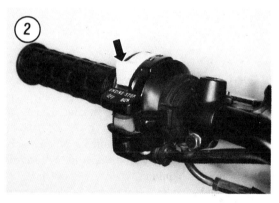

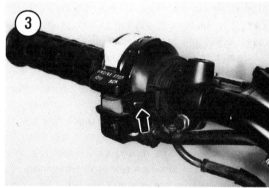

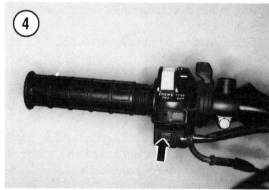

6B. On 1990-on models, move the choke lever to the fully ON position (**Figure 3**).

NOTE
Do not operate the starter motor for more than 5 seconds at a time. Wait approximately 10 seconds between starting attempts.

7A. If using the electric starter, press the starter button (**Figure 4**) and start the engine. Do not open the throttle.

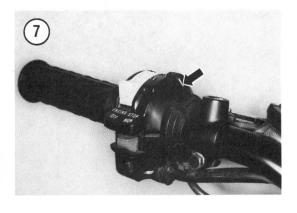

7B. If using the recoil starter, perform the following:

  a. Remove the seat as described in Chapter Fourteen.
  b. Lift the cylinder head decompression lever (**Figure 5**) all the way to the UP position. Do not open the throttle.
  c. Pull the recoil starter rope handle (**Figure 6**) slowly until the decompression lever returns to its normal position with a "click."
  d. Allow the recoil starter rope to return to its normal position within the housing.
  e. Pull the recoil starter rope handle (**Figure 6**) slowly until you feel the starter engage. With the starter engaged, pull up on the handle forcefully to start the engine. Let the rope retrace into the housing.
  f. Repeat this step if the engine fails to start.
  g. After the engine is running, install the seat.

NOTE
When a cold engine is started with the throttle open and the choke ON, a lean mixture will result and cause hard starting.

8. After the engine has started, return the choke knob or lever to the halfway position.

9. After approximately 30 seconds, push the choke knob or lever to the fully OFF position. If the idling is rough, open the throttle lightly until the engine warms up.

Starting a Warm Engine

1. Apply the parking brake.

2. Shift the transmission into NEUTRAL.

3. Move the engine stop switch to the RUN position.

4. Turn the fuel shutoff valve to the ON position.

5. Install the ignition key and turn the ignition switch to ON.

6A. On 1987-1989 models, push the choke knob out to the OFF position.

6B. On 1990-on models, move the choke lever to the fully OFF position (**Figure 7**).

7. Open the throttle slightly and perform Step 7 for *Starting a Cold Engine.*

Starting a Flooded Engine

If the engine will not start after a few attempts, it may be flooded. If you smell gasoline after attempting to start the engine, and the engine did not start, the engine is probably flooded.

1. Make sure the choke knob, or lever, is in the OFF position.

2. Open the throttle all the way and perform Step 7 for *Starting a Cold Engine* deleting the reference *do not open the throttle*.

EMERGENCY TROUBLESHOOTING

When the ATV is difficult to start, or won't start at all, it doesn't help to wear down the battery by using the electric starter. Check for obvious problems even before getting out your tools. Go down the following list step-by-step. Do each one; you may be embarrassed to find the engine stop switch off, but that is better than wearing down the battery or your arm with the recoil starter. Go down the following list step-by-step. Do each one while remembering the 3 engine operating requirements described under *Operating Requirements* earlier in this chapter.

WARNING
Do not use an open flame to check in the tank. A serious explosion is certain to result.

1. Is there fuel in the tank? Open the filler cap (A, **Figure 8**) and rock the ATV side to side. Listen for fuel sloshing around.

2. Check that the fuel tank vent tube (B, **Figure 8**) is not clogged. Remove the tube from the filler cap and fuel tank, thoroughly wipe off one end of the tube and blow through it. If the tube is clear, make sure the opening in the filler cap is clear.

3. Is the fuel supply valve in the ON position? Turn the valve to the ON position (or the RES position). This will ensure you get the last remaining gas.

4. Is the vacuum line attached to the fuel pump and to the intake tube on the cylinder head?

5. Is the engine stop switch (**Figure 2**) in the correct position? The engine should start and operate when the switch is in the RUN position. This switch is used primarily as an emergency or safety switch. Check that the switch is in the RUN position when starting

the engine. Test the switch as described under *Switches* in Chapter Nine.

6. Make sure the spark plug cap is on tight. Push the spark plug cap (**Figure 9**) on and slightly rotate it to clean the electrical connection between the plug and the connector.

7. Is the choke lever (**Figure 7**) in the right position? The choke knob, or lever, should be OFF for a warm engine and ON for a cold engine (**Figure 3**).

ENGINE STARTING TROUBLESHOOTING

An engine that refuses to start or is difficult to start is very frustrating. More often than not, the problem is very minor and can be found with a simple and logical troubleshooting approach.

First, review the steps under *Engine Starting Procedures* in this chapter. If the engine will not start by following the engine starting steps, continue with this section.

The following are beginning points from which to isolate engine starting problems.

NOTE
Do not operate the starter motor for more than 5 seconds at a time. Wait approximately 10 seconds between starting attempts.

Engine Fails to Start (Spark Test)

Perform the following spark test to determine if the ignition system is operating properly.

1. Remove the spark plug from the cylinder head as described in Chapter Three.

NOTE
*If the spark plug is wet after attempting to start the engine or if it appears fouled, refer to **Fuel System** in this chapter.*

2. Connect the spark plug wire and connector to a spark plug and touch the spark plug base to a good ground like the engine cylinder head. Position the spark plug so you can see the electrode.

WARNING
During the next step, do not hold the spark plug or connector with your fingers or a serious electrical shock may result. If necessary, use a pair of insulated pliers to hold the spark plug or wire. The high voltage generated by the ignition system could produce serious or fatal shocks.

3. Crank the engine over with the electric or recoil starter. A fat blue spark should be evident across the spark plug electrode. If the spark is good, continue with Step 4. If the spark is weak or if there is no spark, perform Step 6.

NOTE
*Refer to **Engine Will Not Crank** in this chapter if the starter motor will not operate, or if the starter motor (or recoil starter) appears to operate correctly but the engine does not turn while cranking.*

4. Check engine compression as described in Chapter Three. If the compression is good, perform Step

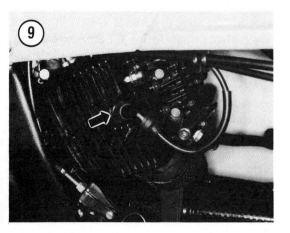

5. If the compression is low, check for one or more of the following:
  a. Leaking cylinder head gasket.
  b. Cracked or warped cylinder head.
  c. Worn piston rings, piston and cylinder.
  d. Valve stuck open.
  e. Seized valve(s).
  f. Worn or damaged valve seat(s).
  g. Incorrect valve timing.

5. Disconnect the fuel tube from the carburetor and insert the open end into a clear, glass container. Turn the fuel valve to ON, RES and OFF. A steady flow of fuel should be noticed with the fuel valve in the ON and RES positions. The fuel flow should stop with the fuel valve in the OFF position. If the fuel flow is okay, perform Step 6. If there is no fuel flow or if the flow is slow and intermittent, check for one or more of the following conditions:
  a. Empty fuel tank.
  b. Plugged fuel tank cap vent hole.
  c. Clogged fuel filter or fuel line.
  d. Stuck or clogged fuel valve.

6. If the spark is weak or if there is no spark, note the following:
  a. If there is no spark, there may be a problem in the input side of the ignition system CDI unit, pickup coil, neutral switch or reverse switch. Test these parts as described in Chapter Nine.
  b. If there is no spark at the spark plug, the spark plug is probably faulty or there is a problem with the spark plug wire or plug cap. Replace the spark plug and retest. If there is still no spark at that one plug, test the spark plug wire and plug cap as described in Chapter Nine. If those test good, the problem may be in the primary side of the ignition system (ignition coil or CDI unit). Test these parts as described in Chapter Nine.

Engine is Difficult to Start

Check for one or more of the following possible malfunctions:
  a. Fouled spark plug.
  b. Improperly adjusted choke.
  c. Intake manifold air leak.
  d. Contaminated fuel system.
  e. Improperly adjusted carburetor.
  f. Ignition system malfunction.
  g. Weak ignition coil.

h. Poor compression.

i. Engine and transmission oil too heavy.

Engine Will Not Crank

Check for one or more of the following possible malfunctions:

a. Blown fuse.

b. Discharged battery.

c. Defective starter motor, starter relay or start switch.

d. Defective recoil starter.

e. Seized piston.

f. Seized crankshaft bearings.

g. Broken connecting rod.

h. Locked-up transmission or clutch assembly.

ENGINE PERFORMANCE

In the following check list, it is assumed that the engine runs, but is not operating at peak performance. This will serve as a starting point from which to isolate a performance malfunction. Where ignition timing is mentioned as a problem, remember that there is no method of adjusting the ignition timing. If you check the ignition timing with a timing light as described in Chapter Three and it is incorrect, there is a faulty part within the ignition system. The individual parts must be checked and the faulty part(s) replaced.

Engine Will Not Start or Is Hard to Start

a. Fuel tank empty.

b. Obstructed fuel line, fuel shutoff valve or fuel filter.

c. Sticking float valve in carburetor.

d. Carburetor incorrectly adjusted.

e. Improper starter valve (choke) operation.

f. Improper throttle operation.

g. Fouled or improperly gapped spark plug.

h. Ignition timing incorrect.

i. Broken or shorted ignition coil.

j. Weak or faulty CDI unit or pickup coil.

k. Improper valve timing.

l. Clogged air filter element.

m. Contaminated fuel.

n. Engine flooded with fuel.

o. Faulty fuel pump.

Engine Starts but Then Stops

a. Incorrect choke adjustment.

b. Incorrect pilot air screw setting (closed).

c. Incorrect ignition timing.

d. Contaminated fuel.

e. Intake manifold air leak.

f. Faulty fuel pump.

Engine Will Not Idle

a. Carburetor incorrectly adjusted (too lean or too rich).

b. Fouled or improperly gapped spark plug.

c. Leaking head gasket or vacuum leak.

d. Ignition timing incorrect.

e. Improper valve timing.

f. Obstructed fuel line or fuel shutoff valve.

g. Low engine compression.

h. Starter valve (choke) stuck in the open position.

i. Incorrect pilot screw adjustment.

j. Clogged slow jet in the carburetor.

k. Clogged air filter element.

l. Valve(s) and valve seat(s) require service.

Poor High Speed Performance

1. Test the following ignition system components as described in Chapter Nine:

a. CDI unit.

b. Pickup coil.

c. Ignition coil.

2. Disconnect the fuel hose from the carburetor and insert the open end into a clear, glass container. Turn the fuel valve to ON, RES and OFF. A steady flow of fuel should be noticed with the fuel valve in the ON and RES positions. The fuel flow should stop with the fuel valve in the OFF position. If the fuel flow is okay, perform Step 3. If there is no fuel flow or if the flow is slow and intermittent, check for one or more of the following conditions:

a. Empty fuel tank.

b. Plugged fuel tank cap vent hole.

c. Clogged fuel filter or fuel line.

d. Stuck or clogged fuel valve.

3. Remove the carburetor as described in Chapter Eight. Then remove the float bowl and check for contamination and plugged jets. If any contamination is found, disassemble and clean the carburetor. You should also pour out and discard the remaining

fuel in the fuel tank and flush the fuel tank thoroughly. If no contamination is found and the jets are not plugged, perform Step 4.

4. Incorrect valve timing and worn or damaged valve springs can cause poor high-speed performance. If the valve timing was set just prior to the ATV experiencing this type of problem, the valve timing may be incorrect. If the valve timing was not set or changed, and you performed all of the other inspection procedures in this section without locating the problem area, the cylinder head cover should be removed and the valve train assembly inspected. Refer to Chapter Four.

Low Speed or Poor Engine Power

1. Check the clutch adjustment and operation. If the clutch slips, refer to *Clutch* in this chapter.
2. If Step 1 did not locate the problem, test ride the ATV and accelerate lightly. If the engine speed increased according to throttle position, perform Step 3. If the engine speed did not increase, check for one or more of the following problems:
   a. Clogged or damaged air filter.
   b. Restricted fuel flow.
   c. Clogged fuel tank cap vent.
   d. Incorrect choke adjustment or operation.
   e. Clogged or damaged muffler.
3. Check for one or more of the following problems:
   a. Low engine compression.
   b. Fouled spark plug.
   c. Clogged carburetor jet(s).
   d. Incorrect ignition timing.
   e. Incorrect oil level (too high or too low).
   f. Contaminated oil.
   g. Worn or damaged valve train assembly.
   h. Engine overheating.

Engine Overheating

   a. Obstructed cooling fins on the cylinder head and cylinder.
   b. Incorrect carburetor adjustment or jet selection.
   c. Improper spark plug heat range.
   d. Oil level low.
   e. Oil not circulating properly.
   f. Valves leaking.
   g. Heavy engine carbon deposits.
   h. Dragging brake(s).
   i. Clutch slipping.

Excessive Exhaust Smoke and Engine Runs Roughly

   a. Clogged air filter element.
   b. Carburetor adjustment incorrect mixture too rich.
   c. Choke not operating correctly.
   d. Water or other contaminants in fuel.
   e. Clogged fuel line.
   f. Spark plugs fouled.
   g. Ignition coil defective.
   h. Loose or defective ignition circuit wire.
   i. Short circuit from damaged wire insulation.
   j. Loose battery cable connection(s).
   k. Valve timing incorrect.

Engine Lacks Acceleration

   a. Carburetor mixture too lean.
   b. Clogged fuel line.
   c. Improper ignition timing.
   d. Dragging brake(s).
   e. Slipping clutch.

Engine Backfires

   a. Faulty ignition system component.
   b. Carburetor improperly adjusted.
   c. Lean fuel mixture.

Engine Misfires During Acceleration

   a. Faulty ignition system component.
   b. Lean fuel mixture.

ENGINE NOISES

Often the first evidence of an internal engine problem is a strange noise. That knocking, clicking or tapping sound which you never heard before may be warning you of impending trouble.

While engine noises can indicate problems, they are difficult to interpret correctly; inexperienced mechanics can be seriously misled by them.

Professional mechanics often use a special stethoscope (which looks like a doctor's stethoscope) for isolating engine noises. You can do nearly as well with a "sounding stick" which can be an ordinary piece of doweling, or a section of small hose. By placing one end in contact with the area to which you want to listen and the other end to the front of your ear (not directly on your ear), you can hear sounds emanating from that area. The first time you do this, you may be confused at the strange sounds coming from even a normal engine. If you can, have an experienced friend or mechanic help you sort out the noises.

Consider the following when troubleshooting engine noises:

1. *Knocking or pinging during acceleration*-Caused by using a lower octane fuel than recommended. May also be caused by poor fuel. Pinging can also be caused by a spark plug of the wrong heat range or carbon build-up in the combustion chamber. Refer to Correct Spark Plug Heat Range and Compression Test in Chapter Three.

2. *Slapping or rattling noises at low speed or during acceleration*-May be caused by piston slap, i.e., excessive piston-cylinder wall clearance.

> *NOTE*
> *Piston slap is easier to detect when the engine is cold and before the piston has expanded. Once the engine has warmed up, piston expansion reduces piston-to-cylinder clearance.*

3. *Knocking or rapping while decelerating*-Usually caused by excessive rod bearing clearance.

4. *Persistent knocking and vibration occurring every crankshaft rotation*-Usually caused by worn rod or main bearing(s). Can also be caused by broken piston rings or damaged piston pins.

5. *Persistent vibration occurring at all engine speeds*. Can be caused by improper installation of the balancer system components or damaged parts within the balancer system. Correct immediately.

6. *Rapid on-off squeal*-Compression leak around cylinder head gasket(s) or spark plug(s).

7. *Valve train noise*-Check for the following:
   a. Valve sticking in guide.
   b. Low oil pressure.

ENGINE LUBRICATION

An improperly operating engine lubrication system will quickly lead to engine seizure. The engine oil level should be checked weekly and topped up as described in Chapter Three. Oil pump service is described in Chapter Five.

Oil Consumption High or Engine Smokes Excessively

a. Worn valve guides.
b. Worn or damaged piston rings.

Excessive Engine Oil Leaks

a. Clogged air filter breather hose.
b. Loose engine parts.
c. Damaged gasket sealing surfaces.

Black Smoke

a. Clogged air filter.
b. Incorrect carburetor fuel level (too high).
c. Choke stuck closed.
d. Incorrect main jet (too large).

White Smoke

a. Worn valve guide.
b. Worn valve oil seal.
c. Worn piston ring oil ring.
d. Excessive cylinder and/or piston wear.

Oil Pressure Too High

a. Clogged oil filter.
b. Clogged oil gallery or metering orifices.
c. Pressure relief valve stuck closed.

Low Oil Pressure

a. Low oil level.
b. Damaged oil pump.
c. Clogged oil screen.
d. Clogged oil filter.
e. Internal oil leakage.
f. Pressure relief valve stuck open.

No Oil Pressure

a. Damaged oil pump.
b. Excessively low oil level.
c. No oil in crankcase.
d. Internal oil leakage.
e. Damaged oil pump drive shaft.

Oil Level Too Low

a. Oil level not maintained at correct level.
b. Worn piston rings.
c. Worn cylinder.
d. Worn valve guides.
e. Worn valve stem seals.
f. Piston rings incorrectly installed during engine overhaul.
g. External oil leakage.

Oil Contamination

a. Blown cylinder head gasket.
b. Oil and filter not changed at specified intervals or when abnormal operating conditions demand more frequent changes.

CLUTCH

The basic clutch troubles and causes are listed in this section.

Rough Clutch Operation

This condition can be caused by excessively worn, grooved or damaged clutch housing slots.

Clutch Slippage

If the engine sounds like it is winding out without accelerating, the clutch is probably slipping. Some of the main causes of clutch slipping are:
a. Centrifugal clutch weights not operating correctly.
b. Worn clutch plates.
c. Weak clutch springs.
d. Clutch mechanism not properly adjusted.
e. Loose clutch lifter bolts.
f. Damaged clutch lifter.
g. Engine oil additive being used (clutch plates contaminated).

GEARSHIFT LINKAGE

The gearshift linkage assembly connects the gearshift pedal (external shift mechanism) to the shift drum (internal shift mechanism).

The gearshift mechanism can only be examined once the engine has been removed from the frame and the crankcase disassembled. Common gearshift linkage troubles and checks to make are listed below.

Transmission Jumps out of Gear

a. Loose stopper arm bolt.
b. Damaged stopper arm.
c. Weak or damaged stopper arm spring.
d. Loose or damaged shifter cam.
e. Bent shift fork shaft(s).
f. Bent or damaged shift fork(s).
g. Worn gear dogs or slots.
h. Damaged shift drum grooves.

Difficult Shifting

a. Damaged clutch system.
b. Incorrect oil viscosity.
c. Bent shift fork shaft(s).
d. Bent or damaged shift fork(s).
e. Worn gear dogs or slots.
f. Damaged shift drum grooves.

TRANSMISSION

Transmission symptoms are sometimes hard to distinguish from clutch symptoms. Common transmission troubles and checks to make are listed below. Refer to Chapter Seven for transmission service procedures. Prior to working on the transmission, make sure the clutch and gearshift linkage assembly are not causing the trouble.

Difficult Shifting

a. Damaged clutch system.
b. Incorrect oil viscosity.
c. Bent shift fork shaft(s).
d. Bent or damaged shift fork(s).
e. Worn gear dogs or slots.
f. Damaged shift drum grooves.

Jumps out of Gear

a. Loose or damaged shift drum stopper arm.
b. Bent or damaged shift fork(s).
c. Bent shift fork shaft(s).

d. Damaged shift drum grooves.

e. Worn gear dogs or slots.

f. Broken shift linkage return spring.

Incorrect Shift Lever Operation

a. Bent shift lever.

b. Stripped shift lever splines.

c. Damaged shift lever linkage.

Excessive Gear Noise

a. Worn bearings.

b. Worn or damaged gears.

c. Excessive gear backlash.

ELECTRICAL TROUBLESHOOTING

This section describes the basics of electrical troubleshooting, how to use test equipment and the basic test procedures with the various pieces of test equipment.

Electrical troubleshooting can be very time-consuming and frustrating without proper knowledge and a suitable plan. Refer to the wiring diagrams at the end of the book and at the individual system diagrams included with the *Charging System*, *Ignition System* and *Starting System* sections in this chapter. Wiring diagrams will help you determine how the circuit should work by tracing the current paths from the power source through the circuit components to ground. Also check any circuits that share the same fuse, ground or switch, etc. If the other circuits work properly, the shared wiring is okay and the cause must be in the wiring used only by the suspect circuit. If all related circuits are faulty at the same time the probable cause is a poor ground connection or a blown fuse(s).

As with all troubleshooting procedures, analyze typical symptoms in a systematic procedure. Never assume anything and don't overlook the obvious like a blown fuse or an electrical connector that has separated. Test the simplest and most obvious cause first and try to make tests at easily accessible points on the ATV.

Preliminary Checks and Precautions

Prior to starting any electrical troubleshooting procedure perform the following:

a. Check the main fuse; make sure it is not blown. Replace if necessary.

b. Inspect the battery. Make sure it is fully charged, the electrolyte level is correct and that the battery leads are clean and securely attached to the battery terminals. Refer to *Battery* in Chapter Nine.

c. Disconnect each electrical connector in the suspect circuit and check that there are no bent metal pins on the male side of the electrical connector (**Figure 10**). A bent pin will not connect to its mating receptacle in the female end of the connector, causing an open circuit.

d. Check each female end of the connector. Make sure that the metal connector on the end of each wire (**Figure 11**) is pushed all the way into the plastic connector. If not, carefully push them in with a narrow blade screwdriver.

e. Check all electrical wires where they enter the individual metal terminal in both the male and female plastic connector.

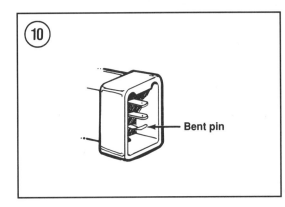

Bent pin

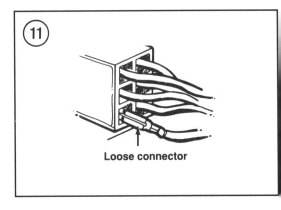

Loose connector

f. Make sure all electrical connectors within the connector are clean and free of corrosion. Clean, if necessary, and pack the connectors with a dielectric grease.

g. After all is checked out, push the connectors together and make sure they are fully engaged and locked together (**Figure 12**).

h. Never pull on the electrical wires when disconnecting an electrical connector—pull only on the connector plastic housing.

i. Never use a self-powered test light on circuits that contain solid-state devices. The solid-state devices may be damaged.

TEST EQUIPMENT

Test Light or Voltmeter

A test light can be constructed of a 12-volt light bulb with a pair of test leads carefully soldered to the bulb. To check for battery voltage (12 volts) in a circuit, attach one lead to ground and the other lead to various points along the circuit. Where battery voltage is present the light bulb will light.

A voltmeter is used in the same manner as the test light to find out if battery voltage is present in any given circuit. The voltmeter, unlike the test light, will also indicate how much voltage is present at each test point. When using a voltmeter, attach the red lead (+) to the component or wire to be checked and the negative (−) lead to a good ground.

Self-powered Test Light and Ohmmeter

A self-powered test light can be constructed of a 12-volt light bulb, a pair of test leads and a 12-volt battery. When the test leads are touched together the light bulb will go on.

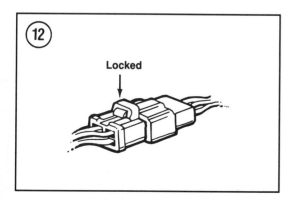

Use a self-powered test light as follows:

a. Touch the test leads together to make sure the light bulb goes on. If not, correct the problem prior to using it in a test procedure.

b. Disconnect the ATV's battery or remove the fuse(s) that protects the circuit to be tested.

c. Select 2 points within the circuit where there should be continuity.

d. Attach one lead of the self-powered test light to each point.

e. If there is continuity, the self-powered test light bulb will come on.

f. If there is no continuity, the self-powered test light bulb will not come on indicating an open circuit.

An ohmmeter can be used in place of the self-powered test light. The ohmmeter, unlike the test light, will also indicate how much resistance is present between each test point. Low resistance means good continuity in a complete circuit. Before using an ohmmeter, it must first be calibrated (except digital ohmmeters). This is done by touching the leads together and turning the ohms calibration knob until the meter reads zero.

> *CAUTION*
> *An ohmmeter must never be connected to any circuit which has power applied to it. Always disconnect the battery negative (−) lead before using the ohmmeter.*

Jumper Wire

When using a jumper wire always install an inline fuse/fuse holder (available at most auto supply stores or electronic supply stores) to the jumper wire. Never use a jumper wire across any load (a component that is connected and turned on). This would result in a direct short and will blow the fuse(s) and/or damage components and wiring in that circuit.

BASIC TEST PROCEDURES

Voltage Testing

Unless otherwise specified, all voltage tests are made with the electrical connector still connected. Insert the test leads into the backside of the connector and make sure the test lead touches the wire or metal terminal within the connector. If the test lead only touches the wire insulation, you will get a false reading.

Always check both sides of the connector as one side may be loose or corroded thus preventing current flow through the connector. This type of test can be performed with a test light or a voltmeter. A voltmeter will give the best results.

NOTE
If using a test light, it doesn't make any difference which test lead is attached to ground.

1. Attach the negative test lead (if using a voltmeter) to a good ground (bare metal). If necessary, scrape away paint from the frame or engine (retouch later with paint). Make sure the part used for ground is *not* insulated with a rubber gasket or rubber grommet.

2. Attach the positive test lead (if using a voltmeter) to the point (electrical connector, etc.) you want to check.

3. Turn the ignition switch on. If using a test light, the test light will come on if voltage is present. If using a voltmeter, note the voltage reading. The reading should be within 1 volt of battery voltage (12 volts). If the voltage is considerably less than battery voltage there is a problem in the circuit.

Voltage Drop Test

A voltage drop of 1 volt or more means there is a problem in the circuit. All components within the circuit are designed for low resistance in order to conduct electricity within a minimum loss of voltage.

1. Connect the voltmeter positive test lead to the end of the wire or switch closest to the battery.

2. Connect the voltmeter negative test lead to the other end of the wire or switch.

3. Turn the components on in the circuit.

4. The voltmeter should indicate battery voltage. If there is a drop of 1 volt or more, there is a problem within the circuit.

5. Check the circuit for loose or dirty connections within an electrical connector(s).

Continuity Test

A continuity test is made to determine if the circuit is complete with no opens in either the electrical wires or components within that circuit.

Unless otherwise specified, all continuity tests are made with the electrical connector disconnected. Insert the test leads into the backside of the connector and make sure the test lead touches the electrical wire or metal terminal within the connector. If the test lead only touches the wire insulation, you will get a false reading.

Always check both sides of the connectors as one side may be loose or corroded thus preventing electrical flow through the connector. This type of test can be performed with a self-powered test light or an ohmmeter. An ohmmeter will give the best results.

If using an analog ohmmeter, calibrate the meter by touching the leads together and turning the ohms calibration knob until the meter reads zero. This is necessary to get accurate results.

1. Disconnect the battery negative lead as described under *Battery* in Chapter Three.

2. Attach one test lead (test light or ohmmeter) to one end of the part of the circuit to be tested.

3. Attach the other test lead to the other end of the part of the circuit to be tested.

4. The self-powered test light will come on if there is continuity. The ohmmeter will indicate either a low or no resistance (means good continuity in a complete circuit) or infinite resistance (means an open circuit).

Testing for a Short with a Self-powered Test Light or Ohmmeter

This test can be performed with either a self-powered test light or an ohmmeter.

1. Disconnect the battery negative lead as described under *Battery* in Chapter Three.

2. Remove the blown fuse from the fuse receptacle.

3. Connect one test lead of the test light or ohmmeter to the load side (battery side) of the fuse terminal in the fuse receptacle.

4. Connect the other test lead to a good ground (bare metal). If necessary, scrape away paint from the frame or engine (retouch later with paint). Make sure the part used for a ground is not insulated with a rubber gasket or rubber grommet.

5. With the self-powered test light or ohmmeter attached to the fuse terminal and ground, wiggle the wiring harness relating to the suspect circuit at 6 in. (15.2 cm) intervals. Start next to the fuse panel and work your way away from the fuse panel. Watch the self-powered test light or ohmmeter as you progress along the harness.

6. If the test light blinks or the needle on the ohmmeter moves, there is a short-to-ground at that point in the harness.

Testing For a Short with a Test Light or Voltmeter

This test can be performed with either a test light or voltmeter.

1. Remove the blown fuse from the fuse receptacle.
2. Connect the test light or voltmeter across the fuse terminals in the fuse receptacle. Turn the ignition switch on and check for battery voltage (12 volts).
3. With the test light or voltmeter attached to the fuse terminals, wiggle the wiring harness relating to the suspect circuit at 6 in. (15.2 cm) intervals. Start next to the fuse panel and work your way away from the fuse panel. Watch the test light or voltmeter as you progress along the harness.

4. If the test light blinks or the needle on the voltmeter moves, there is a short-to-ground at that point in the harness.

ELECTRICAL PROBLEMS

If light bulbs burn out frequently, the cause may be excessive vibration, a loose connection that permits sudden current surges or the installation of the wrong type of bulb.

Most light and ignition problems are caused by loose or corroded ground connections. Check these prior to replacing a light bulb or electrical component.

CHARGING SYSTEM TROUBLESHOOTING

The charging system (**Figure 13**) consists of the battery, magneto and a voltage regulator/rectifier. A 20 amp main fuse protects the circuit.

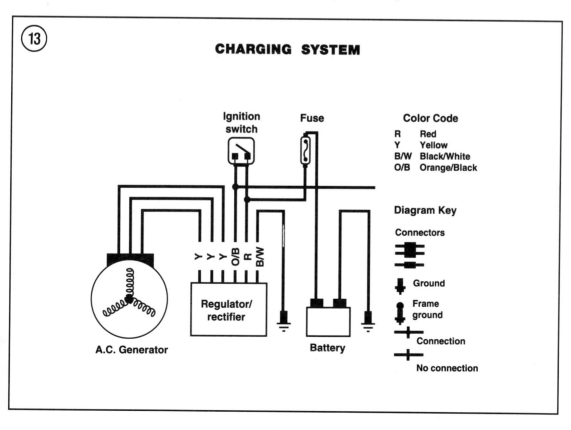

CHARGING SYSTEM

Ignition switch

Fuse

Color Code
R   Red
Y   Yellow
B/W   Black/White
O/B   Orange/Black

Diagram Key

Connectors

Ground

Frame ground

Connection

No connection

Regulator/ rectifier

A.C. Generator

Battery

Alternating current generated by the A.C. generator is rectified to direct current. The voltage regulator maintains the voltage to the battery and additional electrical loads (lights, ignition, etc.) at a constant voltage regardless of variations in engine speed and load.

The basic charging system complaints are:

a. Battery discharging.

b. Battery overcharging.

Battery Discharging

1. Check all of the connections. Make sure they are tight and free of corrosion.

2. Perform the *Charging System Leakage Test* as described in Chapter Nine. Note the following:

a. Current leakage under 1.2 mA, perform Step 3.

b. Current leakage 1.2 mA or higher, perform Step 4.

3. Perform the *Regulator/Rectifier Unit Resistance Test* as described in Chapter Nine. Note the following:

a. If the resistance readings are correct, perform the *Wiring Harness Test* as described in Chapter Nine. If the wiring harness tests are correct, the ignition switch is probably faulty; test the ignition switch as described in Chapter Nine.

b. If the resistance readings are incorrect, replace the regulator/rectifier unit and retest.

4. Perform the *Charging Voltage Test* in Chapter Eight. Note the following:

a. If the test readings are correct, perform Step 5.

b. If the test readings are incorrect, perform Step 6.

5. Test the battery with a battery tester and note the following:

NOTE
If you do not have access to the battery tester, remove the battery from the ATV and take it to a Suzuki dealer for testing.

a. If the test readings are correct, the battery is faulty or the charging system is being overloaded, probably from electrical accessory items.

b. If the test readings are incorrect, check for an open circuit in the wiring harness and for dirty or loose-fitting terminals; clean and repair as required.

6. Perform the battery charging line and ground line tests as described under *Wiring Harness Test* in Chapter Nine. Note the following:

a. If the test readings are correct, perform Step 7.

b. If the test readings are incorrect, check for an open circuit in the wiring harness and for dirty or loose-fitting terminals; clean and repair as required.

7. Perform the charging coil line tests as described under *Wiring Harness Test* in Chapter Nine. Note the following:

a. If the test readings are incorrect, perform Step 8.

b. If the test readings are correct, perform Step 9.

8. Perform the *Charging Coil Resistance Test* as described in Chapter Nine. Note the following:

a. If the test readings are correct, check for a dirty or loose-fitting magneto electrical connector; clean and repair as required.

b. If the test readings are incorrect, replace the magneto assembly as described in Chapter Nine.

9. Perform the *Regulator/Rectifier Unit Resistance Test* as described in Chapter Nine. Note the following:

a. If the resistance readings are correct, the battery is faulty. Replace the battery and retest.

b. If the resistance readings are incorrect, replace the regulator/rectifier unit and retest.

Battery Overcharging

If the battery is overcharging, the regulator/rectifier unit is faulty. Replace the regulator/rectifier unit as described in Chapter Nine.

IGNITION SYSTEM TROUBLESHOOTING

All models are equipped with a capacitor discharge ignition (CDI) system shown in **Figure 14**. This solid state system uses no contact points or other moving parts. Because of the solid state design, problems with the CDI system are relatively few. However, when problems do arise they cause one of the following:

a. Weak spark.

b. No spark.

It is possible to check a CDI system that:

a. Has no spark.

b. Has broken or damaged wires.

c. Has a weak spark.

It is difficult to check a CDI system that malfunctions due to:

a. Vibration problems.

b. Component that malfunctions only when the engine is hot or under a load.

Prior to troubleshooting the ignition system, perform the following:

1. Check the battery to make sure it is fully charged and in good condition. A weak battery will result in slow engine cranking speed.

2. Perform the spark test as described under *Engine Fails to Start (Spark Test)* in this chapter. Then refer to the appropriate ignition system complaint.

3. Because a loose or dirty electrical connector can prevent the ignition system from operating properly,

check for dirty or loose-fitting connector terminals. The ignition system electrical diagram and the wiring diagrams at the end of this book can be used to locate the appropriate electrical connectors. Also, refer to *Preliminary Checks and Precautions* under *Electrical Troubleshooting* in this chapter for additional information.

No Spark at The Spark Plug

1. Check for dirty or loose-fitting connector terminals as previously described. Clean and repair as required.

NOTE
If the ignition system does not operate properly after inspecting and cleaning

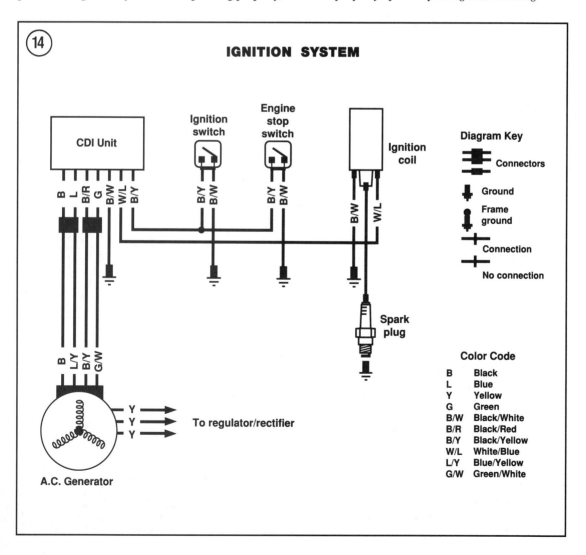

IGNITION SYSTEM

the connector terminals, proceed with Step 2.

2. Measure the CDI unit resistance as described under *CDI Unit Resistance Test* in Chapter Nine. Note the following:
   a. If the resistance reading is incorrect, the CDI unit is faulty and should be replaced.
   b. If the resistance reading is correct, check for an open circuit between the CDI unit and the pickup coil assembly.

> *NOTE*
> *The CDI unit is located on the right-hand side of the fuel tank (**Figure 15**) under the front fender.*

> *NOTE*
> *When switching between ohmmeter scales, always cross the test leads and zero the meter to assure a correct reading.*

3. Measure the pickup coil resistance as described under *Pickup Coil Resistance Test* in Chapter Nine. Note the following:
   a. If the resistance reading is incorrect, the pulse generator is faulty and should be replaced.
   b. If the resistance reading is correct, check for an open circuit between the CDI unit and the pulse generator.

> *NOTE*
> *The pulse generator connector (**Figure 16**) is located on the front right-hand side of the frame.*

4. Test the neutral switch as described in Chapter Nine. Note the following:
   a. If the neutral switch is faulty, replace it and retest.
   b. If the neutral switch is okay, check for an open circuit between the neutral switch and the ignition switch.

5. Measure the coil's secondary resistance as described under *Ignition Coil Resistance Test* in Chapter Nine. Note the following:
   a. If the test results are incorrect, perform Step 6.
   b. If the test results are correct, repeat the spark test by switching the ignition coils. If you now have a spark, the original coil is faulty and should be replaced.

6. Remove the spark plug wire from the ignition coil and repeat the test made in Step 5. Note the following:
   a. If the test results are still incorrect, the ignition coil is faulty and should be replaced.
   b. If the test results are now correct, check for poor contact between the spark plug wire and coil. If this is okay, the spark plug wire is faulty and should be replaced.

ELECTRIC STARTER SYSTEM TROUBLESHOOTING

The electric starting system (**Figure 17**) consists of the starter motor, starter gears, starter relay, starter button, ignition switch, neutral switch, reverse switch, main fuse and battery.

When the starter button is pressed, it allows current flow through the solenoid coil. The coil contacts close, allowing electricity to flow from the battery to the starter motor.

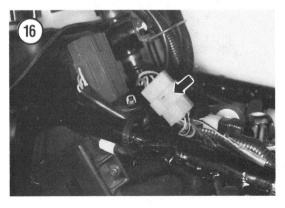

CAUTION
Do not operate the starter for more than 5 seconds at a time. Let it rest approximately 10 seconds, then use it again.

The starter should turn when the starter button is depressed when the transmission is in neutral. If the starter does not operate properly, perform the following test procedures. Starter troubleshooting is grouped under the following:

a. Starter motor does not turn.

b. Starter motor turns slowly.

c. Starter motor turns but the engine does not.

d. Starter motor and engine turn but the engine does not start.

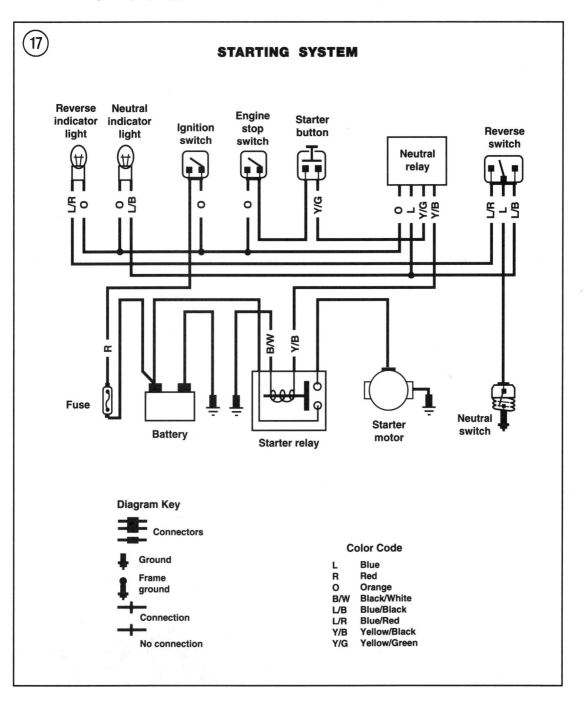

1. Check the battery to make sure it is fully charged and in good condition. Refer to Chapter Three for battery service.

2. Check the starter electrical cables for loose or damaged connections.

3. Check the battery electrical cables for loose or damaged connections. Then check the battery state of charge as described under *Battery Testing* in Chapter Nine.

4. If the starter does not operate correctly after making these checks and adjustments, perform the test procedure that best describes the starting trouble.

Starter Motor Does Not Turn

1. Remove the front fender as described in Chapter Fourteen to expose the starter relay switch (**Figure 18**).

2. Check the starter relay connector for dirty or loose-fitting terminals. Clean and repair as required.

3. Check the starter relay switch. Turn the ignition switch on and depress the starter switch button. When the starter button is depressed, the starter relay switch should click once. Note the following:
   a. If there was a click, perform Step 4.
   b. If there was no click, perform Step 5.

> *CAUTION*
> *Because of the large amount of current that will flow from the battery to the starter in Step 4, large cables should be used to make the connections.*

4. Remove the starter from the ATV as described in Chapter Nine. Using an auxiliary battery, apply battery voltage directly to the starter. The starter should turn when battery voltage is directly applied. Note the following:
   a. If the starter motor does not turn, disassemble and inspect the starter motor as described in Chapter Nine. Test the starter components and replace worn or damaged parts as required.
   b. If the starter motor turns, check for loose or damaged starter cables. If the cables are okay, check the starter relay switch as described in Chapter Nine. Replace the starter relay switch if necessary.

5. Remove the starter relay switch (**Figure 18**). Note the following:

   a. Connect the positive (+) lead of a fully charged 12-volt battery to the starter relay switch Red wire terminal and the battery negative (–) wire to the black/yellow lead terminal.
   b. Connect an ohmmeter between the battery lead terminal and the starter motor lead terminal.
   c. There should be continuity when the battery leads are connected to the starter relay switch and no continuity when they are disconnected.

6. If continuity was shown in each test, perform Step 7. If there is no continuity in one or more tests, check for dirty or loose-fitting terminals; clean and repair as required and retest. Then check for a short circuit in the wiring. If the connectors and wiring are okay, test the following components as described in Chapter Nine:
   a. Clutch switch.
   b. Neutral switch.
   c. Neutral switch diode.

7. Pull the rubber cover away from the starter relay switch electrical connector to expose the wire terminals in the connector (**Figure 19**). Then connect a voltmeter between the starter relay switch connector yellow/black terminal (+) and the black/white ground (–). Turn the ignition switch to ON and the engine stop switch to RUN. Press the starter button and read the voltage indicated on the voltmeter. It should be battery voltage. Turn the ignition switch off and note the following:
   a. If battery voltage is shown, perform Step 8.
   b. If no battery voltage is shown, check for a blown main fuse. See *Fuses* in Chapter Nine. If the fuse is okay, check for an open circuit in the wiring harness or for dirty or loose-fitting terminals. If the wiring and connectors are okay, check for a faulty ignition and/or starter switch as described in Chapter Nine.

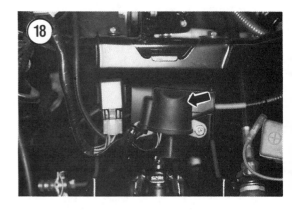

8. Test the starter relay switch as described in Chapter Nine. Note the following:

  a. If the starter relay switch is normal, check for dirty or loose-fitting terminals in its connector block.

  b. If the starter relay switch is faulty, replace it and retest.

Starter Motor Turns Slowly

If the starter motor turns slowly and all engine components and systems are normal, perform the following:

1. Test the battery as described in Chapter Three.

2. Check for the following:

  a. Loose or corroded battery terminals.

  b. Loose or corroded battery ground cable.

  c. Loose starter motor cable.

3. Remove, disassemble and bench test the starter as described under *Starter* in Chapter Nine.

4. Check the starter for binding during operation. Disassemble the starter and check the armature shaft for bending or damage. Also check the starter clutch as described in Chapter Four.

Starter Motor Turns but the Engine Does Not

If the starter motor turns but the engine does not, perform the following:

1. If the starter motor is running backward and the starter was just reassembled or if the starter motor cables were disconnected and then reconnected to the starter:

  a. The starter motor was reassembled incorrectly.

  b. The starter motor cables were incorrectly installed.

2. Check for a damaged starter clutch (Chapter Four).

3. Check for a damaged or faulty starter pinion gear (Chapter Four).

4. Check for damaged starter reduction gears (Chapter Four).

Starter Relay Switch Clicks but Engine Does Not Turn Over

1. Excessive reduction gear friction.

2. Crankshaft cannot turn over because of mechanical failure.

CARBURETOR TROUBLESHOOTING

The following lists isolate basic carburetor problems under specific complaints.

Engine Will Not Start

If the engine will not start and you have determined that the electrical and mechanical systems are working correctly, check the following:

1. If there is no fuel going to the carburetor, note the following:

  a. Clogged fuel tank breather cap hole.

  b. Clogged fuel tank-to-carburetor tube.

  c. Clogged fuel shutoff valve filter screen.

  d. Faulty fuel pump.

2. If the engine is flooded (too much fuel), note the following:

  a. Flooded carburetor. Fuel valve in carburetor stuck open.

  b. Clogged air filter element.

3. If you have not located the problem in Step 1 or Step 2, check for the following:

  a. Contaminated or deteriorated fuel.

  b. Intake manifold air leak.

  c. Clogged pilot or choke circuit.

Engine Starts but Idles and Runs Poorly or Stalls Frequently

An engine that idles roughly or stalls may have one or more of the following problems:

  a. Clogged air cleaner.

b. Contaminated fuel.

c. Incorrect pilot screw adjustment.

d. Faulty fuel pump.

e. Incorrect idle speed.

f. Bystarter or slow circuit clogged.

g. Loose, disconnected or damaged fuel and emission control vacuum hoses.

h. Intake air leak.

i. Lean fuel mixture.

j. Rich fuel mixture.

Incorrect Fast Idle Speed

A fast idle speed can be due to one of the following problems:

a. Faulty bystarter valve.

b. Incorrect choke cable free play.

c. Incorrect carburetor synchronization.

Poor Gas Mileage and Engine Performance

Poor gas mileage and engine performance can be caused by infrequent engine tune-ups. Check your records to see when your ATV was last tuned up and compare against the recommended tune-up service intervals in Chapter Three. If the last tune-up was within the specified service intervals, check for one or more of the following problems:

a. Clogged air filter.

b. Clogged fuel system.

c. Loose, disconnected or damaged fuel vacuum hoses.

Rich Fuel Mixture

A rich carburetor fuel mixture can be caused by one or more of the following conditions:

a. Clogged or dirty air filter.

b. Worn or damaged fuel valve and seat.

c. Clogged air jets.

d. Incorrect float level (too high).

e. Starter valve damaged or stuck ON.

f. Flooded carburetor.

Lean Fuel Mixture

A lean carburetor fuel mixture can be caused by one or more of the following conditions:

a. Clogged carburetor air vent hole.

b. Clogged fuel filter.

c. Restricted fuel line.

d. Intake air leak.

e. Incorrect float level (too low).

f. Worn or damaged fuel valve.

g. Faulty throttle valve.

h. Faulty vacuum piston.

Engine Backfires

a. Lean fuel mixture.

b. Incorrect carburetor adjustment.

Engine Misses During Acceleration

When there is a pause before the engine responds to the throttle, the engine is missing. An engine miss can occur when starting from a dead stop or at any speed. An engine miss may be due to one of the following:

a. Lean fuel mixture.

b. Faulty ignition coil secondary wires; check for cracking, hardening or bad connections.

c. Faulty vacuum hoses; check for kinks, splits or bad connections.

d. Vacuum leaks at the carburetor and/or intake manifold.

e. Fouled spark plug.

f. Low engine compression. Check engine compression as described in Chapter Three. Low compression can be caused by worn engine components.

g. Faulty fuel pump.

EXCESSIVE VIBRATION

If mounting hardware is okay, vibration can be difficult to find without disassembling the engine.

Usually this is caused by loose engine mounting hardware.

FRONT SUSPENSION AND STEERING

Poor handling may be caused by improper tire pressure, a damaged or bent frame or front steering components, worn front suspension arms, worn wheel bearings or dragging brakes.

ATV Steers to One Side

a. Uneven air pressure in front tires.
b. Bent frame.
c. Worn or damaged front wheel bearings.
d. Damaged steering shaft holders.
e. Incorrectly installed wheels.

Suspension Noise

a. Loose mounting fasteners.
b. Damaged front and/or rear shock absorber.

Wobble/Vibration

a. Loose front or rear wheels.
b. Loose or damaged wheel bearing(s).
c. Damaged wheel rim(s).
d. Damaged tire(s).
e. Loose suspension arm pivot bolts.

Hard Suspension

a. Excessive tire pressure.

b. Bent damper rod(s).
c. Incorrect shock adjustment.
d. Damaged shock absorber bushing(s).
e. Damaged shock absorber bearing.

Soft Suspension

a. Insufficient tire pressure.
b. Weak or damaged shock absorber spring(s).
c. Damaged shock absorber(s).
d. Incorrect shock absorber adjustment.
e. Leaking damper unit(s).

BRAKE PROBLEMS

Sticking drum brakes may be caused by worn or weak return springs, dry pivot and camshaft bushings or improper adjustment. Grabbing brakes may be caused by greasy linings which must be replaced. Brake grab may also be due to an out-of-round drum. Glazed linings will cause loss of stopping power.

CHAPTER THREE

LUBRICATION, MAINTENANCE AND TUNE-UP

If this is your first experience with an ATV or motorcycle, you should become acquainted with products that are available in auto or motorcycle parts and supply stores. Look into the tune-up tools and parts and check out the different lubricants, locking compounds and greases. Also check engine degreasers, like Gunk or Bel-Ray Degreaser, for cleaning your engine prior to working on it.

The more you get involved in your ATV the more you will want to work on it. Start by doing simple tune-up, lubrication and maintenance. Tackle more involved jobs as you gain experience.

The Suzuki ATV is a relatively simple machine but to gain the utmost in safety, performance and useful life from it, it is necessary to make periodic inspections and adjustments. It frequently happens that minor problems are found during such inspections that are simple and inexpensive to correct at the time. If these problems are not corrected, it could lead to major problems.

This chapter explains lubrication, maintenance and tune-up procedures required for all Suzuki LT-F250, LT-4WD and LT-4WDX models. **Table 1** is a suggested factory maintenance schedule. **Tables 1-7** are located at the end of this chapter.

PRE-CHECKS

The following checks should be performed prior to the first ride of the day.

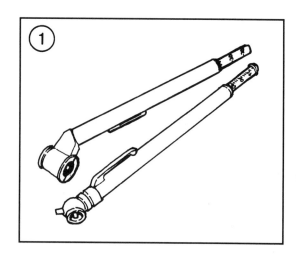

1. Inspect all fuel lines and fittings for leakage.

2. Make sure the fuel tank is full of fresh gasoline.

3. Make sure the engine oil level is correct. Add oil if necessary.

4. Check the oil level in the front differential unit.

5. Make sure the air filter is clean.

6. Check the operation of the clutch and adjust if necessary.

7. Check the throttle and the brake levers. Make sure they operate properly with no binding.

8. Check the brake fluid level in the front brake reservoir. Add fluid if necessary.

9. Inspect the front and rear suspension; make sure it has a good solid feel with no looseness.

10. Check tire pressure; refer to **Table 2**.

11. Check the exhaust system for damage.

12. Check the tightness of all fasteners, especially engine mounting hardware.

13. Make sure the headlight and taillight work.

SERVICE INTERVALS

The service intervals shown in **Table 1** are recommended by the factory. Strict adherence to these recommendations will insure long service from your Suzuki ATV. However, if the vehicle is run in an area of high humidity, the lubrication and maintenance must be done more frequently to prevent possible rust damage. This is especially true if you have run the ATV through water (especially saltwater).

For convenience when maintaining your vehicle, most of the services shown in **Table 1** are described in this chapter. However, some procedures which require more than minor disassembly or adjustment are covered elsewhere in the appropriate chapter.

TIRES AND WHEELS

Tire Pressure

Tire pressure should be checked and adjusted to maintain the smoothness of the tire, good traction and handling and to get the maximum life out of the tire. A simple, accurate gauge (**Figure 1**) can be purchased for a few dollars and should be carried in your tool box in the tow vehicle. The appropriate tire pressures are shown in **Table 2**.

> *NOTE*
> *After checking and adjusting the air pressure, make sure to install the air valve cap (**Figure 2**). The cap prevents small pebbles and dirt from collecting in the valve stem; this could allow air leakage or result in incorrect tire pressure readings.*

> *NOTE*
> *A loss of air pressure may be due to a loose or damaged valve core. Put a few drops of water on the top of the valve core. If the water bubbles, tighten the valve core and recheck. If air is still leaking from the valve after tightening it, replace the valve stem assembly.*

> *WARNING*
> *Always inflate both front tires to the same pressure and the rear tires to the same pressure (front and rear air pressures are different). If the ATV is run with unequal air pressures, it will cause the vehicle to run toward one side and cause poor handling.*

> *CAUTION*
> *Do not over inflate the stock tires as they will be permanently distorted and damaged. If overinflated, they will bulge out similar to inflating an inner tube that is not within the constraints of a tire. If this happens, the tire **will not** return to its original contour.*

Tire Inspection

The tires take a lot of punishment due to the variety of terrain they are subjected to. Inspect the tires for the following:

a. Deep cuts and imbedded objects (i.e., stones, nails, etc.). If you find a nail or other object in a tire, mark its location with a light crayon prior to removing it. This will help to locate the hole for repair. Refer to Chapter Ten for tire changing and repair information.
b. Cracks.
c. Separating plies.
d. Sidewall damage.

Tread Depth

Suzuki recommends replacing any tire that has only 4 mm (3/16 in.) of tread left (**Figure 3**). Refer to Chapter Ten for tire changing and repair information.

Rim Inspection

Frequently inspect the condition of the wheel rims, especially the outer side. If the wheel has hit a tree or large rock, rim damage may be sufficient to cause an air leak or knock it out of alignment. Improper wheel alignment can cause severe vibration and result in an unsafe riding condition.

Make sure that the wheel lug nuts (**Figure 4**) and hub cotter pins are securely in place on all 4 wheels.

BATTERY

The battery is an important component in the electrical system. It is also the one most frequently neglected. In addition to checking and correcting the battery electrolyte level on a weekly basis, the battery should be cleaned and inspected at periodic intervals listed in **Table 1**.

The battery should be checked periodically for electrolyte level, state of charge and corrosion. During hot weather periods, frequent checks are recommended. If the electrolyte level is below the fill line, add distilled water as required. To assure proper mixing of the water and acid, operate the engine immediately after adding water. *Never* add battery acid instead of water; this will shorten the battery's life.

> *CAUTION*
> *If it becomes necessary to remove the battery breather tube when performing any of the following procedures, make*

sure to route the tube correctly during installation to prevent electrolyte or gas from spewing onto the battery compartment of the front fender assembly or any other component. Incorrect breather tube routing can cause structural and/or cosmetic damage.

Battery Removal/Installation and Electrolyte Level Check

The electrolyte level can be checked with the battery installed, by removing the front cover. The electrolyte level should be maintained between the 2 marks on the battery case (**Figure 5**). If the electrolyte level is low, it's a good idea to remove the battery from the ATV so it can be thoroughly serviced and checked.

1. Remove the screws and washers securing the front cover (**Figure 6**). Slide the front cover forward and out through the front rack and remove it.
2. Unhook the battery hold down strap (**Figure 7**) and remove it.

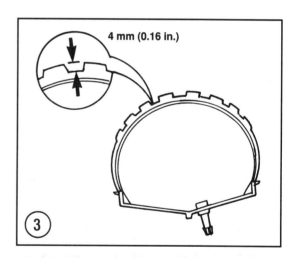

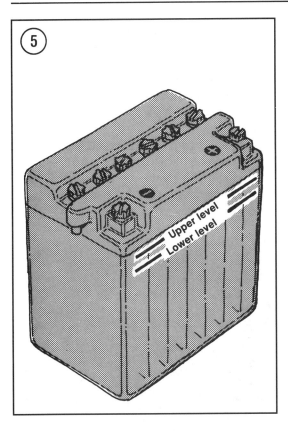

3. First disconnect the battery negative (–) lead (A, **Figure 8**) then the positive (+) lead (B, **Figure 8**) from the battery.

4. Disconnect the battery vent tube from the battery (C, **Figure 8**). Leave the vent tube attached to the front fender assembly.

5. Pull the battery straight up and out of its compartment in the front fender assembly. Wipe off any of the highly corrosive residue that may have dripped from the battery during removal.

6. Set the battery on some newspapers or shop cloths to protect the workbench surface from any spilled acid residue.

7. The electrolyte level should be maintained between the 2 marks on the battery case (**Figure 9**).

WARNING
Protect your eyes, skin and clothing. If electrolyte gets into your eyes, flush your eyes thoroughly with clean water and get prompt medical attention.

CAUTION
Be careful not to spill battery electrolyte on plastic or painted surfaces. The liquid is highly corrosive and will damage

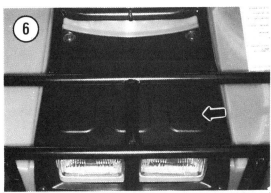

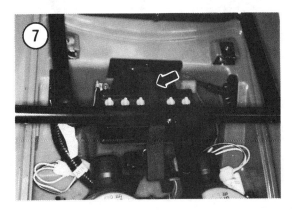

the finish. If it is spilled, wash it off immediately with soapy water and thoroughly rinse with clean water.

8. Rinse the battery off with clean water and wipe dry.

9. If the electrolyte level is low, remove the caps (**Figure 10**) from the battery cells and add distilled water to correct the level. Never add electrolyte (acid) to correct the level.

NOTE
After distilled water has been added, reinstall the battery caps and gently shake the battery for several minutes to mix the existing electrolyte with the new water.

10. After the fluid level has been corrected and the battery allowed to stand for a few minutes, remove the battery caps and check the specific gravity of the electrolyte with a hydrometer (**Figure 11**). See *Battery Testing* in this chapter.

CAUTION
*If distilled water has been added to a battery in freezing or near freezing weather, dress warmly and then ride the ATV for a **minimum of 30 minutes**. This will help mix the water thoroughly into the electrolyte in the battery. Distilled water is lighter than electrolyte and will float on top of the electrolyte if it is not mixed in properly. If the water stays on the top, it may freeze and fracture the battery case, ruining the battery.*

11. After the battery has been refilled, recharged or replaced, install it as follows:

a. Clean the battery terminals (**Figure 12**) of all corrosion and/or oxidation. After a thorough cleaning, coat the terminals with a thin layer of dielectric grease to retard corrosion and decomposition of the terminals.

b. Visually inspect the battery cable connectors for corrosion and/or damage. If necessary, clean the cable connectors prior to attaching them to the battery.

c. Position the battery on the ground with the negative (–) terminal (A, **Figure 8**) toward the *left-hand* side of the ATV. The positive (+) terminal and the breather outlet are on the right-hand side (B, **Figure 8**).

d. Make sure the breather tube (**Figure 13**) is in place in the front fender assembly prior to installing the battery.

e. Carefully lower the battery straight down into its compartment in the front fender assembly and attach the breather tube to the battery (C, **Figure 8**).

f. Attach the red positive (+) cable and bolt first (B, **Figure 8**) then the black negative (–) cable (A, **Figure 8**). Tighten the bolts securely.

g. Hook the battery hold down strap (**Figure 7**) and make sure it is secured properly.

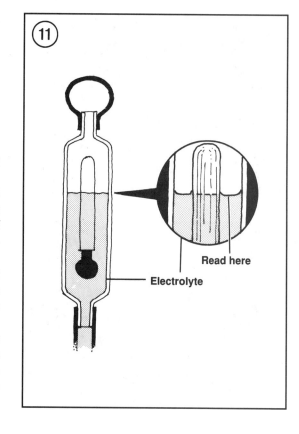

Read here
Electrolyte

h. Slide the front cover through the front rack and secure it with the screws and washers. Tighten the screws securely.

Testing

Hydrometer testing is the best way to check battery condition. Use a hydrometer with numbered graduations from 1.100 to 1.300 rather than one with color-coded bands. To use the hydrometer, squeeze the rubber ball, insert the tip into the cell and release the pressure on the ball. Draw enough electrolyte to float the weighted float inside the hydrometer. Note the number in line with the surface of the electrolyte; this is the specific gravity for this cell. Squeeze the rubber ball again and return the electrolyte to the cell from which it came.

The specific gravity of the electrolyte in each battery cell is an excellent indication of that cell's condition. A fully charged cell will read 1.260-1.280, while a cell in good condition reads from 1.230-1.250 and anything below 1.140 is discharged.

Specific gravity varies with temperature. For each 10° the electrolyte temperature exceeds 80° F (27°

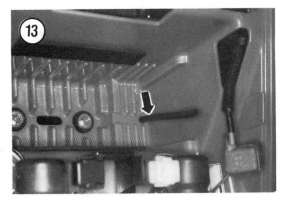

C), add 0.004 to readings indicated on the hydrometer. Subtract 0.004 for each 10° below 80° F (27° C).

If the cells test in the poor range, the battery requires recharging. The hydrometer is useful for checking the progress of the charging operation. **Table 3** shows approximate state of charge.

Charging

WARNING
During the charging process, highly explosive hydrogen gas is released from the battery. The battery should be charged only in a well-ventilated area away from any open flames (including pilot lights on home gas appliances). Do not allow any smoking in the area. Never check the charge by arcing (connecting pliers or other metal objects) across the terminals; the resulting spark can ignite the hydrogen gas.

CAUTION
*Do **NOT** use an automotive-type battery charger as you will run the risk of overheating the battery and causing internal plate damage. Use only a small trickle charger designed specifically for use on motorcycle batteries.*

CAUTION
Always remove the battery from the front fender assembly before connecting the battery charger. Never recharge a battery in the vehicle; the corrosive mist that is emitted during the charging process will corrode all surrounding surfaces.

1. Connect the positive (+) charger lead to the positive (+) battery terminal and the negative (–) charger lead to the negative (–) battery terminal.
2. Remove all vent caps from the battery, set the charger to 12 volts and switch the charger ON. If the output of the charger is variable, it is best to select a low setting—1 1/2 to 2 amps. Normally, a battery should be charged at a slow charge rate of 1/10 its given capacity.

CAUTION
The electrolyte level must be maintained at the upper level during the charging cycle; check and refill as necessary.

3. The charging time depends on the discharged condition of the battery. The chart in **Figure 14** can be used to determine approximate charging times at different specific gravity readings. For example, if the specific gravity of your battery is 1.180, the approximate charging time would be 6 hours.

4. After the battery has been charged for about 6 hours, turn the charger OFF, disconnect the leads and check the specific gravity of each cell. It should be within the limits specified in **Table 3**. If it is, and remains stable for 1 hour, the battery is considered charged.

5. To ensure good electrical contact, cables must be clean and tight on the battery's terminals. If the cable terminals are badly corroded, even after performing the above cleaning procedures, the cables should be disconnected, removed from the ATV and cleaned separately with a wire brush and a baking soda solution. After cleaning, apply a very thin coating of dielectric grease, petroleum jelly (Vaseline) or silicone spray to the battery terminals before reattaching the cables.

NEW BATTERY INSTALLATION

When replacing the old battery, be sure to charge it completely (specific gravity 1.260-1.280) before installing it in the ATV. Failure to do so or using the battery with a low electrolyte level will permanently damage the new battery.

NOTE
Recycle your old battery. When you replace the old battery, be sure to turn in the old battery at that time. The lead plates and the plastic case can be recycled. Most motorcycle dealers will accept your old battery in trade when you purchase a new one, but if they will not, many automotive supply store certainly will. Never place an old battery in your household trash since it is illegal, in most states, to place any acid or lead (heavy metal) contents in landfills. There is also the danger of the battery being crushed in the trash truck and spraying acid on the truck operator.

BATTERY ELECTRICAL CABLE CONNECTORS

To ensure good electrical contact between the battery and the electrical cables, the cables must be clean and free of corrosion.

1. If the electrical cable terminals are badly corroded, disconnect them from the vehicle's electrical system.

2. Thoroughly clean each connector with a wire brush and then with a baking soda solution. Rinse thoroughly with clean water and wipe dry with a clean cloth.

3. After cleaning, apply a thin layer of dielectric grease to the battery terminals before reattaching the cables.

4. If disconnected, connect the electrical cables to the ATV's electrical system.

5. After connecting the electrical cables, apply a light coating of dielectric grease to the electrical

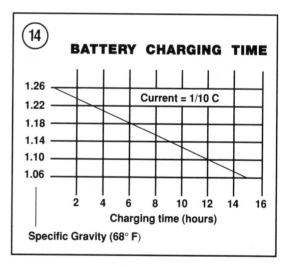

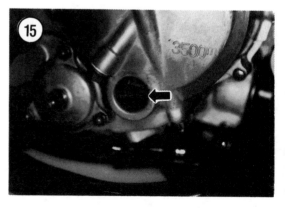

terminals of the battery to retard corrosion and de-composition of the terminals.

PERIODIC LUBRICATION

Oil

Oil is classified according to its viscosity, which is an indication of how thick it is. The Society of Automotive Engineers (SAE) system distinguishes oil viscosity by numbers. Thick oils have higher viscosity numbers than thin oils. For example, SAE 5 oil is a thin oil while SAE 90 oil is relatively thick. If the oil has been tested in cold weather, it is denoted with a "W" after the number as "SAE 10W."

Grease

A good quality grease (preferably waterproof) should be used. Water does not wash grease off parts as easily as it washes oil off. In addition, grease maintains its lubricating qualities better than oil on long and strenuous rides. In a pinch, though, the

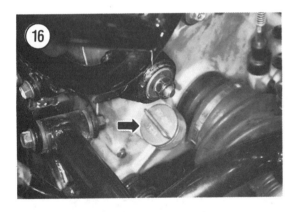

wrong lubricant is better than none at all. Correct the situation as soon as possible.

Engine Oil Level Check and Adding Oil

Engine oil level is checked with the viewing port on the right-hand crankcase half next to the oil filter cover.

1. Start the engine and let it warm up approximately 2-3 minutes.
2. Shut off the engine and let the oil settle for at least 1 minute.
3. Place the ATV on level ground and apply the parking brake.
4. Look at the oil level inspection window. The oil level should be between the 2 lines (**Figure 15**). If the level is below the lower "H" line, add the recommended engine oil to correct the level.
5. Remove the oil filler cap (**Figure 16**).
6. Insert a funnel into the oil fill hole and fill the engine with the correct viscosity and quantity of oil. Refer to **Table 4**.
7. Remove the funnel, then install the oil filler cap and tighten securely.
8. Repeat Steps 1-4 and recheck the oil level.

Engine Oil and Filter Change

Regular oil changes will contribute more to engine longevity than any other maintenance performed. The recommended oil and filter change interval is listed in **Table 1**. This assumes that the vehicle is operated in moderate climates. If it is operated under dusty conditions, the oil will get dirty more quickly and should be changed more frequently than recommended.

Use only a high quality detergent 10W/40 motor oil with an API classification of SF or SG. The classification is stamped or printed on top of the can or on the label on plastic bottles (**Figure 17**). Try to use the same brand of oil at each oil change.

CAUTION
Do not use any friction reducing additives in the oil as it will cause clutch slippage. Also, do not use an engine oil with graphite added.

NOTE
*Never dispose of motor oil in the trash, on the ground, or down a storm drain. Many service stations accept used motor oil and waste haulers provide curbside used motor oil collection. Do not combine other fluids with motor oil to be recycled. To locate a recycler, contact the American Petroleum Institute (API) at **www.recycleoil.org**.*

To change the engine oil and filter, you will need the following:

  a. Drain pan.

  b. Funnel.

  c. Can opener or pour spout.

  d. 17 mm wrench.

  e. Oil (refer to **Table 4** for quantity).

There are a number of ways to discard the old oil safely. Some service stations and oil retailers will accept your used oil for recycling; some may even give you money for it. Never drain the oil onto the ground.

1. Place the ATV on level ground.

2. Set the parking brake, start the engine and let it reach operating temperature.

3. Shut it off and place a drain pan under the engine.

4. Remove the 17 mm drain plug that is accessible through the hole in the engine skid plate (**Figure 18**).

5. Remove the oil filler cap; this will speed up the flow of oil.

6. Let it drain for at least 15-20 minutes.

7. Turn both the ignition switch and the engine kill switch to the OFF position and depending on model, pull on the recoil starter or use the electric starter a couple of times to help drain any remaining oil.

CAUTION
Do not let the engine start and run without oil in the crankcase. Make sure the ignition switch and engine kill switch are in the OFF position.

NOTE
*The area where the oil filter (**Figure 19**) is located on the engine is obstructed by the right-hand rear wheel. To make filter change easier, it is suggested that the right-hand rear wheel be removed for this procedure.*

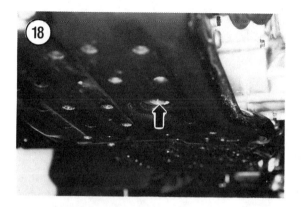

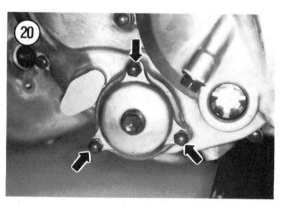

8. Remove the right-hand rear wheel as described in Chapter Twelve.

NOTE
Step 9 is performed with the engine removed from the frame for clarity. It is not necessary to remove the engine for this procedure.

9. To remove the oil filter, perform the following:

a. Remove the nuts (**Figure 20**) securing the filter cover on the right-hand crankcase cover and remove the filter cover and spring.

b. Remove the filter, place it in a reclosable plastic bag, then discard it properly.

c. Thoroughly clean out the filter receptacle (A, **Figure 21**) in the crankcase cover with a shop cloth and solvent. If necessary, scrape out any oil sludge with a broad-tipped, dull screwdriver.

d. Remove the filter cover O-ring seal (A, **Figure 22**) from the filter cover. A new O-ring seal must be installed every time the filter is replaced.

e. Make sure the small O-ring seal (B, **Figure 21**) is in place in the crankcase cover.

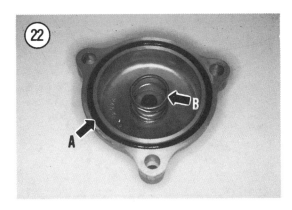

f. Position the new filter with the open end (**Figure 23**) going in first, toward the engine.

g. Install the new filter (**Figure 24**) into the crankcase cover.

h. Make sure the O-ring seal (A, **Figure 22**) is in place in the filter cover.

i. If removed, install the spring (B, **Figure 22**) on the filter cover.

j. Apply a light coat of gasket sealer to the threaded studs on the crankcase cover.

k. Install the cover and nuts (**Figure 20**). Tighten the nuts securely.

10. Install the drain plug and tighten to the torque specification listed in **Table 5**.

11. Insert a funnel into the oil fill hole and fill the engine with the correct weight and quantity oil. Refer to **Table 4** for quantity.

12. Screw in the oil filler cap (**Figure 16**) securely.

13. If the engine has been rebuilt or disassembled, turn both the ignition switch and the engine kill switch to the OFF position. Then, depending on model, pull on the recoil starter or use the electric starter a couple of times to help distribute the oil throughout the engine.

14. Install the right-hand rear wheel as described in Chapter Twelve.

15. Start the engine and let it run at moderate speed and check for leaks.

16. Turn the engine off and check for correct oil level; adjust as necessary.

Front Differential Gear Unit
(4-wheel Drive Models)

Oil level check

The oil level should be checked at the interval indicated in **Table 1**. The final drive unit should be

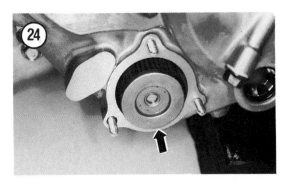

cool. If the ATV has been run, allow it to cool down, then check the oil level. When checking or changing the final drive oil, do not allow any dirt or foreign matter to enter the case opening.

1. Place the ATV on level ground and set the parking brake.

2. Wipe the area around the oil fill cap clean and unscrew the oil fill cap (A, **Figure 25**).

3. The oil level is correct if the oil is up to the lower edge of the fill cap hole. If the oil level is low, add a good quality of SAE 90 hypoid gear oil until the oil level is correct. Refer to **Table 4** for specified quantity.

4. Install the oil fill cap and tighten to the torque specification listed in **Table 5**.

Oil change

Change the front differential gear oil at the factory recommended interval (**Table 1**), or whenever the oil becomes contaminated.

To drain the oil you will need the following:

a. Drain pan.

b. Funnel.

c. Oil (refer to **Table 4** for quantity).

Discard old oil in the same manner as outlined in *Engine Oil and Filter Change* in this chapter.

1. Ride the ATV until normal operating temperature is reached. Usually 15-20 minutes of stop-and-go riding is sufficient.

2. Place the ATV on level ground and set the parking brake.

3. Place a drain pan under the drain bolt.

4. Remove the oil fill cap (A, **Figure 25**) and the drain bolt (B, **Figure 25**).

5. Let the oil drain for at least 15-20 minutes to ensure that the majority of the oil has drained out.

6. Inspect the sealing washer on the drain bolt and the O-ring seal on the fill cap; replace if necessary.

7. Install the drain bolt and tighten to the torque specification listed in **Table 5**.

8. Insert a funnel into the oil fill hole.

NOTE
To measure the correct amount of fluid, use a plastic baby bottle. These have measurements in milliliters (ml) and fluid ounces (oz.) on the side.

9. Add hypoid gear oil rated API GL-5 until the oil level is correct. Refer to **Table 4** for quantity.

10. Remove the funnel and make sure the oil comes up to the bottom of the oil fill cap hole. Add additional oil if necessary.

11. Install the oil fill cap and tighten to the torque specification listed in **Table 5**.

12. Test ride the ATV and check for leaks. After the test ride, recheck the oil level and adjust if necessary.

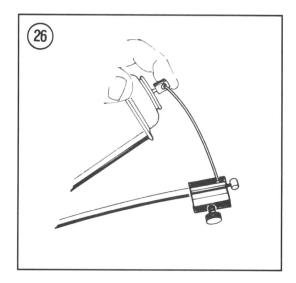

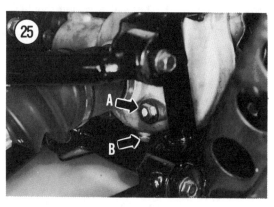

Control Cables

The control cables should be lubricated every 30 days of operation. They should be also inspected at this time for fraying and the cable sheath should be checked for chafing. The cables are relatively inexpensive and should be replaced when found to be faulty.

The cable should be lubricated with a cable lubricant and a cable lubricator.

CAUTION
*If the stock cable has been replaced with nylon-lined cables, do **not** oil them as described in the following procedure. Oil and most cable lubricants will cause the liner to expand, pinching the liner against the cable. Nylon-lined cables are normally used dry. When servicing nylon-lined cables, follow the cable manufacturer's instructions.*

NOTE
The main cause of cable breakage or cable stiffness is improper lubrication. Maintaining the cables as described in this section will assure long service life.

1. Disconnect the cables from the throttle, choke and rear brake lever.

2. Attach a lubricator following its manufacturer's instructions.

3. Insert the nozzle of the lubricant can in the lubricator (**Figure 26**), press the button on the can and hold it down until the lubricant begins to flow out of the other end of the cable.

NOTE
Place a shop cloth at the end of the cable(s) to catch all excess lubricant.

4. Remove the lubricator, reconnect the cable(s) and adjust the cable(s) as described in this chapter.

Miscellaneous Lubrication Points

Lubricate the front brake lever, rear brake hand lever and rear brake pedal pivot points. Use SAE 10W/40 engine oil.

PERIODIC MAINTENANCE

Front Drum Brake Fluid Level Check and Adding Brake Fluid

The fluid level should be between the upper and lower mark within the reservoir. If the brake fluid level reaches the lower level mark (**Figure 27**) on the side of the master cylinder reservoir, the fluid level must be corrected by adding fresh brake fluid.

1. Place the ATV on level ground and set the parking brake.

2. Position the handlebars so the front master cylinder reservoir is in its normal riding position.

3. Clean the top of the master cylinder of all dirt and foreign matter.

4. Remove the screws securing the cover (**Figure 28**). Remove the cover and the diaphragm.

5. Add brake fluid (**Figure 29**) until the level is to the upper level line within the master cylinder res-

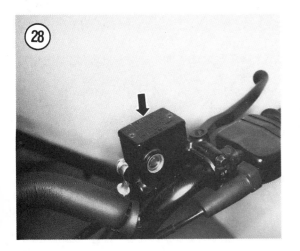

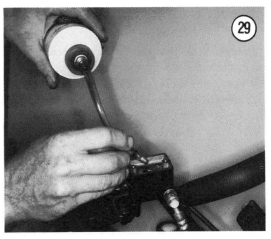

ervoir (**Figure 30**). Use fresh brake fluid from a sealed brake fluid container.

> *WARNING*
> *Use brake fluid from a sealed container and clearly marked DOT 4 only. Others may vaporize and cause brake failure. Do not intermix different brands or types of brake fluid as they may not be compatible. Do not intermix a silicone based (DOT 5) brake fluid as it can cause brake component damage leading to brake system failure.*

> *CAUTION*
> *Be careful when handling brake fluid. Do not spill it on painted or plated surfaces or plastic parts as it will destroy the surface. Wash the area immediately with soapy water and thoroughly rinse it off.*

6. Reinstall the diaphragm and the top cover (**Figure 28**). Tighten the screws securely.

Front Drum Brake Hoses and Lines

Carefully inspect the hydraulic brake hoses and lines between the front master cylinder and each front wheel cylinder. See **Figure 31** and **Figure 32**. If there is any leakage, tighten the connections and bleed the brakes as described under *Bleeding the System* in Chapter Thirteen. If this does not stop the leak or if a brake hose(s) or line(s) are obviously damaged, cracked or chafed, replace the brake line or hose and bleed the system.

Front Drum Brake Fluid Change

Every time the reservoir cap is removed, a small amount of dirt and moisture enters the brake fluid. The same thing happens if a leak occurs or any part of the hydraulic system is loosened or disconnected. Dirt can clog the system and cause unnecessary wear. Water in the brake fluid vaporizes at high temperature, impairing the hydraulic action and reducing the brake's stopping ability.

To maintain peak performance, change the brake fluid as indicated in **Table 1**. To change brake fluid, follow the *Bleeding the System* procedure in Chapter Thirteen. Continue adding new fluid to the master

cylinder and bleeding out at the front wheel cylinder until the fluid leaving the cylinder is clean and free of contaminants.

> *WARNING*
> *Use brake fluid from a sealed container and clearly marked DOT 4 only. Others may vaporize and cause brake failure. Do not intermix different brands or types of brake fluid as they may not be compatible. Do not intermix a silicone based (DOT 5) brake fluid as it can*

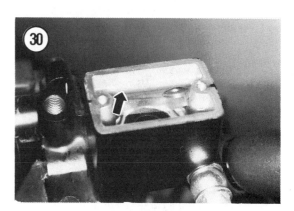

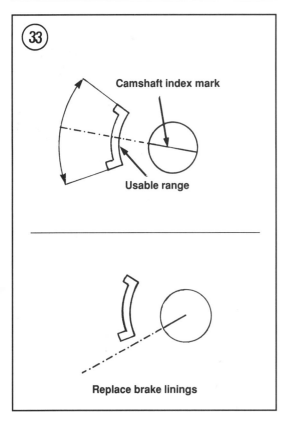

Camshaft index mark

Usable range

Replace brake linings

cause brake component damage leading to brake system failure.

Front Drum Brake Lining Inspection

The front drum brakes are not equipped with wear indicators as is the rear brake. The only way to inspect the front brake linings is to remove the front wheel and brake drum and measure the thickness of the lining. This procedure is covered in Chapter Thirteen.

Rear Drum Brake Lining Inspection

At the interval indicated in **Table 1**, inspect the rear brake lining wear indicator. Apply the rear brake fully; the index line on the brake arm camshaft should be within the range of the cast-in depression on the brake backing plate (**Figure 33**). If alignment is out of range, replace the rear brake shoes as described in Chapter Thirteen.

Rear Drum Brake Pedal Adjustment

The rear brake pedal adjustment should be inspected at the interval indicated in **Table 1** and adjusted if necessary to maintain the proper amount of free play. Free play is the distance the pedal travels from the at-rest position to the applied position when the pedal is lightly depressed by hand.

The brake pedal should travel about 20-30 mm (0.8-1.2 in.) before the brake shoes come in contact with the brake drum, but must not be adjusted so closely that the brake shoes contact the brake drum with the pedal relaxed.

1. Remove the bolts securing the right-hand side mudguard (**Figure 34**) and remove the mudguard.

2. First adjust the brake pedal so it is aligned with the top surface of the footpeg. Perform the following:

    a. Loosen the locknut and turn the adjust bolt (**Figure 35**) in either direction until the brake pedal is level with the footpeg.

    b. Tighten the locknut securely.

3. To adjust the free play, perform the following:

a. Loosen the locknut (A, **Figure 36**) and turn the adjust bolt (B, **Figure 36**) in either direction to achieve the correct amount of free play.

b. Tighten the locknut (A, **Figure 36**) securely.

Rear Drum Brake Lever and Parking Brake Adjustment

The rear brake lever adjustment should be inspected at the interval indicated in **Table 1** and adjusted if necessary to maintain the proper amount of free play. Free play is the distance the lever travels when the lever is pulled lightly in toward the hand grip.

The brake lever should travel only about 3-7 mm (0.1-032 in.) to take up the slack in the brake cable.

NOTE
Adjust the rear brake pedal free play prior to adjusting the rear drum brake lever.

If adjustment is necessary, perform the following.

1. Loosen the locknut (A, **Figure 37**) and turn the adjuster nut (B, **Figure 37**) until the slack is taken up in the cable.

2. Hold onto the adjuster and tighten the locknut securely.

Clutch Mechanism Adjustment

The clutch mechanism free play should be checked at the interval indicated in **Table 1**.

This adjustment pertains only to the manual clutch as the centrifugal clutch requires no adjustment. Since there is no clutch cable, the mechanism is the only component requiring adjustment. This adjustment takes up slack due to clutch component wear.

1. Place the ATV on level ground and set the parking brake.

2. Remove the right rear wheel as described under *Rear Wheel Removal/Installation* in Chapter Twelve.

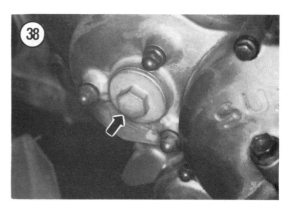

3. Unscrew and remove the clutch adjuster cover (**Figure 38**).

4. Loosen the locknut (A, **Figure 39**).

5. Loosen the release screw (B, **Figure 39**), then tighten it until *slight* resistance is felt, then *stop*.

6. From this point, turn the release screw clockwise 0-1/8 of a turn. Hold onto the release screw and tighten the locknut (**Figure 40**).

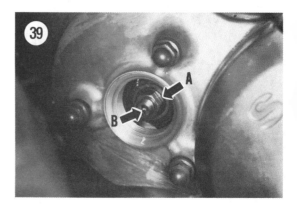

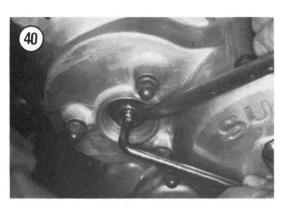

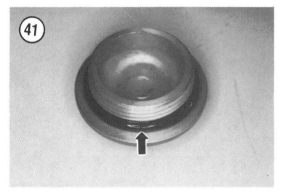

B A

NOTE
Make sure the release screw does not move when tightening the locknut or the adjustment will be incorrect.

7. After adjustment is completed, check that the locknut is tight.

8. Install a new gasket on the clutch adjuster cover and install the cover. Tighten the cover bolts securely.

9. Inspect the O-ring seal (**Figure 41**) on the clutch adjuster cover for hardness or deterioration. Replace if necessary.

10. Install the clutch adjuster cover and tighten securely.

11. Install the right-hand rear wheel as described in Chapter Twelve.

12. Test ride the ATV and make sure the clutch is operating correctly. Readjust if necessary.

Throttle Lever Adjustment

The throttle cable free play should be checked at the interval indicated in **Table 1**. The throttle cable should have 0.5-1.0 mm (0.02-0.04 in.) of free play measured where the cable moves in and out of the adjuster.

1. At the throttle lever, slide the rubber boot (**Figure 42**) off of the adjuster on the throttle cable.

2. Loosen the locknut and turn the adjuster in or out to obtain the correct amount of cable free play. Hold the adjuster and tighten the locknut.

3. If the proper amount of free play cannot be achieved by using this adjustment procedure, the cable has stretched to the point that it needs to be replaced. Refer to Chapter Eight for this service procedure.

4. Slide the rubber boot back onto the adjuster.

5. Check the throttle cable from the right-hand grip to carburetor. Make sure it is not kinked or chafed. Replace as necessary.

Throttle Limiter Adjustment

The throttle limiter can be adjusted to restrict engine RPM according to rider's skill and experience.

To adjust the limiter, loosen the locknut (A, **Figure 43**) and turn the limiter screw (B, **Figure 43**) in or out to obtain the desired position. Turning the screw in restricts the engine RPM and turning the screw out allows a higher engine RPM.

Choke Lever Adjustment
(1990-on Models)

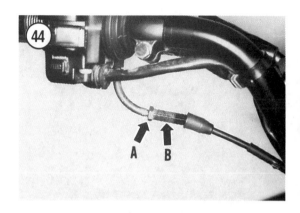

The choke cable free play should be checked at the interval indicated in **Table 1**. The choke cable should have 0.5-1.0 mm (0.02-0.04 in.) of free play measured where the cable moves in and out of the adjuster.

1. At the choke lever, loosen the locknut (A, **Figure 44**) and turn the adjuster (B, **Figure 44**) in or out to obtain the correct amount of cable free play. Hold the adjuster and tighten the locknut.

2. If the proper amount of free play cannot be achieved by using this adjustment procedure, the cable has stretched to the point that it needs to be replaced. Refer to Chapter Eight for this service procedure.

3. Check the choke cable from the left-hand grip to carburetor. Make sure it is not kinked or chafed. Replace as necessary.

Air Filter Element Cleaning

The air filter element should be removed and cleaned at the interval indicated in **Table 1** and replaced if it is damaged or starts to deteriorate.

The air filter removes dust and abrasive particles before the air enters the carburetor and engine. Without the air filter, very fine particles could enter the engine and cause rapid wear of the piston rings, cylinder and bearings. They also might clog small passages in the carburetor. Never run the ATV without the element installed.

Proper air filter servicing can ensure long service from your engine.

1. Place the ATV on level ground and set the parking brake.

2. Remove the seat as described in Chapter Fourteen.

3. Remove the screws (A, **Figure 45**) securing the air filter case cover (B, **Figure 45**) and remove the cover.

4. Pull up and remove the air filter element holder (A, **Figure 46**).

5. Remove the air filter assembly (B, **Figure 46**) from the air box.

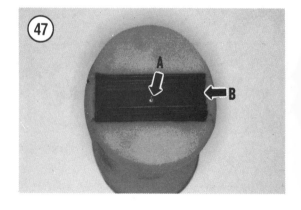

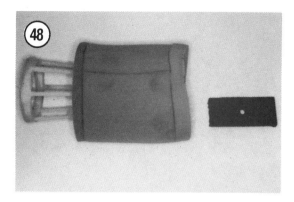

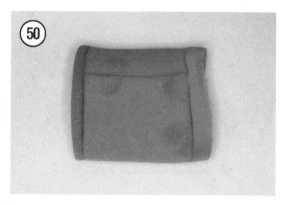

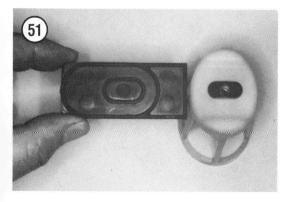

6. Remove the screw (A, **Figure 47**) securing the element guide (B, **Figure 47**) and remove the guide.
7. Carefully slide the foam element off the element holder (**Figure 48**).
8. Wipe out the interior of the air box (**Figure 49**) with a shop rag dampened in cleaning solvent. Remove any foreign matter that may have passed through a broken element.
9. Clean the element gently in cleaning solvent until all dirt is removed. Do not twist or wring the element because it will tear or damage the individual cells in the foam element. Thoroughly dry with a clean shop cloth until all solvent residue is removed. Let it dry for about 1 hour.
10. Inspect the element (**Figure 50**); if it is torn or broken in any area it should be replaced. Do not run with a damaged element as it will allow dirt to enter the engine.
11. Oil the element as follows:
  a. Pour a small amount of clean SAE 10W/40 engine oil or special foam air filter oil onto the element and work it into the porous foam material. Do not oversaturate the element as too much oil will restrict air flow. The element will be discolored by the oil and should have an even color indicating that the oil is distributed evenly.
  b. Let it dry for another hour prior to installation. If installed too soon, the chemical carrier in the special foam air filter oil will be drawn into the engine and may cause damage.
12. Inspect the guide and element holder (**Figure 51**) for wear or damage. Replace if necessary.
13. Carefully slide the foam element onto the element holder (**Figure 48**).
14. Install the element guide (B, **Figure 47**) and tighten the screw securely (A, **Figure 47**).
15. Remove the plug from the air box drain tube (**Figure 52**) and drain out any residue that has col-

lected in the air box. Reinstall the plug and make sure the clamps are installed on the plug.

16. Install the air filter assembly (B, **Figure 46**) into the air box. Push it forward until it is correctly seated in the air box.

17. Position the air filter element holder with the angle side (**Figure 53**) facing toward the element and insert the holder (**Figure 54**). Push the holder all the way down until it completely seats.

18. Inspect the seal around the perimeter of the cover (**Figure 55**). Replace if necessary.

19. Install the air filter case cover (B, **Figure 45**) and screws (A, **Figure 45**) and tighten securely.

20. Install the seat as described in Chapter Fourteen.

Fuel Shutoff Valve and Filter Removal/Installation

The fuel filter is an integral part of the fuel shutoff valve. The fuel filter traps particles in the fuel which might otherwise enter the carburetor. This could cause the float needle to stay in the open position or clog one of the jets.

1. Remove the front fender (A, **Figure 56**) as described under *Front Fender Removal/Installation* in Chapter Fourteen.

2. Disconnect the battery negative lead as described under *Battery* in this chapter.

3. Turn the fuel shutoff valve to the OFF position.

4. At the fuel pump, disconnect the fuel line going from the fuel pump to the shutoff valve.

5. Place the loose end of the fuel line in an approved gasoline storage container. If the gasoline is kept clean, it can be reused.

6. Remove the fuel filler cap (B, **Figure 56**) this will speed up the flow of fuel in the next step.

7. Turn the fuel shutoff valve to the RES position and drain the fuel from the tank. The fuel tank must be empty to perform this procedure.

8. Remove the fuel line from the container and reconnect it to the fuel pump.

9. Disconnect the fuel line (A, **Figure 57**) from the shutoff valve and plug the fuel line to prevent any residual fuel from draining out and to keep out foreign matter.

10. Remove the screws and lockwashers securing the fuel shutoff valve (B, **Figure 57**) to the fuel tank and carefully remove it from the fuel tank.

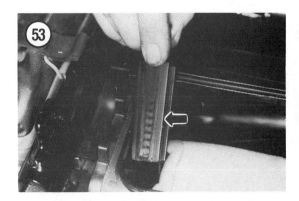

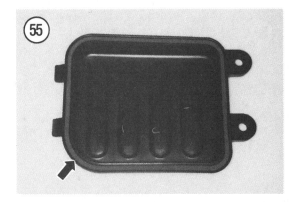
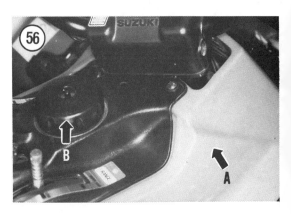

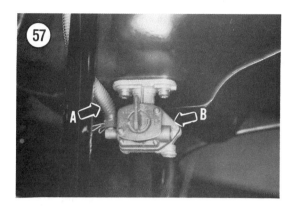

11. Clean the filter screens on both the ON and RES pickup tubes of the shutoff valve with a medium soft toothbrush and blow out with compressed air.

12. Inspect both filters for damage. If either is damaged, replace the fuel filter assembly. The filters cannot be replaced individually.

13. Install by reversing the removal steps while noting the following:

    a. Be sure the fuel line is connected securely to the fuel filter assembly.

    b. Check for fuel leakage after installation is completed.

Fuel Line Inspection

Inspect the fuel line from the fuel shutoff valve to the fuel pump and to the carburetor. If any are cracked or starting to deteriorate they must be replaced. Make sure the small hose clamps are in place and holding securely.

> *WARNING*
> *A damaged or deteriorated fuel line presents a very dangerous fire hazard to both the rider and the vehicle if fuel should spill onto a hot engine or exhaust pipe.*

Crankcase Breather System

The ATV has a very basic crankcase breather system consisting of a single hose (**Figure 58**) going from the crankcase to the air filter case.

Make sure the air filter case hose clamp (**Figure 59**) and the crankcase hose clamp (**Figure 60**) are tight and check the hose for deterioration. Replace as necessary. Check that the hose is not clogged or crimped.

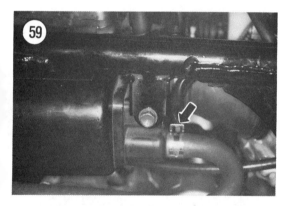

Remove the drain plug (**Figure 61**) from the end of the air filter air box drain hose and drain out all

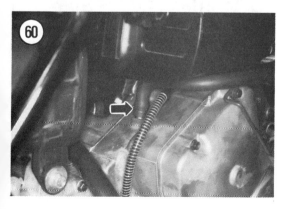

residue. This cleaning should be done more frequently if a considerable amount of riding is done at full throttle or in the rain.

Wheel Bearings

There is no factory-recommended interval for cleaning and repacking the wheel bearings. They should be serviced whenever they are removed from the wheel hub, or whenever there is the likelihood of water contamination (especially saltwater). The correct service procedures are covered in Chapter Ten and Chapter Twelve.

Steering System and
Front Suspension Inspection

The steering system and front suspension should be checked at the interval indicated in **Table 1**.
1. Visually inspect all components of the steering system. Pay close attention to the tie-rods and steering shaft, especially after a hard spill or collision. If any signs of damage are apparent, the steering components must be repaired as described in Chapter Ten.
2. Check the tightness of the handlebar holder bolts securing the handlebar.
3. Remove the rubber cover on each hub and make sure the front spindle nuts are tight and that the cotter pins are in place.

> *CAUTION*
> *If any of the previously mentioned bolts and nuts are loose, refer to Chapter Ten for correct procedures and torque specifications.*

Front Wheel Toe-in Adjustment

The front wheel toe-in alignment should be checked at the interval indicated in **Table 1**.
1. Inflate the front tires to the recommended tire pressure. Refer to **Table 2**.
2. Place the ATV on level ground and set the parking brake. Block the rear wheels so the vehicle will not roll in either direction.
3. Have an assistant (approximate weight of 165 lb.) sit on the seat.
4. Turn the handlebar so the wheels are at the straight ahead position.
5. Hold a scribe (**Figure 62**), white crayon or white tire marker against the center of the front tire and spin the wheel slowly. Make sure the line is visible at both the front and rear of the tire. Repeat for the other tire.

6. Carefully measure the distance between the center line of both front tires at the front and the rear as shown in **Figure 63**. The front dimension "A" should be less than the rear dimension "B" by the dimension listed in **Table 6**. This amount of toe-in is necessary for proper steering. Too much toe-in can cause excessive tire wear and hard steering. Too little toe-in will allow the front end to wander.
7. If adjustment is necessary, loosen the adjustment sleeve locknuts and turn the sleeves as required to set the correct toe in. Adjust the toe so the handlebar is centered when the vehicle is ridden in a straight line on a flat surface. If necessary, test ride the vehicle and repeat the toe adjustment as required to center the handlebar.
8. Tighten the adjustment sleeve locknuts securely.

Rear Suspension Check

1. Visually inspect all components of the rear suspension system. If any signs of damage are apparent, the rear suspension components must be repaired as described in Chapter Twelve.
2. Remove the rubber hub covers and make sure the rear spindle nuts are tight and that the cotter pin is in place on each side.

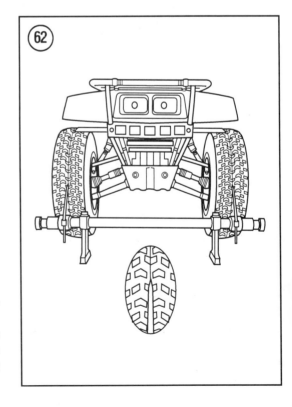

CAUTION
If any of the previously mentioned bolts and nuts are loose, refer to Chapter Twelve for correct procedures and torque specifications.

Nuts, Bolts and Other Fasteners

Constant vibration can loosen many of the fasteners on the ATV. Check the tightness of all fasteners, especially those on:

a. Engine mounting hardware.
b. Engine crankcase covers.
c. Handlebar and front steering components.
d. Gearshift levers.
e. Brake pedal and lever.
f. Exhaust system.

ENGINE TUNE-UP

A complete tune-up should be performed at the interval indicated in **Table 1**. More frequently tune-ups may be required if the ATV is ridden primarily in dusty areas or at construction sites.

The number of definitions of the term "tune-up" is probably equal to the number of people defining it. For the purposes of this book, a tune-up is general adjustment and maintenance to ensure peak engine performance. Have new parts on hand before you begin.

Table 7 summarizes tune-up specifications.

The air filter element should be cleaned or replaced prior to doing other tune-up procedures as described in this chapter.

Because different systems in an engine interact, the procedures should be done in the following order.

a. Clean or replace the air filter element.
b. Check and tighten, if necessary, the cylinder head nuts, cylinder nuts and exhaust pipe nuts.
c. Check and adjust the valve clearance.
d. Run a compression test.
e. Check or replace the spark plug.
f. Adjust the carburetor idle speed.

To perform a tune-up on your Suzuki, you will need the following tools and equipment:

a. 18 mm spark plug wrench.
b. Socket wrench and assorted sockets.
c. Flat feeler gauge.
d. Wire type spark plug feeler gauge and gap adjusting tool.
e. Compression gauge.
f. Portable tachometer.

Cylinder Head Nuts, Cylinder Nuts and Exhaust System Bolts and Nuts

The cylinder head nuts, cylinder nuts and exhaust system bolts and nuts should be tightened at the interval indicated in **Table 1**.

1. Place the ATV on level ground and set the parking brake. Block the rear wheels so the vehicle will not roll in either direction.
2. Remove the rear fender as described under *Rear Fender Removal/Installation* in Chapter Fourteen.
3. Remove the spark plug (this will make it easier to rotate the engine).
4. Remove the cylinder head cover as described in Chapter Four.

NOTE
Figure 64 and Figure 65 are shown with the engine removed from the frame

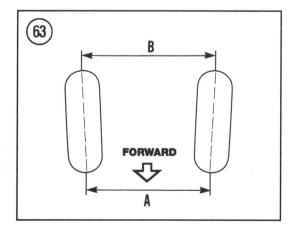

*for clarity. It is not necessary to remove
the engine for this procedure.*

5. In a criss-cross pattern, loosen the 8 mm cylinder
head nuts (**Figure 64**) at the top of the cylinder head
and the 6 mm nuts (**Figure 65**) on the left-hand side
of the cylinder head and cylinder.

6. After the cylinder head nuts have all been loosened, first tighten the upper 8 mm nuts in a crisscross pattern and then the 6 mm nuts on the side of
the cylinder to the torque specification listed in
Table 5.

7. Install the cylinder head cover as described in
Chapter Four.

8. Tighten the nuts (**Figure 66**) securing the exhaust
pipe to the cylinder head. Tighten the nuts to the
torque specification listed in **Table 5**.

9. Tighten the muffler-to-exhaust pipe clamp bolt
(**Figure 67**) to the torque specification listed in
Table 5.

10. Tighten the bolt (**Figure 68**) securing the muffler assembly to the crankcase to the torque specification listed in **Table 5**.

Valve Clearance Adjustment

Valve clearance adjustment must be made with the
engine at room temperature (below 95° F [35° C]).
The correct valve clearance for all models is listed
in **Table 7**. The exhaust valve is located on the front,
or lower side, of the engine and the intake valve is
at the rear, or upper side, of the engine.

1. Place the ATV on level ground and set the parking brake.

2. Remove the seat and rear fender as described
under *Rear Fender Removal/Installation* in Chapter
Fourteen.

3. Remove the spark plug as described in this chapter. This will make it easier to rotate the engine in the
following steps.

4. Remove the bolts securing the recoil starter assembly (**Figure 69**) and remove the assembly and
gasket.

5. On models so equipped, remove the exhaust pipe
heat shield (**Figure 70**).

6. Use a 17 mm wrench, remove the timing hole cap
located on the left-hand crankcase cover. Refer to A,
Figure 71.

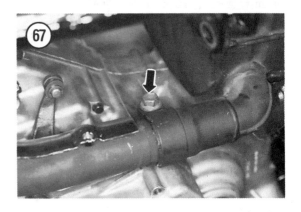

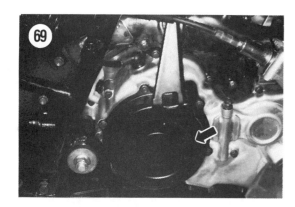

NOTE
The following steps are shown with the engine removed from the frame. It is not necessary to remove the engine for this procedure.

7. Use a 17 mm wrench and remove both valve adjuster caps (**Figure 72**).

NOTE
*In the following step, it is very difficult to look directly down into the crankcase cover opening to view the "T" mark on the rotor. It is suggested that a small mirror be used to get a better view of the timing mark within the hole. Be sure to hold the mirror correctly to get a "**straight on view**" of the rotor for correct alignment.*

8. Using the nut on the recoil starter cup (B, **Figure 71**), rotate the engine until the "T" timing mark (A, **Figure 73**) on the rotor aligns with the index mark on the crankcase (B, **Figure 73**). The piston must be at top dead center (TDC) on the compression stroke.

NOTE
A cylinder at TDC of its compression stroke will have free play in both of its rocker arms, indicating that both the intake and exhaust valves are closed.

9. With the engine timing mark on the "T," if both rocker arms are not loose; rotate the engine an additional 360° until both valves have free play.
10. Check the clearance of both the intake and exhaust valves by inserting a flat feeler gauge between

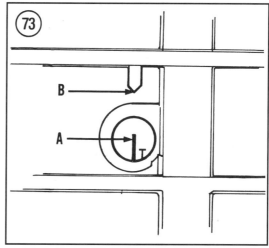

the rocker arm pad and the camshaft lobe (**Figure 74**). When the clearance is correct, there will be a slight resistance on the feeler gauge when it is inserted and withdrawn.

11A. If using the special valve adjusting tool to correct the clearance, perform the following:

   a. Use a wrench and back off the locknut.

   b. Screw the adjuster (A, **Figure 75**) in or out until there is a slight resistance felt on the feeler gauge (**Figure 74**).

   c. Hold the adjuster to prevent it from turning further and tighten the locknut securely (B, **Figure 75**).

   d. Then recheck the clearance to make sure the adjuster (A, **Figure 76**) did not slip when the locknut (B, **Figure 76**) was tightened. Readjust if necessary.

11B. If the special tool is not used to correct the clearance, perform the following:

   a. Use a box wrench (A, **Figure 77**) and back off the locknut.

   b. Use a screwdriver (B, **Figure 77**) and screw the adjuster in or out until there is a slight resistance felt on the feeler gauge (**Figure 74**).

   c. Hold the adjuster to prevent it from turning further and tighten the locknut securely.

   d. Then recheck the clearance to make sure the adjuster (A, **Figure 76**) did not slip when the locknut (B, **Figure 76**) was tightened. Readjust if necessary.

12. Rotate the engine 360° and repeat Step 11 to make sure the adjustment is correct. Readjust if necessary.

13. Inspect the O-ring seal (**Figure 78**) on both valve adjuster caps. Replace if necessary.

14. Install both valve adjuster caps (**Figure 72**) and tighten securely.

15. Install the timing hole cap on the left-hand crankcase cover. Refer to A, **Figure 71** and **Figure 79** and tighten to the torque specification listed in **Table 5**.

16. If so equipped, install the exhaust pipe heat shield (**Figure 70**).

17. Install the recoil starter assembly (**Figure 69**) and gasket. Tighten the bolts securely.

18. Install the spark plug as described in this chapter.

19. Install rear fender and seat as described in Chapter Fourteen.

Compression Test

Check compression pressure at the interval indicated in **Table 1**. Record the results and compare them at the next check interval. A running record will show trends in deterioration so that corrective action can be taken before complete failure occurs to a given set of parts.

The results, when properly interpreted, can indicate general cylinder, piston ring and valve condition.

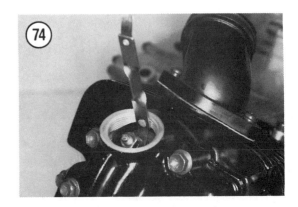

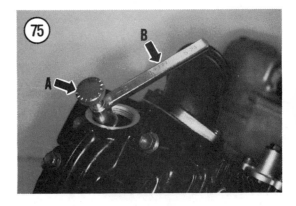

1. Place the ATV on level ground and set the parking brake.

2. Warm the engine and let it reach normal operating temperature.

3. Fully open the throttle lever and move the choke lever (or knob) to the completely open position.

4. Disconnect the spark plug wire and remove the spark plug as described in this chapter.

5. Connect a compression gauge to the cylinder following its manufacturer's instructions.

6. Have an assistant operate the recoil starter or electric starter several times.

> *NOTE*
> *If you perform this operation by yourself, make sure the compression gauge does not leak around the spark plug hole. This will give a false reading. On recoil starter equipped models this is difficult as you must work on both sides of the vehicle at the same time.*

> *CAUTION*
> *Do not turn the engine over more than absolutely necessary.*

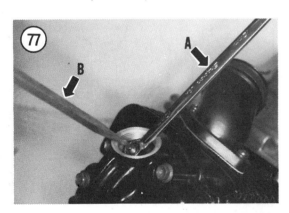

When the spark plug lead is disconnected the electronic ignition will produce the highest voltage possible; the ignition coil may overheat and be damaged.

7. Remove the compression gauge and record the reading. The readings are listed in **Table 7**. If the reading is higher than normal, there may be a buildup of carbon deposits in the combustion chamber or on the piston crown.

If a low reading (10% or more) is obtained it indicates a leaking cylinder head gasket, valve or piston ring trouble. If the gasket is okay, then determine which other component is faulty. Pour about one teaspoon of engine oil through the spark plug hole onto the top of the piston. Turn the engine over once to distribute the oil, then take another compression reading. If the compression increases significantly, the valves are good but the piston rings are defective. If compression does not increase, the valves require servicing. A valve could be hanging open but not burned or a piece of carbon could be on a valve seat.

Spark Plug Selection

Spark plugs are available in various heat ranges. They can be hotter or colder than the plugs originally installed at the factory.

Select a plug of the heat range designed for the loads and conditions under which the ATV will be run. Use of incorrect heat range can cause a seized piston, scored cylinder wall or damaged piston crown.

> *NOTE*
> *Higher plug numbers designate colder plugs; lower plug numbers designate hotter plugs. For example, an NGK*

D7EA plug is hotter than a NGK D8EA plug.

In general, use a hot plug for low speeds and low temperatures. Use a cold plug for high speeds, high engine loads and high temperatures. The plug should operate hot enough to burn off unwanted deposits, but not so hot that it is damaged or causes preignition. A spark plug of the correct heat range will show a light tan color on the portion of the insulator within the cylinder after the plug has been in service.

The reach (length) (**Figure 80**) of a plug is also important. A longer than normal plug could interfere with the piston, causing permanent and severe damage; refer to **Figure 81**.

Refer to **Table 7** for Suzuki factory recommended spark plug heat ranges

Spark Plug Removal/Cleaning

1. Grasp the spark plug lead (**Figure 82**) as near the plug as possible and pull it off the plug. If it is stuck to the plug, twist it slightly to break it loose.
2. Blow away any dirt that has accumulated in the spark plug well.

CAUTION
The dirt could fall into the cylinder when the plug is removed, causing serious engine damage.

3. Remove the spark plug with a spark plug wrench.

NOTE
If the plug is difficult to remove, apply penetrating oil, like WD-40 or Liquid Wrench around the base of the plug and let it soak in about 10-20 minutes.

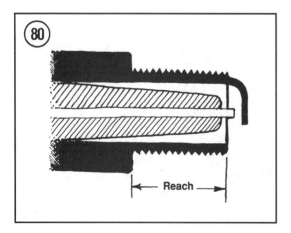

4. Inspect the plug carefully. Look for a broken center porcelain, excessively eroded electrodes and excessive carbon or oil fouling. If present, replace the plug. If deposits are light, the plug may be cleaned in solvent with a wire brush. Regap the plug as explained in the following section.

NOTE
Spark plug cleaning with the use of a sand-blast type device is not recommended. While this type of cleaning is thorough, the plug must be perfectly free of all abrasive cleaning material when done. If not, it is possible for the cleaning material to fall into the engine during operation and cause damage.

Gapping and Installing the Plug

A spark plug should be carefully gapped to ensure a reliable, consistent spark. You must use a special spark plug gapping tool and a wire feeler gauge.

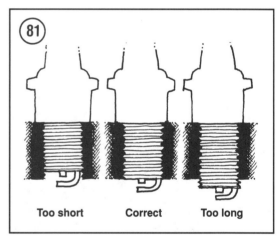

Too short   Correct   Too long

1. Remove the new spark plug from its box. *Do not screw on the small piece that is loose in the box* (**Figure 83**); it is not used.

2. Insert a wire feeler gauge between the center and side electrode of the plug (**Figure 84**). The correct gap is listed in **Table 7**. If the gap is correct, you will feel a slight drag as you pull the wire through. If there is no drag, or the gauge won't pass through, bend the side electrode *with a gapping tool* (**Figure 85**) to set the proper gap.

3. Put a small drop of oil or aluminum antiseize compound on the threads of the spark plug.

4. Screw the spark plug in by hand until it seats. Very little effort is required. If force is necessary, you may have the plug cross threaded; unscrew it and try again.

NOTE
If a spark plug is difficult to install, the cylinder head threads may be dirty or slightly damaged. To clean the threads, apply grease to the threads of a spark plug tap and screw it carefully into the cylinder head. Turn the tap slowly until it is completely installed. If the tap cannot be installed, the threads are severely damaged and must be repaired.

5. Use a spark plug wrench and tighten the plug an additional 1/4 to 1/2 turn after the gasket has made contact with the head. If you are installing an old plug and reusing the old gasket, only tighten an additional 1/4 turn.

CAUTION
Do not over tighten the spark plug. Besides making the plug difficult to remove, the excessive torque will squash the gasket and destroy its sealing ability.

6. Install the spark plug lead; make sure it is on tight.

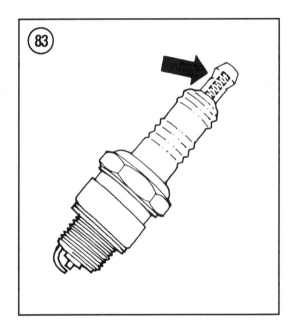

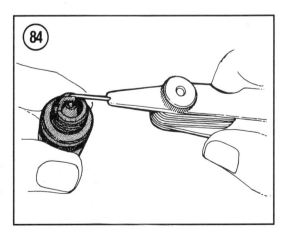

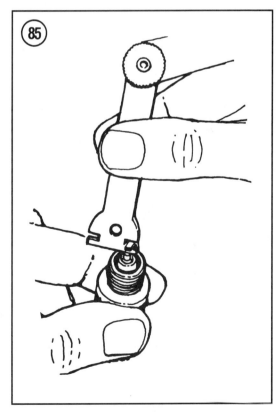

SPARK PLUG CONDITION

NORMAL

- Identified by light tan or gray deposits on the firing tip.
- Can be cleaned.

GAP BRIDGED

- Identified by deposit buildup closing gap between electrodes.
- Caused by oil or carbon fouling. If deposits are not excessive, the plug can be cleaned.

OIL FOULED

- Identified by wet black deposits on the insulator shell bore and electrodes.
- Caused by excessive oil entering combustion chamber through worn rings and pistons, excessive clearance between valve guides and stems or worn or loose bearings. Can be cleaned. If engine is not repaired, use a hotter plug.

CARBON FOULED

- Identified by black, dry fluffy carbon deposits on insulator tips, exposed shell surfaces and electrodes.
- Caused by too cold a plug, weak ignition, dirty air cleaner, too rich a fuel mixture or excessive idling. Can be cleaned.

LEAD FOULED

- Identified by dark gray, black, yellow or tan deposits or a fused glazed coating on the insulator tip.
- Caused by highly leaded gasoline. Can be cleaned.

WORN

- Identified by severely eroded or worn electrodes.
- Caused by normal wear. Should be replaced.

FUSED SPOT DEPOSIT

- Identified by melted or spotty deposits resembling bubbles or blisters.
- Caused by sudden acceleration. Can be cleaned.

OVERHEATING

- Identified by a white or light gray insulator with small black or gray brown spots and with bluish-burnt appearance of electrodes.
- Caused by engine overheating, wrong type of fuel, loose spark plugs, too hot a plug or incorrect ignition timing. Replace the plug.

PREIGNITION

- Identified by melted electrodes and possibly blistered insulator. Metallic deposits on insulator indicate engine damage.
- Caused by wrong type of fuel, incorrect ignition timing or advance, too hot a plug, burned valves or engine overheating. Replace the plug.

3

Reading Spark Plugs

Much information about engine and spark plug performance can be determined by careful examination of the spark plug. This information is more valid after performing the following steps.

1. Ride the ATV a short distance at full throttle in any gear.

2. Turn the ignition switch to the OFF position before closing the throttle and simultaneously shift to NEUTRAL; coast and brake to a stop.

3. Remove the spark plug and examine it. Compare it to **Figure 86**. If the insulator is white or burned, the plug is too hot and should be replaced with a colder one.

A too-cold plug will have sooty or oily deposits ranging in color from dark brown to black. Replace with a hotter plug and check for too-rich carburetion or evidence of oil blow-by at the piston rings.

If the plug has a light tan or gray colored deposit and no abnormal gap wear or electrode erosion is evident, the plug and the engine are running properly.

If the plug exhibits a black insulator tip, a damp and oily film over the firing end and a carbon layer over the entire nose, it is oil fouled. An oil fouled plug can be cleaned, but it is better to replace it.

Ignition Timing

All models are equipped with a capacitor discharge ignition system (CDI). This system uses no breaker points, and ignition timing is fixed. Suzuki does not provide any service information for checking ignition timing. If you feel that any of the ignition system components are not operating properly, refer to Chapter Nine and perform the service procedures relating to the ignition system.

Engine Idle Speed Adjustment

Before making this adjustment, the air filter must be clean and the engine must have adequate compression; see *Compression Test* in this chapter.

1. Place the ATV on level ground and set the parking brake. Block the rear wheels so the vehicle will not roll in either direction.

2. Start the engine and let it reach normal operating temperature. Shut the engine off.

3. Connect a portable tachometer following its manufacturer's instructions.

4A. On 1988-1989 models, perform the following:

> *CAUTION*
> *The pilot screw can be damaged if the pilot screw is tightened too hard against the seat.*

   a. For preliminary adjustment, carefully turn the pilot adjust screw (A, **Figure 87**) in until it *lightly* seats, then *stop*. From this position, back out the pilot screw the number of turns indicated in **Table 7**.

   b. Start the engine and turn the idle adjust screw (B, **Figure 87**) to achieve the idle speed listed in **Table 7**.

   c. Turn the pilot screw (A, **Figure 87**) 1/2 turn in either direction (from the setting achieved in sub-step 4A a.) to achieve the highest engine rpm.

   d. Open and close the throttle a couple of times; check for variation in idle speed. Readjust if necessary.

   e. Turn the idle adjust screw (B, **Figure 87**) to achieve the idle speed listed in **Table 7**.

4B. On 1990-on models, perform the following:

   a. Turn the idle adjust screw (**Figure 88**) to achieve the idle speed listed in **Table 7**.

b. Open and close the throttle a couple of times; check for variation in idle speed. Readjust if necessary.

> *WARNING*
> *With the engine idling, move the handlebar from side to side. If idle speed increases during this movement, the throttle cable needs adjusting or may be incorrectly routed through the frame. Correct this problem immediately. Do not ride the vehicle in this unsafe condition.*

5. Turn the engine off and disconnect the portable tachometer.

Exhaust System Draining and Carbon Removal

Under some working conditions, the ATV may be run at slow speeds for long periods of time. This will sometimes cause the buildup of carbon and oil residue in the muffler portion of the exhaust system.

> *NOTE*
> *To maximize the amount of sludge to be drained from the muffler, the engine must have been run allowing the exhaust system to heat up. By doing this the sludge will be thinned by the heat and the maximum amount will be drained out.*

1. Start the engine and allow it to reach normal operating temperature. Shut off the engine and allow the exhaust system to cool down sufficiently to allow working on the rear portion of the muffler.

2. Place a shop rag under the drain plug to catch any oil and moisture sludge that drains out.

3. Unscrew the drain plug and gasket (**Figure 89**) from the end of the muffler and allow all sludge to drain out. Leave the plug out until all sludge has drained out.

4. Start the engine and rev it several times to blow out any accumulation of carbon and oil sludge. Shut off the engine.

5. Inspect the gasket for damage and replace if necessary.

6. Install the drain plug and gasket and tighten securely.

Table 1 MAINTENANCE SCHEDULE*

Prior to each ride	Inspect tires and rims and check inflation pressure
	Check steering for smooth operation
	  with no excessive play or restrictions
	Check brake operation and front brake for
	  fluid leakage
	Check fuel supply. Make sure there is enough fuel
	  for the intended ride
	Check for fuel leakage
	Check all lights for proper operation
	Check engine oil level
	Check front differential oil level (4-wheel drive)
	Check for smooth throttle operation
	Check gearshift pedal operation

**Initial 100 miles (200 km)
  or 1 month of operation**
	Inspect tires and rims and check inflation pressure
	Replace engine oil and filter
	Check front differential oil level
	Check engine idle speed; adjust if necessary
	Check valve clearance; adjust if necessary
	Check clutch operation; adjust if necessary
	Check throttle lever action and free play;
	  adjust if necessary
	Check rear brake pedal free play; adjust if necessary
	Check fluid level in front brake master cylinder;
	  add fluid if necessary
	Check battery electrolyte level; add distilled water
	  if necessary
	Inspect entire brake system
	Check all hoses--fuel, vacuum and brake
	Check tightness of all fasteners,
	  especially engine mounting bolts and nuts
	Inspect steering for smooth operation;
	  adjust if necessary

**Every 600 miles (1,000 km)
  or 3 months of operation**
	Change engine oil and oil filter
	Clean and oil air filter element (perform sooner
	  if used in wet or dusty terrain)
	Check cylinder head nuts and exhaust pipe nuts;
	  tighten if necessary
	Check valve clearance; adjust if necessary
	Inspect spark plug; regap if necessary
	Check battery electrolyte level, add distilled water
	  if necessary
	Inspect brake hoses for cracked or swollen ends;
	  replace if necessary
	Check brake fluid level in front master cylinder;
	  add fluid if necessary
	Inspect fuel lines for chafed, cracked or
	  swollen ends; replace if necessary
	Check throttle operation; adjust if necessary
	Check oil level in front differential unit;
	  add oil if necessary (4-wheel drive models)
	Check drum brake lining wear indicator
	Check and adjust rear brake pedal free play
	Lubricate rear brake pedal and shift lever
	Check tire and wheel condition
	Inspect front steering for looseness
	Check wheel bearings for smooth operation
	Check engine mounting bolts for tightness
	Check chassis bolts for tightness

(continued)

Table 1 MAINTENANCE SCHEDULE* (continued)

Every 1,200 miles (2,000 km) or 6 months of operation	Check throttle lever action and free play; adjust if necessary Check engine idle speed; adjust if necessary Check clutch operation; adjust if necessary Check oil level in front differential unit; add oil if necessary (4-wheel drive models) Inspect all suspension components for wear or damage Inspect all suspension components mounting bolts and nuts for tightness
Every 4,000 miles (6,000 km)	Replace spark plug
Every year	Replace front differential oil (4-wheel drive models)
Every 2 years	Replace hydraulic brake fluid
Every 4 years	Replace fuel hoses Replace flexible brake hoses

* This Suzuki factory suggested maintenance schedule should be considered as a guide to general maintenance and lubrication intervals. Harder than normal use and exposure to mud, water, sand, high humidity, etc. will naturally dictate more frequent attention to most maintenance items.

Table 2 TIRE INFLATION PRESSURE (COLD)*

	Tire pressure			
	Front tires		**Rear tires**	
Load capacity	**kPa**	**psi**	**kPa**	**psi**
LT-F250 models				
All loads	25	3.6	25	3.6
LT-4WD models				
Up to 80 kg (175 lb.)	30	4.4	20	2.9
80-172 kg (175-380 lb.)	35	5.1	20	2.9
LT-4WDX models				
All loads up to 177 kg (90 lb.) maximum	30	4.4	27.5	4.0

* Tire inflation pressure for factory equipped tires. Aftermarket tires may require different inflation pressure.

Table 3 BATTERY STATE OF CHARGE

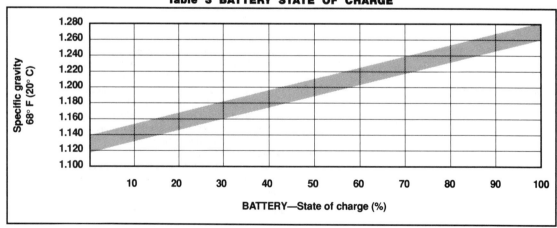

Table 4 REFILL CAPACITIES AND SPECIFICATIONS

	Capacity	Type
Fuel tank		85-95 octane
Including reserve	12 liters (3.2 U.S gal.)	or higher
Reserve only	2.0 liters (2.1 U.S qt.)	
Engine oil		SAE 10W/40
Oil change	3,500 ml (3.7 U.S. qts.)	
Oil and filter change	3,600 ml (3.8 U.S. qts.)	
Engine overhaul	3,860 ml (4.1 U.S. qts.)	
Front differential	150 ml (5.1 U.S. oz)	Hypoid gear oil
(4-wheel drive)		SAE 90 (GL-5)

Table 5 TUNE-UP AND MAINTENANCE TIGHTENING TORQUES

Item	N·m	ft.-lb.
Cylinder head 8 mm nuts		
250 cc	18-23	13-16.5
280 cc	21-25	15-18
Cylinder head-to-cylinder 6 mm nuts	7-11	5-8
Cylinder to-crankcase 6 mm nuts	7-11	5-8
Timing hole cap (17 mm)	20-25	14.5-18.0
Engine oil drain plug	18-23	13-16.5
Front differential		
Fill cap	20-30	14.5-21.5
Drain bolt	20-30	14.5-21.5
Exhaust system		
Exhaust pipe-to-cylinder head nuts	9-12	6.5-8.5
Muffler-to-exhaust pipe bolt	18-23	13-16.5
Muffler mounting bolts	18-28	13-20

Table 6 FRONT SUSPENSION TOE-IN DIMENSION

Model	Dimension
Shaft-driven	15-21 mm (0.6-0.8 in.)
Chain-driven	11-19 mm (0.4-0.7 in.)

Table 7 TUNE-UP SPECIFICATIONS

Valve clearance	
Intake	0.03-0.08 mm (0.001-0.003 in.)
Exhaust	0.08-0.13 mm (0.003-0.005 in.)
Compression pressure (at sea level)	
Standard	1,000-1,400 kPa (142-199 psi)
Service limit (min.)	800 kPa (114 psi)
Spark plug standard type	
U.S. models	NGK D7EA, ND X22ES-U
Canadian models	NGK DR7EA, ND X22ESR-U
Spark plug gap	0.6-0.7 mm (0.024-0.028 in.)
Idle speed	
250 cc models	1,350-1,450 rpm
280 cc models	1,400-1,600 rpm
Pilot screw initial opening	
250 cc models	2 turns out
280 cc models	2 5/8 turns out

ENGINE TOP END

All models covered in this book are equipped with an air-cooled, 4-stroke, single cylinder engine with a single overhead camshaft. The crankshaft is supported by 2 main ball bearings in a vertically split crankcase.

The camshaft is chain-driven from the sprocket on the left-hand side of the crankshaft and operates rocker arms that are individually adjustable.

Engine lubrication is by wet sump with the oil pump located on the right-hand side of the engine next to the clutch. The oil pump delivers oil under pressure throughout the engine and is gear driven by a gear on the crankshaft.

This chapter contains information for removal, inspection, service and reassembly of the top end of the engine. The removal and installation of the engine assembly are covered in Chapter Five.

Table 1 (250 cc engine) and **Table 2** (280 cc engine) provides specifications for the top end of the engine and **Table 3** lists all of the engine torque specifications. **Tables 1-3** are located at the end of this chapter.

Before beginning work, re-read Chapter One of this book. You will do a better job with this information fresh in your mind.

Throughout the text there is frequent mention of the right-hand and left-hand side of the engine. This refers to the engine as it sits in the ATV's frame, not as it sits on your workbench. The right- and left-hand refers to a rider sitting on the seat facing forward.

ENGINE PRINCIPLES

Figure 1 explains how the engine works. This will be helpful when troubleshooting or repairing the engine.

ENGINE COOLING

Cooling is provided by air passing over the cooling fins on the engine cylinder head and cylinder. It is very important to keep these fins free from buildup of dirt, oil, grease and other foreign matter. Brush

①
4-STROKE PRINCIPLES

4

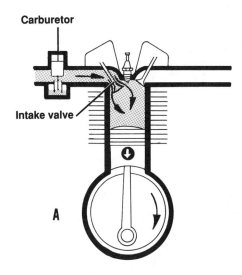

Carburetor

Intake valve

A

As the piston travels downward, the exhaust valve is closed and the intake valve opens, allowing the new air-fuel mixture from the carburetor to be drawn into the cylinder. When the piston reaches the bottom of its travel (BDC), the intake valve closes and remains closed for the next 1 1/2 revolutions of the crankshaft.

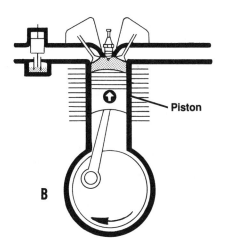

Piston

B

While the crankshaft continues to rotate, the piston moves upward, compressing the air-fuel mixture.

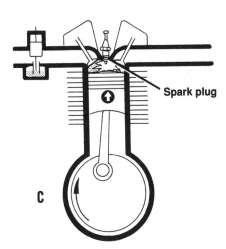

Spark plug

C

As the piston almost reaches the top of its travel, the spark plug fires, igniting the compressed air-fuel mixture. The piston continues to top dead center (TDC) and is pushed downward by the expanding gases.

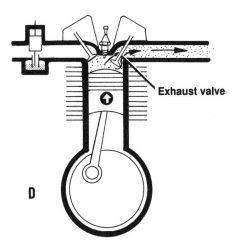

Exhaust valve

D

When the piston almost reaches BDC, the exhaust valve opens and remains open until the piston is near TDC. The upward travel of the piston forces the exhaust gases out of the cylinder. After the piston has reached TDC, the exhaust valve closes and the cycle starts all over again.

out the fins with a whisk broom or small, stiff paint brush.

> *CAUTION*
> *Remember, these fins are thin in order to dissipate heat and may be damaged if struck too hard.*

CLEANLINESS

Repairs go much faster and easier if the engine is clean before you begin work. This is especially important when servicing the engine's top end. If the top end is being serviced while the engine is installed in the frame, note that dirt trapped underneath the fuel tank and frame members can fall into the cylinder and crankcase openings. Thoroughly clean the engine and surrounding area prior to starting work on the upper end of the engine.

SERVICING ENGINE IN FRAME

The following components can be serviced while the engine is mounted in the frame (the ATV's frame is a great holding fixture for breaking loose stubborn bolts and nuts):

   a. Camshaft.
   b. Cylinder head.
   c. Cylinder.
   d. Carburetor.
   e. Recoil starter.
   f. A.C. generator assembly.
   g. Clutch assembly(ies).
   h. Starter motor.

CYLINDER HEAD COVER

Removal

> *CAUTION*
> *To prevent any warpage and damage, remove the cylinder head cover only when the engine is at room temperature.*

1. Place the ATV on level ground and set the parking brake. Block the rear wheels so the vehicle will not roll in either direction.

2. Remove the seat and rear fender as described under *Rear Fender Removal/Installation* in Chapter Fourteen.

3. Drain the engine oil as described under *Engine Oil and Filter Change* in Chapter Three.

4. Remove the spark plug as described under *Spark Plug* in Chapter Three. This will make it easier to rotate the engine in the following steps.

5. Remove the bolts securing the recoil starter assembly (**Figure 2**) and remove the assembly and gasket.

6. Using a 17 mm wrench, remove the timing hole cap located on the left-hand crankcase cover. Refer to A, **Figure 3** and **Figure 4**.

7. Remove the exhaust system as described under *Exhaust System Removal/Installation* in Chapter Eight.

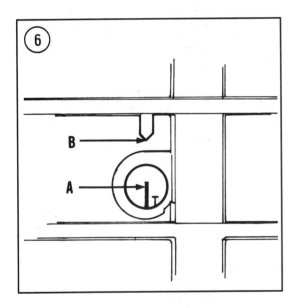

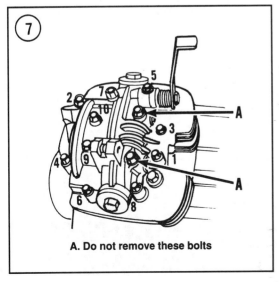

A. Do not remove these bolts

NOTE
The following steps are shown with the engine removed from the frame. It is not necessary to remove the engine for this procedure.

8. Use a 17 mm wrench and remove both valve adjuster caps (**Figure 5**).

NOTE
In the following step, it is very difficult to look directly down into the crankcase cover opening to view the "T" mark on the rotor. It is suggested that a small mirror be used to get a better view of the timing mark within the hole. Be sure to hold the mirror correctly to get a "straight on view" of the rotor for correct alignment.

9. Using the nut on the recoil starter cup (B, **Figure 3**), rotate the engine until the "T" timing mark (A, **Figure 6**) on the rotor aligns with the index mark on the crankcase (B, **Figure 6**). The piston must be at top dead center (TDC) on the compression stroke.

NOTE
A cylinder at TDC of its compression stroke will have free play in both of its rocker arms, indicating that both the intake and exhaust valves are closed.

10. With the engine timing mark on the "T," if both rocker arms are not loose; rotate the engine an additional 360° until both valves have free play. Realign the "T" timing mark.

NOTE
*Do not remove the 2 bolts (A, **Figure 7**) with the conically recessed heads as they hold the rocker arm shafts in position.*

11. Loosen the cylinder head cover bolts in the order indicated in **Figure 7**.

NOTE
Prior to removing the cylinder head bolts, cut a cardboard template the approximate size of the cylinder head cover. Punch holes in the template for each bolt location and place the bolts in the template holes as they are removed. This will greatly speed up the assembly time by eliminating the search for the correct bolt.

12. Remove the cylinder head bolts and washers (A, **Figure 8**), then remove the cylinder head cover (B, **Figure 8**). It may be necessary to tap around the perimeter of the cover with a plastic or soft-faced mallet to break the cover loose from the cylinder head. Don't lose the locating dowels.

CAUTION
Never use a screwdriver or similar sharp tool to loosen or pry off the cylinder head cover. Serious and very expensive damage to the cylinder head cover and cylinder head will result.

Inspection

If oil leakage is visible between the cylinder head cover and the cylinder head, the sealing surface of the cylinder head cover may be warped or damaged. Inspect the sealing surface of the cylinder head cover for scoring or other signs of damage.

Because the cylinder head and cylinder head cover are machined as a set during manufacture, they must be replaced as a set if either is damaged or defective.

1. Remove all traces of sealant residue from the cylinder head and cylinder head cover (**Figure 9**) mating surfaces.

2. Thoroughly clean the cylinder head cover in solvent and dry with compressed air.

3. After the cylinder head cover has been cleaned, place the cylinder head cover gasket surface on a flat surface plate. Measure the warp by inserting a flat feeler gauge between the surface plate and the cylinder head cover at several locations around the perimeter (**Figure 10**). There should be no warpage. The maximum allowable distortion is listed in **Table**

1 or **Table 2**. If the cylinder head cover is warped or distorted beyond the limit, the cylinder head cover and cylinder head must be replaced as a set.

4. Remove and inspect the rocker arms as described in this chapter.

Installation

The piston must be at TDC on the compression stroke. Refer to the *Cylinder Head Removal* procedure in this chapter.

1. Make sure all sealant residue is removed from the sealing surfaces of the cylinder head and cylinder head cover. Spray both sealing surfaces with contact cleaner.

2. Apply a thin even coat of Suzuki Bond 1207B, Three Bond 1104 or equivalent to the cylinder head sealing surface.

3. Lubricate the rocker arm pads, the camshaft bearing journals and bearing surfaces in the cylinder head cover (**Figure 11**) with molybdenum disulfide grease.

4. Install the camshaft rubber end cap (**Figure 12**) into the cylinder head cover.

5. Make sure the locating dowels (**Figure 13**) are in place.

6. Install the cylinder head cover and press it into position.

7. Install a new copper washer under cylinder head bolt No. 2 and No. 6 as shown in **Figure 14** and **Figure 15**. Install all bolts and washers.

NOTE
The torque pattern for tightening the bolts is different than the pattern used for removal.

8. Tighten the cylinder head cover bolts in 2-3 stages in the torque pattern indicated in **Figure 16**. Tighten to the torque specification listed in **Table 3**.

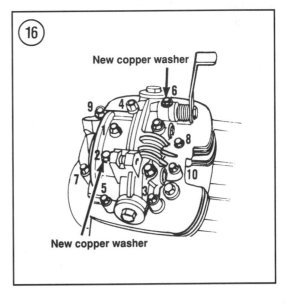

9. Inspect the O-ring seal (**Figure 17**) on both valve adjuster caps. Replace if necessary.

10. Install both valve adjuster caps (**Figure 18**) and tighten securely.

11. Inspect the gasket (**Figure 19**) on the timing hole cover. Replace if necessary.

12. Install the timing hole cap (**Figure 20**) on the left-hand crankcase cover and tighten to the torque specification listed in **Table 3**.

13. Install the exhaust system as described in Chapter Eight.

14. Install the recoil starter assembly and gasket. Tighten the bolts securely.

15. Install the spark plug as described in this chapter.

16. Install rear fender and seat as described in Chapter Fourteen.

17. Refill the engine with new oil as described in Chapter Three.

Disassembly/Inspection/Assembly

It is suggested that one rocker arm assembly be disassembled, inspected and then assembled to avoid the intermixing of parts. This is especially true with a well run-in engine (high mileage). Once wear patterns are developed on these parts, they should only be installed as they were removed or excessive wear may occur.

If you remove both rocker arm assemblies at the same time, mark them in sets with "In" (intake) or "Ex" (exhaust) so they will be reinstalled in the correct location in the cylinder head (**Figure 21**). The exhaust rocker arm has a pad where the decompression shaft rides.

1. Remove the rocker arm shaft bolts (**Figure 22**) and the gasket/washers. Discard the gasket/washers.

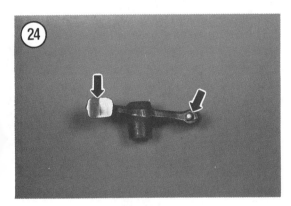

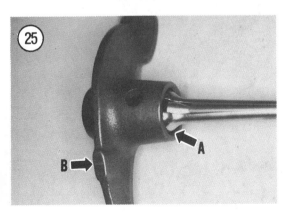

2. Tap on the side of the cylinder head cover, next to the rocker arm shafts, with a plastic mallet and the rocker arm shafts will work their way out of the cylinder head. Using a pair of pliers, carefully withdraw the rocker arm shaft, rocker arm and wave washer.

3. Withdraw the decompression shaft (**Figure 23**).

4. Wash all parts in cleaning solvent and thoroughly dry.

5. Inspect the rocker arm pad where it rides on the cam lobe and where the adjuster rides on the valve stem (**Figure 24**). If the pad is scratched or unevenly worn, inspect the cam lobe for scoring, chipping or flat spots. Replace the rocker arm if defective.

6. Measure the inside diameter of the rocker arm bore with a small hole gauge (A, **Figure 25**), then measure the small hole gauge with a micrometer (**Figure 26**). Check against the dimensions in **Table 1** or **Table 2**. Replace if excessively worn.

7. Inspect the rocker arm shaft for signs of wear or scoring. Measure the outside diameter (**Figure 27**) with a micrometer and check against the dimensions in **Table 1** or **Table 2**. Replace if excessively worn.

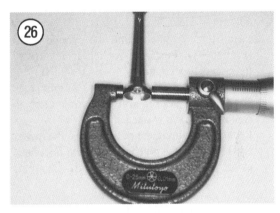

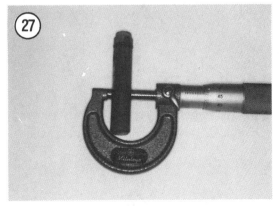

8. Inspect the rocker arm shaft threaded hole (A, **Figure 28**) for wear or damage. If damage is minimal, clean up with a metric tap.

9. Install a new O-ring seal (B, **Figure 28**) on the rocker arm shaft to prevent an oil leak.

10. Coat the decompression shaft with Suzuki Moly Paste or equivalent (molybdenum disulfide grease).

11. Install the decompession shaft and correctly position the return spring on the cylinder head cover boss (**Figure 29**).

12. Coat the rocker arm shafts and rocker arm bores with Suzuki Moly Paste or equivalent (molybdenum disulfide grease).

13. Install the exhaust valve rocker arm and shaft assembly as follows:

NOTE
The exhaust rocker arm has the decompression shaft contact pad (B, Figure 25).

a. Position the exhaust rocker arm shaft with the O-ring end facing out and with the retaining bolt hole located so it will align with the bolt hole in the cylinder head cover. Partially insert the rocker arm shaft into the cylinder head (**Figure 30**).

b. Install the rocker arm into the cylinder head (**Figure 31**). Push the rocker arm partway through the rocker arm.

c. Insert the wave washer (**Figure 32**) into place and slide the rocker arm in a little more to capture the wave washer.

d. Recheck the alignment of the hole in the rocker arm shaft with the bolt hole in the cylinder head cover. Push the rocker arm in until it bottoms out.

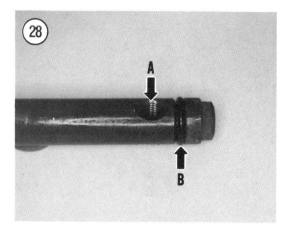

e. Install a new gasket/washer (**Figure 33**) under the bolt and install the rocker arm shaft bolt. Tighten the rocker arm shaft bolt to the torque specification listed in **Table 3**.

14. Install the intake valve rocker arm and shaft assembly as follows:

a. Position the intake rocker arm shaft with the O-ring end facing out and with the retaining bolt hole located so it will align with the bolt hole in the cylinder head cover. Partially insert the rocker arm shaft into the cylinder head (**Figure 34**).

b. Install the rocker arm into the cylinder head (**Figure 35**). Push the rocker arm partway through the rocker arm.

c. Insert the wave washer (**Figure 36**) into place and slide the rocker arm in a little more to capture the wave washer.

d. Recheck the alignment of the hole in the rocker arm shaft with the bolt hole in the cylinder head cover. Push the rocker arm in until it bottoms out.

e. Install a new gasket/washer (**Figure 33**) under the bolt and install the rocker arm shaft bolt. Tighten the rocker arm shaft bolt to the torque specification listed in **Table 3**.

15. After installing both rocker arm and shaft assemblies, refer to **Figure 37** and make sure the wave washers are installed correctly.

4

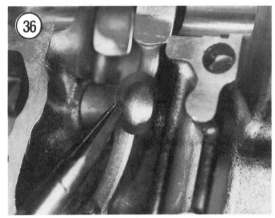

CAMSHAFT

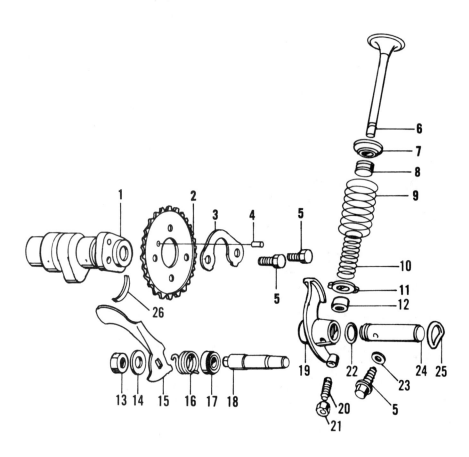

1. Camshaft	13. Nut
2. Camshaft sprocket	14. Washer
3. Lockwasher	15. Decompression lever
4. Drive pin	16. Spring
5. Bolt	17. Oil seal
6. Valve	18. Decompression shaft
7. Spring seat	19. Rocker arm
8. Oil seal	20. Adjust screw
9. Spring	21. Locknut
10. Inner spring	22. O-ring
(1987 models only)	23. Washer
11. Valve spring retainer	24. Rocker arm shaft
12. Keepers	25. Wave washer

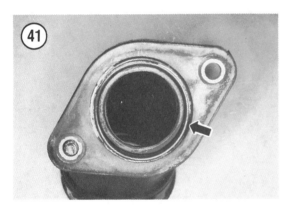

CYLINDER HEAD AND CAMSHAFT

Removal

Refer to **Figure 38** for this procedure.

CAUTION
To prevent any warpage and damage, remove the cylinder head and cam only when the engine is at room temperature.

NOTE
This procedure is shown with the engine removed from the frame. It is not necessary to remove the engine for this procedure.

1. Place the ATV on level ground and set the parking brake.

2. Remove the cylinder head cover (A, **Figure 39**) as described in this chapter.

3. Remove the carburetor as described under *Carburetor Removal/Installation* in Chapter Eight.

4. Remove the screen (**Figure 40**) from the intake pipe.

5. Remove the screw (B, **Figure 39**) from each side securing the intake pipe (C, **Figure 39**) and remove the intake pipe. Don't lose the O-ring (**Figure 41**) in the intake pipe recess.

6. Remove the camshaft drive chain tensioner assembly from the cylinder as described in this chapter.

7. If still installed, remove the camshaft end cap (**Figure 42**). Sometimes the end cap will stay with the cylinder head cover.

8. Flatten the locking tabs (**Figure 43**) of the lockwasher on the camshaft sprocket bolts.

9. Rotate the engine until one of the camshaft sprocket bolts is exposed. Remove that bolt (**Figure 44**).

10. Again rotate the engine until the other camshaft sprocket bolt is exposed. Remove that bolt (A, **Figure 45**) and lockwasher (B, **Figure 45**). Discard the lockwasher as a new one must be installed during installation.

> *NOTE*
> *A small drive pin is used to keep the sprocket aligned with the camshaft. The drive pin may remain with the sprocket or the camshaft (**Figure 46**). Take care not to drop the drive pin into the crankcase.*

11. Gently pry the camshaft sprocket (**Figure 47**) free from the camshaft. Disengage the drive chain from the sprocket and remove the sprocket. Remove the drive pin from either the camshaft or sprocket.

12. Attach a piece of wire to the drive chain and tie it to the exterior of the engine. This will prevent the chain from falling into the crankcase.

> *CAUTION*
> *If the crankshaft must be rotated when the camshaft is removed, pull up on the cam chain and keep it taut while rotating the crankshaft. Make certain that the drive chain is positioned correctly on the crankshaft timing sprocket. If this is not done, the drive chain may become kinked and may damage both the chain and the timing sprocket on the crankshaft.*

13. Remove the bolt and washer (**Figure 48**) securing the camshaft chain tensioner guide assembly to the cylinder head and remove the camshaft chain

tensioner guide (A, **Figure 49**) from the cylinder head

14. Remove the camshaft (B, **Figure 49**) from the cylinder head.

15. Remove the camshaft locating "C" ring (**Figure 50**).

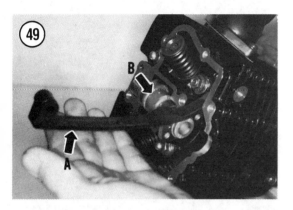

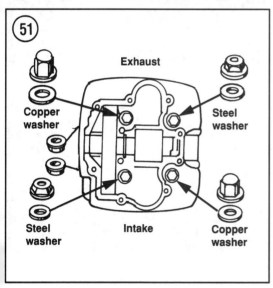

NOTE
*Prior to removing the cap nuts, the plain nuts, the steel washers and copper washers, note the location of the washers and nuts as shown in (**Figure 51**). They must be installed on the same crankcase stud from which they were removed. If installed incorrectly, an oil leak will result.*

16. In a crisscross pattern, remove the nuts and washers (**Figure 52**) securing the cylinder head.

17. Use a box-end wrench and loosen, then remove the cylinder head-to-cylinder nuts (**Figure 53**).

18. Loosen the cylinder head by tapping around the perimeter with a rubber or soft-faced mallet. If necessary, *gently* pry the head loose with a broad-tipped screwdriver.

CAUTION
Remember the cooling fins are fragile and may be damaged if tapped or pried on too hard. Never use a metal hammer.

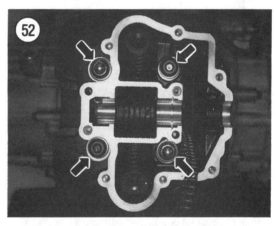

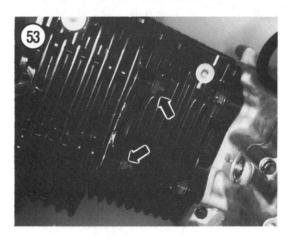

4

19. Lift the cylinder head (A, **Figure 54**) straight up and off the crankcase studs. Guide the camshaft chain (B, **Figure 54**) through the opening in the cylinder head and retie the wire to the exterior of the engine. This will prevent the drive chain from falling down into the crankcase.

20. Remove the cylinder head gasket and discard it. Don't lose the locating dowels.

21. Place a clean shop cloth into the cam chain opening in the cylinder to prevent the entry of foreign matter.

Cylinder Head Inspection

Because the cylinder head and cylinder head cover are machined as a set during manufacture, they must be replaced as a set if either is damaged or defective.

1. Remove all traces of gasket material from the cylinder head-to-cylinder head cover mating surface (**Figure 55**).

2. Remove all traces of gasket material from the cylinder head-to-cylinder mating surface.

3. *Without removing the valves,* remove all carbon deposits from the combustion chamber and valve ports with a wire brush. A blunt screwdriver or chisel may be used if care is taken not to damage the head, valves and spark plug threads.

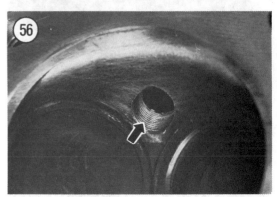

4. Examine the spark plug threads (**Figure 56**) in the cylinder head for damage. If damage is minor or if the threads are dirty or clogged with carbon, use a spark plug thread tap to clean the threads following its manufacturer's instructions. If thread damage is severe, refer further service to a dealer or competent machine shop.

5. Inspect the threads on the short cylinder head-to-cylinder threaded studs for damage (**Figure 57**). Clean up with an appropriate size metric die if

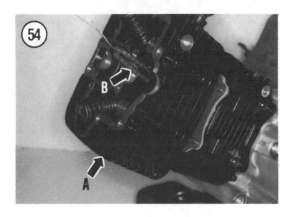

necessary. Make sure the studs are tightly secured into the cylinder head.

6. Inspect the exhaust pipe threaded studs (**Figure 58**) for damage. Clean up with an appropriate size metric die if necessary. Make sure the studs are tightly secured into the cylinder head.

7. After the carbon is removed from the combustion chamber and the valve intake and exhaust ports,

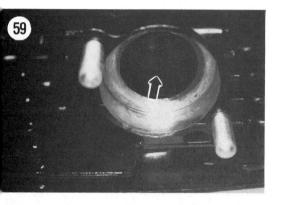

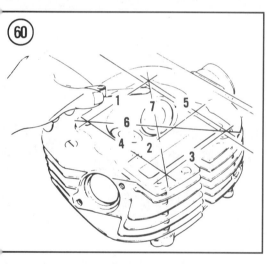

clean the entire head in cleaning solvent. Blow dry with compressed air.

8. Clean away all carbon from the piston crown. Do not remove the carbon ridge at the top of the cylinder bore.

9. Check for cracks in the combustion chamber and exhaust port (**Figure 59**). A cracked head must be replaced.

10. After the head has been thoroughly cleaned, place a straightedge across the cylinder head-to-cylinder gasket surface at several points (**Figure 60**). Measure the warp by inserting a flat feeler gauge between the straightedge and the cylinder head at each location (**Figure 61**). There should be no warpage; if a small amount is present, it can be resurfaced by a dealer or qualified machine shop. Replace the cylinder head and cylinder head cover as a set if the gasket surface is warped to or beyond the limit listed in **Table 1** or **Table 2**.

11. Inspect the cam bearing surfaces in the cylinder head (**Figure 62**) and cylinder head cover (**Figure 63**) for wear or scoring. Replace the cylinder head and cylinder head cover as a set if the bearing surfaces are worn or scored.

Camshaft Inspection

1. Inspect the camshaft bearing journals (A, **Figure 64**) for wear.

2. Measure all camshaft bearing journals with a micrometer. Refer to **Figure 65** and **Figure 66**. Compare to the dimensions given in **Table 1** or **Table 2**. If worn to the service limit or less the camshaft must be replaced.

3. Check the camshaft lobes (B, **Figure 64**) for wear. The lobes should show no signs of scoring and the edges should be square. Slight damage may be removed with a silicone carbide oilstone. Use No. 100-120 grit stone initially, then polish with a No. 280-320 grit stone.

4. Even though the camshaft lobe surface appears to be satisfactory, with no visible signs of wear, the camshaft lobes must be measured with a micrometer (**Figure 67**). Compare to the dimensions given in

Table 1 or **Table 2**. If worn to the service limit or less, the camshaft must be replaced.

5. Inspect the camshaft end-float locating groove (A, **Figure 68**) for wear or damage. If worn or damaged, replace the camshaft.

6. Make sure the oil control holes (B, **Figure 68**) are clear. Clean out with a piece of wire and solvent, then blow out with compressed air.

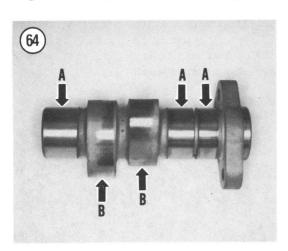

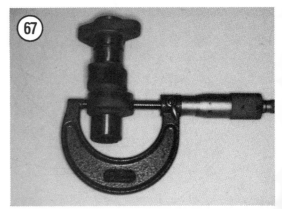

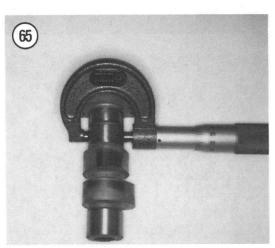

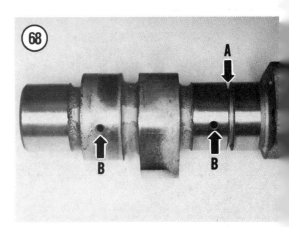

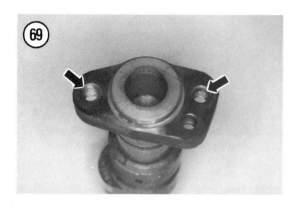

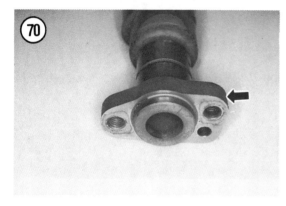

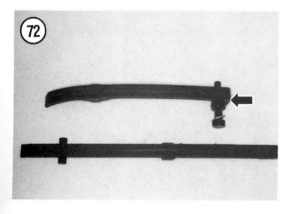

7. Inspect the sprocket mounting bolt threaded holes (**Figure 69**) for damage. Clean up with an appropriate size metric tap if necessary.

8. Inspect the sprocket mounting flange (**Figure 70**) for cracks, warpage or damage. Replace the camshaft if necessary.

9. Inspect the camshaft sprocket teeth (**Figure 71**) for wear; replace if necessary. If the teeth are damaged, inspect the camshaft drive chain (see Chapter Five) for damage also. If either part is damaged, both should be replaced as a set.

10. Inspect the camshaft chain tensioner guide (**Figure 72**) for wear or damage. Replace if necessary.

4

Camshaft Bearing Clearance Measurement

This procedure requires the use of a Plastigage set. The camshaft must be installed into the cylinder head. Before installing the camshaft, wipe all oil residue from the camshaft bearing journals and bearing surfaces in the cylinder head and camshaft bearing cap.

1. Install the camshaft into the cylinder head with the lobes facing up. Do not attach the drive sprocket to the camshaft.

2. Make sure the locating dowels are in place in the cylinder head.

3. Place a strip of Plastigage material on top of each camshaft center and end bearing journals, parallel to the camshaft.

4. Install the cylinder head cover (**Figure 73**) and press it into position.

5. Install the washers and nuts.

6. Tighten the cylinder head cover bolts in 2-3 stages in the torque pattern indicated in **Figure 74**. Tighten to the torque specification listed in **Table 3**.

> *CAUTION*
> *Do not rotate the camshaft with the Plastigage material in place.*

7. Loosen the cylinder head cover nuts in a crisscross pattern, then remove the nuts and washers.

8. Carefully pull the cylinder head cover straight up and off of the camshaft and cylinder head.

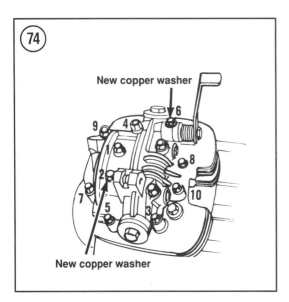

New copper washer

New copper washer

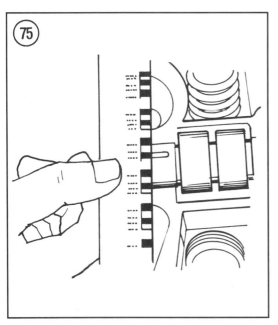

9. Measure the width of the flattened Plastigage material at the widest point, according to the manufacturer's instructions (**Figure 75**).

> *CAUTION*
> *Be sure to remove all traces of Plastigage material from the bearing journals in the cylinder head and cylinder head cover. If any material is left in the en-*

*gine, it can plug up an oil control orifice
and cause severe engine damage.*

10. Remove *all* Plastigage material from the camshaft.

11. If the oil clearance is greater than specified in **Table 1** or **Table 2**, and the camshaft bearing journal outside diameter dimensions are within specification as described under *Camshaft Inspection*, replace the cylinder head and cylinder head cover as a set.

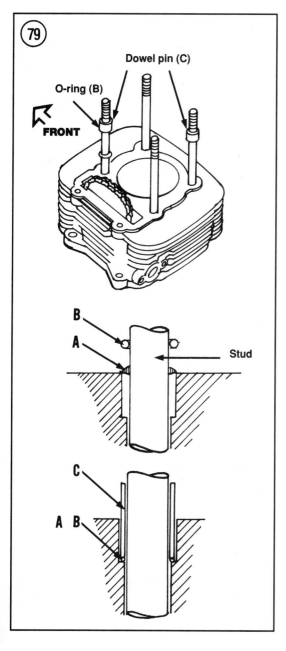

79

Dowel pin (C)

O-ring (B)

FRONT

B
A

Stud

C

A B

Installation

1. Remove the clean shop cloth from the cam chain opening in the cylinder.

CAUTION
When rotating the crankshaft, keep the cam chain taut and engaged with the timing sprocket on the crankshaft.

2. The engine must be at top dead center (TDC) for the following steps for correct valve timing. Hold the cam chain out and taut while rotating the crankshaft to avoid damage to the chain and/or the crankcase.

3. If the engine has been rotated since the cylinder head was removed, using the nut on the recoil starter cup (**Figure 76**), rotate the engine until the "T" timing mark aligns with the index mark on the crankcase (**Figure 77**).

4. Make sure the camshaft chain guide locating pins are properly positioned in the cylinder receptacles (**Figure 78**).

5A. On LT-4WDX (280 cc) models, perform the following:

    a. On the lower left-hand crankcase stud only, apply Suzuki Bond No. 1216 (part No. 09280-05006) sealant, or equivalent, around the perimeter of the crankcase stud (A, **Figure 79**).

    b. Install the O-ring seal (B, **Figure 79**) onto the crankcase stud and slide it onto the sealant.

    c. Install the locating dowel (C, **Figure 79**) onto the crankcase stud. Using the locating dowel, push the O-ring seal and sealant down into the receptacle in the cylinder head. Slowly push the locating dowel down until it bottoms out.

    d. Install the other locating dowel and a new head gasket.

5B. On all other models, install a new head gasket (A, **Figure 80**) and the locating dowels (B, **Figure 80**).

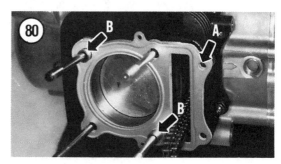

80

6. Install the cylinder head (A, **Figure 81**) onto the crankcase studs. Carefully guide the camshaft chain (B, **Figure 81**) up through the camshaft chain cavity on the side of the cylinder head while pushing the cylinder head down into position.

7. Guide the short threaded studs through the base gasket (**Figure 82**) being careful not to damage the gasket surfaces.

8. Tie the wire attached to the camshaft chain to the exterior of the engine (**Figure 83**).

NOTE
In Step 9, the cap nuts, the plain nuts, the steel washers and copper washers must be installed in the on the same crankcase stud from which they were removed. If installed incorrectly, an oil leak will result.

9. Install the copper washers (**Figure 84**) and cap nuts (**Figure 85**) onto the crankcase studs as shown. Do not tighten the cap nuts at this time.

10. Install the steel washers (**Figure 86**) and plain nuts (**Figure 87**) onto the crankcase studs as shown. Do not tighten the plain nuts at this time.

11. Tighten the 4 upper nuts gradually in 2-3 steps in a crisscross pattern to the torque specification listed in **Table 3**.

12. Install the lower nuts (**Figure 88**) on the right-hand side of the cylinder head, securing the cylinder head to the cylinder.

CAUTION
Use only a box-end wrench to tighten the lower nuts. The cylinder may be damaged if you use a socket or open-end wrench since the nut is very close to the cylinder wall.

13. Using a box-end wrench (**Figure 89**), tighten the 2 lower nuts to the torque specification listed in **Table 3**.

14. Apply some cold grease to the groove in the cylinder head and install the camshaft locating "C" ring (**Figure 90**). Make sure it is seated correctly. This C-clip controls end float of the camshaft and must be installed.

15. Position the camshaft chain tensioner guide as shown (A, **Figure 91**) and install it into the cylinder head. Push it down into position and align the bolt hole with the hole in the cylinder head. Install the bolt and washer (**Figure 92**) securing the camshaft chain tensioner assembly and tighten securely.

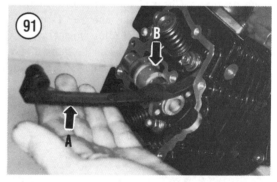

NOTE
*Make sure the "T" timing mark is still aligned with the index mark on the crankcase (**Figure 93**). This is necessary for proper camshaft timing.*

16. Install the camshaft (B, **Figure 91**) and position it with the sprocket locating pin (A, **Figure 94**) facing up and align the timing marks (B, **Figure 94**) with the top surface of the cylinder head.

17. Make sure the locating pin (**Figure 95**) is still in place in the sprocket mounting boss.

18. Carefully pull the camshaft drive chain up and place it over the end of the camshaft (**Figure 96**).

19. Position the camshaft sprocket so the drive pin hole is located at approximately the 12 o'clock position.

20. Install and mesh the drive sprocket with the drive chain.

21. Slide the camshaft sprocket over the shoulder on the camshaft. The drive pin hole in the sprocket and the drive pin in the camshaft should align and the camshaft must be indexed into the C-clip in the cylinder head. Push the sprocket onto the camshaft until it bottoms out.

22. Install the camshaft chain tensioner assembly as described in this chapter.

23. At this time make sure the timing marks are still aligned properly. Check all timing marks as follows:

   a. Refer to Step 3 and make sure the "T" mark is still properly aligned. Readjust if necessary.

   b. Make sure the index marks on the camshaft are perfectly aligned with the top surface of the cylinder head.

   c. Readjust if any timing marks are not aligned correctly.

CAUTION
Very expensive damage could result from improper camshaft and camshaft chain alignment. Recheck your work several times to be sure alignment is correct.

24. When all timing marks are aligned correctly, perform the following:

    a. Apply a blue Loctite (No. 242) to one of the cam sprocket bolts.

    b. Position the new lockwasher so it will cover the camshaft drive pin (A, **Figure 97**) and install the lockwasher (B, **Figure 97**).

    c. Install the bolt (C, **Figure 97**) into the exposed bolt hole. Do not tighten the bolt at this time.

    d. Rotate the engine one full turn to expose the other bolt hole.

    e. Apply a blue Loctite (No. 242) to the other cam sprocket bolt and install the bolt (**Figure 98**).

    f. Tighten this bolt to the torque specification listed in **Table 3**.

    g. Rotate the engine one full turn to expose the first bolt and remove it.

    h. Tighten this bolt to the torque specification listed in **Table 3**.

    i. Fold over the locking tab onto a flat on each of the bolts (**Figure 99**).

25. Make one final check to make sure alignment is correct. The "T" timing mark must be aligned with the crankcase mark and the index marks on the end of the cam shaft must be perfectly aligned with the top surface of the cylinder head.

26. Install the camshaft end cap (**Figure 100**).

27. Install the cylinder head cover as described in this chapter.

28. Make sure the intake pipe mating surface on the cylinder head (**Figure 101**) is clean to ensure a good air-tight seal.

29. Inspect the O-ring seal (**Figure 102**) for deterioration or damage. Replace if necessary.

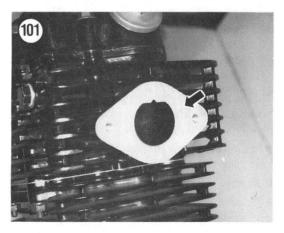

30. Install the O-ring (**Figure 103**) in the intake pipe recess and apply a light coat of clean engine oil to it after installation.

31. Install the intake pipe (A, **Figure 104**) onto the cylinder and install the 2 screws (B, **Figure 104**). Tighten the screws securely to ensure an air-tight fit.

32. Install the screen (**Figure 105**) into the intake pipe.

33. Install the carburetor as described in Chapter Eight.

34. Adjust the valves as described in Chapter Three.

VALVES AND VALVE COMPONENTS

General practice among those who do their own service is to remove the cylinder head and take it to a machine shop or dealer for inspection and service. Since the cost is relative to the required effort and equipment, this is the best approach even for experienced mechanics.

This procedure is included for those who chose to do their own valve service.

Refer to **Figure 106** for this procedure.

Valve Removal

1. Remove the cylinder head and camshaft as described in this chapter.

> *CAUTION*
> *To avoid loss of spring tension, do not compress the springs any more than necessary to remove the keepers.*

2. Compress the valve springs with a valve compressor tool (**Figure 107**). Remove the valve keepers and release the compression. Remove the valve compressor tool.

3A. On 1987 250 cc and all 280 cc models, remove the valve spring retainer and the outer and inner valve springs.

3B. On all other models, remove the valve spring retainer and the valve spring.

4. Prior to removing the valve, remove any burrs from the valve stem (**Figure 108**). Otherwise the valve guide will be damaged.

5. Remove the valve.

6. Remove the oil seal and spring seats from the valve guide.

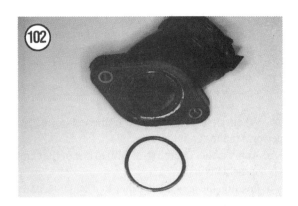

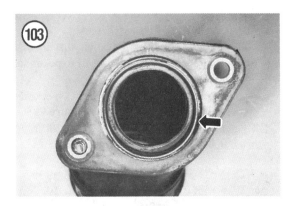

106

VALVES AND VALVE COMPONENTS

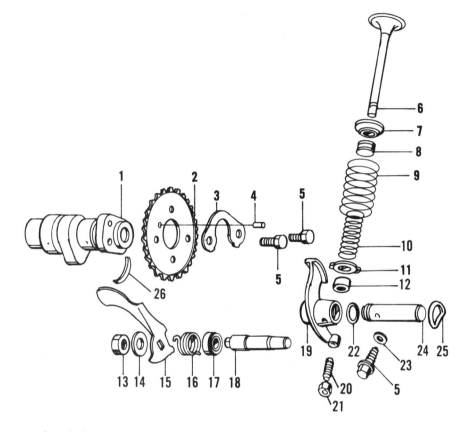

4

1. Camshaft
2. Camshaft sprocket
3. Lockwasher
4. Drive pin
5. Bolt
6. Valve
7. Spring seat
8. Oil seal
9. Spring

10. Inner spring
    (1987 models only)
11. Valve spring retainer
12. Keepers
13. Nut
14. Washer
15. Decompression lever
16. Spring
17. Oil seal

18. Decompression shaft
19. Rocker arm
20. Adjust screw
21. Locknut
22. O-ring
23. Washer
24. Rocker arm shaft
25. Wave washer

 107

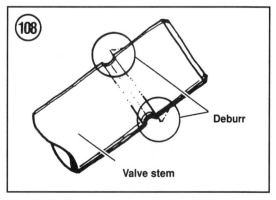 108

Deburr

Valve stem

7. Repeat Steps 2-6 for the remaining valve assembly.

8. Mark all parts (**Figure 109**) as they are disassembled so that they will be installed in their same locations. The exhaust valve is adjacent to the exhaust port and the intake valve is located next to the intake pipe.

Valve Inspection

1. Clean the valves with a soft wire brush and solvent.

2. Inspect the contact surface of each valve (**Figure 110**) for burning or pitting. Unevenness of the contact surface is an indication that the valve is not serviceable. The valve contact surface *cannot* be ground and must be replaced if defective.

3. Measure each valve stem for wear (**Figure 111**). If worn to the wear limit listed in **Table 1** or **Table 2** or less, the valve must be replaced.

4. Measure the valve stem radial runout with a dial indicator as shown in **Figure 112**. If the runout exceeds the wear limit listed in **Table 1** or **Table 2**, the valve must be replaced.

5. Measure the valve head radial runout with a dial indicator as shown in **Figure 113**. If the runout exceeds the wear limit listed in **Table 1** or **Table 2**, the valve must be replaced.

6. Measure the valve head thickness as shown in **Figure 114**. If the head thickness is less than the wear limit listed in **Table 1** or **Table 2**, the valve must be replaced.

7. Remove all carbon and varnish from each valve guide with a stiff spiral wire brush.

8. To measure valve stem-to-valve guide clearance with the wobble or tilt method, perform the following:

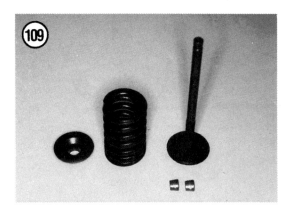

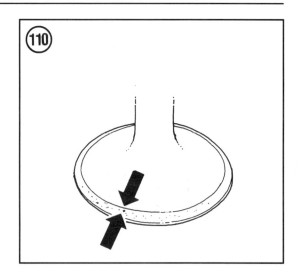

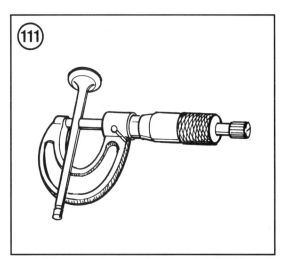

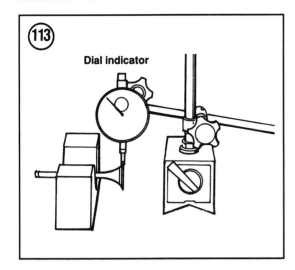

Dial indicator

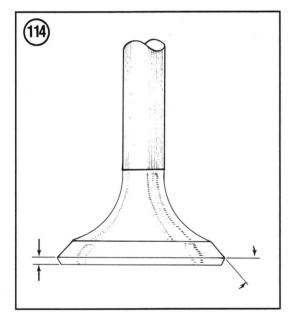

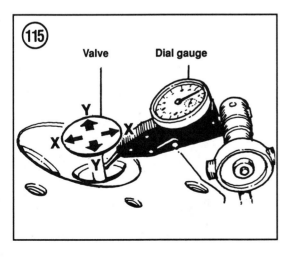

Valve   Dial gauge

a. Insert a *new* valve in a guide.

b. Hold the valve with the head just slightly off the valve seat and rock it sideways in 2 directions, "X" and "Y," perpendicular to each other as shown in **Figure 115**.

c. If the valve-to-valve guide clearance exceeds the limit listed in **Table 1** or **Table 2**, replace the valve guide.

9. Measure each valve spring free length with a vernier caliper (**Figure 116**). The spring(s) should be within the length specified in **Table 1** or **Table 2** with no signs of bends or distortion (**Figure 117**). Replace defective spring(s).

4

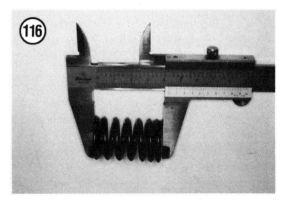

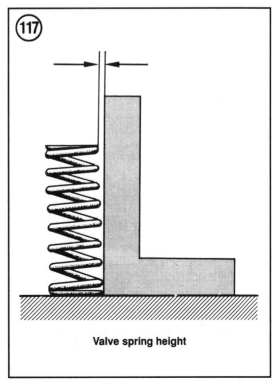

Valve spring height

10. Check the valve spring retainer and valve keepers. If they are in good condition, they may be reused; replace as necessary.

11. Inspect the valve seats (**Figure 118**) in the cylinder head. If worn or burned, they must be reconditioned as described in this chapter.

Valve Installation

1. If removed, install a new seal on each valve guide and push it down until it bottoms out.

2. Install the spring seat (**Figure 119**) and push it down until it bottoms out.

3. Coat the valve stems with molybdenum disulfide grease. To avoid damage to the valve stem seal, turn the valve slowly while inserting the valve into the cylinder head (**Figure 120**). Push the valve all the way in until it bottoms out.

4. Position the valve springs with their closer wound coils (**Figure 121**) facing the cylinder head.

5A. On 1987 250 cc and all 280 cc models, install the inner valve spring and the outer valve spring.

5B. On all other models, install the valve spring (**Figure 122**).

6. Position the valve spring retainer with the small shoulder side facing the valve springs and install the valve spring retainer (**Figure 123**) on top of the valve spring(s).

> *CAUTION*
> *To avoid loss of spring tension, do not compress the springs any more than necessary to install the keepers.*

7. Compress the valve springs with a compressor tool (**Figure 107**).

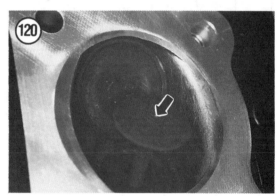

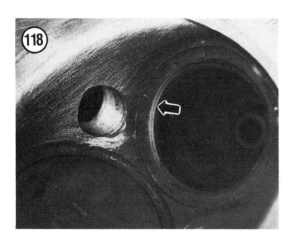

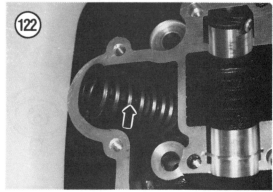

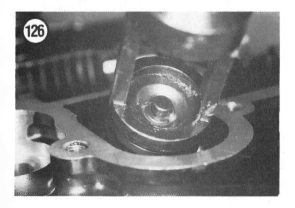

8. Apply a small amount of cold grease to the valve keeper and install both keepers. Refer to **Figure 124** and **Figure 125**. Make sure the keepers fit snug into the rounded groove in the valve stem (**Figure 126**).

9. Remove the compression tool.

10. After the spring has been installed, gently tap the end of the valve stem with a soft aluminum or brass drift and hammer. This will ensure that the keepers are properly seated.

11. Repeat for the other valve assembly if necessary.

12. Install the cylinder head as described in this chapter.

Valve Guide Replacement

When valve guides are worn so that there is excessive valve stem-to-guide clearance or valve tipping, the guides must be replaced. This job should only be done by a dealer as special tools are required as well as considerable expertise. If the valve guide is replaced, also replace the respective valve.

The following procedure is provided if you choose to perform this task yourself.

> *CAUTION*
> *There **may** be a residual oil or solvent odor left in the oven after heating the cylinder head. If you use a household oven, first check with the person who uses the oven for food preparation to avoid getting into trouble.*

1. If still installed, remove the screws securing the intake pipe (**Figure 127**) and remove from the cylinder head.

2. The valve guides (**Figure 128**) are installed with a slight interference fit. Place the cylinder head in a heated oven (or on a hot plate). Heat the cylinder head to a temperature between 120-150° C (248-302° F). An easy way to check the proper temperature is to drop tiny drops of water on the cylinder head; if they sizzle and evaporate immediately, the temperature is correct.

> *CAUTION*
> *Do not heat the cylinder head with a torch (propane or acetylene); never bring a flame into contact with the cylinder head or valve guide. The direct heat will destroy the case hardening of the valve guide and will likely cause warpage of the cylinder head.*

3. Remove the cylinder head from the oven and hold onto it with kitchen pot holders, heavy gloves or heavy shop cloths—*it is very hot.*

4. While heating up the cylinder head, place the new valve guides in a freezer (or refrigerator) if possible. Chilling them will slightly reduce their overall diameter while the hot cylinder head is slightly larger due to heat expansion. This will make valve guide installation much easier.

5. Turn the cylinder head upside down on wooden blocks. Make sure the cylinder is properly supported on the wooden blocks.

6. From the combustion chamber side of the cylinder head, drive out the old valve guide with a hammer and valve guide arbor (**Figure 129**). Use Suzuki special tool, Valve Guide Remover/Installer (part No. 09916-44910). Remove the special tool.

7. Remove and discard the valve guide. *Never* reinstall a valve guide that has been removed as it is no longer true nor within tolerances.

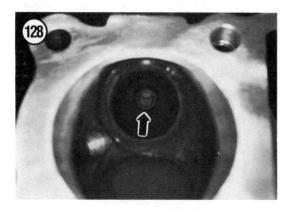

8. Inspect the valve guide receptacle in the cylinder head for damage. After the valve guide has been removed, ream the valve guide receptacle in the cylinder head as follows:

   a. Use Suzuki special tool, 11.3 mm Reamer (part No. 09916-34561) and Handle (part No. 09916-34541).

   b. Apply cutting oil to both the valve guide receptacle and to the reamer.

> *CAUTION*
> *Always rotate the reamer **clockwise**. If the reamer is rotated counterclockwise,*

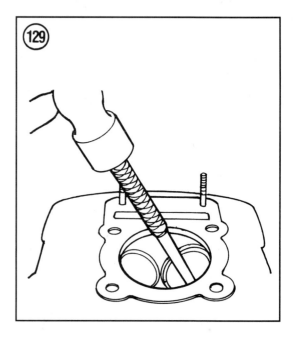

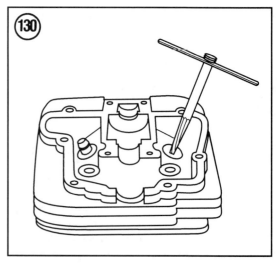

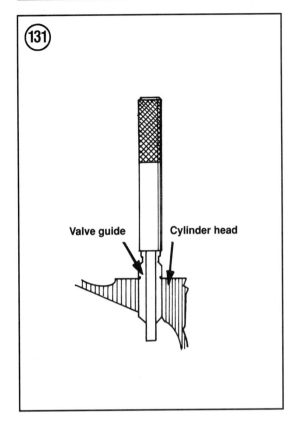

Valve guide   Cylinder head

damage to a valve guide receptacle will occur.

c. Rotate the reamer *clockwise* (**Figure 130**). Continue to rotate the reamer and work it down through the entire length of the valve guide receptacle in the cylinder head. Apply additional cutting oil during this procedure.

d. Rotate the reamer *clockwise* until the reamer has traveled all the way through the valve guide receptacle in the cylinder head.

e. While rotating the reamer *clockwise*, withdraw the reamer from the valve guide receptacle. Remove the reamer.

CAUTION
Failure to apply fresh engine oil to both the valve guide and the valve guide hole in the cylinder head will result in damage to the cylinder head and/or the new valve guide.

9. Turn the cylinder head so the combustion chamber side is facing down.

10. Apply fresh engine oil to the new valve guide and the valve guide receptacle in the cylinder head.

NOTE
The same tool is used for removal and installation of the valve guide. The same valve guide (same part No.) is used for both intake and exhaust valves.

11. From the top side (valve spring side) of the cylinder head, use Suzuki special tool, Valve Guide Remover/Installer (part No. 09916-44910) and hammer and drive in the new valve guide (**Figure 131**). Drive the guide in until the valve guide shoulder bottoms out on the cylinder head surface (**Figure 132**). Remove the special tool.

12. After installation, ream the new valve guide as follows:

a. Use Suzuki special tool, 5.5 Reamer (part No. 09916-34550) and Handle (part No. 09916-34541).

b. Apply cutting oil to both the new valve guide and the valve guide reamer.

CAUTION
Always *rotate the valve guide reamer* ***clockwise***. *If the reamer is rotated counterclockwise, damage to a good valve guide will occur.*

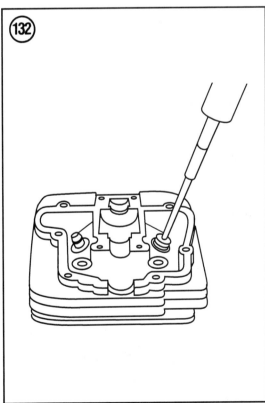

c. Rotate the reamer *clockwise* (**Figure 133**). Continue to rotate the reamer and work it down through the entire length of the new valve guide. Apply additional cutting oil during this procedure.

d. Rotate the reamer *clockwise* until the reamer has traveled all the way through the new valve guide.

e. While rotating the reamer *clockwise*, withdraw the reamer from the valve guide. Remove the reamer.

13. If necessary, repeat Steps 1-12 for the other valve guide.

14. Thoroughly clean the cylinder head and valve guides with solvent to wash out all metal particles. Dry with compressed air. Apply a light coat of engine oil to all bare metal surfaces to prevent any rust formation.

15. Reface the valve seats as described in this chapter.

16. Make sure the intake pipe mating surface on the cylinder head is clean to ensure a good airtight seal.

17. Inspect the O-ring seal (**Figure 134**) for deterioration or damage. Replace if necessary.

18. Install the O-ring (**Figure 135**) in the intake pipe recess and apply light coat of clean engine oil to it after installation.

19. Install the intake pipe (**Figure 127**) onto the cylinder and install the 2 screws. Tighten the screws securely to ensure an airtight fit.

20. Install the screen into the intake pipe.

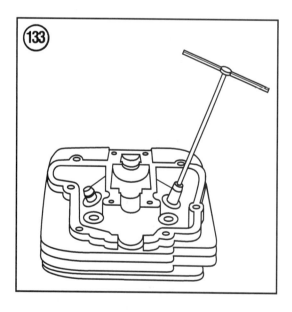

Valve Seat Inspection

1. Remove the valves as described in this chapter.

2. The most accurate method for checking the valve seal is to use Prussian Blue or machinist's dye,

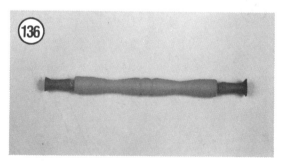
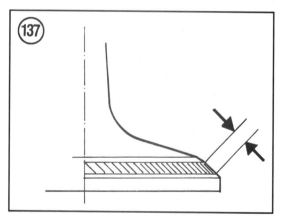

available from auto parts stores or machine shops. To check the valve seal with Prussian Blue or machinist's dye, perform the following:

a. Thoroughly clean off all carbon deposits from the valve face with solvent or detergent, then thoroughly dry.

b. Spread a thin layer of Prussian Blue or machinist's dye evenly on the valve face.

c. Moisten the end of a suction cup valve tool (**Figure 136**) and attach it to the valve. Insert the valve into the guide.

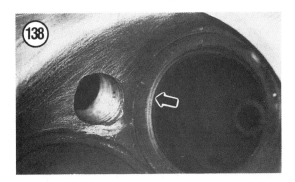

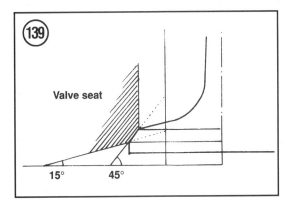

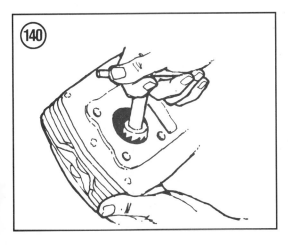

d. Using the suction cup tool, tap the valve up and down in the cylinder head. Do *not* rotate the valve or a false indication will result.

e. Remove the valve and examine the impression left by the Prussian Blue or machinist's dye. If the impression left in the dye (on the valve or in the cylinder head) is not even and continuous and the valve seat width (**Figure 137**) is not within specified tolerance listed in **Table 1** or **Table 2**, the cylinder head valve seat must be reconditioned.

3. Closely examine the valve seat (**Figure 138**) in the cylinder head. It should be smooth and even with a polished seating surface.

4. If the valve seat is okay, install the valves as described in this chapter.

5. If the valve seat is not correct, recondition the valve seat as described in this chapter.

Valve Seat Reconditioning

Special valve cutter tools and considerable expertise are required to recondition the valve seats in the cylinder heads properly. You can save considerable money by removing the cylinder head and taking just the cylinder head to a dealer or machine shop and have the valve seats ground.

The following procedure is provided if you choose to perform this task yourself.

The following tools will be required:

a. Valve seat cutters (see a Suzuki dealer for part numbers).

b. Vernier caliper.

c. Machinist's blue.

d. Valve lapping stick.

The valve seat for both the intake and exhaust valves are machined to the same angles. The valve contact surface is cut to a 45° angle and the area above the contact surface (closest to the combustion chamber) is cut to a 15° angle (**Figure 139**).

1. Carefully rotate and insert the solid pilot into the valve guide. Make sure the solid pilot is correctly seated.

2. Using the 45° cutter, descale and clean the seat to remove roughness and clean the valve seat with one or two turns (**Figure 140**).

CAUTION
Measure the valve seat contact area in the cylinder head after each cut to make sure the contact area is correct and to

prevent removing too much material. If too much material is removed, the cylinder head must be replaced.

3. If the seat is still pitted or burned, turn the 45° cutter additional turns until the surface is clean. Refer to the previous CAUTION to avoid removing too much material from the cylinder head.

4. Remove the valve cutter, T-handle and solid pilot from the cylinder head.

5. Inspect the valve seat-to-valve face impression as follows:

   a. Spread a thin layer of Prussian Blue or machinest's dye evenly on the valve face.

   b. Moisten the suction cup tool and attach it to the valve. Insert the valve into the guide.

   c. Using the suction cup tool, tap the valve up and down in the cylinder head. Do *not* rotate the valve or a false indication will result.

   d. Remove the valve and examine the impression left by the Prussian Blue or machinest's dye.

   e. Measure the valve seat width by measuring the impression the dye left on the valve face. See **Figure 141** and **Figure 137**.

6. If the contact area is too *high* on the valve, or if it is too wide, use the 15° cutter and remove a portion of the top area of the valve seat material to lower and narrow the contact area (**Figure 137**).

7. If the contact area is too *low* on the valve, or if it is too narrow, use the 45° cutter and remove a portion of the lower area of the valve seat material to raise and widen the contact area (**Figure 142**).

8. After the desired valve seat position and width is obtained, use the 45° cutter and very lightly clean off any burrs that may have been caused by the previous cuts.

CAUTION
*Do **not** use any valve lapping compound after the final cut has been made.*

9. Check that the finish has a smooth surface. It should *not* be shiny or highly polished. The final seating will take place when the engine is first run.

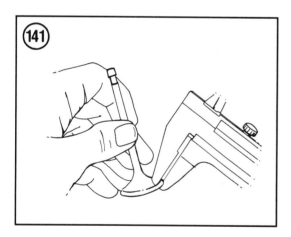

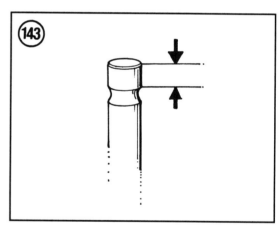

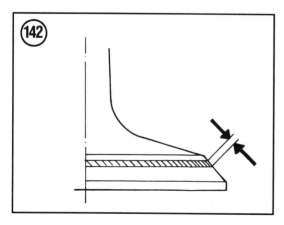

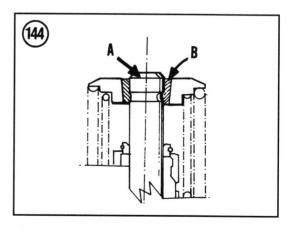

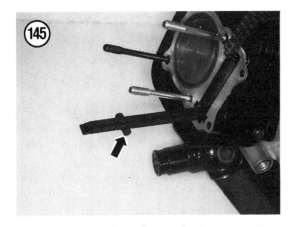

10. Repeat Steps 1-9 for the remaining valve seat.

11. Thoroughly clean the cylinder head and all valve components in solvent or detergent and hot water.

12. Install the valve assemblies as described in this chapter and fill the ports with solvent to check for leaks. If any leaks are present, the valve seats must be inspected for foreign matter or burrs that may be preventing a proper seal.

13. If the cylinder head and valve components were cleaned in detergent and hot water, apply a light coat of engine oil to all bare metal surfaces to prevent any rust formation.

14. If the end of the valve stem must be resurfaced, refer to the following:

   a. The valve stem can be resurfaced only to the point where there is a *minimum* dimension of 2.7 mm (0.11 in.) (**Figure 143**). If the finished dimension is less than specified, the valve must be replaced.

   b. After installing the valve that has had its stem resurfaced, check that the face (A, **Figure 144**) of the valve stem is above the keepers (B, **Figure 144**). If not, the valve must be replaced.

CYLINDER

Removal

1. Remove the cylinder head cover and cylinder head as described in this chapter.

2. Remove the camshaft chain front guide (**Figure 145**).

3. Use a box-end wrench and remove the nuts (**Figure 146**) securing the cylinder to the crankcase.

4. Loosen the cylinder by tapping around the perimeter with a rubber or plastic mallet. If necessary, *gently* pry the cylinder loose with a broad-tipped screwdriver.

5. Pull the cylinder straight out and off of the crankcase studs and piston. Work the cam chain wire through the opening in the cylinder.

6. Remove the cylinder base gasket and discard it. Remove the dowel pins from the crankcase studs.

7. Install a piston holding fixture under the piston to protect the piston skirt from damage. This fixture may be purchased or may be a homemade unit of wood. See **Figure 147** for basic dimensions.

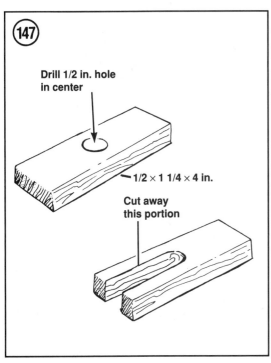

Drill 1/2 in. hole in center

1/2 × 1 1/4 × 4 in.

Cut away this portion

8. Place a clean shop cloth (**Figure 148**) into the openings in the crankcase to prevent the entry of foreign material.

9. Inspect the cylinder as described in this chapter.

Installation

1. If used, remove the clean shop cloth (**Figure 148**) from the openings in the crankcase opening.

2. Apply a liberal coat of clean engine oil to the cylinder wall, especially at the lower end where the piston will be entering.

3. Also apply clean engine oil to the piston and piston rings. This will make it easier to guide the piston into the cylinder bore.

4. Make sure the piston ring end gaps are *not* lined up with each other—they must be staggered.

5. Check that the top surface of the crankcase (**Figure 149**) and the bottom surface of the cylinder (**Figure 150**) are clean prior to installing a new base gasket.

6. If removed, install the locating dowels (A, **Figure 151**).

7. Install a new cylinder base gasket (B, **Figure 151**).

8. Install the cylinder and slide it down onto the crankcase studs (**Figure 152**).

9. Start the cylinder down over the piston. Compress each piston ring with your fingers as it enters the cylinder (**Figure 153**).

10. Push the cylinder down past the piston rings (**Figure 154**).

11. Carefully feed the cam chain and wire (A, **Figure 155**) up through the opening in the cylinder and tie it to the engine.

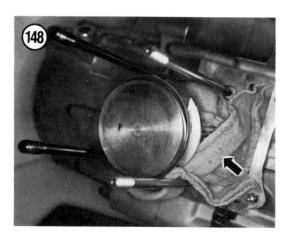

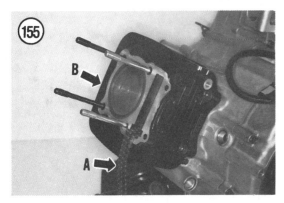

12. Slide the cylinder down until it bottoms on the piston holding fixture.

13. Remove the piston holding fixture and push the cylinder down into place on the crankcase until it bottoms out (B, **Figure 155**).

14. Install the lower nuts (**Figure 146**) securing the cylinder to the crankcase and tighten only finger-tight at this time.

15. Install the camshaft chain front guide. Make sure the locating pins are properly positioned in the cylinder receptacles (**Figure 156**). If improperly installed, it will interfere and bind with the cam chain.

16. Install the cylinder head and cylinder head cover as described in this chapter.

> *CAUTION*
> *Use only a box-end wrench to tighten the lower nuts. The cylinder may be damaged if you use a socket or open-end wrench since the nut is very close to the cylinder wall.*

17. Tighten the cylinder-to-crankcase lower nuts (**Figure 157**), installed in Step 13, to the torque specification listed in **Table 3**.

18. Follow the *Break-in Procedure* in this chapter if the cylinder was rebored, honed or a new piston or piston rings were installed.

Inspection

The following procedure requires the use of highly specialized and expensive measuring instruments. If such equipment is not readily available, have the measurements performed by a dealer or qualified machine shop.

1. Thoroughly clean the cylinder head and cylinder with solvent. Then, using a *dull* gasket scraper, carefully remove all gasket material from the cylinder head (**Figure 158**) and cylinder base (**Figure 150**). Do not nick or gouge the gasket surfaces or oil and air leakage will result.

CAUTION
The cooling fins on the cylinder must be thin to dissipate heat effectively. Remember this when cleaning the cylinder to prevent damage.

2. Thoroughly clean the cooling fins of all road dirt and debris. Be sure to remove any mud that may be imbedded in the fins that are closest to the road surface.

3. Inspect the cooling fins (**Figure 159**) for cracks or damage. Several chipped or missing fins are acceptable. If a large portion of several fins, in the same area have broken off, the cylinder should be replaced to avoid a hot spot.

4. Inspect the threaded holes (**Figure 160**) in the cylinder for the camshaft tensioner for damage. Clean out the threads with the appropriate size metric tap if necessary, then clean out with solvent and compressed air.

5. After the cylinder has been thoroughly cleaned, place a straight edge across the cylinder-to-cylinder head gasket surface at several points. Measure the warp by inserting a flat feeler gauge between the straightedge and the cylinder head at each location (**Figure 161**). There should be no warpage; if a small amount is present, it can be resurfaced by a dealer or qualified machine shop. Replace the cylinder if the gasket surface is warped to or beyond the limit listed in **Table 1** or **Table 2**.

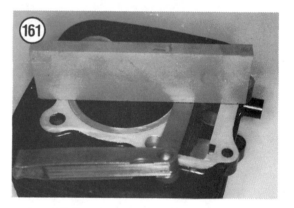

6. Measure the cylinder bore with a cylinder gauge (**Figure 162**) or inside micrometer at the points shown in **Figure 163**. Measure in 2 axes—in line

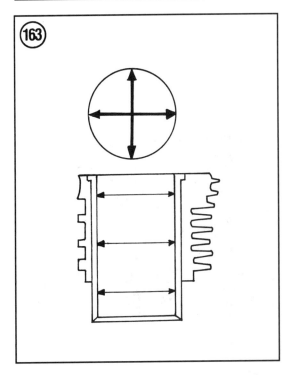

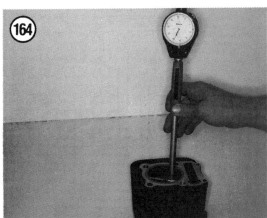

with the piston-pin (**Figure 164**) and at 90° to the pin. If the taper or out-of-round is 0.10 mm (0.004 in.) or greater, the cylinder must be rebored to the next oversize and a new piston installed.

7. If the cylinders are not worn past the service limit, thoroughly check the bore surface (**Figure 165**) for scratches or gouges. If damaged in any way, the bore will require boring and reconditioning.

> *NOTE*
> *The new piston should be obtained before the cylinder is rebored so that the piston can be measured; slight manufacturing tolerances must be taken into account to determine the actual size and working clearance.*

> *NOTE*
> *The maximum wear limit on the cylinder is listed in **Table 1** or **Table 2**. If the cylinder is worn to this limit, it must be replaced. Never rebore a cylinder if the finished rebore diameter will be this dimension or greater.*

8. If the cylinder requires reboring, remove all dowel pins from the cylinder prior to taking it to a dealer or machine shop for service.

9. After the cylinder has been serviced, perform the following:

> *CAUTION*
> *A combination of soap and hot water is the only solution that will completely clean cylinder walls. Solvent and kerosene cannot wash fine grit out of cylinder crevices. Any grit left in the cylinders will act as a grinding compound and cause premature wear to the new rings.*

a. Wash each cylinder bore in hot soapy water. This is the only way to clean the cylinders of the fine grit material left from the bore and honing procedure.

b. Also wash out any fine grit material from the cooling cores surrounding each cylinder.

c. After washing the cylinder walls, run a clean white cloth through each cylinder wall. It should *not* show any traces of grit or debris. If the rag is the slightest bit dirty, the wall is not thoroughly cleaned and must be rewashed.

d. After the cylinder is cleaned, lubricate the cylinder walls with clean engine oil to prevent the cylinder liners from rusting.

10. Inspect the camshaft chain front guide (**Figure 166**) for wear or damage. Replace if necessary.

PISTON, PISTON PIN AND PISTON RINGS

The piston is made of an aluminum alloy, and the piston pin is made of steel. The piston pin is a precision fit and is held in place by a clip at each end of the piston pin bore.

Piston Removal

1. Remove the cylinder head cover, cylinder head and cylinder as described in this chapter.

2. Stuff clean shop cloths into the cylinder bore crankcase openings (**Figure 167**) to prevent objects from falling into the crankcase.

3. Mark an arrow on the piston crown indicating the direction of the piston in the engine.

4. If necessary, remove the piston rings as described in this chapter.

5. Before removing the piston, hold the rod tightly and rock the piston as shown in **Figure 168**. Any rocking motion (do not confuse with the normal sliding motion) indicates wear on the piston pin, piston pin bore or connecting rod small-end bore (more likely a combination of these).

6. Remove the clips from each side of the piston pin bore with a small screwdriver, scribe or needlenose pliers (**Figure 169**). Hold your thumb over one edge of the clip when removing it to prevent the clip from springing out.

7. Use a proper size wooden dowel or socket extension and push out the piston pin.

CAUTION
Be careful when removing the pin to avoid damaging the connecting rod. If

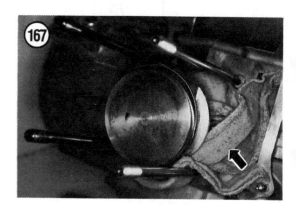

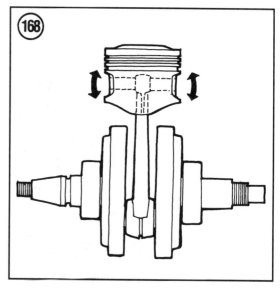

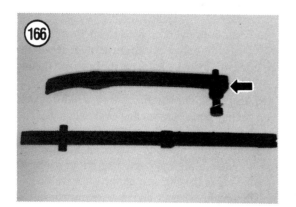

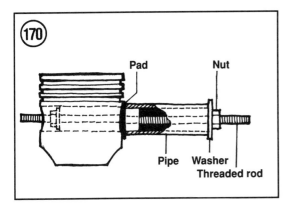

Pad   Nut

Pipe   Washer
Threaded rod

it is necessary to tap the pin gently to remove it, be sure that the piston is properly supported so that lateral shock is not transmitted to the connecting rod lower bearing.

8. If the piston pin is difficult to remove, heat the piston and pin with a butane torch. The pin will probably push right out. Heat the piston to only about 140° F (60° C), i.e., until it is too warm to touch, but not excessively hot. If the pin is still difficult to push out, use a homemade tool as shown in **Figure 170**.

9. Lift the piston off the connecting rod and inspect it as described in this chapter.

10. If the piston is going to be left off for some time, place a piece of foam insulation tube over the end of the rod to protect it.

11. Apply molybdenum disulfide grease to the inside surface of the connecting rod piston pin bore.

12. Oil the piston pin with assembly oil or fresh engine oil and install it in the piston until its end extends slightly beyond the inside of the boss (**Figure 171**).

13. Correctly position the piston-to-connecting rod as follows:

  a. Refer to arrow mark made during disassembly and install the piston with the arrow toward the front of the engine.

  b. If a new piston is being installed, position the piston with the "arrow" mark on the crown (**Figure 172**) pointing toward the *exhaust valve side* of the cylinder.

14. Place the piston over the connecting rod.

15. Line up the piston pin with the hole in the connecting rod. Push the piston pin through the connecting rod and into the other side of the piston until it is even with the piston pin clip grooves.

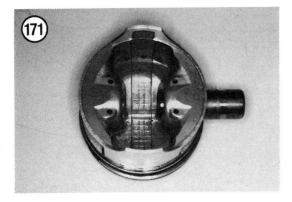

> *CAUTION*
> *If it is necessary to tap the piston pin into the connecting rod, do so gently with a block of wood or a soft-faced hammer. Make sure you support the piston to prevent the lateral shock from being transmitted to the connecting rod lower bearing.*

> *NOTE*
> *In the next step, install the clips with the gap away from the cutout in the piston (**Figure 173**).*

16. Install a *new* piston pin clip in both ends of the pin boss. Make sure they are seated in the grooves in the piston.

17. Check the installation by rocking the piston back and forth around the pin axis and from side to side along the axis. It should rotate freely back and forth but not from side to side.

18. If removed, install the piston rings as described in this chapter.

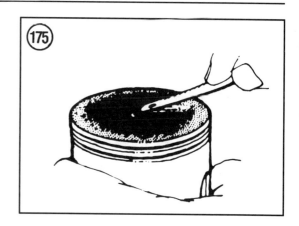

Inspection

1. Carefully clean the carbon from the piston crown (**Figure 174**) with a chemical remover or with a soft scraper (**Figure 175**). Do not remove or damage the carbon ridge around the circumference of the piston above the top ring. If the piston, rings and cylinder are found to be dimensionally correct and can be reused, removal of the carbon ring from the top of the piston or the carbon ridge from the top of the cylinder will promote excessive oil consumption.

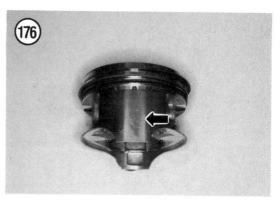

> *CAUTION*
> *Do not wire brush the piston skirts (**Figure 176**) or ring lands. The wire brush removes aluminum and increases piston clearance. It also rounds the corners of the ring lands, which results in decreased support for the piston rings.*

2. Examine each ring groove for burrs, dented edges and excessive wear. Pay particular attention to the top compression ring groove as it usually wears more than the other grooves.

3. If damage or wear indicates piston replacement, select a new piston as described under *Piston Clearance Measurement* in this chapter.

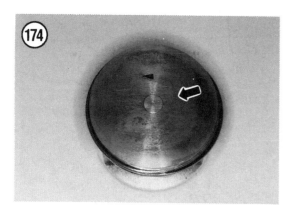

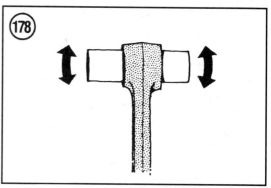

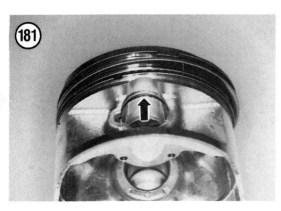

4. Oil the piston pin and install it in the connecting rod (**Figure 177**). Slowly rotate the piston pin and check for radial and axial play (**Figure 178**). If any play exists, the piston pin should be replaced, providing the connecting rod bore is in good condition.

5. Check the oil control holes in the piston for carbon or oil sludge buildup. Refer to **Figure 179** and **Figure 180**. Clean the holes with a small diameter drill bit and blow out with compressed air.

6. Check the piston skirt (**Figure 176**) for galling and abrasion which may have been caused by piston seizure. If light galling is present, smooth the affected area with No. 400 emery paper and oil or a fine oilstone. However, if galling is severe or if the piston is deeply scored, replace it.

7. Inspect the piston pin clip groove (**Figure 181**) on each side of the piston. If either groove is damaged, replace the piston.

8. If damage or wear indicates piston replacement, select a new piston as described under *Piston Clearance Measurement* in this chapter.

9. Inspect the piston pin for chrome flaking or cracks. Replace if necessary.

10. Measure the inside diameter (**Figure 182**) of the piston pin bore with a snap gauge and measure the outside diameter of the piston pin with a micrometer (**Figure 183**). Compare with dimensions given in **Table 1** or **Table 2**. Replace the piston and piston pin as a set if either or both are worn.

Piston Clearance

1. Make sure the piston and cylinder wall are clean and dry.

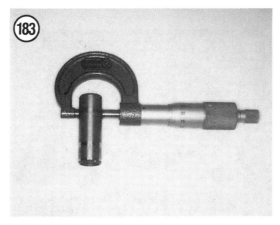

2. Measure the inside diameter of the cylinder bore at a point 13 mm (1/2 in.) from the upper edge with a bore gauge (**Figure 184**).

3. Measure the outside diameter of the piston across the skirt (**Figure 185**) at a right angle to the piston pin. Measure at a distance 18 mm (0.70 in.) up from the bottom of the piston skirt.

4. Piston clearance is the difference between the maximum piston diameter and the minimum cylinder diameter. Subtract the dimension of the piston from the cylinder dimension and compare to the dimension listed in **Table 1** or **Table 2**. If the clearance exceeds that specified, the cylinder should be rebored to the next oversize and a new piston installed.

5. To establish a final overbore dimension with a new piston, add the piston skirt measurement to the specified clearance. This will determine the dimension for the cylinder overbore size. Remember, do not exceed the cylinder maximum service limit inside diameter indicated in **Table 1** or **Table 2**.

Piston Installation

1. Apply molybdenum disulfide grease to the inside surface of the piston pin bore in the connecting rod.

2. Oil the piston pin with assembly oil and install it in the piston until its end extends slightly beyond the inside of the boss (**Figure 171**).

3. Place the piston over the connecting rod with the arrow (**Figure 186**) on the piston crown directed upward toward the front of the engine.

4. Line up the piston pin with the hole in the connecting rod. Push the piston pin through the connecting rod and into the other side of the piston until it is even with the piston pin clip grooves.

CAUTION
If it is necessary to tap the piston pin into the connecting rod, do so gently with a block of wood or a soft-faced hammer. Make sure you support the piston to prevent the lateral shock from being transmitted to the connecting rod bearing.

NOTE
In the next step, install the clips with the gap away from the cutout in the piston (Figure 173).

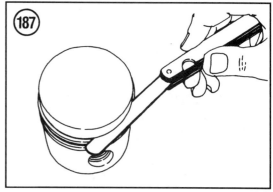

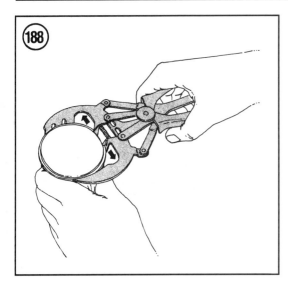

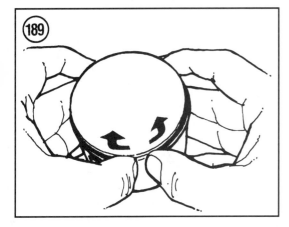

5. Install new piston pin clips in both ends of the pin boss. Make sure they are seated in the grooves in the piston.

6. Check the installation by rocking the piston back and forth around the pin axis and from side to side along the axis. It should rotate freely back and forth but not from side to side.

7. Install the piston rings as described in this chapter.

8. Install the cylinder, cylinder head and cylinder head cover as described in this chapter.

Piston Ring
Removal/Inspection/Installation

WARNING
The edges of all piston rings are very sharp. Be careful when handling them to avoid cutting fingers.

1. Measure the side clearance of each ring in its groove with a flat feeler gauge (**Figure 187**) and compare to dimensions given in **Table 1** or **Table 2**. If the clearance is greater than specified, the rings must be replaced. If the clearance is still excessive with the new rings, the piston must also be replaced.

2. Remove the old rings with a ring expander tool (**Figure 188**) or by spreading the ends with your thumbs just enough to slide the ring up over the piston (**Figure 189**). Repeat for the remaining rings.

3. Carefully remove all carbon buildup from the ring grooves with a broken piston ring (**Figure 190**).

4. Inspect the grooves carefully for burrs, nicks or broken and cracked lands. Recondition or replace the piston if necessary.

5. Roll each ring around its piston groove as shown in **Figure 191** to check for binding. If there is any binding, reclean the ring groove with solvent as there

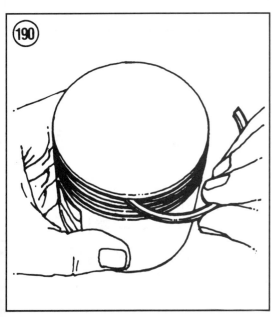

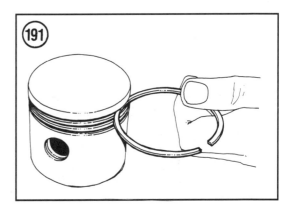

may still be a carbon or oil sludge buildup that was not previously removed. After cleaning with solvent, reclean the groove with a broken piston ring (**Figure 190**).

6. Measure the thickness of each ring with a micrometer (**Figure 192**) and compare to dimensions in **Table 1** or **Table 2**. If the thickness is less than specified, the ring(s) should be replaced.

7. Next, measure the free end gap of each ring with a vernier caliper (**Figure 193**) and compare to dimensions in **Table 1** or **Table 2**. If the gap is greater than specified, the ring(s) should be replaced.

8. After measuring the free end gap, place each ring, one at a time, into the bottom of the cylinder bore and push it in about 20 mm (5/8 in.) with the crown of the piston to ensure that the ring is square in the cylinder bore. Measure the gap with a flat feeler gauge (**Figure 194**) and compare to dimensions in **Table 1** or **Table 3**. If the gap is greater than specified, the ring(s) should be replaced.

9. When installing new rings, measure their end gap as described in Step 7 and Step 8 and compare to dimensions listed in **Table 1** or **Table 2**. If the gap is less than specified, return the ring(s) for another set.

10. Install the oil ring spacer first (A, **Figure 195**) then both side rails (B, **Figure 195**). Suzuki factory new oil ring side rails do not have top and bottom designations and can be installed either way. If reassembling used parts, install the side rails in the same position from which they were removed.

NOTE
*Position the top and second ring with the "R" mark (**Figure 196**) facing toward the piston crown.*

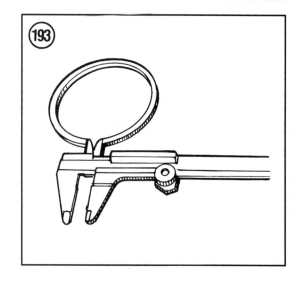
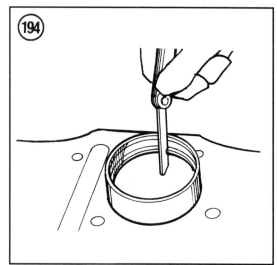
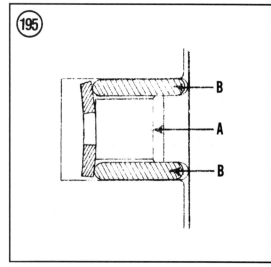
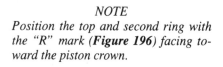
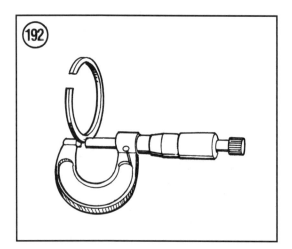

11. Install the second compression ring (with the slight side taper), then the top (**Figure 197**) by carefully spreading the ends with your thumbs and slipping the rings over the top of the piston. Remember that the marks on the piston rings are toward the top of the piston.

12. Make sure the rings are seated completely in their grooves (**Figure 198**) all the way around the piston and that the ends are distributed around the piston as shown in **Figure 199**. The important thing

is that the ring gaps are not aligned with each other when installed to prevent compression pressure from escaping.

13. If installing oversize rings, check the ring number (A, **Figure 200**) to make sure the correct rings are being installed. The ring oversize numbers should be the same as the piston oversize number.

14. If installing an oversize oil ring assembly, check the paint spot (B, **Figure 200**) to make sure the correct oil ring is being installed. The paint color spots are as follows:

  a. No paint spot: standard size.

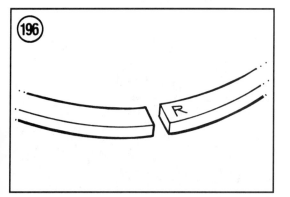

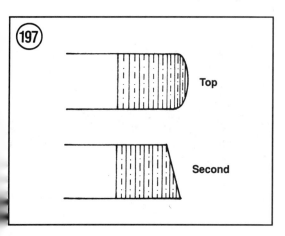

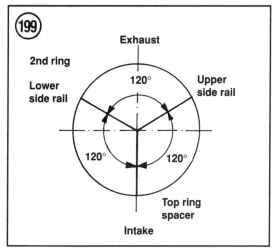

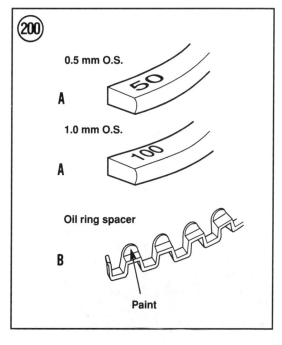

b. Red: 0.5 mm oversize.

c. Yellow: 1.0 mm oversize.

15. If new rings were installed, measure the side clearance of each ring in its groove with a flat feeler gauge (**Figure 187**) and compare to dimensions given in **Table 1** or **Table 2**.

16. After the rings are installed, apply clean engine oil to the rings. Rotate the rings several complete revolutions in their respective grooves. This will assure proper oiling when the engine is first started after piston service.

17. If new rings were installed, the cylinder must be deglazed or honed. This will help to seat the new rings. Refer honing to a Suzuki dealer or competent machine shop. After honing, measure the end gap clearance of each ring (**Figure 194**) and compare to dimensions in **Table 1** or **Table 2**.

> *CAUTION*
> *If the cylinder was deglazed or honed, clean the cylinder as described under* ***Cylinder Inspection*** *in this chapter.*

18. Follow the *Break-in Procedure* in this chapter if a new piston or new piston rings were installed or if the cylinder has been deglazed or honed.

CAMSHAFT CHAIN TENSIONER ADJUSTER

Removal/Installation

1. Place the ATV on level ground and set the parking brake. Block the rear wheels so the vehicle will not roll in either direction.

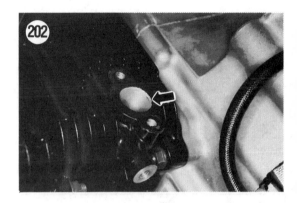

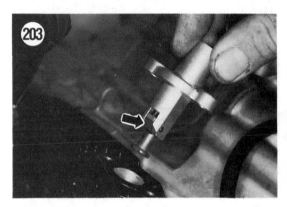

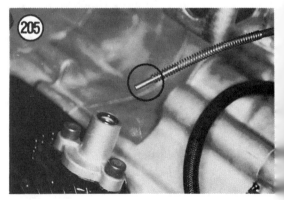

CAMSHAFT CHAIN TENSION ADJUSTER

1.
2.
3.
4.
5.
6.
7.
8.
9.
10.
11.

7. Camshaft chain tensioner guide
1. Center bolt
2. Plunger
3. O-ring
4. Bolt
5. Adjuster body
6. Gasket
8. Washer
9. Bolt
10. Camshaft drive chain
11. Camshaft chain guide

2. Remove the seat and rear fender as described under *Rear Fender Removal/Installation* in Chapter Fourteen.

WARNING
If the engine has just been shut off, the exhaust system will be hot. Since the tensioner assembly is adjacent to the exhaust system heat guard, protect your hands and arms accordingly.

NOTE
This procedure is shown with the engine removed from the frame. It is not necessary to remove the engine for this procedure.

3. Loosen the center bolt (A, **Figure 201**) then remove the mounting bolts (B, **Figure 201**) securing the camshaft chain tension adjuster assembly. Remove the assembly and gasket and discard the gasket.

4. Install a new gasket (**Figure 202**).

5. Use a small flat-bladed screwdriver and release the ratchet. Press the plunger into the body and release the ratchet. The plunger will now stay in the body until the assembly is installed in the cylinder.

6. Position the tensioner body with the ratchet surface (**Figure 203**) facing toward the top of the engine and install the tensioner body into the cylinder.

7. Install the mounting bolts (B, **Figure 201**) and tighten to the torque specification listed in **Table 3**.

8. Apply a light coat of clean engine oil to the O-ring, then install a new O-ring (**Figure 204**) on the body.

9. Install the spring and plunger (**Figure 205**) into the tensioner body, then install the center bolt (**Figure 206**). Tighten to the torque specification listed in **Table 3**.

10. Install the rear fender and seat as described in Chapter Fourteen.

Disassembly/Inspection/Assembly

Refer to **Figure 207** for this procedure.

1. Unscrew the center bolt and remove the O-ring, plunger and spring from the tensioner adjuster body (**Figure 208**).

2. Clean all parts in solvent and thoroughly dry with compressed air.

3. Inspect the tension adjuster body and mounting bosses (**Figure 209**) for damage or excessive wear. Replace the worn parts as necessary.

4. Inspect the end of the plunger (A, **Figure 210**) and the ratchet teeth (B, **Figure 210**) for wear or damage. If either is damaged, replace the tension adjuster body.

5. Inspect the O-ring for deterioration and hardness; replace if necessary.

6. Use a small flat-bladed screwdriver and release the ratchet (A, **Figure 211**). Press the plunger (B, **Figure 211**) into the body and release the ratchet. The plunger will now stay in the body until the assembly is installed in the cylinder.

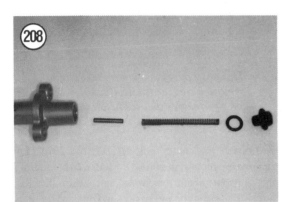

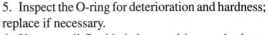

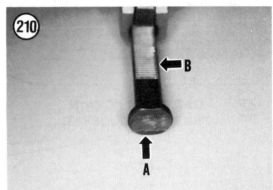

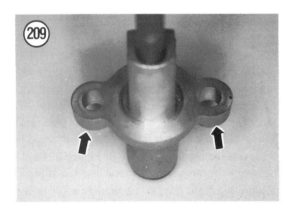

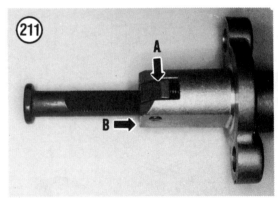

Table 1 ENGINE SERVICE SPECIFICATIONS (250 CC ENGINE)

Item	Specifications	Wear limit
General		
Type	4-stroke, air-cooled, SOHC	
Number of cylinders	1	
Bore and stroke	66.0 × 72.0 mm (2.598 × 2.835 in.)	
Displacement	246 cc (15.0 cu. in.)	
Compression ratio	8.5 to 1	
Compression pressure (at sea level)		
Standard	1,000-1,400 kPa (142-199 psi)	
Service limit (min.)	800 kPa (114 psi)	
Lubrication	Wet sump	
Cylinder		
Bore	66.000-66.015 mm (2.5985-2.5990 in.)	66.090 mm (2.602 in.)
Out of round	—	0.05 mm (0.002 in.)
Piston/cylinder clearance	0.04-0.05 mm (0.0016-0.0020 in.)	0.120 mm (0.005 in.)
Piston		
Diameter	65.955-69.970 mm (2.5966-2.5972 in.)	65.880 mm (2.5937 in.)
Piston pin bore diameter	16.002-16.008 mm (0.6300-0.6302 in.)	16.030 mm (0.6311 in.)
Piston pin diameter	15.996-16.000 mm (0.6298-0.6299 in.)	15.980 mm (.06291 in.)
Piston rings		
Number of rings		
Compression	2	
Oil control	1	
Ring free end gap		
Top	Approx. 7.5 mm (0.30 in.)	6.0 mm (0.24 in.)
Second	Approx. 9.4 mm (0.37 in.)	7.5 mm (0.30 in.)
Ring end gap (in cylinder bore)		
Top and second	0.10-0.25 mm (0.004-0.010 in.)	0.70 mm (0.028 in.)
Ring side clearance		
Top	—	0.180 mm (0.0071 in.)
Second	—	0.150 mm (0.0059 in.)
Ring thickness		
Top	0.97-0.99 mm (0.038-0.039 in.)	—
Second	1.17-1.19 mm (0.046-0.047 in.)	—
Connecting rod		
Small end inner diameter	16.006-16.014 mm (0.6302-0.6305 in.)	16.040 mm (0.6315 in.)
Camshaft		
Cam lobe height		
Intake	34.166-34.206 mm (1.3451-1.3467 in.)	33.870 mm (1.3335 in.)
Exhaust	33.464-33.504 mm (1.3175-1.3191 in.)	33.170 mm (1.3059 in.)
	(continued)	

Table 1 ENGINE SERVICE SPECIFICATIONS (250 CC ENGINE) (continued)

Item	Specifications	Wear limit
Camshaft (continued)		
Cam journal outer diameter	21.959-21.980 mm (0.8645-0.8654 in.)	—
Cam journal holder inner diameter	22.012-22.025 mm (0.8666-0.8671 in.)	—
Cam journal oil clearance	0.032-0.066 mm (0.0013-0.0026 in.)	0.150 mm (0.0059 in.)
Runout	—	0.10 mm (0.004 in.)
Valves		
Valve stem outer diameter		
Intake	5.460-5.475 mm (0.2150-0.2156 in.)	—
Exhaust	5.445-5.460 mm (0.2144-0.2150 in.)	—
Valve guide inner diameter		
Intake and exhaust	5.500-5.512 mm (0.2165-0.2170 in.)	—
Stem to guide clearance		
Intake	0.025-0.052 mm (0.0010-0.0020 in.)	0.35 mm (0.014 in.)
Exhaust	0.040-0.067 mm (0.0016-0.0026 in.)	0.35 mm (0.014 in.)
Valve seat width		
Intake and exhaust	0.9-1.1 mm (0.035-0.043 in.)	—
Valve stem runout	—	0.05 mm (0.002 in.)
Valve head thickness	—	0.5 mm (0.02 in.)
Valve stem end length	—	2.7 mm (0.11 in.)
Valve head radial runout	—	0.03 mm (0.001 in.)
Valve seat width	0.9-1.1 mm (0.035-0.043 in.)	—
Valve springs free length (intake and exhaust)		
Inner spring	—	35.1 mm (1.38 in.)
Outer spring	—	39.9 mm (1.57 in.)
Rocker arm assembly		
Rocker arm bore I.D.	12.000-12.012 mm (0.4724-0.4729 in.)	—
Rocker arm shaft O.D.	11.966-11.984 mm (0.4711-0.4718 in.)	—
Cylinder head and cover warpage	—	0.05 mm (0.002 in.)

Table 2 ENGINE SERVICE SPECIFICATIONS (280 CC ENGINE)

Item	Specifications	Wear limit
General		
Type	4-stroke, air-cooled, SOHC	
Number of cylinders	1	
Bore and stroke	68.5 × 76.0 mm (2.697 × 2.992 in.)	
Displacement	280 cc (17.1 cu. in.)	
Compression ratio	8.9 to 1	
	(continued)	

Table 2 ENGINE SERVICE SPECIFICATIONS (280 CC ENGINE) (continued)

Item	Specifications	Wear Limit
General (continued)		
Compression pressure (at sea level)		
Standard	1,000-1,400 kPa (142-199 psi)	
Service limit (min.)	800 kPa (114 psi)	
Lubrication	Wet sump	
Cylinder		
Bore	68.500-68.515 mm (2.6968-2.6974 in.)	68.580 mm (2.700 in.)
Out of round	—	0.05 mm (0.002 in.)
Piston/cylinder clearance	0.06-0.07 mm (0.0024-0.0028 in.)	0.120 mm (0.005 in.)
Piston		
Diameter	68.445-68.460 mm (2.6947-2.6953 in.)	68.380 mm (2.6921 in.)
Piston pin bore diamter	17.002-17.008 mm (0.6694-0.6696 in.)	17.030 mm (0.6705 in.)
Piston pin diameter	16.996-17.000 mm (0.66913-0.66929 in.)	16.980 mm (0.6685 in.)
Piston rings		
Number of rings		
Compression	2	
Oil control	1	
Ring free end gap		
Top	Approx. 7.8 mm (0.31 in.)	6.2 mm (0.25 in.)
Second	Approx. 9.1 mm (0.36 in.)	7.3 mm (0.29 in.)
Ring end gap (in cylinder bore)		
Top	0.15-0.30 mm (0.006-0.012 in.)	0.70 mm (0.028 in.)
Second	0.50-0.65 mm (0.020-0.026 in.)	0.70 mm (1.000 in.)
Ring side clearance		
Top	—	0.180 mm (0.0071 in.)
Second	—	0.150 mm (0.0059 in.)
Ring thickness		
Top	0.97-0.99 mm (0.038-0.039 in.)	—
Second	1.17-1.19 mm (0.046-0.047 in.)	—
Connecting rod		
Small end inner diameter	17.002-17.014 mm (0.6695-0.6698 in.)	17.040 mm (0.6709 in.)
Camshaft		
Cam lobe height		
Intake	34.112-34.152 mm (1.3430-1.3446 in.)	33.820 mm (1.3315 in.)
Exhaust	33.790-33.830 mm (1.3303-1.3319 in.)	33.490 mm (1.3185 in.)
Cam journal outer diameter	21.959-21.980 mm (0.8645-0.8654 in.)	—
Cam journal holder inner diameter	22.012-22.025 mm (0.8666-0.8671 in.)	—

(continued)

4

Table 2 ENGINE SERVICE SPECIFICATIONS (280 CC ENGINE) (continued)

Item	Specifications	Wear limit
Camshaft		
Cam journal oil clearance	0.032-0.066 mm (0.0013-0.0026 in.)	0.150 mm (0.0059 in.)
Runout	—	0.10 mm (0.004 in.)
Valves		
Valve stem outer diameter		
Intake	5.460-5.475 mm (0.2150-0.2156 in.)	—
Exhaust	5.445-5.460 mm (0.2144-0.2150 in.)	—
Valve guide inner diameter		
Intake and exhaust	5.500-5.512 mm (0.2165-0.2170 in.)	—
Stem to guide clearance		
Intake	0.025-0.052 mm (0.0010-0.0020 in.)	0.35 mm (0.014 in.)
Exhaust	0.040-0.067 mm (0.0016-0.0026 in.)	0.35 mm (0.014 in.)
Valve seat width		
Intake and exhaust	0.9-1.1 mm (0.035-0.043 in.)	—
Valve stem runout	—	0.05 mm (0.002 in.)
Valve head thickness	—	0.5 mm (0.02 in.)
Valve stem end length	—	2.7 mm (0.11 in.)
Valve head radial runout	—	0.03 mm (0.001 in.)
Valve seat width	0.9-1.1 mm (0.035-0.043 in.)	—
Valve springs free length (intake and exhaust)		
Inner spring	—	35.1 mm (1.38 in.)
Outer spring	—	39.9 mm (1.57 in.)
Rocker arm assembly		
Rocker arm bore I.D.	12.000-12.012 mm (0.4724-0.4729 in.)	—
Rocker arm shaft O.D.	11.966-11.984 mm (0.4711-0.4718 in.)	—
Cylinder head and cover warpage	—	0.05 mm (0.002 in.)

Table 3 ENGINE TIGHTENING TORQUE

Item	N·m	ft.-lb.
Cylinder head cover bolt	9-11	6.5-8
Cylinder head 8 mm nuts		
250 cc	18-23	13-16.5
280 cc	21-25	15-18
Cylinder head-to-cylinder 6 mm nuts	7-11	5-8
Cylinder-to-crankcase 6 mm nuts	7-11	5-8
Timing hole cap (17 mm)	20-25	14.5-18.0
Engine oil drain plug	18-23	13-16.5
Camshaft sprocket bolts	10-12	7-8.5
Rocker arm shaft bolt	9-11	6.5-8
Camshaft tensioner		
Body mounting bolts	8-12	6-12
Center bolt	7-9	5-6

CHAPTER FIVE

ENGINE LOWER END

5

This chapter contains information for removal, inspection, service and reassembly of the lower end of the engine. Although the clutch and transmission are located within the lower end of the engine, they are covered in Chapter Six and Chapter Seven to simplify this material.

Table 1 provides specifications for the lower end of the engine and **Table 2** lists the torque specifications. **Table 1** and **Table 2** are located at the end of this chapter.

Before beginning work, read Chapter One again. You will do a better job with this information fresh in your mind.

Throughout the text there is frequent mention of the right-hand and left-hand side of the engine. This refers to the engine as it sits in the ATV's frame, not as it sits on your workbench. The right- and left-hand refers to a rider sitting on the seat facing forward.

SERVICING ENGINE IN FRAME

NOTE
If you are just removing the engine and are not planning to disassemble it, there is no need to remove any of the external components. The engine assembly is small enough that external components can be left on during engine removal.

The following components can be serviced while the engine is mounted in the frame (the ATV's frame is a great holding fixture for breaking loose stubborn bolts and nuts):

a. Camshaft.
b. Cylinder head.
c. Cylinder.
d. Carburetor.
e. Recoil starter.
f. AC generator.
g. Clutch assembly(ies).
h. Starter motor.

ENGINE

Removal/Installation

CAUTION
*Self-locking nuts are used on the engine mounting bolts. Suzuki recommends that all self-locking nuts be discarded once they have been removed. The self-locking portion of the nut is damaged once it has been removed from the bolt and will no longer properly lock onto the bolt threads. Always install **new** self-locking nuts. **Never** reinstall a used nut*

once it has been removed as it will not retain its final tightening torque.

1. Drain the engine oil as described in Chapter Three.

2. Remove the seat, the front fender and the rear fender as well as the rear storage box and heat shield as described in Chapter Fourteen.

3. Remove the nut (A, **Figure 1**) from the engine front lower mounting through bolt. It is not necessary to remove the bolt unless the bolt has been installed from the left-hand side; if so remove the bolt as well as the nut.

4. Loosen the center mounting bolts (**Figure 2**).

5. Loosen then remove the upper and lower bolts (B, **Figure 1**) securing the frame left-hand side bridge to the frame.

6. It is not necessary to disconnect the rear brake cable (C, **Figure 1**) from the left-hand side bridge.

7. Remove the bolts loosened in Step 4.

8. Remove the left-hand side bridge away from the frame. Move the bridge along with the rear brake cable forward and rest it on the foot rest assembly.

9. Remove the long spacer (**Figure 3**) from the front through bolt.

10. Remove the exhaust system as described in Chapter Eight.

11. Remove the carburetor as described in Chapter Eight.

12. Disconnect the spark plug lead and tie it up out of the way.

13. Disconnect the battery negative lead as described under *Battery* in Chapter Three.

14. Remove the recoil starter assembly as described in this chapter.

15. Remove the air filter air box as described under *Air Filter Air Box Removal/Installation* in Chapter Eight.

16. Disconnect the reverse control cable, transmission control cable and the sub-transmission control cable as described in Chapter Seven.

17. On the right-hand side of the crankcase, slide the rubber boot (A, **Figure 4**) up on the speedometer cable. Remove the set screw (B, **Figure 4**) and withdraw the speedometer cable (C, **Figure 4**) from the speedometer gear box.

18. On LT-4WDX (280 cc) models, remove the oil cooler from the frame and engine as described in this chapter.

> *NOTE*
> *After disconnecting the following electrical wires, move the loose ends out of the way and secure them to the frame. This will help to eliminate them catching on the engine assembly during removal from the frame.*

19. Disconnect the following electrical wires from the engine:

   a. Starter motor.

   b. A.C. generator and pickup coil.

   c. Neutral switch.

   d. Reverse switch.

   e. Engine ground.

   f. Oil indicator light thermo switch (LT-4WDX [280 cc] models).

20. Remove the rear suspension arm assemblies as described under *Rear Suspension Arm Removal/Installation* in Chapter Twelve.

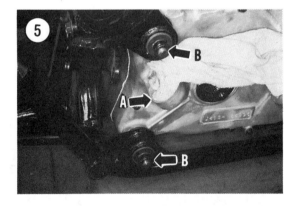

21. Remove both rear drive axle assemblies as described under *Rear Drive Axle Removal/Installation* in Chapter Twelve.

22. On 4-wheel drive models, remove the drive shaft as described under *Drive Shaft Removal/Installation* in Chapter Eleven.

> *NOTE*
> *The removal of the oil filler cap is necessary to achieve clearance to remove the entire engine assembly from the frame. This is a very small part but it is necessary for engine removal in most cases.*

23. If the cylinder head assembly is still installed, remove the oil filler cap and insert a clean shop cloth in to the opening (A, **Figure 5**).

> *NOTE*
> *The LT-F4WDX (280 cc) models are equipped with a washer under the engine mounting through-bolt heads and nuts.*

24. Remove the nuts (B, **Figure 5**) from the rear through mounting bolts.

25. Apply duct tape or place shop rags on the frame lower rails as the engine will rest on the frame rails after the mounting bolts are removed.

26. Withdraw the rear through-bolts from the frame and engine and let the engine rest on the frame.

27. Withdraw the front lower through-bolt (**Figure 6**) from the frame and engine. Don't lose the short spacer on the right-hand side between the engine and frame. The nut (A, **Figure 1**) was removed from this bolt in Step 3.

28. Install both the short spacer, the long spacer (**Figure 3**) and nut onto the front lower bolt to avoid misplacing them.

> *CAUTION*
> *The following step requires the aid of a helper to remove the engine assembly from the frame safely. Due to the overall length of the engine, as well as the weight, it is suggested that at least one helper, preferably 2 assist you in the removal of the engine.*

29. Pull the engine slightly forward, then out of the left-hand side of the frame. Take it to a workbench for further disassembly.

30. Install by reversing these removal steps while noting the following.

> *NOTE*
> *On LT-F4WDX (280 cc) models, be sure to install a washer under the engine mounting through-bolt heads and the nuts.*

a. Install *new self-locking nuts* on the engine mounting through-bolts.

b. Tighten the mounting bolt nuts to the torque specification in **Table 2**.

c. Make sure all electrical connectors are free of corrosion and are tight.

d. Fill the engine with the recommended type and quantity of oil; refer to Chapter Three.

e. Start the engine and check for leaks.

RIGHT-HAND CRANKCASE COVER

Removal

1. Remove the seat and the rear fender as described under *Rear Fender Removal/Installation* in Chapter Fourteen.

2. Remove the right-hand rear wheel as described under *Rear Wheel Removal/Installation* in Chapter Twelve.

3. Remove the right-hand shock absorber as described under *Shock Absorber Removal/Installation* in Chapter Twelve.

4. Let the right-hand rear suspension arm pivot down until it stops.

5. Remove the cotter pin, washer, pivot pin and washer, then disconnect the rear brake cable from the rear brake pedal (A, **Figure 7**).

6. Loosen the locknut, disconnect the rear brake cable from the bracket (B, **Figure 7**).

7. Remove the tie wrap (A, **Figure 8**) move the brake cable (B, **Figure 8**) and hose (C, **Figure 8**) out of the way.

> *NOTE*
> *The following steps are shown with the engine removed from the frame and with the top end of the engine removed. It is not necessary to remove the engine nor any of these components for this procedure.*

8. To remove the oil filter, perform the following:

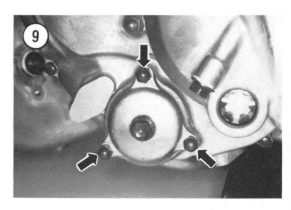

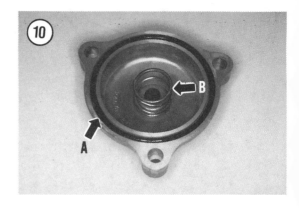

a. Remove the nuts (**Figure 9**) securing the filter cover on the right-hand crankcase cover and remove the filter cover and spring.

b. Remove the filter, place it in a reclosable plastic bag, then discard it properly. Always install a new filter whenever the crankcase cover is removed. The filter is inexpensive and installing a new one helps ensure a long service life from the engine.

c. Remove the filter cover O-ring seal (A, **Figure 10**) from the filter cover. A new O-ring seal must be installed every time the filter is replaced.

9. On LT-F4WDX (280 cc) models, disconnect the oil cooler line from the cover as described in this chapter.

10. Note the location of the wiring and cable guide (**Figure 11**) on the right-hand crankcase cover.

NOTE
*Note the location of the metal washers (A, **Figure 12**) and gasket washers (B, **Figure 12**) under the right-hand crankcase bolts. These washers must be reinstalled in the same location to avoid an oil leak.*

11. Using a crisscross pattern, loosen then remove the bolts (**Figure 12**) securing the right-hand crankcase cover.

12. Carefully tap around the perimeter of the cover with a soft-faced mallet to loosen it from the crankcase mating surface.

NOTE
Some small parts of the clutch lifting mechanism may fall out when the right-hand crankcase cover is removed. If this happens, installation of these parts is covered in the installation procedure. Place these loose parts in a reclosable plastic bag to avoid misplacing them.

CAUTION
*There is one **long, thin threaded stud** attached to the crankcase. The oil filter cover lower rear nut attaches to this stud. Do not bend this stud while removing the right-hand crankcase cover.*

13. Carefully pull the right-hand crankcase cover and gasket straight out away from the crankcase and the one long threaded stud attached to the crankcase. Don't lose the location dowels.

Inspection

1. Clean the right-hand crankcase cover in solvent and thoroughly dry with compressed air.

2. Clean off all old gasket residue from the mating surface of the right-hand crankcase cover and the right-hand crankcase. All gasket residue must be removed to prevent an oil leak.

3. Thoroughly clean out the filter receptacle (A, **Figure 13**) in the crankcase cover with a shop cloth

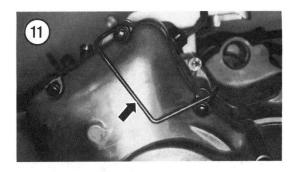

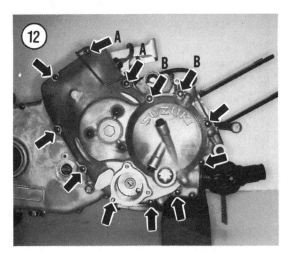

and solvent and if necessary scrape out any oil sludge with a broad tipped dull screwdriver.

4. Make sure the oil control openings (**Figure 14**) and oil control path (**Figure 15**) are open and clear. If necessary, clean out with solvent and compressed air.

5. If the oil control openings and control path were clogged in Step 4, inspect the mating oil control openings and control paths (**Figure 16**) in the right-hand crankcase half. If necessary, clean out these areas also.

6. Inspect the bearing (**Figure 17**) where the end of the crankshaft rides. The bearing must rotate smoothly with no signs of pitting, galling or play when rotated. Replace the bearing if necessary.

7. Remove the plugs in the end of the oil galleys. Refer to B, **Figure 13** and **Figure 18**. Clean out the galleys with solvent and blow out with compressed air. Install the plugs (and gasket, if so equipped) and tighten securely.

Installation

1. If removed, install the clutch lifting components in the right-hand crankcase cover as described under *Clutch Lifting Mechanism Installation* in Chapter Six.

2. If removed, install the locating dowels (A, **Figure 19**), then install a new gasket (B, **Figure 19**) onto the crankcase cover.

3. Move the crankcase cover into position. Align the hole (A, **Figure 20**) with the long threaded stud (B, **Figure 20**) attached to the crankcase.

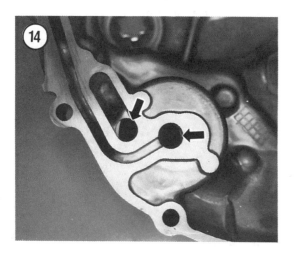

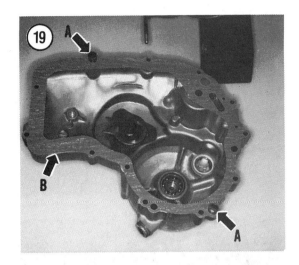

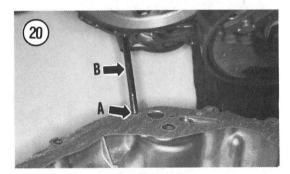

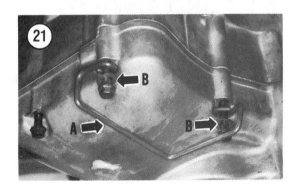

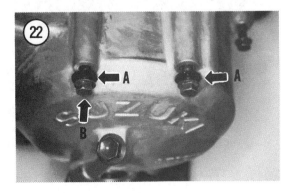

4. Push the right-hand crankcase cover straight onto the crankcase until it stops.

> *NOTE*
> *Prior to tightening the bolts, install all bolts and check that the bolt heads are all the same distance from the bolt boss on the crankcase cover. If any bolts are higher or lower than the others, switch the bolts around until all are of the same distance.*

5. Hold the cover in place and install the bolts. Install the wiring and cable guide (A, **Figure 21**), metal washers (B, **Figure 21**) and bolts.

> *CAUTION*
> *Be sure install the gasket washers (A, **Figure 22**) on these 2 top bolts prior to installation. If the gasket washers are not installed, it will result in an oil leak.*

6. When installing the long bolt (B, **Figure 22**) through the crankcase cover in this location, hold the bolt straight out while inserting it. The threaded hole in the crankcase for this bolt is set quite away back from the mating surface of the cover. If the bolt is not inserted straight into the cover and crankcase the bolt will miss the threaded hole, leading to the assumption that the bolt is too short.

7. Using a crisscross pattern, tighten the bolts securely in 2-3 stages.

8. On LT-F4WDX (280 cc) models, connect the oil cooler lines onto the cover as described in this chapter.

9. To install the oil filter, perform the following:
   a. Make sure the small O-ring seal (**Figure 23**) is in place in the crankcase cover.

b. Position the *new* filter with the open end (**Figure 24**) going in first, toward the engine.

c. Install a new filter (**Figure 25**) into the crankcase cover.

d. Make sure the O-ring seal (A, **Figure 10**) is in place in the filter cover.

e. If removed, install the spring (B, **Figure 10**) on the filter cover.

f. Apply a light coat of gasket sealer to the threaded studs on the crankcase cover.

g. Install the cover and nuts (**Figure 9**). Tighten the nuts securely.

LEFT-HAND CRANKCASE COVER

Removal

1. Remove the engine from the frame as described in this chapter.

2. Shift the transmission into gear.

3. Remove the bolt (A, **Figure 26**), then remove the sub-transmission gearshift lever (B, **Figure 26**) from the end of the gearshift shaft.

4. Remove the nut (**Figure 27**) and lockwasher (**Figure 28**) securing the recoil starter cup.

5. Remove the recoil starter cup (**Figure 29**) from the end of the crankshaft.

6. Remove the bolts (**Figure 30**) securing the exhaust system hanger plate (A, **Figure 31**) and remove the hanger plate.

> *NOTE*
> *The following steps are shown with the top end of the engine removed. It is not necessary to remove any of these components for this procedure.*

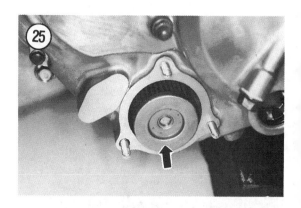
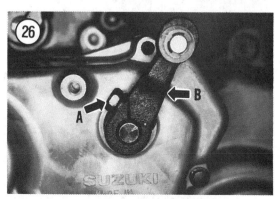

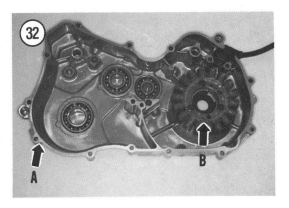

7. Using a crisscross pattern, loosen, then remove the bolts securing the left-hand crankcase cover (B, **Figure 31**).

8. Carefully tap around the perimeter of the cover with a soft-faced mallet to loosen it from the crankcase.

9. Carefully pull the left-hand crankcase cover and gasket straight out away from the crankcase. Don't lose the location dowels.

Inspection

1. Clean the left-hand crankcase cover in solvent and thoroughly dry with compressed air.

2. Clean off all old gasket residue from the mating surface of the left-hand crankcase cover (A, **Figure 32**) and the left-hand crankcase. All gasket residue must be removed to prevent an oil leak.

3. Inspect the bearings for the sub-transmission shafts and shift linkage. Refer to **Figure 33** and **Figure 34**. The bearings must rotate smoothly with no signs of pitting, galling or play when rotated. Replace the bearing(s) if necessary.

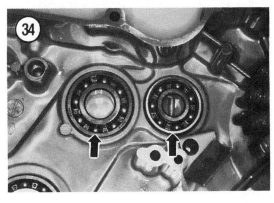

4. Inspect the oil seal for the sub-transmission shift shaft (**Figure 35**) and the crankshaft (**Figure 36**). Check for hardness, deterioration and wear. Replace if necessary.

5. Make sure the AC generator stator assembly (B, **Figure 32**) mounting bolts and the small oil baffle plate bolt (**Figure 37**) are tight. If necessary, tighten the bolts securely.

6. Apply a light coat of silicone sealant to the top surface of the stator assembly electrical harness rubber grommet and to the crankcase sealing surface on each side of the grommet (**Figure 38**). This is necessary to prevent an oil leak.

Installation

1. Apply a *small* amount of silicone sealant to several locations on the backside of the new gasket to hold it in place.

2. Install a new gasket (**Figure 39**) onto the crankcase cover.

3. If removed, install the locating dowels onto the crankcase. Refer to **Figure 40** and **Figure 41**.

4. Move the crankcase cover into position. Push the left-hand crankcase cover straight onto the crankcase until it stops.

NOTE
*Prior to tightening the bolts, install all bolts and check that the bolt heads are all the same distance from the bolt boss on the crankcase cover (**Figure 42**). If any bolts are higher or lower than the others, switch the bolts around until all are of the same height.*

5. Hold the cover in place and install the bolts.

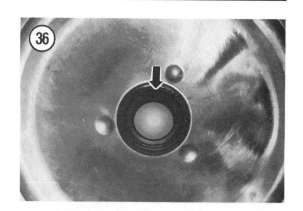

6. Install the exhaust system hanger plate (A, **Figure 43**) and bolts (B, **Figure 43**).

7. Using a crisscross pattern, tighten the bolts securely in 2-3 stages.

8. Install the recoil starter cup (**Figure 29**) onto the end of the crankshaft.

9. Make sure the transmission is still in gear. This will keep the crankshaft from rotating while tightening the recoil starter mounting nut.

10. Install the lockwasher (**Figure 28**) and the nut (**Figure 27**) securing the recoil starter cup.

11. Tighten the nut to the torque specification listed in **Table 2**.

12. Align the index mark on the sub-transmission gearshift lever with the line on the end of the gearshift shaft (A, **Figure 44**) and install the gearshift lever (B, **Figure 44**) onto the gearshift shaft. Install and tighten the bolt (C, **Figure 44**) securely.

13. Install the engine in the frame as described in this chapter.

RECOIL STARTER

Removal/Installation

1. Place the ATV on level ground and set the parking brake. Block the rear wheels so the vehicle will not roll in either direction.

2. Remove the seat and rear fender as described in Chapter Fourteen.

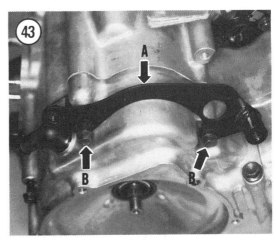

3. Remove the bolts securing the recoil starter assembly and remove the assembly and gasket (A, **Figure 45**).

4. Install by reversing these removal steps while noting the following:

  a. Be sure to install a new gasket on the assembly prior to installation.

  b. Install the gasket washer under the center rear bolt (B, **Figure 45**).

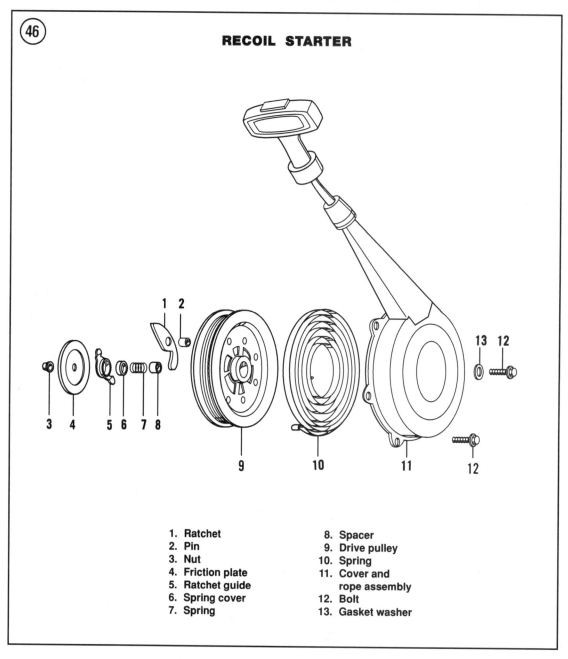

RECOIL STARTER

1. Ratchet	8. Spacer
2. Pin	9. Drive pulley
3. Nut	10. Spring
4. Friction plate	11. Cover and
5. Ratchet guide	rope assembly
6. Spring cover	12. Bolt
7. Spring	13. Gasket washer

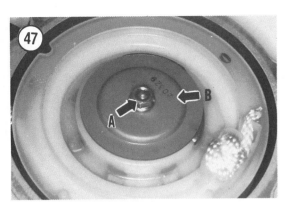

Disassembly and Starter Rope Removal

Refer to **Figure 46** for this procedure.

> *WARNING*
> *The return spring is under pressure and may jump out during the disassembly procedure. It is a very strong spring and may cut fingers or cause eye damage if not handled properly. Wear safety glasses and gloves when disassembling and assembling.*

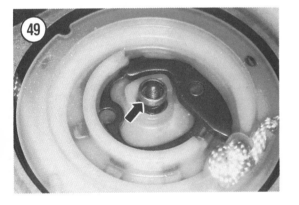

1. Remove and discard the gasket.
2. Remove the nut (A, **Figure 47**) and friction plate (B, **Figure 47**).
3. Remove the ratchet guide (**Figure 48**).
4. Remove the spring cover (**Figure 49**), spring (**Figure 50**) and spacer (**Figure 51**) from the center bolt.
5. Remove the ratchet (**Figure 52**) and the pin (**Figure 53**).

> *WARNING*
> *The recoil spring may jump out at this time—protect yourself accordingly.*

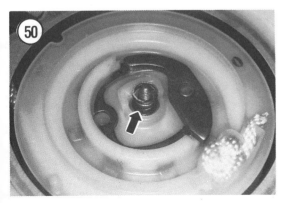

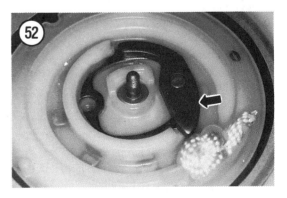

6. Slowly remove the drive pulley (A, **Figure 54**) and rope assembly out of the cover and disengage it from the recoil spring.

7. Remove the cover (A, **Figure 55**) from the starter handle and untie the knot in the starter rope or cut the rope.

8. Remove the starter handle (B, **Figure 55**) from the rope.

9. Untie and remove the starter rope (B, **Figure 54**) from the drive pulley.

10. If necessary, remove the recoil spring from the cover.

> *NOTE*
> *It is a good idea to replace the starter rope every time the recoil starter is disassembled.*

11. Clean all parts in solvent and thoroughly dry.

12. Inspect all moving parts (**Figure 56**) for wear or damage and replace as necessary.

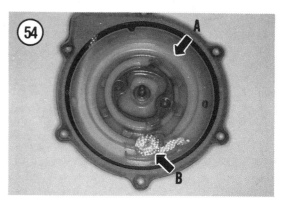

**Assembly and
Starter Rope Installation**

1. If removed, install the recoil spring into the cover as follows:

  a. Apply multipurpose grease to the housing shaft (A, **Figure 57**).

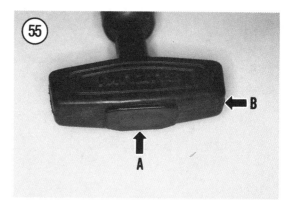

> *WARNING*
> *This step requires an assistant as it is very dangerous, and almost impossible, to try to install the spring by yourself. Both your assistant and yourself must wear eye and hand protection as the recoil spring could jump out at any time—**protect yourself accordingly**.*

  b. Have the assistant hold onto the cover so it will not rotate.

  c. Hook the end of the spring onto the outer hook (B, **Figure 57**) in the cover.

  d. Hold the end of the spring in place and start feeding the spring into the housing in a clockwise direction.

  e. As you feed the spring into the housing, have the assistant hold the spring down after each loop is installed. The spring must be continually held in place or it will jump out.

  f. Continue to feed the spring in and hold it down until the entire spring is installed.

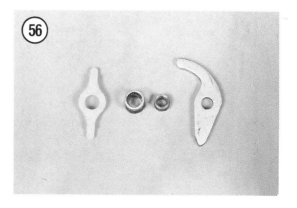

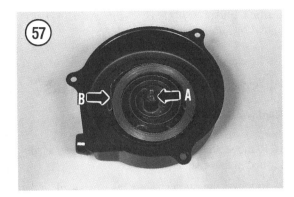

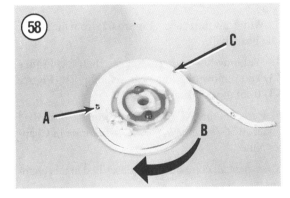

g. After the spring is completely installed, do not move the cover and spring assembly as the spring is under pressure and could jump out at any time. *Protect yourself and your assistant accordingly.*

2. Install a new starter rope in the drive pulley (A, **Figure 58**). Tie a special knot at the end (**Figure 59**). Apply heat to the knot (a match is sufficient) and *slightly* melt the nylon rope. This will hold the knot securely.

3. Coil the rope onto the drive pulley in a *clockwise* direction (B, **Figure 58**).

4. Position the end of the rope in the drive pulley so the starter grip end in located within the notch (C, **Figure 58**) in the drive pulley.

5

5. Feed the rope out through the hole in the cover and attach a pair of vise-grip pliers to the loose end of the rope so it will not slip back through the hole in the case.

6. Install the drive pulley into the cover and spring assembly while rotating it in a *clockwise* direction. Make sure the rope is positioned up through the notch in the drive pulley. The tab (A, **Figure 60**) on the bottom of the drive pulley must engage with the hook (B, **Figure 60**) in the end of the recoil spring.

7. Apply a light coat of multipurpose grease to the pin and the ratchet. Install the pin (**Figure 53**) and the ratchet (**Figure 52**).

8. Onto the center bolt, install the spacer (**Figure 51**) and the spring cover (**Figure 49**).

9. Install the ratchet guide (**Figure 48**).

10. Install the friction plate (B, **Figure 47**) and nut (A, **Figure 47**). Tighten the nut securely.

11. After the recoil starter is assembled, the spring tension must be set as follows:

a. Rotate the drive pulley (A, **Figure 61**) until the notch (B) is aligned with the area in the cover where the rope exits.

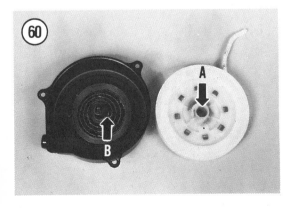

b. Pull the handle end of the rope up out of the drive pulley and into the notch (B, **Figure 61**) in the drive pulley.

c. Within the cover, hold the rope up and make sure it stays in the notch in the drive pulley. The rope must stay in the notch during the next step or all rope slack (out past the cover) will be taken up.

d. Rotate the drive pulley *clockwise* (C, **Figure 61**) 3 to 4 complete revolutions to wind-up the spring.

e. Move the rope out of the notch in the drive pulley and down into the drive pulley.

f. Hold the drive pulley in this position. Do not let go or the drive pulley will rotate counterclockwise and unwind.

g. With the drive pulley and spring in this position, pull the rope out an additional 1/2 in. (12.7 mm). Release, then reinstall the vise-grip pliers onto the rope where it exits the cover. The rope must be held in this position until the end of the rope is knotted and installed in the starter handle.

12. Install the rope through the starter handle (B, **Figure 55**) and tie the end using the same special knot as shown in **Figure 59**). Apply heat to the knot (a match is usually sufficient) and *slightly* melt the nylon rope. This will hold the knot securely. Install the cover (A, **Figure 55**) in the starter handle. Remove the vise-grip pliers from the rope.

13. After assembly is complete, check the operation of the recoil starter by pulling on the starter handle. Make sure the drive pulley rotates freely and returns completely. Also make sure the ratchet moves out and in correctly. If either does not operate correctly, disassemble and correct the problem.

14. Inspect the slots in the starter cup. If they are damaged, the starter cup should be replaced as de-scribed under *Left-hand Crankcase Cover Removal/Installation* in this chapter.

STARTER CLUTCH AND GEARS

Removal/Installation

1. Remove the left-hand crankcase cover as described in this chapter.

2. Remove the starter motor as described under *Starter Motor Removal/Installation* in Chapter Nine.

3. Withdraw the spacer (**Figure 62**) from the starter idle gear shaft.

4. Withdraw the starter idle gear shaft (A, **Figure 63**) and remove the idle gear assembly (B, **Figure 63**) from the crankcase.

5. Remove the AC generator rotor as described under *AC Generator Removal/Installation* in Chapter Nine.

6. Inspect all components as described in this chapter.

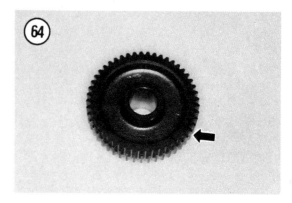

7. Install by reversing these removal steps. Position the starter idle gear with the larger diameter gear (Figure 64) going on last and install it onto the shaft.

Disassembly/Inspection/Assembly

Refer to **Figure 65** for this procedure.

1. Set the rotor and starter driven gear on the workbench with the rotor facing down.

2. Inspect the one-way clutch as follows:
   a. Rotate the starter driven gear (A, **Figure 66**) *clockwise* (B, **Figure 66**); it should rotate.
   b. Rotate the starter driven gear (B, **Figure 66**) *counterclockwise* (C, **Figure 66**); it should not move.
   c. If the one-way clutch fails either of these tests, replace the one-way clutch.

3. Rotate the starter driven gear (A, **Figure 66**) *clockwise* (C, **Figure 66**) and pull it up at the same

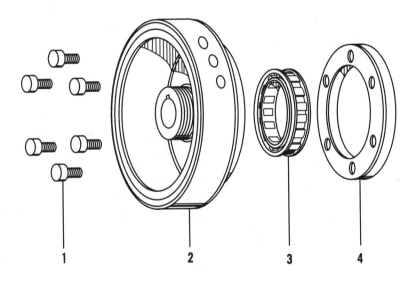

STARTER CLUTCH

1. Bolt
2. AC generator rotor
3. One-way clutch
4. Starter clutch holder

time. Remove the gear from the backside of the AC generator rotor.

4. Inspect both gears on the starter idle gear (**Figure 67**) for wear or damage. Replace if necessary.

5. Inspect the starter driven gear (A, **Figure 68**) for wear, chipped or missing teeth. Replace the gear if necessary.

6. Inspect the starter driven gear needle bearing (**Figure 69**) for wear or damage. It must rotate freely with no binding. Replace if necessary.

7. Inspect the starter driven gear outer surface (B, **Figure 68**) where it rides on the one-way clutch. If the surface is damaged, replace the gear.

8. Inspect the starter driven gear inner surface where it rides on the needle bearing. If the surface is damaged, replace the gear.

9. Inspect the rollers (**Figure 70**) of the one-way clutch for burrs, wear or damage. If necessary, remove the one-way clutch as follows:

   a. Use a 29 mm offset box wrench on the center raised shoulder (A, **Figure 71**) of the AC generator rotor. Hold the rotor stationary while loosening the Allen bolts in the next step.

CAUTION
The Phillips head screws have a locking agent applied to them during installation. Use an impact driver or air tool to loosen the screws. The screw heads will probably be damaged if removal is tried using a hand-held, regular Phillips head screwdriver.

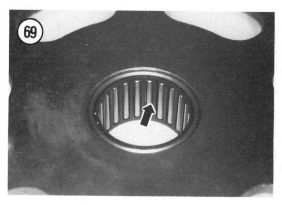

   b. Loosen, then remove the Allen bolts (B, **Figure 71**) securing the starter clutch holder and one-way clutch to the backside of the AC generator rotor. Remove the box wrench.

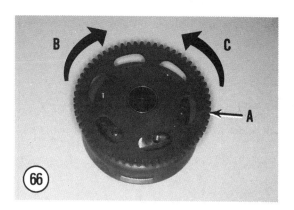

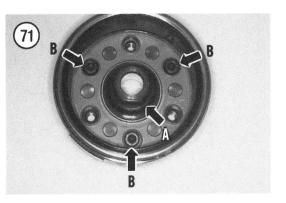

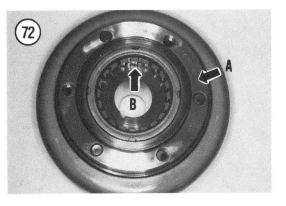

c. Remove the starter clutch holder (A, **Figure 72**) and the one-way clutch (B, **Figure 72**) from the backside of the AC generator rotor.

d. Install the one-way clutch (B, **Figure 72**) with the flange side facing the AC generator rotor. Install the starter clutch holder (A, **Figure 72**) and align the bolt holes.

e. Apply red Loctite (No. 271) to the Allen bolt threads prior to installation, then install the bolts (B, **Figure 71**). Use the same tool set up used for loosening the bolts and tighten to the torque specification listed in **Table 2**.

10. Rotate the starter driven gear (A, **Figure 66**) *clockwise* (B, **Figure 66**) and push it down at the same time. Install the gear into the backside of the AC generator rotor. Make sure the gear does not rotate *counterclockwise* (C, **Figure 66**). If the gear can rotate *counterclockwise*, the one-way clutch is installed backward and must be repositioned. Reposition the one-way clutch at this time.

OIL PUMP

The oil pump is located on the right-hand side of the engine behind the clutch assemblies.

Removal

1. Remove both clutch assemblies as described in Chapter Six.

2. Remove the E-clip (**Figure 73**) securing the oil pump driven gear and remove the driven gear (**Figure 74**).

3. Remove the drive pin (A, **Figure 75**) from the oil pump drive shaft.

CAUTION
The Phillips head screws have a locking agent applied to them during installa-

tion. Use an impact driver or air tool to loosen the screws. The screw heads will probably be damaged if removal is tried using a hand-held, regular Phillips head screwdriver.

4. Use an impact driver or air tool and loosen the Phillips head screws (B, **Figure 75**) securing the oil pump.

5. Remove the screws and the oil pump assembly.

Inspection

The oil pump cannot be disassembled for inspection or service and must be replaced as a unit. If the engine is undergoing a complete overhaul, replace the oil pump.

If abnormal oil pressure is suspected, have the oil pressure checked by a Suzuki dealer; a special low pressure gauge and adaptor are required to perform this test.

Inspect the oil pump driven gear (**Figure 76**) for wear, chipped or missing teeth. Replace the gear if necessary.

Installation

1. If a new oil pump is being installed or the existing oil pump was cleaned in solvent, the oil pump must be primed. Apply fresh engine oil into one of the openings in the backside of the oil pump until it runs out the other opening. Rotate the drive shaft several times by hand to make sure the internal rotors within the oil pump are coated with oil.

2. Install the oil pump onto the right-hand crankcase.

3. Apply blue Loctite (No. 242) to the screw threads securing the oil pump. Tighten the screws to the torque specification listed in **Table 2**.

4. Make sure the drive pin is installed and centered (**Figure 77**) in the oil pump shaft.

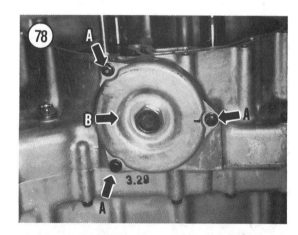

5. Align the groove in the oil pump driven gear with the pin in the oil pump shaft and install the oil pump driven gear (**Figure 74**).

6. Install the E-clip (**Figure 73**) securing the oil pump driven gear. Make sure the E-clip is secure in the shaft.

7. Install the clutch assemblies as described in Chapter Six.

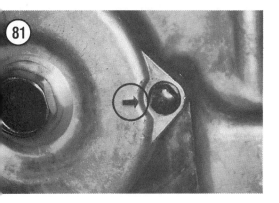

OIL STRAINER

Removal/Installation

NOTE
This procedure is shown with the engine removed and partially disassembled for clarity. The oil strainer can be removed with the engine in the frame.

1. Drain the engine oil as described under *Engine Oil and Filter Change* in Chapter Three.
2. Remove the screws (A, **Figure 78**) securing the oil strainer cap (B, **Figure 78**) and remove the cap.
3. Remove the screws (A, **Figure 79**) securing the oil strainer screen (B, **Figure 79**) and remove the screen.
4. Install the oil strainer screen and tighten the screws securely.
5. Install a new O-ring seal (**Figure 80**) into the groove in the oil strainer cap. Apply a light coat of grease to the O-ring seal.
6. Position the oil strainer cap so the arrow (**Figure 81**) is pointing toward the front of the engine and install the cap. Install the screws and tighten securely.
7. Refill the engine with the specified type and quantity of engine oil as described in Chapter Three.

Inspection

1. Clean the oil strainer cap (**Figure 82**) and strainer screen (**Figure 83**) of all sludge, dirt and foreign matter. Use solvent and thoroughly dry with compressed air.
2. Inspect the strainer screen (**Figure 84**) for deterioration or any holes. Replace the strainer if necessary.

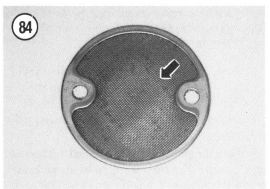

3. Remove the O-ring seal (**Figure 80**) from the groove in the oil strainer cap. Install a new O-ring seal every time the cap is removed to prevent an oil leak.

4. Clean out the oil strainer cavity (A, **Figure 85**) in the right-hand crankcase half. Make sure the oil hole (B, **Figure 85**) is clear. If necessary, clean out the oil hole with a piece of wire and re-clean with solvent. If the crankcase is separated, blow dry with compressed air. Do *not* use compressed air if the crankcase is still assembled as you will force any dirt up into the crankcase.

5. Inspect the oil strainer cap for damage that could lead to an oil leak. Replace the cap if necessary.

OIL COOLER
(LT-F4WDX [280 CC] MODELS)

Refer to **Figure 86** for this procedure.

The oil hoses are long and are secured to the frame and ignition coil bracket at several places. It is suggested that each hose be removed separately while carefully noting the path of the hose through the frame. If possible, take a Polaroid photo of the hose routing especially if the hose(s) is going to be left off for some time.

1. Remove the seat, rear fender and front fender as described in Chapter Fourteen.

2. Drain the engine oil as described in Chapter Three.

3. Place a drain pan under the front right-hand side of the engine to catch any residual engine oil as the oil cooler hoses are disconnected from the engine.

NOTE
This procedure represents removal of the entire oil cooler system including both hoses. If only the oil cooler or one of the hoses requires replacing, perform only the steps necessary for the removal of that specific component.

4. Remove the tie-wraps securing both oil hoses to the frame and other components. Reinstall the tie wraps in their existing locations on the frame. This will be a reminder of the correct location and will save time during installation.

5. Remove the oil hose fitting bolts and disconnect the oil cooler hoses from the right-hand crankcase cover and crankcase. Discard the O-ring seal from

the fitting(s) as a new seal(s) must be used during installation.

6. Drain any residual oil from the hose(s) into the drain pan. Place the loose end of the oil hose(s) in reclosable plastic bags and close the bag around the hose. This will eliminate oil from draining onto the frame during removal.

7. Remove the bolts securing the oil cooler guard to the frame and remove the guard.

8. Remove the oil hose fitting bolts and disconnect the oil hose(s) from the top of the oil cooler. Discard the O-ring seal from each fitting as new seals must be installed. Place the loose end of the oil hose(s) in reclosable plastic bags and close the bag around the hose. This will eliminate oil from draining onto the frame during removal.

9. Remove the oil hose(s) from the frame. Wipe off any oil that may have dripped from the oil hose(s) or plastic bag(s) during removal.

10. Remove the 4 bolts securing the oil cooler assembly to the frame. Don't lose the collar in the rubber grommet on the frame mounting tabs.

11. Remove the oil cooler assembly from the frame and hold it in an upright position since it is still full of oil.

12. Turn the oil cooler over and drain the remaining oil into the drain pan.

13. Install by reversing these removal steps while noting the following:

   a. Install a new O-ring seal at each oil hose fitting and apply a light coat of clean engine oil to each one prior to installation.

   b. On oil hose No. 2, align the white paint mark on the hose with the clamp on the ignition coil bracket. Tighten the clamp securely.

   c. On the oil hose No. 1 front lower fitting, apply liquid sealant to the bolt threads prior to instal-

lation on the crankcase. This is necessary to prevent an oil leak.

d. After the oil hose(s) is installed, make sure there are no sharp bends or kinks that would restrict the oil flow.

e. Tighten the oil hose fitting bolts to the torque specification listed in **Table 2**.

f. Refill the engine with oil as described in Chapter Three.

Inspection

1. Remove the bolt securing the screen to the front surface of the oil cooler and remove it. Clean all road dirt and debris from the screen.

2. Use duct tape, or equivalent, and close off the oil hose fitting openings on top of the oil cooler to prevent the entry of water and foreign matter while cleaning the exterior of the oil cooler.

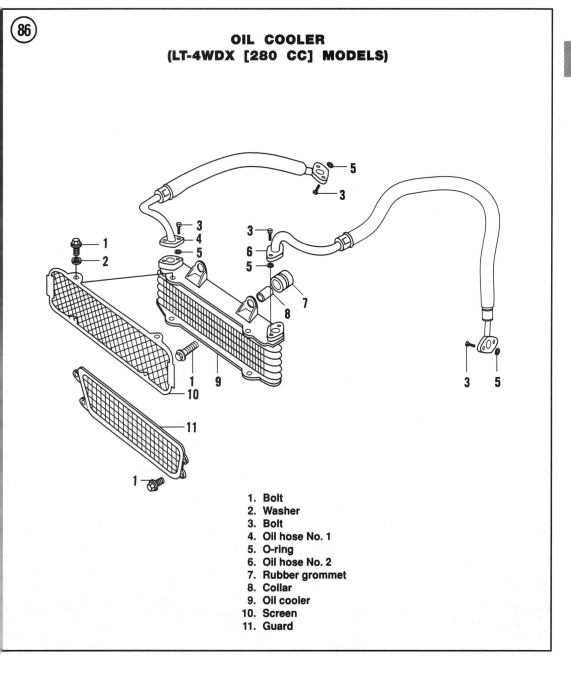

(86)

5

OIL COOLER
(LT-4WDX [280 CC] MODELS)

1. Bolt
2. Washer
3. Bolt
4. Oil hose No. 1
5. O-ring
6. Oil hose No. 2
7. Rubber grommet
8. Collar
9. Oil cooler
10. Screen
11. Guard

3. If compressed air is available, use short spurts of air directed to the *backside* of the oil cooler and blow out dirt, bugs and debris.

4. Flush off the exterior of the oil cooler with a garden hose on low pressure. Spray both the front and the back to remove all road dirt, bugs and debris. Carefully use a whisk broom or stiff paint brush to remove any stubborn dirt.

> *CAUTION*
> *Do not press too hard or the cooling fins and tubes may be damaged causing a leak. Do not use a wire brush.*

5. Carefully straighten out any bent cooling fins with a broad tipped screwdriver or putty knife.

6. Check the entire cooler for cracks or leakage. Check the oil hose fittings mounting surfaces for damage.

7. Inspect the upper and lower mounting tabs. Check for cracks or fractures and repair if necessary. If the condition of the oil cooler is doubtful, replace it as it cannot be serviced.

8. To prevent oxidation to the oil cooler, touch up any area where the black paint is worn off. Use a good-quality spray paint and apply several *light*

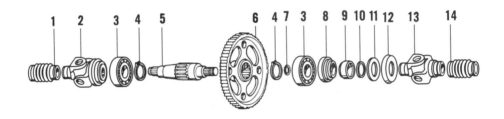

REAR FINAL DRIVEN GEAR

1. Rubber boot
2. Universal joint
3. Bearing
4. Circlip
5. Rear final drive shaft
6. Rear final driven gear
7. C-ring
8. Oil seal
9. Spacer
10. O-ring
11. Washer
12. Collar
13. Universal joint
14. Rubber boot

coats of paint. Do not apply heavy coats as this will cut down on the cooling efficiency of the oil cooler.

NOTE
Do not hesitate to replace an oil hose(s). If the hose condition is doubtful in any way, replace it. You don't want to lose oil pressure and the resulting loss of engine oil while on a ride or on the job site.

9. Inspect the entire length of both oil hoses. Check for cuts, cracks, abrasions or deterioration. Check

the hose fitting at each end for damage. Replace the oil hose(s) if damaged, as they cannot be serviced.

SUB-TRANSMISSION OUTPUT SHAFT AND REAR FINAL DRIVEN GEAR

Removal/Installation

Refer to **Figure 87** for this procedure.

NOTE
This procedure is shown on a 4-wheel drive model. The only difference is the addition of the bevel gear on the end of the sub-transmission output shaft.

1. Remove the engine from the frame and disassemble the crankcase as described in this chapter.
2. On 4-wheel drive models, remove the secondary driven output shaft (**Figure 88**) as described in this chapter.
3. Pull the sub-transmission output shaft assembly (A, **Figure 89**) straight up and out of the left-hand crankcase half.
4. Pull the rear final drive shaft assembly (**Figure 90**) straight up and out of the left-hand crankcase half.
5. Inspect both shaft assemblies as described in this chapter.
6. Apply clean engine oil to both shaft bearings (A, **Figure 91**) in the left-hand crankcase half.
7. Position the rear final drive shaft assembly with the short end of the shaft (B, **Figure 91**) going in first and install the shaft assembly. Push it down into the bearing until it seats completely (**Figure 92**).
8. After the shaft is installed, rotate it slowly to make sure it rotates smoothly.
9. Position the sub-transmission output shaft assembly with the long splined end of the shaft (**Figure 93**) going in first and install the shaft assembly.

Push it down, mesh it with the final drive shaft gear (B, **Figure 89**) and into the bearing until it seats completely (A, **Figure 89**).

10. After the shaft is installed, rotate the sub-transmission output shaft assembly and the rear final drive shaft assembly slowly to make sure they both rotate smoothly.

11. Assemble the crankcase and install the engine into the frame as described in this chapter.

Sub-transmission Output Shaft Inspection

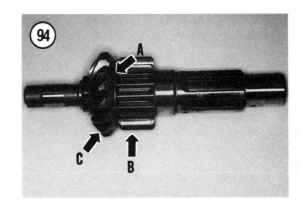

> *NOTE*
> *On 4-wheel drive models, do not disassemble the sub-transmission output shaft assembly. A shim (A, **Figure 94**) is located between the shaft straight-cut gear (B, **Figure 94**) and the bevel gear (C, **Figure 94**). If this portion of the shaft is disassembled, the shim will have to be replaced and the gear backlash inspected. There are 10 different shims available with a 0.05 mm thickness variation between each one. If the sub-transmission output shaft assembly requires service, refer this procedure to a Suzuki dealer service department.*

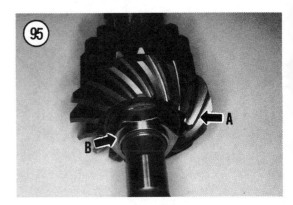

1. Inspect the sub-transmission output shaft assembly for external damage.
2. On 4-wheel drive models, perform the following:
   a. Inspect the bevel gear (A, **Figure 95**) for burrs, pitting or roughness. Minor roughness can be cleaned up with an oilstone but there's little point in attempting to remove deep scars. If any of the teeth are chipped or missing, replace the gear. If damage is severe, inspect the mating bevel gear on the secondary driven output shaft as it may also require replacement.

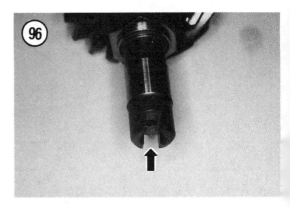

   b. Make sure the nut (B, **Figure 95**) securing the bevel gear is tight. Tighten if necessary to the torque specification listed in **Table 2**.
3. Inspect the speedometer gear drive slot (**Figure 96**) in the end of the shaft for wear or damage.
4. Inspect the straight-cut gear (B, **Figure 94**) for burrs pitting or roughness. Minor roughness can be cleaned up with an oilstone but there's little point in attempting to remove deep scars. If any of the teeth are chipped or missing, replace the gear. If damage is severe, inspect the mating rear final driven gear as it may also require replacement.

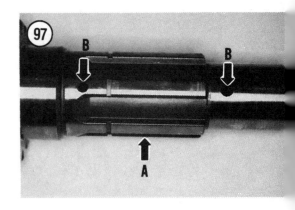

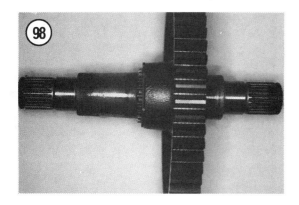

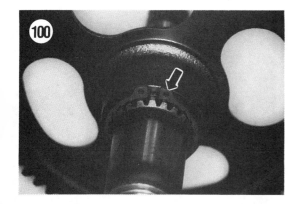

5. Check the outer splines (A, **Figure 97**) on the shaft for excessive wear or burrs. Replace if necessary.

6. Make sure the oil holes (B, **Figure 97**) are clear. Clean out with a piece of wire and solvent, then blow out with compressed air.

Rear Final Driven Shaft Assembly Inspection

1. Inspect the rear final driven shaft assembly (**Figure 98**) for external damage.

2. Inspect the gear (**Figure 99**) for burrs, pitting or roughness. Minor roughness can be cleaned up with an oilstone but there's little point in attempting to remove deep scars. If one of the teeth are chipped or missing, replace the gear. If damage is severe, inspect the mating straight-cut gear on the secondary driven output shaft as it may also require replacement.

3. Make sure each circlip securing the rear final driven gear to the shaft are in place and are correctly seated in their grooves. Refer to **Figure 100** and **Figure 101**. If necessary, replace the circlip(s).

4. Make sure the stopper ring (**Figure 102**) is in place on each end of the rear final driven shaft assembly. The ring must be secure. If loose, replace the stopper ring(s).

SECONDARY DRIVEN OUTPUT SHAFT (4-WHEEL DRIVE MODELS)

Removal/Installation

1. Remove the engine from the frame and separate the crankcase as described in this chapter.

2. Carefully pull the secondary driven output shaft (**Figure 88**) straight up and out of the left-hand crankcase half.

3. Remove the C-ring (**Figure 103**) from the left-hand crankcase half.

4. Inspect the assembly as described in this chapter.

5. If the secondary driven output shaft was cleaned in solvent during the inspection procedure, apply fresh engine oil to both bearings and spin the bearings *slowly* to make sure the rollers, balls and races are covered with oil.

6. Install the C-ring (**Figure 103**) into the left-hand crankcase half. Both ends of the C-ring must be flush with the top surface of the crankcase—do not allow the ends to stick up as they may interfere with the installation of the right-hand crankcase half.

7. Make sure the front ball bearing set-ring groove (**Figure 104**) is clean. This is necessary as the set-ring must fit all the way down into the groove.

8. Install the secondary driven output shaft (**Figure 88**) straight down into the left-hand crankcase half. Check for the following:

   a. Properly mesh both bevel gears (A, **Figure 105**).

   b. Make sure the groove in the rear roller bearing is positioned correctly in the crankcase C-ring (B, **Figure 105**).

   c. Hold down the center (A, **Figure 106**) of the secondary driven output shaft to keep both bearings in place in the crankcase. Slowly rotate the universal joint end of the shaft (B, **Figure 106**) with the other hand. Make sure it rotates freely and that the bevel gear is properly rotating the sub-transmission shaft.

   d. Rotate the front ball bearing until the locating pin is located within the receptacle (**Figure 107**) in the left-hand crankcase half.

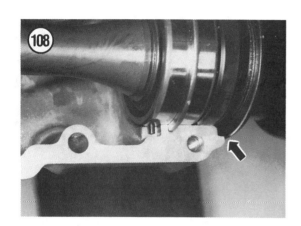

e. Make sure the front oil seal (**Figure 108**) is positioned correctly against the receptacle in the left-hand crankcase half.

9. Assemble the crankcase and install the engine into the frame as described in this chapter.

Inspection

Refer to **Figure 109** for this procedure.

NOTE
Do not disassemble the universal joint end of the secondary driven output

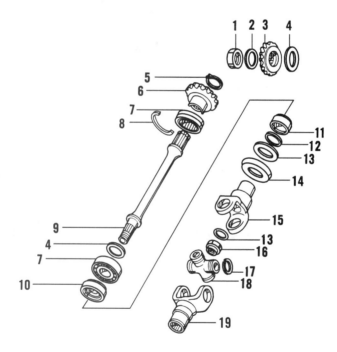

SECONDARY DRIVEN OUTPUT SHAFT

1. Nut	10. Oil seal
2. Washer	11. Spacer
3. Secondary drive bevel gear	12. O-ring
4. Shim	13. Washer
5. Circlip	14. Collar
6. Output shaft bevel gear	15. Secondary driven output shaft yoke
7. Bearing	16. Nut
8. C-ring	17. C-ring
9. Secondary driven output shaft	18. U-joint star
	19. Propeller shaft yoke

shaft. A shim is located between the shaft shoulder and the front ball bearing. If this portion of the shaft is disassembled, the shim will have to be replaced and the gear backlash inspected. There are 10 different shims available with a 0.05 mm thickness variation between each one. If the universal joint requires service, refer this procedure to a Suzuki service department. The rear roller bearing can be replaced without upsetting the gear backlash.

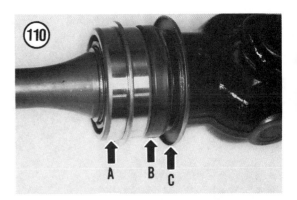

1. Inspect the secondary driven output shaft assembly for external damage.

2. Check the front ball bearing (A, **Figure 110**) for roughness and play by rotating it slowly by hand. If any roughness or play can be felt in the bearing, it must be replaced.

3. Inspect the oil seal (B, **Figure 110**) for hardness or deterioration. Replace the seal if necessary.

4. Inspect the collar (C, **Figure 110**) for wear or damage. This collar protects the oil seal and if distorted in any way it may damage the oil seal leading to an engine oil leak. Replace the collar if necessary.

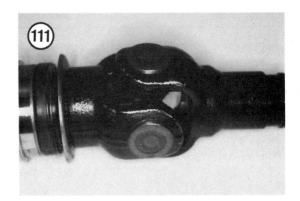

5. Inspect the universal joint (**Figure 111**) as follows:

   a. Check the exterior for cracks or damage.

   b. Move each universal joint in a circular motion and check for excessive wear or play.

   c. Inspect the inner splines (**Figure 112**) for wear or damage. If damage is severe, inspect the outer splines (**Figure 113**) on the propeller shaft as it may also be damaged and require replacement.

   d. The universal joint can be disassembled and serviced or replaced. Refer either of these procedures to a Suzuki service department.

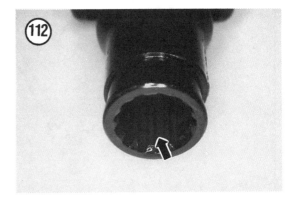

6. Slide the rear roller bearing (**Figure 114**) off the shoulder of the bevel gear. Inspect the rollers (**Figure 115**) for evidence of wear, pitting or excessive heat (bluish tint). Replace the bearing as described in this chapter.

7. Inspect the bevel gear (A, **Figure 116**) for burrs pitting or roughness. Minor roughness can be cleaned up with an oilstone but there's little point in attempting to remove deep scars. If any of the teeth are chipped or missing, replace the gear. If damage is severe, inspect the mating bevel gear on the subtransmission shaft as it may also require replacement.

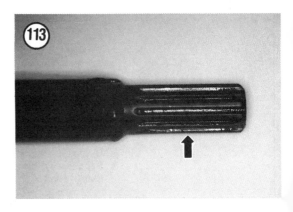

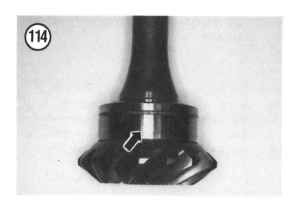

CAUTION
If the locating pin works loose and falls out when the engine is operating it can become entangled in lower end engine components. It may also allow the bearing outer race to rotate along with the bearing. For the bearing to operate correctly, the outer race must remain stationary.

8. Make sure the locating pin (**Figure 117**) is secured in place in the ball bearing. If necessary, tighten the pin in the bearing hole.

Rear Roller Bearing and Bevel Gear Replacement

1. Remove the circlip (B, **Figure 116**) from the shaft. Discard the circlip as a new one must be installed.
2. Slide the bevel gear (A, **Figure 118**) and the roller bearing (B, **Figure 118**) off the shaft splines. Slide the roller bearing off the bevel gear shoulder.
3. Apply clean engine oil to the rollers within the bearing.
4. Position the bearing with the C-ring groove side (**Figure 119**) going on first and install the bearing.

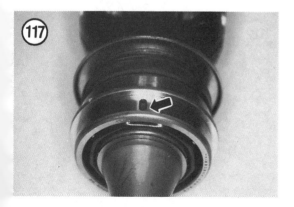

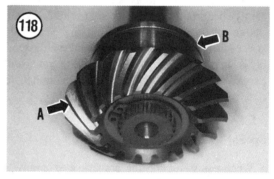

Rotate the bearing on the shaft and check for smooth operation.

5. Install the bevel gear (A, **Figure 116**) onto the shaft splines and push it on until it bottoms out on the bearing.

6. Install a new circlip (B, **Figure 116**) and make sure it is correctly seated in the shaft groove.

CRANKCASE AND CRANKSHAFT

Disassembly of the crankcase—splitting the cases—and removal of the crankshaft assembly require that the engine be removed from the frame. However, many of the attached assemblies should be removed with the engine in the frame.

The crankcase is made in 2 halves of precision die cast aluminum alloy and is of the "thin-walled" type. To avoid damage, do not hammer or pry on any of the interior or exterior projected walls. These areas are easily damaged. The cases are split vertically down the centerline of the connecting rod. The cases are assembled *without* a gasket; only gasket sealer is used while dowel pins align the crankcase halves when they are bolted together. The crankcase halves are sold as a matched set only; if one crankcase half is damaged, both halves must be replaced.

The crankshaft assembly is made up of 2 full-circle flywheels pressed together on a solid crankpin. The connecting rod big end bearing on the crankpin is a needle bearing assembly. The crankshaft assembly is supported in 2 ball bearings in the crankcase. Service to the crankshaft assembly is limited to removal and replacement.

Special Tools

When disassembling the crankcase assembly, a few special tools are required. These tools allow easy disassembly and assembly of the engine crankcase without using a hammer or prying. Remember, the crankcase halves can be easily damaged by improper disassembly and assembly techniques. If you are not equipped to service the crankcase halves, refer this service to a Suzuki dealer service department.

    a. When handling the crankcase assembly, two 4 × 4 wooden blocks or a wooden fixture of 2 × 4 in. wood as shown in **Figure 120** will assist in engine disassembly and assembly and will help

to prevent damage to the crankshaft and transmission shafts.

NOTE
The following special tools are not always necessary due to the condition of the crankcase halves, the crankshaft bearings and the crankshaft. In some cases the crankcase can be separated and the crankshaft removed and installed without the use of these special tools. This depends on the condition of

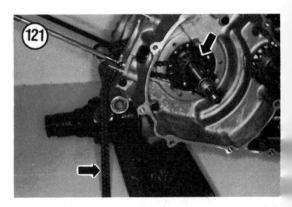

the engine. If you are having trouble removing or installing the crankshaft, use the special tools or take the crankcase to a dealer and have them perform this operation for you.

b. Suzuki crankcase separating tool (part No. 09920-13120), or equivalent. This tool threads into the right-hand crankcase and is used to separate the crankcase halves and to press the crankshaft out of the left-hand crankcase. The tool is very simple in design and a similar type

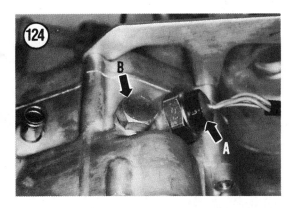

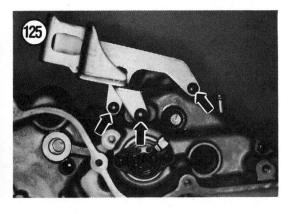

of tool, such as a steering wheel puller may be substituted.

c. Suzuki crankshaft installing tool set (part No. 09910-32812). This tool set is used to press the crankshaft back into the left-hand crankcase half.

Crankcase Disassembly

The procedure which follows is presented as a complete, step-by-step, major lower end rebuild that should be followed if an engine is to be completely reconditioned. However, if you're replacing a part that you know is defective, the disassembly should be carried out only until the failed part is accessible; there is no need to disassemble the engine beyond that point so long as you know the remaining components are in good condition and that they were not affected by the failed part.

Remember that the right- and left-hand side of the engine relates to the engine as it sits in the ATV's frame, not as it sits on your workbench.

1. Remove all exterior engine assemblies as described in this chapter and other related chapters.

2. Remove the engine as described in this chapter.

3. Remove the camshaft drive chain (**Figure 121**) from the left-hand end of the crankshaft.

4. Slide the oil pump drive gear (**Figure 122**) off the right-hand end of the crankshaft.

5. Remove the bolts (A, **Figure 123**) securing the speedometer drive gear housing and remove the housing (B, **Figure 123**) and gasket.

6. Unscrew and remove the reverse switch (A, **Figure 124**) and the reverse cam detent (B, **Figure 124**).

7. Before removing the crankcase screws, cut a cardboard template approximately the size of the crankcase and punch holes in the template for each screw location. Place each screw in the template hole as it is removed. This will speed up the assembly time by eliminating the search for the correct length screw.

8. Remove the bolts (**Figure 125**) securing the reverse shift cable bracket and remove the bracket (A, **Figure 126**).

CAUTION
In Step 9 and Step 10, to prevent crankcase warpage, loosen all bolts in 2-3 stages in a crisscross pattern.

9. Remove the following bolts from the left-hand crankcase half that secure the crankcase halves together:

    a. Five upper rear perimeter bolts (B, **Figure 126**).

    b. Two bolts (**Figure 127**) in the AC generator area.

    c. One bolt (**Figure 128**) next to the engine front mounting bolt boss.

    d. One bolt (**Figure 129**) next to the sub-transmission shafts.

    e. Four lower front perimeter bolts (**Figure 130**).

10. Remove the following bolts from the right-hand crankcase half that secure the crankcase halves together:

    a. Two front bolts (**Figure 131**).

    b. Four rear bolts (**Figure 132**). Don't lose the copper washer under the larger hex bolt (W, **Figure 132**).

NOTE
*Set the engine on wooden blocks or fabricate a holding fixture of 2 × 4 in. wood as shown in (**Figure 120**) or two 4 × 4 wooden blocks.*

CAUTION
*Perform the next step directly over and close to the workbench as the crankcase halves may separate easily. **Do not** hammer on the crankcase halves or they will be damaged.*

11. Place the crankcase assembly on the wooden box or wooden blocks on its left-hand side with the right-hand side facing up.

12. Hold onto the right-hand crankcase and studs and tap on the right-hand end of the crankshaft and

transmission shafts with a plastic or rubber mallet until the crankshaft and crankcase separate.

13. If the crankcase and crankshaft will not separate using this method, check to make sure that all screws are removed. If you still have a problem, it may be necessary to use a puller to remove the right-hand crankcase half. Many universal pullers are available or use the Suzuki Crankcase Separating Tool (part No. 09920-13120). If the proper tools are not available, take the crankcase assembly to a dealer and

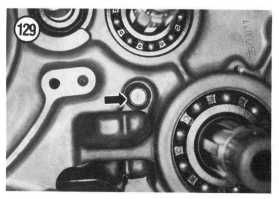

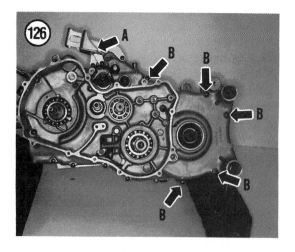

have it separated. Do not risk expensive crankcase damage with improper tools or techniques.

NOTE
Never pry between case halves. Doing so may result in oil leaks, requiring replacement of the case halves as a set.

14. Don't lose the locating dowels if they are loose in the case. They do not have to be removed from the case if they are secure.

15. Remove the transmission, shift drum and shift fork shaft assemblies as described under *Transmission and Internal Shift Mechanism Removal* in Chapter Seven.

16. The crankshaft can be removed at this time, if desired. The crankshaft is installed in the left-hand crankcase main bearing with an interference fit. Install the same puller used during crankcase separation in the threaded holes in the outer surface of

the left-hand crankcase and carefully *push* the crankshaft out of the left-hand main bearing.

CAUTION
Do not try to drive the crankshaft out of the main bearing with a hammer or the crankshaft alignment may be disturbed.

17. Remove the 3 mounting bolt rubber bushings from both crankcase halves.

18. Inspect the crankcase halves and crankshaft as described in this chapter.

Crankcase Assembly

1. Perform the inspection procedures to make sure all worn or defective parts have been repaired or replaced. All parts should be thoroughly cleaned before assembly and clean engine oil applied to all bearings in both crankcase halves.

2. Install the crankcase bearings, if removed, as described in this chapter.

3. Install new crankcase oil seals, if removed, as described in this chapter.

4. Pack the crankcase oil seals with a heat-durable grease.

5. Apply assembly oil to the inner race of all bearings in both crankcase halves.

NOTE
Set the left-hand crankcase half assembly on wooden blocks or the wooden holding fixture shown in the disassembly procedure.

6. If removed, install the crankshaft as follows:

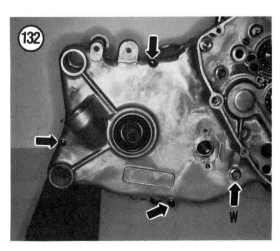

a. Position the crankshaft with the tapered end (AC generator side) going in first (**Figure 133**).

b. Gradually lower the assembly into the left-hand crankcase (**Figure 134**) while centering the connecting rod small end in the crankcase cut-out (**Figure 135**).

> *CAUTION*
> *Do not attempt to drive the crankshaft into the left-hand main bearing with a hammer or mallet or the crankshaft alignment will be disturbed.*

c. Push the crankshaft assembly down until it bottoms out. Recheck that the connecting rod small end is still centered in the crankcase cut-out (**Figure 136**).

d. Hold onto the connecting rod small end and slowly rotate the crankshaft to make sure it rotates freely with no binding.

7. Install the mounting bolt rubber bushings into both crankcase halves.

8. Install the transmission, shift drum and shift fork shaft assemblies as described under *Transmission and Internal Shift Mechanism Installation* in Chapter Seven.

> *NOTE*
> *Make sure the mating surfaces are clean and free of all old sealant material. Make sure you get a leak-free seal.*

9. Apply a light coat of sealant to the sealing surface of the left-hand crankcase half. Use a nonhardening sealant like Three-4 bond or equivalent.

10. If removed, install the front locating dowel (**Figure 137**) and the rear locating dowel (**Figure 138**). Push the locating dowels down until they bottom out in their receptacle.

11. Set the right-hand crankcase half over the left-hand crankcase half on the blocks. Push it down squarely into place until it reaches the crankshaft bearing. There is usually about 1/2 in. (12.7 mm) left to go (**Figure 139**).

12. Lightly tap the case halves together with a plastic or rubber mallet until they seat.

> *CAUTION*
> *Crankcase halves should fit together without force. If the crankcase halves do not fit together completely, do not attempt to pull them together with the crankcase screws. Separate the crank-*

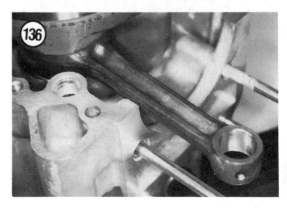

case halves and investigate the cause of the interference. If the transmission shafts were disassembled, recheck to make sure that a gear is not installed backward. Do not risk damage by trying to force the crankcase halves together.

13. After the crankcase halves are completely assembled, rotate the crankshaft and transmission shafts to make sure there is no binding. If any is present, disassemble the crankcase and correct the problem.

NOTE
Tighten all bolts finger-tight. Do not tighten to the torque specification until all bolts are installed and in the correct location.

14. Install the following bolts into the right-hand crankcase half:

    a. Two front bolts (**Figure 131**).

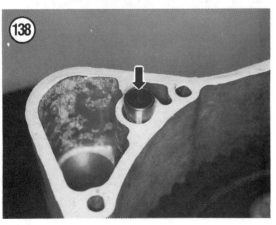

    b. Four rear bolts (**Figure 132**). Be sure to install the copper washer under the larger hex bolt (w, **Figure 132**).

15. Turn the crankcase over.

16. Install the following bolts into the left-hand crankcase half:

    a. Install the reverse shift cable bracket (A, **Figure 126**).

    b. Five upper rear perimeter bolts (B, **Figure 126**).

    c. Two bolts (**Figure 127**) in the AC generator area.

    d. One bolt (**Figure 128**) next to the engine front mounting bolt boss.

    e. One bolt (**Figure 129**) next to the sub-transmission shafts.

    f. Four lower front perimeter bolts (**Figure 130**).

CAUTION
To prevent crankcase warpage, tighten the bolts in 2-3 stages in a crisscross pattern.

17. Tighten the 8 mm bolt on each side first, then the 6 mm bolts to the torque specification listed in **Table 2**.

18. After the crankcase halves are completely assembled, again rotate the crankshaft and transmission shafts to make sure there is no binding. If any is present, disassemble the crankcase and correct the problem at this time.

19. Install the reverse switch (A, **Figure 124**) and the reverse cam detent (B, **Figure 124**).

20. Install the speedometer drive gear housing as follows:

    a. Rotate the sub-transmission shaft until the groove is horizontal (**Figure 140**).

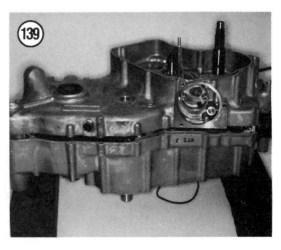

b. Install a new gasket (A, **Figure 141**) onto the speedometer drive gear housing.

c. Rotate the speedometer drive gear bar until it is horizontal (B, **Figure 141**).

d. Install the speedometer drive gear housing onto the crankcase and align the bar with the groove in the shaft. If necessary, slightly rotate the output shaft slightly with needlenose pliers (**Figure 142**) until alignment is correct.

e. Push the housing on until it is flush with the crankcase surface, then install the bolts (A, **Figure 123**). Tighten the bolts securely.

21. Install the oil pump drive gear onto the right-hand end of the crankshaft as follows:

a. Make sure the locating pin (**Figure 143**) is in place in the crankshaft.

b. Position the gear with the gear tooth side going on last.

c. Align the gear notch (A, **Figure 144**) with the locating pin (B, **Figure 144**) on the crankshaft and push the gear on until it bottoms out.

d. After the gear is installed, check the alignment of the gear to the pin (**Figure 145**).

22. Install the camshaft chain (**Figure 146**) onto timing sprocket on the left-hand end of the crankshaft. Make sure it is meshed properly with the sprocket (**Figure 147**).

23. Install the engine as described in this chapter.

24. Install all exterior engine assemblies as described in this chapter and other related chapters.

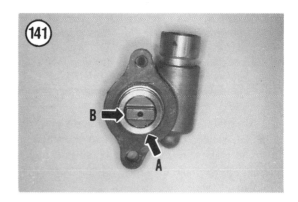

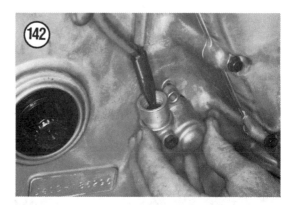

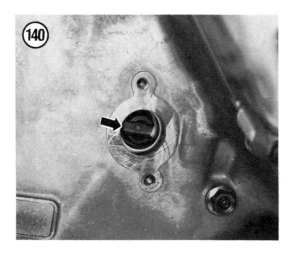

Crankcase Cleaning and Inspection

1. Remove the crankcase oil seals (**Figure 148**) as described under *Bearing and Oil Seal Replacement* in this chapter.

2. Remove the bolts (A, **Figure 149**) securing the oil breather pipe (B, **Figure 149**) and remove the breather pipe.

3. Remove all traces of gasket sealer from all mating surfaces.

4. Clean both crankcase halves inside and out with cleaning solvent.

5. Clean the crankcase bearings (**Figure 150**, typical) with cleaning solvent.

6. After cleaning in solvent, clean the cases and bearings in hot, soapy water and then rinse in clear cold water.

7. Dry the case halves and bearings with compressed air if available. When drying the bearings, do not allow the air jet to spin the bearings, but instead, hold the inner bearing races to prevent them from turning. When the bearings are dry, lubricate them as described in Step 8.

8. Lubricate the bearings and bushings with clean engine oil. Distribute the oil throughout the bearings.

9. Check the crankshaft main bearings, the transmission bearings and the sub-transmission bearings (**Figure 151**) for roughness, pitting, galling and play by rotating them slowly by hand. If any roughness or play can be felt in the bearing it must be replaced. Refer to *Bearing and Oil Seal Replacement* in this chapter for the correct procedure.

10. Carefully inspect the cases for cracks and fractures, especially in the lower areas (**Figure 152**) where they are vulnerable to rock damage. Also check the areas around the stiffening ribs, around bearing bosses and threaded holes. If damage is found, have it repaired by a shop specializing in the welding and machining of precision aluminum castings. If the damaged cases cannot be repaired, they must be replaced as a set.

11. Inspect the machined surfaces for burrs, cracks or other damage. You may be able to repair minor damage with a fine-cut file or oil stone. Otherwise, the mating surface will have to be welded and then machined flat.

12. On 4-wheel drive models, inspect the bearing receptacles (**Figure 153**) for the secondary driven output shaft bearings for wear or damage.

13. Check studs and threaded holes for stripping, cross-threading or deposit buildup. Refer to **Figure 154** and **Figure 155**. Threaded holes should be blown out with compressed air as dirt and sealer in the bottom of the hole may prevent the screw from being torqued properly. If necessary, use a metric tap or die to true up the threads and to remove deposits.

14. Cylinder studs (**Figure 156**) are susceptible to corrosion damage. Replace damaged or questionable studs. Remove studs with a stud remover. If the

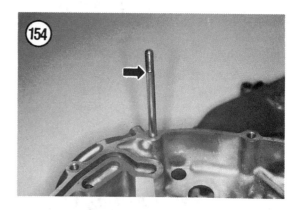

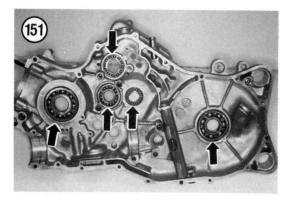

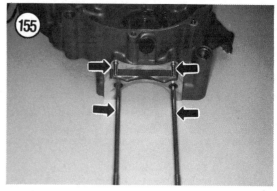

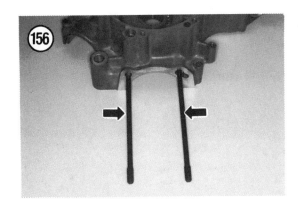

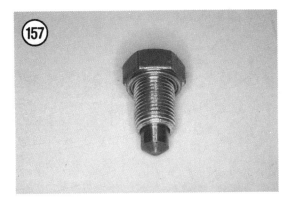

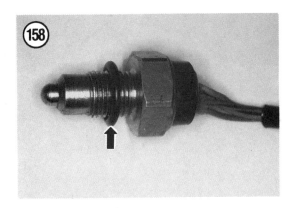

studs are in good condition, make sure they are tight in each case half. Retighten if necessary.

15. Check all bearing retainer plate bolts for wear, damage or looseness. Remove, clean and reinstall with blue Loctite (No. 242). Tighten the bolts securely.

16. Inspect the tip of the reverse cam stopper bolt (**Figure 157**) for wear or damage. Replace if necessary.

17. Inspect the reverse switch for wear or damage. Replace the O-ring seal (**Figure 158**). Replace the switch if necessary.

18. Inspect the mounting bolt rubber bushing receptacles (**Figure 159**) in both crankcase halves for cracks or damage.

19. Inspect the mounting bolt rubber bushings (**Figure 160**) for wear, damage or deterioration. Replace as a set if necessary.

20. Inspect the speedometer drive gear housing (**Figure 161**) for wear or damage. Inspect the speed-

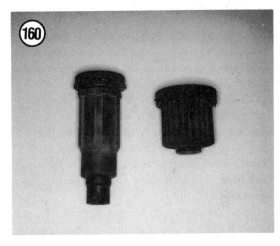

ometer drive gear bar (**Figure 162**) for wear or damage. If any part is worn or damaged, replace the assembly. Replacement parts are not available.

21. Install the oil pipe breather pipe (B, **Figure 149**) onto the right-hand crankcase half. Apply blue Loctite (No. 242) to the bolt threads prior to installation. Install the bolts (A, **Figure 149**) and tighten securely.

Crankshaft Inspection

Because the crankshaft operates under severe stress, service tolerances are critical and must be maintained. A worn connecting rod and lower end bearing or out-of-true crankshaft can cause severe engine damage.

Table 1 lists tolerances and wear limit specifications for the crankshaft. If you do not have all of the measuring tools described in this section, take the crankshaft to a dealer and have them check it for you.

If you are disassembling the engine because of secondary damage that is not related to the crankshaft (e.g. piston seizure, piston skirt damage, etc.), the crankshaft lower end bearing may have been damaged, or it may be contaminated with pieces of the broken piston. Check the connecting rod and lower end bearing carefully.

1. Dip the crankshaft in solvent and thoroughly clean it, then clean with hot soapy water and rinse in clear cold water. Dry with compressed air if available. When the crankshaft is dry, lubricate the bottom end with clean engine oil. Make sure the lower roller bearing is thoroughly coated with the clean engine oil.

2. Check the crankshaft bearing journals (**Figure 163**) for scratches, heat distortion or other defects.

3. Check the crankshaft oil seal surfaces for grooving, pitting or scratches.

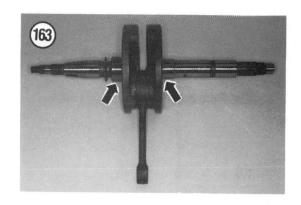
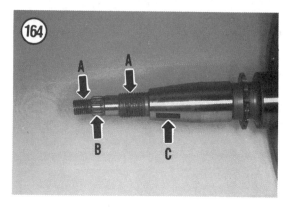
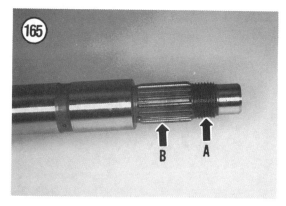

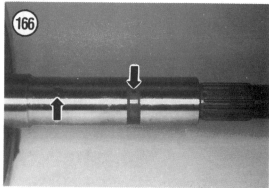

4. Check the crankshaft bearing surfaces for chatter marks and excessive or uneven wear. Minor cases of chatter marks may be cleaned up with 320 grit carborundum cloth. If 320 cloth is used, clean this area of the crankshaft in solvent and recheck the surfaces. If they did not clean up properly, have the crankshaft disassembled and have a dealer replace the damaged part.

5. On the left-hand end, inspect the threads (A, **Figure 164**), splines (B, **Figure 164**) and keyway

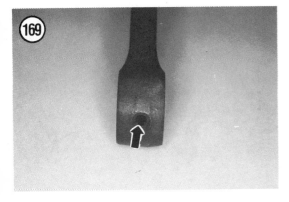

(C, **Figure 164**) for wear or damage. If one half of the crankshaft is damaged, the crankshaft can be disassembled and the damaged part replaced by a Suzuki dealer.

6. On the right-hand end, inspect the threads (A, **Figure 165**) and splines (B, **Figure 165**) for wear or damage. If one half of the crankshaft is damaged, the crankshaft can be disassembled and the damaged part replaced by a Suzuki dealer.

7. Make sure the oil holes (**Figure 166**) are clear. Clean out with a small diameter wire, solvent and compressed air.

8. Inspect the cam chain sprocket (**Figure 167**) for wear or missing teeth. If the sprocket is damaged, the left-hand portion of the crankshaft must be replaced.

9. Check the lower end bearing and connecting rod for signs of heat or damage.

10. Check the connecting rod big end bearing by grasping the rod in one hand and lifting up on it. With the heel of your other hand, rap sharply on the top of the rod. A sharp metallic sound, such as a click, is an indication that the bearing or crankpin, or both, are worn and the crankshaft assembly should be repaired or replaced.

11. Check the connecting rod-to-crankshaft side clearance with a flat feeler gauge (**Figure 168**). Compare to dimensions given in **Table 1**. If the clearance is greater than specified the crankshaft assembly should be repaired or replaced.

12. Make sure the connecting rod small end oil hole (**Figure 169**) is clear. Clean out with a small diameter wire, solvent and compressed air.

13. Oil the piston pin and install it in the connecting rod (**Figure 170**). Slowly rotate the piston pin and

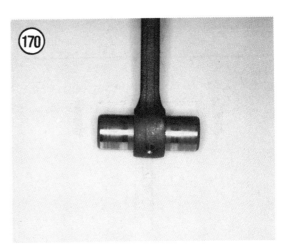

5

check for radial and axial play (**Figure 171**). If any play exists, the piston pin should be replaced, providing the connecting rod bore is in good condition.

14. Measure the inside diameter of the connecting rod small end with a snap gauge (**Figure 172**) and an outside micrometer (**Figure 173**). Compare to dimensions given in **Table 1**. If worn to the service limit the connecting rod portion of the crankshaft assembly must be replaced.

15. Check the crankshaft runout with a dial indicator and V-blocks. Refer to **Figure 174**, **Figure 175** and **Figure 176**. Have a dealer retrue the crankshaft assembly if the runout exceeds the service limit listed in **Table 1**.

16. The crankshaft in this engine is very wide to accommodate the recoil starter cup and the clutch assembly. If any of the previous dimensions are off by the slightest amount, it may cause a considerable amount of damage or destruction of the engine. If necessary, have the crankshaft rebuilt by a dealer.

17. Inspect the camshaft drive chain (**Figure 177**) for damaged pins or links. Measure the camshaft chain for stretching as follows:

   a. Place the chain in a flat surface and pull the chain taut to remove all slack.

   b. Use a vernier caliper and measure the distance between 21 pins as shown in **Figure 178**.

   c. Repeat Steps 17a and 17b several times at various locations around the chain. This type of chain rarely wears and stretches evenly.

   d. If the chain has stretched to the service limit listed in **Table 1** or greater, replace the chain.

18. Inspect the oil pump drive gear (**Figure 179**) for chipped or missing teeth. Make sure the locating pin groove (**Figure 180**) is not damaged. Replace the gear if necessary.

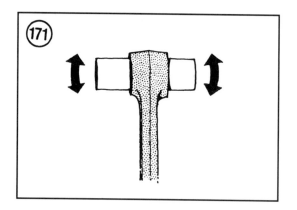

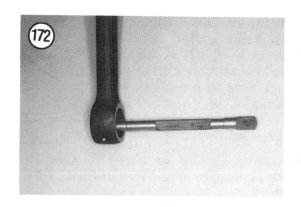

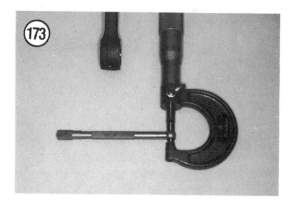

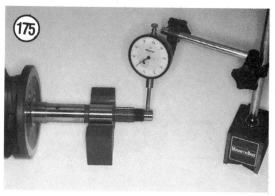

Bearing and Oil Seal Replacement

When removing oil seals from the crankcase halves, note the direction in which the lip of each seal faces (**Figure 181**, typical) to ensure proper installation. Likewise, when removing the bearing, note and record the direction of the manufacturer's name and size code (**Figure 182**, typical) to ensure proper installation.

1. Pry out the oil seal (**Figure 181**) with a screwdriver, taking care not to damage the crankcase bore. Pad the pry area under the screwdriver with a shop

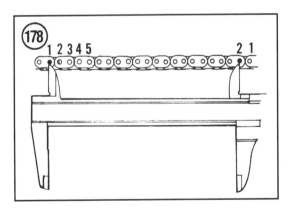

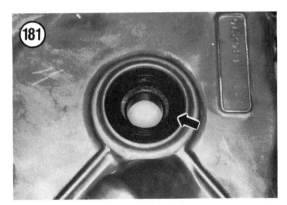

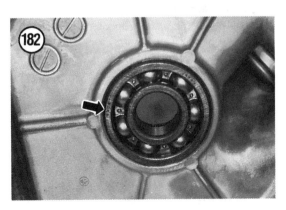

cloth to avoid damaging the crankcase. If the seal is old and difficult to remove, heat the cases as described later and use an awl to punch a small hole in the steel backing of the seal. Install a small sheet metal screw part way into the seal and pull the seal out with a pair of pliers.

CAUTION
Do not install the screw too deep or it may contact and damage the bearing behind it.

2. On a bearing so equipped, remove the screws (**Figure 183**) securing the bearing retainer plate(s) and remove the retainer plate(s). If the bearing is not going to be replaced, check the retaining screws for tightness.

CAUTION
Before heating the crankcase halves in this procedure to remove the bearings, wash the cases thoroughly with hot water and detergent. Rinse and rewash the cases as required to remove all traces of oil and other chemical deposits.

CAUTION
*Even after the cases have been thoroughly washed, there **may** be a slight residual oil or solvent odor left in the oven after heating the crankcase. If you use a household oven, first check with the person who uses the oven for food preparation to avoid getting into trouble.*

3A. The bearings are installed with a slight interference fit. The crankcase must be heated in an oven or hot plate to a temperature of about 215° F (100° C). An easy way to check the proper temperature is to drop tiny drops of water on the case; if they sizzle and evaporate immediately, the temperature is correct. Heat only one case at a time.

CAUTION
Do not heat the cases with a torch (propane or acetylene); never bring a flame into contact with the bearing or case. The direct heat will destroy the case hardening of the bearing and will likely cause warpage of the case.

3B. If you have access to a hydraulic press, it can be used instead of heat to remove and install the bearings and oil seals.

4. Remove the case from the oven or hot plate and hold onto the 2 crankcase studs with a kitchen pot holder, heavy gloves or heavy shop cloths—*it is hot.*

5. Remove the oil seals if not already removed.

6. Hold the crankcase with the bearing side down and tap it squarely on a piece of soft wood. Continue to tap until the bearing(s) fall out. Repeat for the other case half.

CAUTION
Be sure to tap the crankcase squarely on the piece of wood. Avoid damaging the sealing surface of the crankcase.

7. If the bearings are difficult to remove, they can be gently tapped out with a suitable size socket or piece of pipe the same size as the bearing inner race.

NOTE
If the bearings or seals are difficult to remove or install, don't take a chance on expensive damage. Have the work performed by a dealer or competent machine shop.

8. While heating up the crankcase halves, place the new bearings in a freezer if possible. Chilling them will slightly reduce their overall diameter while the hot crankcase is slightly larger due to heat expansion. This will make bearing installation much easier.

NOTE
Prior to installing the new bearing(s) or oil seal(s) apply a light coat of lithium-based grease to the inside and outside to aid in installation. Be sure to apply

the same grease to the lips of the new grease seals.

NOTE
*Install new bearing so that the manufacturer's name and size code face in the same direction recorded during disassembly. If you did not note this information prior to removing the bearings, install the bearings so that their marks are visible after the bearing has been installed. Refer to **Figure 182**, typical.*

9. While the crankcase is still hot, press each new bearing(s) into place in the crankcase by hand until it seats completely. Install the bearings by hand, if possible. If necessary, lightly tap the bearing(s) into the case with a socket placed on the outer race. *Do not* install new bearings by driving on the inner bearing race. Install the bearing(s) until it seats completely. If the bearing will not seat, remove it and cool it again. Reheat the crankcase and install the bearing again.

10. Oil seals are best installed with a special tool available at a dealer or motorcycle supply store. However, a proper size socket or piece of pipe can be substituted. Make sure that the bearings and seals are not cocked in the crankcase hole and that they are seated properly.

BREAK-IN PROCEDURE

If the rings were replaced, a new piston installed, the cylinder rebored or honed or major lower end work performed, the engine should be broken in just as though it were new. The performance and service life of the engine depends greatly on a careful and sensible break-in.

For the first 5-10 hours of operation, no more than one-third throttle should be used and speed should be varied as much as possible within the one-third throttle limit. Prolonged steady running at one speed, no matter how moderate, is to be avoided as well as hard acceleration.

Following the first 5-10 hours of operation more throttle should not be used until the ATV has run for 100 hours and then it should be limited to short bursts of speed until 150 hours have been logged.

The single-grade oils recommended for break-in and normal use provide a better bedding pattern for rings and cylinder than do multi-grade oils. As a result, piston ring and cylinder bore life are greatly increased. During this period, oil consumption will be higher than normal. It is therefore important to check frequently and correct the oil level. At no time, during the break-in or later, should the oil level be allowed to drop below the bottom line on the dipstick; if the oil level is low, the oil will become overheated resulting in insufficient lubrication and increased wear.

After 10 Hours Of Operation Service

It is essential that the oil be changed and the oil filter rotor and filter screen be cleaned after the first 10 hours of operation. In addition, it is a good idea to change the oil and oil filter at the completion of the 100 hours of operation to ensure that all of the particles produced during break-in are removed from the lubrication system. The small added expense may be considered a smart investment that will pay off in increased engine life.

Table 1 ENGINE SERVICE SPECIFICATIONS

Item	Specification	Wear limit
Connecting rod **Small end inner diameter**		
250 cc	16.006-16.014 mm (0.6302-0.6305 in.)	16.040 mm (0.6315 in.)
280 cc	17.006-17.014 mm (0.6694-0.6696 in.)	17.040 mm (0.6709 in.)
Big end side clearance	0.10-0.45 mm (0.004-0.018 in.)	1.00 mm (0.039 in.)
	(continued)	

Table 1 ENGINE SERVICE SPECIFICATIONS (continued)

Item	Specification	Wear limit
Crankshaft runout		
Right-hand side	—	0.08 mm (0.003 in.)
Left-hand side	—	0.05 mm (0.002 in.)
Camshaft chain wear limit		
20-pitch length	—	129.0 mm (5.08 in.)

Table 2 ENGINE TIGHTENING TORQUES

Item	N·m	ft.-lb.
Engine mounting bolts and nuts		
Left-hand side frame		
bridge bolts	60-70	43.5-50.5
LT-F250		
Front bolt and nut	80-95	58-68.5
Rear bolts and nuts	80-95	58-68.5
LT-4WD		
Front bolt and nut	60-72	43.5-52.0
Rear bolts and nuts	80-95	58-68.5
LT-4WDX		
Front bolt and nut	60-72	43.5-52.0
Rear bolts and nuts	64-76	46.5-55
Recoil starter cup nut	30-35	21.5-25.5
Starter clutch holder		
Allen bolts	23-28	16.5-20
Oil pump mounting bolts	7-10	5-7
Sub-transmission output		
shaft bevel gear nut	90-110	65-79.5
Crankcase bolts		
6 mm	9-13	6.5-9.5
8 mm	20-24	14.5-17.5
Oil cooler hose fitting bolts	9-10	6.5-8
Engine oil drain plugs		
12 mm	18-23	13-16.5
14 mm	20-25	14.5-18
Reverse switch stopper bolt	20-25	14.5-18

CLUTCH

6

This chapter contains service procedures for the centrifugal and mechanical clutch assemblies. **Table 1** and **Table 2** are at the end of this chapter.

CLUTCH OPERATION

The clutch assemblies on all models consists of a centrifugal clutch and a manual clutch. The centrifugal clutch is mounted on the right-hand end of the crankshaft. The main components of this clutch are the primary drive gear, clutch shoe assembly and a one-way clutch which allows the primary drive gear to rotate in one direction only. The primary drive gear is not driven directly by the crankshaft, but by the centrifugal clutch weights attached to a hub that is splined to the crankshaft. As the engine rpm increases, the centrifugal weights are forced out against the primary drive gear, thus driving and rotating the primary drive gear. When engine speed

decreases; 3 perimeter coil springs retract the weights to disengage the weights from the primary drive gear. A gear on the backside of the primary drive gear meshes with the gear on the manual clutch outer housing. The one-way clutch not only allows the outer housing to rotate in one direction, but also allows engine compression to be used to slow down the vehicle when the centrifugal clutch weights are not engaged (when coasting).

The manual clutch is a wet multi-plate type and is activated by the gearshift linkage. The clutch outer housing is driven by the centrifugal clutch while the clutch center is splined to the transmission main shaft. When the gearshift lever is moved to shift gears it also activates the clutch lifting mechanism, releasing the clutch.

Both clutch mechanisms can be removed with the engine in the frame and both clutch types are immersed in the oil supply they share with the engine and transmission.

CENTRIFUGAL CLUTCH

Removal

Refer to **Figure 1** for this procedure.

1. Place the ATV on level ground and set the parking brake. Block the front wheels so the vehicle will not roll in either direction.

2. Drain the engine oil as described under *Engine Oil and Filter Change* in Chapter Three.

3. Remove the right-hand crankcase cover as described under *Right-hand Crankcase Cover Removal/Installation* in Chapter Five.

NOTE
The following steps are shown with the engine removed from the frame for clarity.

4. Place a soft copper washer (copper penny) or shop cloth into mesh with the gears on the backside of the centrifugal primary drive gear and the clutch

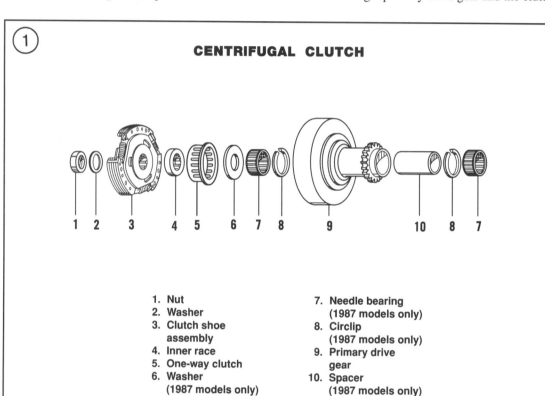

CENTRIFUGAL CLUTCH

1. Nut
2. Washer
3. Clutch shoe assembly
4. Inner race
5. One-way clutch
6. Washer (1987 models only)
7. Needle bearing (1987 models only)
8. Circlip (1987 models only)
9. Primary drive gear
10. Spacer (1987 models only)

outer housing. This will prevent the primary drive gear from turning in the next step.

CAUTION
*The nut in the following step has **left-hand** threads. Loosen it by turning it **clockwise**.*

5. Remove the nut (**Figure 2**) securing the centrifugal primary drive gear to the crankshaft. Remember, turn the wrench *clockwise*.

6. Remove the lockwasher (**Figure 3**).

7. Slide off the clutch shoe assembly (**Figure 4**). There is no spring tension to worry about during the removal of this component.

NOTE
Proceed to Step 9 unless the manual clutch is going to be removed also.

6

8. If the manual clutch is going to be removed, perform the following:

NOTE
Loosen the locknut at this time, as you will need the primary drive gear to aid in loosening the locknut.

   a. Place a soft copper washer (or copper penny) or shop cloth into mesh with the gears on the backside of the centrifugal primary drive gear and the clutch outer housing. This is to keep the manual clutch outer housing from rotating while removing the locknut.

   b. Remove the bolts securing the lifter plate (**Figure 5**) and remove the lifter plate assembly (A, **Figure 6**).

   c. Remove the clutch springs (**Figure 7**).

   d. Loosen the clutch locknut (**Figure 8**).

e. Remove the copper washer (or copper penny) or shop cloth from the backside of the centrifugal primary drive gear and the clutch outer housing.

9. Slide off the primary drive gear (B, **Figure 6**) and one-way clutch assembly.

NOTE
*On 1988-on models, the spacer, circlip and inner needle bearings are replaced by internal pressed-in bushings that remain with the primary drive gear during removal. Refer to **Figure 1**.*

10. On 1987 models only, perform the following:
   a. Slide off the spacer.
   b. Slide off the inner needle bearing.

11. Inspect all centrifugal clutch components as described in this chapter.

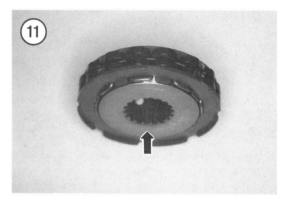

Inspection

1. Clean all parts in petroleum-based solvent such as kerosene and thoroughly dry with compressed air.

2. Rotate the inner race within the one-way clutch (**Figure 9**). It should only rotate *clockwise*. If it will rotate counterclockwise, even the slightest amount, it is defective and must be replaced.

3. Rotate the inner race within the one-way clutch (**Figure 9**). It should only rotate *clockwise* smoothly with no binding or roughness. If necessary, note the orientation of the one-way clutch to the primary drive gear, then remove the one-way clutch and inner race (**Figure 10**) from the primary drive gear and inspect as follows:
   a. Separate the inner race (**Figure 11**) from the one-way clutch.

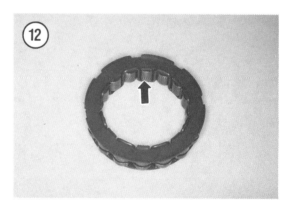

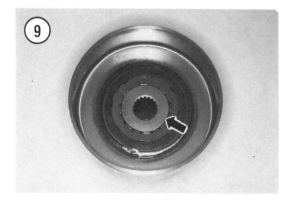

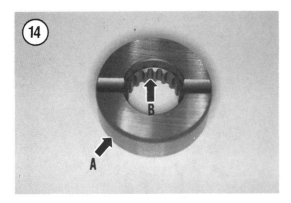

b. Check the rollers (**Figure 12**) in the one-way clutch for uneven or excessive wear. If damaged, inspect the mating surface of the primary drive gear (A, **Figure 13**) and the inner race (A, **Figure 14**) for any wear caused by damaged rollers. Replace the one-way clutch and any related parts if excessive wear or damage is noted.

c. Inspect the inner splines (B, **Figure 14**) of the inner race for wear or damage. Replace if necessary.

d. If all parts are okay, make sure the washer (B, **Figure 13**) is in place, then install the inner race into the one-way clutch and install this assembly into the primary drive gear.

4. Inspect the drive gear teeth on the primary drive gear (**Figure 15**). Remove any small nicks on the gear teeth with an oil stone. If damage is severe, the primary drive gear must be replaced. Also check the teeth on the manual clutch outer housing. It may also need replacing.

5. Inspect the inside contact surface of the primary drive gear (**Figure 16**) for scratches, scoring or heat damage (bluish tint). Abnormal wear is unlikely unless the friction surface of the clutch shoe assembly has worn past the limit and metal-to-metal contact has occurred. Replace the primary drive gear if the shoe surface is not in perfect condition. If there are indications of heat damage, the primary drive gear may be distorted. If so, the primary drive gear must be replaced.

6A. On 1987 models, inspect the primary drive gear needle bearings for wear or damage and replace if necessary.

6B. On 1988-on models, inspect the primary drive gear bushings (**Figure 17**) for wear. If either bushing is worn, replace the primary drive gear.

7. Check the springs (**Figure 18**) on the clutch shoe assembly. If any spring (**Figure 19**) is stretched or

distorted in any way, the clutch shoe assembly must be replaced.

8. Examine the friction lining on the clutch shoe assembly (**Figure 20**). If the shoes are worn so that none of the grooves in the friction material remain (**Figure 21**), the clutch shoe assembly must be replaced.

9. Examine the clutch shoe assembly inner splines (**Figure 22**) for wear or damage. Remove any small nicks on the gear teeth with an oilstone. If damage is severe, the clutch shoe assembly must be replaced.

10. Inspect the clutch lifting mechanism in the clutch cover as described in this chapter.

Installation

1. On 1987 models only, perform the following:
   a. Slide on the inner needle bearing.
   b. Slide on the spacer.

2. Slide on the primary drive gear (B, **Figure 5**) and one-way clutch assembly. On 1987 models, install the outer needle bearing (if removed) into the primary drive gear.

3. On 1987 models only, align the oil hole in the primary drive gear inner race with the hole in the crankshaft, then slide the inner race on all the way.

NOTE
Proceed to Step 5 if the manual clutch was not removed.

4. If the manual clutch was removed, perform the following:
   a. Install the manual clutch assembly as described in this chapter.
   b. Place a soft copper washer (or copper penny) (**Figure 23**) or shop cloth into mesh with the gears on the backside of the centrifugal primary drive gear and the clutch outer housing. This is to keep the manual clutch outer housing from rotating while tightening the locknut.
   c. Install, then tighten the clutch locknut (**Figure 8**).
   d. Temporarily install 2 opposing clutch bolts into the pressure plate. Pull on the bolts and make sure the pressure plate has pulled the friction disc and clutch plates up against the backside of the clutch center. If this is not correct, slightly jiggle the bolts in order to align the notches in the pressure plate with the grooves in the clutch center. Once alignment is correct, pull on the

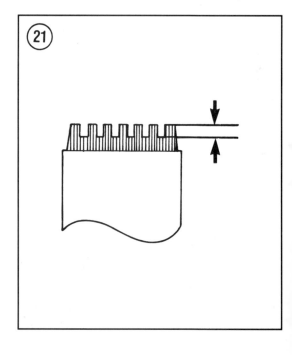

backside of the pressure plate and keep it in this position.

CAUTION
Proper alignment between the pressure plate and the clutch center must be achieved before the clutch springs are installed and the bolts tightened. If the bolts are tightened and the alignment is not correct, the first time the clutch is operated, these 2 parts will shift, the pressure plate will move outward and the clutch bolts will be loose. Clutch operation will be erratic and unsafe.

e. Remove the 2 bolts installed in Sub-step d.

f. Install the clutch springs (**Figure 7**), lifter plate assembly (A, **Figure 5**) and the bolts. Once again, check that the pressure plate is snug up against the friction discs and clutch plates prior to tightening the clutch bolts.

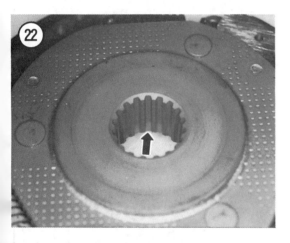

g. Tighten the bolts securely in a crisscross pattern.

h. Remove the copper washer (or copper penny) or shop cloth from the backside of the centrifugal primary drive gear and the clutch outer housing.

NOTE
If the clutch shoe assembly was replaced, apply new engine oil to all surfaces to avoid having the clutch lock up when used for the first time.

5. Slide on the clutch shoe assembly (**Figure 4**) and the lockwasher (**Figure 3**).

CAUTION
*The nut in the following step has **left-hand** threads. Tighten by turning it **counterclockwise**.*

NOTE
It is a good idea to install a new nut every 2nd or 3rd time it is removed.

6. Place a soft copper washer (copper penny) or shop cloth into mesh with the gears on the backside of the centrifugal primary drive gear and the clutch outer housing. This will prevent the primary drive gear from turning in the next step.

7. Install the nut (**Figure 2**) securing the centrifugal primary drive gear to the crankshaft. Remember, turn the wrench *counterclockwise* and tighten the nut to the torque specification listed in **Table 1**.

8. Install the right-hand crankcase cover as described in Chapter Five.

9. Refill the engine with the recommended type and quantity of engine oil as described in Chapter Three.

10. Start the engine and check for oil leaks.

11. Adjust the clutch as described in Chapter Three.

MANUAL CLUTCH

Removal/Disassembly

Refer to **Figure 24** for this procedure.

NOTE
The centrifugal clutch has to be removed prior to removing the manual clutch.

1. Remove the centrifugal clutch (A, **Figure 25**) as described in this chapter.

MANUAL CLUTCH

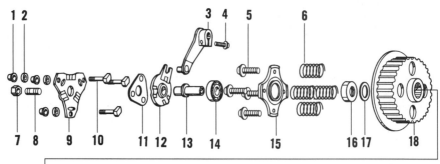

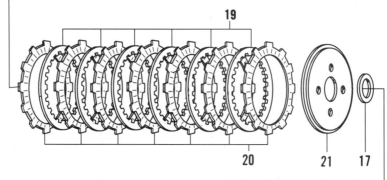

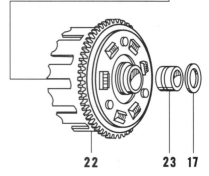

1. Cap nut
2. Laminated washer
3. Shift lever
4. Clamping bolt
5. Spring bolt
6. Spring
7. Locknut
8. Adjust bolt
9. Clutch lifter
10. Special bolt
11. Ball retainer
12. Clutch lifter cam
13. Push piece
14. Ball bearing

15. Lifter plate
16. Locknut
17. Lockwasher
18. Clutch center
19. Clutch plates
20. Friction discs
21. Pressure plate
22. Clutch outer housing
23. Spacer

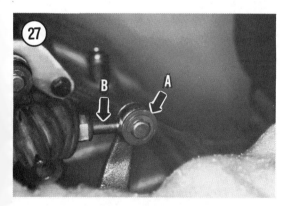

2. Remove the manual clutch lifter plate assembly (**Figure 26**) and the clutch springs as described under *Centrifugal Clutch Removal* in this chapter.

3. On the left-hand side of the engine, perform the following:

    a. Remove the E-clip (A, **Figure 27**) and washer securing the gearshift cable to the gearshift lever.

    b. Disconnect the gearshift cable (B, **Figure 27**) from the lever. Don't lose the bushing that may stay with the cable or on the gearshift lever pivot post.

    c. Reinstall the washer and E-clip onto the gearshift lever pivot post (A, **Figure 28**) to avoid misplacing them.

    d. Remove the bolt (B, **Figure 28**), then remove the gearshift lever (C, **Figure 28**) from the end of the gearshift shaft.

4. Withdraw the shift lever assembly (B, **Figure 25**) from the crankcase.

5. Remove the previously loosened clutch locknut (**Figure 29**).

6. Remove the lockwasher (**Figure 30**).

6

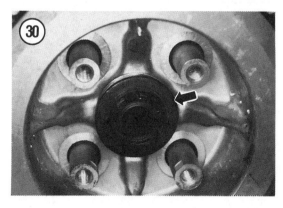

7. Remove the clutch center, plates, discs and pressure plate (**Figure 31**) as an assembly.

8. Remove the thrust washer (**Figure 32**).

9. Remove the clutch outer housing (**Figure 33**) and spacer (**Figure 34**).

10. Remove the thrust washer (**Figure 35**).

11. Inspect all manual clutch components as described in this chapter.

Inspection

1. Clean all parts in a petroleum based solvent such as kerosene and thoroughly dry with compressed air.

2. Measure the free length of each clutch spring as shown in **Figure 36**. If any of the springs are worn to service limit listed in **Table 2** (or less), replace all springs as a set.

3. Check the friction discs (**Figure 37**) and clutch plates (**Figure 38**) for surface damage from heat or lack of oil. Replace any disc and plate that is damaged in any way.

4. Measure the thickness of each friction disc at several places around the disc as shown in **Figure 39**. Replace any disc that is worn to the service limit listed in **Table 2**.

5. Measure the width of the claws on each friction disc as shown in **Figure 40**. Replace any disc that is worn to the service limit listed in **Table 2**.

6. Check the clutch plates for warpage on a surface plate such as a piece of plate glass (**Figure 41**). Replace any that are warped to the service limit listed in **Table 2**.

> *NOTE*
> *If any of the friction discs, clutch plates or clutch springs require replacement, you should consider replacing all of*

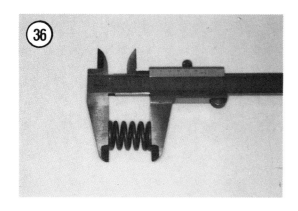

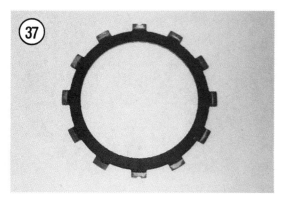

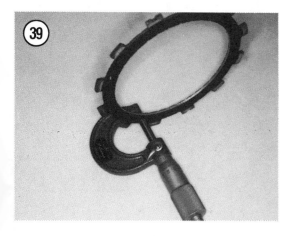

them as a set to retain maximum clutch performance.

7. Inspect the pressure plate grooves (**Figure 42**) and studs (**Figure 43**). If either show signs of wear or galling, the pressure plate should be replaced.

8. Inspect the spring receptacles (**Figure 44**) in the clutch center for wear or damage. Replace the clutch center if necessary.

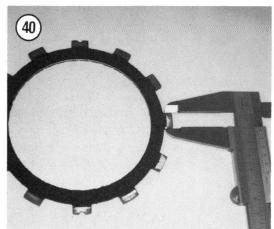

6

9. Inspect the clutch center inner splines (**Figure 45**) and outer grooves (**Figure 46**). If any are damaged, the clutch center should be replaced.

10. Inspect the slots (**Figure 47**) in the clutch outer housing for cracks, nicks or galling where they come in contact with the friction disc tabs. If any severe damage is evident, the housing must be replaced.

CAUTION
*If the clutch outer housing driven gear teeth are severely damaged, inspect the mating teeth (**Figure 48**) on the centrifugal clutch primary drive gear. If necessary, replace this part also.*

11. Inspect the driven gear teeth (**Figure 49**) on the clutch outer housing for damage. Remove any small nicks with an oil stone. If damage is severe, the clutch outer housing must be replaced.

12. Inspect the clutch outer housing damper springs (**Figure 50**). If they are sagged or broken, the clutch outer housing must be replaced.

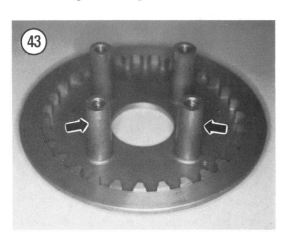

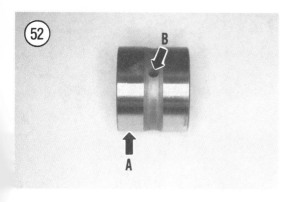

13. Check the inner surface (**Figure 51**) of the clutch outer housing, where the spacer rides, for signs of wear, burrs or heat damage. Replace the clutch outer housing if necessary.

14. Check the outer surface of the spacer (A, **Figure 52**) for wear, burrs or heat damage. Make sure the oil control hole (B, **Figure 52**) is clear. Clean out with solvent, then blow out with compressed air. Replace if necessary.

15. Install the spacer into the clutch outer housing, rotate the spacer (**Figure 53**) and check for wear. Replace either/or both parts if necessary. There are no wear tolerance specifications for either part.

16. Check the clutch push piece (A, **Figure 54**) for wear or damage. Replace if necessary.

17. Check the clutch push piece ball bearing (B, **Figure 54**). Make sure it rotates smoothly with no signs of wear or damage. Replace if necessary.

6

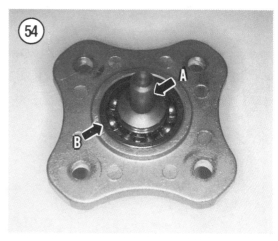

18. Inspect the lifter plate (**Figure 55**) for cracks or damage. Check that the mounting holes are not elongated or damaged. Replace if necessary.

Assembly/Installation

> *NOTE*
> *If new friction discs and clutch plates are being installed, apply new engine oil to all surfaces to avoid having the clutch lock up when used for the first time.*

1. Place the clutch center on your workbench with the outer groove side facing up (**Figure 56**).
2. First install a friction disc (**Figure 57**) and then a clutch plate (**Figure 58**) onto the clutch center.
3. Continue to install a friction disc then a clutch plate, until all are installed. The last item installed is a friction disc (**Figure 59**).
4. Align all the tabs on the friction discs (**Figure 60**). This will make installation easier.
5. Align the punch marks on the clutch center and the pressure plate (**Figure 61**) and install the pressure plate (**Figure 62**).

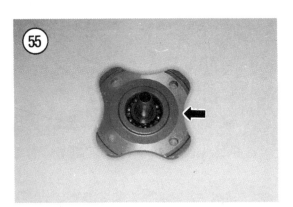

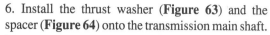

6. Install the thrust washer (**Figure 63**) and the spacer (**Figure 64**) onto the transmission main shaft.

7. Install the clutch outer housing (**Figure 65**) and the thrust washer (**Figure 66**).

8. Slide on the clutch parts (clutch center, friction discs, clutch plates and pressure plate). Push the assembly on slowly, carefully aligning the tabs of the friction discs into the slots in the clutch outer housing (**Figure 67**).

6

9. Position the lockwasher with the dished side facing out and install the lockwasher (**Figure 68**).

10. Install the locknut (**Figure 69**). Do not tighten the locknut at this time. It is to be tightened after the centrifugal clutch is installed.

11. Install the shift lever assembly (A, **Figure 70**) into the crankcase. Push it into the crankcase and align the shift lever finger into mesh with the link arm (**Figure 71**). Push the shift lever assembly in until it bottoms out.

12. On the left-hand side of the engine, perform the following:

    a. Align the punch mark on the gearshift lever with the line on the gearshift shaft and install the lever (A, **Figure 72**).

    b. Install the bolt (B, **Figure 72**) and tighten securely.

    c. Remove the E-ring and washer (C, **Figure 72**) from the gearshift lever pivot post.

    d. If removed install the bushing into the cable pivot end, then apply a light coat of molybdenum disulfide grease to the inner surface of the gearshift cable pivot bushing (**Figure 73**).

    e. Connect the gearshift cable (A, **Figure 74**) onto the lever pivot post. Don't lose the bushing during installation.

    f. Install the washer and E-clip (B, **Figure 74**) securing the gearshift cable to the gearshift lever. Make sure the E-clip is properly installed in the pivot post groove.

13. Install the manual clutch springs (**Figure 75**) and the lifter plate assembly (**Figure 76**) as described under *Centrifugal Clutch Removal* in this chapter.

14. Install the centrifugal clutch (B, **Figure 70**) as described in this chapter.

15. Adjust the clutch as described in Chapter Three.

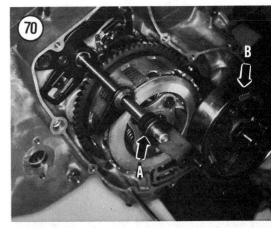

CLUTCH LIFTING MECHANISM

The clutch lifting mechanism is located within both the clutch cover and on the external shift mechanism. When the gearshift lever is moved to shift gears, it also activates the clutch lifting mechanism, releasing the clutch.

Removal

Refer to **Figure 77** for this procedure.

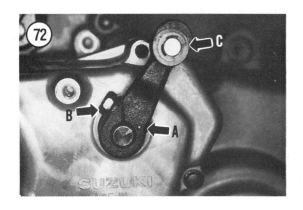

1. Perform Steps 1-9 of *Centrifugal Clutch, Removal* as described in this chapter and remove the right-hand crankcase cover.
2. Remove the clutch lifter cam (**Figure 78**) and the ball retainer (**Figure 79**) from the right-hand crankcase cover.
3. If necessary, remove the cap nuts and special laminated washers (**Figure 80**) securing the clutch lifter assembly in the right-hand crankcase cover.
4. Turn the cover over and remove the clutch lifter assembly (**Figure 81**) from the right-hand crankcase cover.

Inspection

1. Clean all parts in solvent and thoroughly dry with compressed air.
2. Inspect the balls (**Figure 82**) in the ball retainer. They must rotate freely in the ball retainer but not so loose that they will fall out. Check the balls for evidence of wear, pitting or excessive heat (bluish tint). Replace if necessary.
3. Inspect the groves and inside surface of both the clutch lifter cam (A, **Figure 83**) and clutch lifter

6

MANUAL CLUTCH

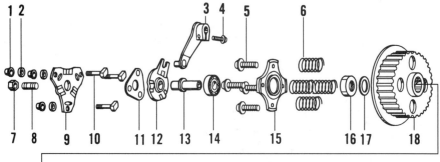

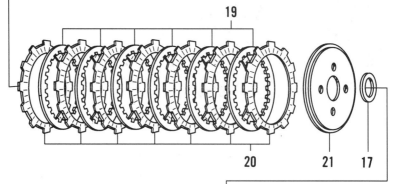

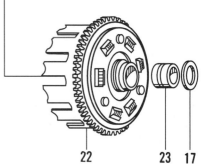

1. Cap nut
2. Laminated washer
3. Shift lever
4. Clamping bolt
5. Spring bolt
6. Spring
7. Locknut
8. Adjust bolt
9. Clutch lifter
10. Special bolt
11. Ball retainer
12. Clutch lifter cam
13. Push piece
14. Ball bearing
15. Lifter plate
16. Locknut
17. Lockwasher
18. Clutch center
19. Clutch plates
20. Friction discs
21. Pressure plate
22. Clutch outer housing
23. Spacer

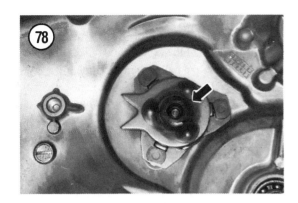

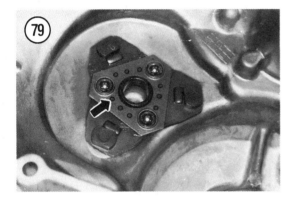

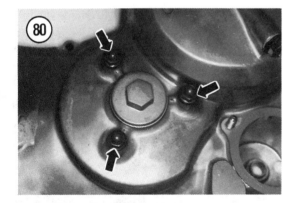

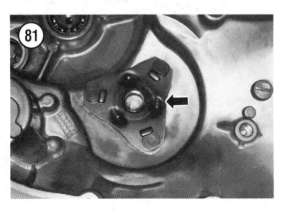

(**Figure 81**) where the balls ride. All surfaces must be smooth and free of burrs or scoring. Replace as necessary.

4. Check the locating notch on the clutch lifter cam (B, **Figure 83**). It cannot show signs of wear or damage as it must fit snugly onto the pin of the clutch release arm of the shift mechanism. If the fit between these 2 parts is sloppy, transmission shifting will be difficult.

5. Inspect the clutch adjustment locknut and threaded stud (**Figure 84**) for wear or damage. Replace if necessary.

NOTE
For optimum performance replace all 3 of these parts if any one of them requires replacement.

6

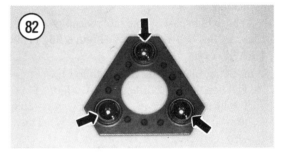

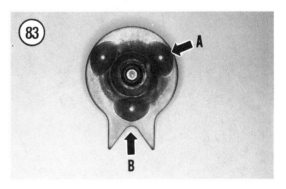

Installation

NOTE
The special washers and cap nuts must be installed on the bolts that are outside of the clutch adjustment cover to prevent an oil leak.

1. If removed, install the clutch lifter assembly in the right-hand crankcase cover. Hold it in place, turn the cover over and install the special laminated washers and nuts (**Figure 80**). Tighten the nuts securely.

2. Apply a light coat of cold molybdenum disulfide grease to the ball receptacles (**Figure 85**) in the clutch lifter.

3. Install the ball retainer and position it so the balls are in the receptacles (**Figure 79**). Push it down so the grease will hold the ball retainer in place during installation.

4. Apply a light coat of cold molybdenum disulfide grease to the ball receptacles (**Figure 86**) in the clutch lifter cam.

5. Install the clutch lifter cam as follows:
   a. Position the clutch lifter cam (A, **Figure 87**) so the locating notch (B, **Figure 87**) is pointing toward the raised boss (C, **Figure 87**). This is necessary for proper alignment of the clutch lifter notch to the shift lever arm pin during installation of the right-hand crankcase cover.
   b. Make sure the balls are in the clutch lifter cam receptacles. Push it down so the grease will hold the clutch lifter cam in place during installation.

6. After these parts are assembled, check that the balls in the ball retainer fit correctly into the recesses in both the clutch lifter cam and the clutch lifter. If not, correct the problem at this time.

7. Perform Steps 8-16 of *Centrifugal Clutch, Installation* as described in this chapter and install the right-hand crankcase cover and other related parts.

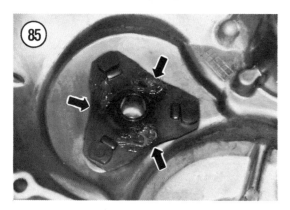

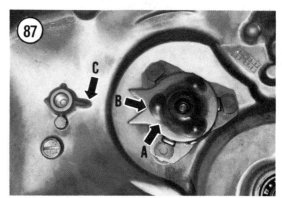

Table 1 CLUTCH TIGHTENING TORQUES		
Item	N·m	ft.-lb.
Clutch locknut		
Manual	60-80	43.5-58
Centrifugal	90-110	65-79.5

Table 2 CLUTCH SERVICE SPECIFICATIONS

Item	Standard	Wear limit
Friction disc thickness	2.7-2.9 mm (0.106-0.114 in.)	2.4 mm (0.094 in.)
Friction disc claw width	11.8-12.0 mm (0.46-0.47 in.)	11.0 mm (0.43 in.)
Clutch plate warpage	—	0.1 mm (0.004 in.)
Clutch springs free length	—	27.4 mm (1.08 in.)
Primary drive gear I.D.	116.00-116.15 mm (4.567-4.573 in.)	Scuffs or scratches on surface

6

TRANSMISSION AND SHIFT MECHANISM

The 5-speed main transmission and internal shift mechanism assemblies are the same for both the 2-wheel drive and the 4-wheel drive models. The sub-transmission is basically the same with 2-wheel drive models having one less gear. Where minor variations occur, they are identified in the following procedures.

Refer to **Table 1** for specifications on the internal shift mechanism. Suzuki does not provide any specifications for transmission components.

To gain access to the sub-transmission it is necessary to remove the engine and remove the left-hand crankcase cover. To gain access to the transmission, internal shift mechanism and output shaft, it is necessary to remove the engine and disassemble the crankcase as described in Chapter Five.

MAIN TRANSMISSION EXTERNAL SHIFT MECHANISM

The external shift mechanism is located on the right-hand side of the crankcase next to the clutch assemblies. To remove the shift drum and shift forks it is necessary to remove the engine and disassemble the crankcase. This procedure is covered under *Transmission and Internal Shift Mechanism* in this chapter.

Removal

Refer to **Figure 1** for this procedure.

1. Place the ATV on level ground and set the parking brake. Block the front wheels so the vehicle will not roll in either direction.

2. Drain the engine oil as described under *Engine Oil and Filter Change* in Chapter Three.

3. Remove the seat and the rear fender as described under *Rear Fender Removal/Installation* in Chapter Fourteen.

4. Remove the right-hand rear wheel as described under *Rear Wheel Removal/Installation* in Chapter Twelve.

5. Remove the right-hand shock absorber as described under *Shock Absorber Removal/Installation* in Chapter Twelve.

6. Let the right-hand rear suspension arm pivot down until it stops.

MAIN TRANSMISSION
EXTERNAL SHIFT MECHANISM

1. Shoulder bolt	20. Reverse gearshift shaft	36. Pin
2. Gear shifter	21. Washer	37. Shift cam
3. Washer	22. Oil seal	38. Bolt
4. Roller	23. Reverse gearshift lever	39. Collar
5. Stud	24. Reverse indicator switch	40. Bearing retainer
6. Gearshift lever (engine side)	25. O-ring	41. Bearing
7. Washer	26. Reverse shift fork	42. Locating pin
8. Collar	27. Shift fork No. 1	43. Gearshift drum
9. E-clip	28. Shift fork No. 2	44. Spring
10. Clamping bolt	29. Shift fork shaft No. 1	45. Pin
11. Return spring	30. Gearshift lever (foot pedal)	46. O-ring
12. Link arm	31. O-ring	47. Neutral switch
13. Gearshift shaft	32. Collar	48. Washer
14. Return spring	33. Bolt	49. Lockwasher
15. Oil seal	34. Bolt	50. Screw
16. Reverse cam stopper	35. Shift cam plate	51. Cam stopper arm
17. Gasket		52. Washer
18. Spring		53. Shift fork No. 3
19. Stopper pin		54. Shift fork shaft No. 2

7

7. Remove the cotter pin, washer, pivot pin and washer, then disconnect the rear brake cable from the rear brake pedal (A, **Figure 2**).

8. Loosen the locknut, disconnect the rear brake cable from the bracket (B, **Figure 2**) and move the brake cable and hose (A, **Figure 3**) out of the way.

9. Remove the right-hand crankcase cover (B, **Figure 3**) as described under *Right-hand Crankcase Cover Removal/Installation* in Chapter Five.

10. On the left-hand side of the engine, perform the following:

   a. Remove the E-clip (A, **Figure 4**) and washer securing the sub-transmission gearshift control cable to the gearshift lever.

   b. Disconnect the control cable (B, **Figure 4**) from the lever. Don't lose the bushing that may stay with the cable or on the gearshift lever pivot post.

   c. Reinstall the washer and E-clip onto the gearshift lever pivot post (A, **Figure 5**) to avoid misplacing them.

   d. Remove the bolt (B, **Figure 5**), then remove the gearshift lever (C, **Figure 5**) from the end of the gearshift shaft.

11. Withdraw the shift lever assembly (**Figure 6**) from the right-hand side of the crankcase.

12. Remove both clutch assemblies as described in Chapter Six.

13. Remove the shoulder bolt (A, **Figure 7**) securing the gear shifter.

14. Lift the short arm of the gear shifter (B, **Figure 7**) away from the shift drum shift cam and remove the gear shifter (C, **Figure 7**). Don't lose the washer on the backside of the gear shifter.

15. Remove the roller (**Figure 8**) from the link arm.

16. Remove the link arm (**Figure 9**) from the crankcase.

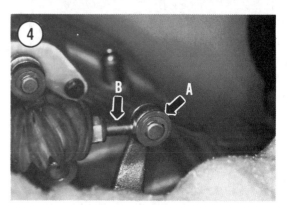

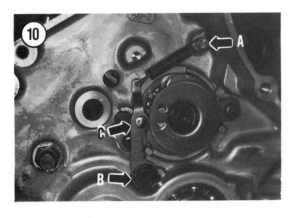

17. Unhook the return spring (A, **Figure 10**) from the post on the crankcase.

18. Remove the bolt (B, **Figure 10**) securing the cam stopper arm and remove the cam stopper arm (C, **Figure 10**) and washer from the crankcase.

NOTE
In Step 19, hold the shift cam assembly together during removal. If the pin retainer moves away from the shift cam, 6 small pins may fall out.

19. Remove the bolt (A, **Figure 11**) securing the shift cam assembly (B, **Figure 11**) and remove the shift cam assembly from the end of the shift drum. If the locating pin (**Figure 12**) in the end of the shift drum is loose, remove it. If not, leave it in place.

20. Inspect the components as described in this chapter.

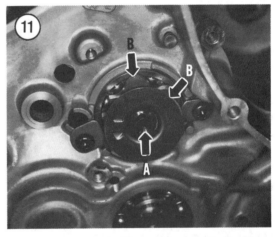

Inspection

1. Inspect the gearshift shaft (**Figure 13**) for bending, wear or other damage; replace if necessary.

2. Make sure the bolt (A, **Figure 14**) securing the shift lever (B, **Figure 14**) is tight. Tighten if necessary.

3. Inspect the return spring (A, **Figure 15**) on the link arm. If broken or weak, it must be replaced.

4. Inspect the bore (B, **Figure 15**) in the link arm where it rides on the gearshift shaft for wear or damage. Replace the link arm if necessary.

5. Install the roller (**Figure 16**) on the link arm and rotate it by hand. It must rotate freely with no binding. Replace the roller if necessary.

6. Inspect the gear shifter (**Figure 17**) for wear or damage. Move the short arm back and forth; it must move freely and then return to its original position. If there is any binding, the gear shifter assembly must be replaced.

7. Inspect the return spring (**Figure 18**) on the gear shifter. If broken or weak, the gear shifter must be replaced.

8. Inspect the bore (**Figure 19**) in the gear shifter where it rides on the shoulder bolt for wear or damage. Replace the gear shifter if necessary.

9. Separate the pin retainer (A, **Figure 20**) from the shift cam (B, **Figure 20**). If necessary, remove the 6 small pins.

10. Inspect the shift cam (A, **Figure 21**), the pin retainer (B, **Figure 21**) and the pins (C, **Figure 21**) for wear or damage. Replace any worn parts.

11. Assemble the 6 pins, the pin retainer (A, **Figure 20**) and the shift cam (B, **Figure 20**).

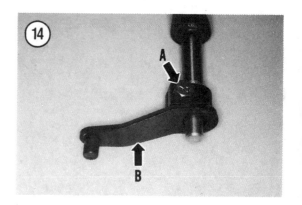

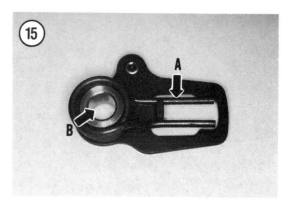

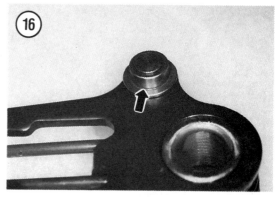

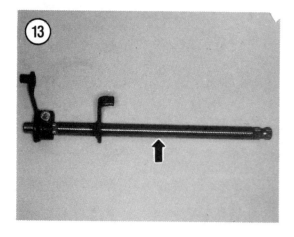

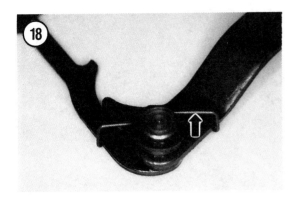

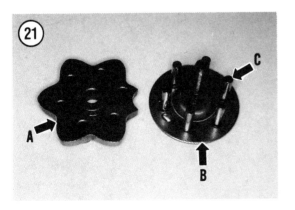

Installation

1. Make sure the locating pin (**Figure 12**) is in place in the end of the shift drum.

2. Align the hole (A, **Figure 22**) in the backside of the shift cam with the pin (B, **Figure 22**) in the end of the shift drum.

3. Apply blue Loctite (No. 242) to the bolt threads prior to installation. Install the shift cam assembly (B, **Figure 11**) and install, but do not tighten the bolt (A, **Figure 11**) securing the shift cam assembly.

4. Align the pin retainer protrusions (A, **Figure 23**) so they are positioned over one of the pins and aligned with the shift cam (B, **Figure 23**) as shown. Tighten the bolt securely.

5. Install the cam stopper arm (C, **Figure 10**) and washer onto the crankcase.

6. Apply blue Loctite (No. 242) to the bolt threads prior to installation. Install the bolt (B, **Figure 10**) securing the cam stopper arm and tighten securely.

7. Move the cam stopper arm against the shift cam and hook the return spring (A, **Figure 10**) onto the post on the crankcase.

7

8. Install the link arm (**Figure 9**) onto the crankcase and position the return spring onto the threaded stud as shown in **Figure 24**.

9. Position the roller with the flange side (**Figure 25**) going on first and install it onto the link arm (**Figure 26**).

10. Install the shoulder bolt through the gear shifter and install the washer on the backside of the gear shifter. Apply blue Loctite (No. 242) to the bolt threads prior to installation on the crankcase.

11. Lift the short arm of the gear shifter (A, **Figure 27**) away from the shift drum shift cam and install the gear shifter (B, **Figure 27**) onto the crankcase.

12. Securely tighten the shoulder bolt (C, **Figure 27**) securing the gear shifter.

13. Move the short arm of the gear shifter into position on the shift cam (B, **Figure 7**).

14. Install both clutch assemblies as described in Chapter Six.

15. Install the shift lever assembly (**Figure 28**) into the crankcase. Push it into the crankcase and align the shift lever finger into mesh with the link arm (**Figure 29**). Push the shift lever assembly in until it bottoms out.

NOTE
*In Step 16, refer to the drawing in **Figure 30** and the photograph in **Figure 31**.*

16. On the left-hand side of the engine, perform the following:

    a. Align the slit on the sub-transmission gearshift lever with the punch mark on the gearshift shaft and install the lever (A, **Figure 31**).

    b. Install the bolt (B, **Figure 31**) and tighten securely.

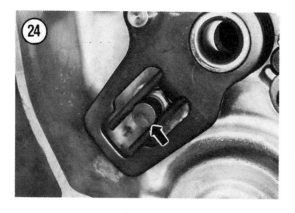

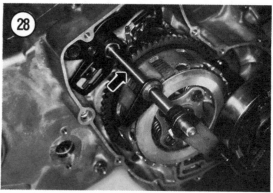

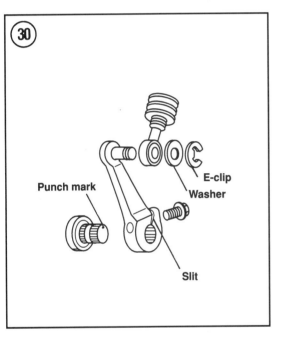

Punch mark

E-clip

Washer

Slit

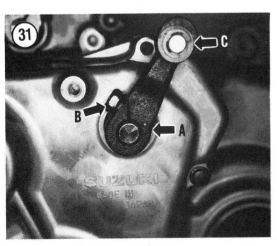

c. Remove the E-ring and washer (C, **Figure 31**) from the gearshift lever pivot post.

d. If removed install the bushing into the control cable pivot end, then apply a light coat of molybdenum disulfide grease to the inner surface of the control cable pivot bushing (**Figure 32**).

e. Connect the control cable (A, **Figure 33**) onto the lever pivot post. Don't lose the bushing during installation.

f. Install the washer and E-clip (B, **Figure 33**) securing the control cable to the sub-transmission gearshift lever. Make sure the E-clip is properly installed in the pivot post groove.

17. Install the right-hand crankcase cover as described under *Right-hand Crankcase Cover Removal/Installation* in Chapter Five.

18. Move the brake cable and hose back into position.

19. Connect the rear brake cable onto the rear brake pedal. Install the washer, pivot pin, washer and new cotter pin. Bend the ends over completely.

20. Move the right-hand rear suspension arm up into position and install the right-hand shock absorber as described in Chapter Twelve.

21. Install the right-hand rear wheel as described in Chapter Twelve.

22. Install the rear fender and seat as described in Chapter Fourteen.

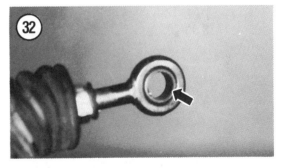

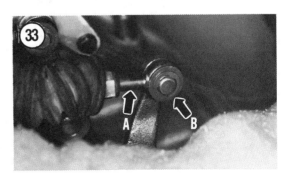

23. Refill the engine with the recommended type and quantity of engine oil as described in Chapter Three.

24. Start the engine and check for oil leaks.

25. Adjust the clutch as described in Chapter Three.

MAIN TRANSMISSION INTERNAL SHIFT MECHANISM

The main transmission used on all models is shown in **Figure 34**. The internal shift mechanisms used on all models is shown in **Figure 35**.

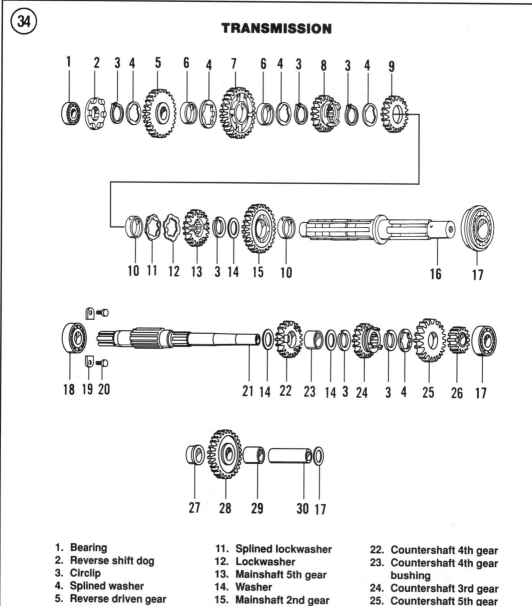

34

TRANSMISSION

1. Bearing
2. Reverse shift dog
3. Circlip
4. Splined washer
5. Reverse driven gear
6. Bushing
7. Mainshaft 1st gear
8. Mainshaft 4th gear
9. Mainshaft 3rd gear
10. Mainshaft 3rd gear bushing
11. Splined lockwasher
12. Lockwasher
13. Mainshaft 5th gear
14. Washer
15. Mainshaft 2nd gear
16. Mainshaft
17. Bearing
18. Bearing
19. Bearing retainer
20. Bolt
21. Countershaft
22. Countershaft 4th gear
23. Countershaft 4th gear bushing
24. Countershaft 3rd gear
25. Countershaft 5th gear
26. Countershaft 2nd gear
27. Bearing
28. Reverse idle gear
29. Reverse idle gear bushing
30. Reverse idle gear shaft

35 MAIN TRANSMISSION
INTERNAL SHIFT MECHANISM

1. Shoulder bolt	20. Reverse gearshift shaft	36. Pin
2. Gear shifter	21. Washer	37. Shift cam
3. Washer	22. Oil seal	38. Bolt
4. Roller	23. Reverse gearshift lever	39. Collar
5. Stud	24. Reverse indicator switch	40. Bearing retainer
6. Gearshift lever (engine side)	25. O-ring	41. Bearing
7. Washer	26. Reverse shift fork	42. Locating pin
8. Collar	27. Shift fork No. 1	43. Gearshift drum
9. E-clip	28. Shift fork No. 2	44. Spring
10. Clamping bolt	29. Shift fork shaft No. 1	45. Pin
11. Return spring	30. Gearshift lever (foot pedal)	46. O-ring
12. Link arm	31. O-ring	47. Neutral switch
13. Gearshift shaft	32. Collar	48. Washer
14. Return spring	33. Bolt	49. Lockwasher
15. Oil seal	34. Bolt	50. Screw
16. Reverse cam stopper	35. Shift cam plate	51. Cam stopper arm
17. Gasket		52. Washer
18. Spring		53. Shift fork No. 3
19. Stopper pin		54. Shift fork shaft No. 2

Removal

1. Remove the engine from the frame as described in Chapter Five.

2. Remove the reverse cam detent (**Figure 36**) and gasket from the right-hand crankcase half.

3. Disassemble the crankcase as described in Chapter Five.

4. Remove the washer (**Figure 37**) from the reverse idle shaft.

5. Remove the reverse idle gear (**Figure 38**) from the reverse idle shaft.

6. Slide the bushing (A, **Figure 39**) and spacer (B, **Figure 39**) off of the reverse idle shaft.

7. Remove the reverse idle shaft (C, **Figure 39**).

8. Remove the shift fork shaft No. 2 (A, **Figure 40**), then the No. 3 shift fork (B, **Figure 40**).

9. Temporarily remove shift fork shaft No. 1 (A, **Figure 41**).

10. Disengage the reverse shift fork (B, **Figure 41**) from the reverse gearshift shaft (C, **Figure 41**).

11. Remove the reverse gearshift shaft and washer (C, **Figure 41**).

12. Reinstall shift fork shaft No. 1 back through the shift forks (A, **Figure 41**). Keep the shift forks engaged with the mainshaft assembly as they will be removed along with the mainshaft as an assembly.

13. Partially pull both the mainshaft/shift fork assembly and the countershaft assembly up from the right-hand crankcase half.

14. Remove the countershaft assembly (A, **Figure 42**) from the right-hand crankcase half.

15. Remove the main shaft assembly/shift fork assembly (B, **Figure 42**) from the right-hand crankcase half.

16. Remove the shift drum (**Figure 43**) from the right-hand crankcase half.

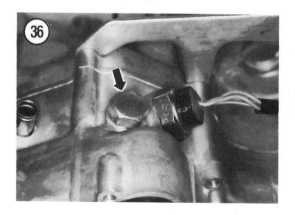

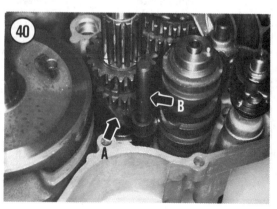

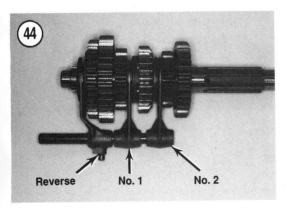

Reverse   No. 1   No. 2

17. If necessary, disassemble and inspect the shift forks and transmission assemblies as described in this chapter.

Installation

1. Coat all bearing and sliding surfaces of the shift drum with assembly oil and install the shift drum (**Figure 43**). Rotate the shift drum to the neutral position. This will make it easier to insert the shift fork pin followers into the shift drum.

2. If the shift forks were removed from the main shaft, or if the shaft was disassembled, install the shift forks into their respective gears as shown in **Figure 44**, then install the No. 1 shift fork shaft.

3. Install the main shaft/shift fork assembly into the right-hand crankcase (**Figure 45**). Do not push the assembly all the way down until the countershaft assembly is installed and meshed with the countershaft assembly.

4. Install the countershaft assembly and mesh it with the main shaft (**Figure 46**). After both shaft assemblies are meshed together, push both assem-

7

blies down into their respective bearings until they bottom out (**Figure 47**).

5. After both assemblies are installed, tap on the end of both shafts with a plastic or rubber mallet to make sure they are completely seated.

6. Withdraw the No. 1 shift fork shaft (**Figure 48**), but leave the shift forks in place.

7. Install the washer (**Figure 49**) on the reverse gearshift shaft, then install the reverse gearshift shaft (**Figure 50**) into the right-hand crankcase.

8. Properly mesh the No. 2 and the No. 3 shift forks with the gearshift drum, then move both forks into alignment with the No. 1 shift fork shaft receptacle in the right-hand crankcase.

9. Properly mesh the reverse shift fork with the reverse shift shaft groove (**Figure 51**), then engage the fork with the gearshift drum (**Figure 52**).

10. Slowly insert the No. 1 shift fork shaft (**Figure 53**) through the reverse shift fork, the No. 2 shift fork and the No. 1 shift fork. Push the shift fork shaft (A, **Figure 54**) all the way down and into the receptacle in the right-hand crankcase.

11. Make sure the shift fork pins are still aligned with the shift drum and that the reverse shift fork is

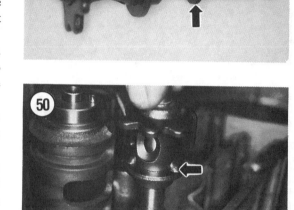

still aligned with the reverse shift shaft (B, **Figure 54**).

12. Install the No. 3 shift fork onto the No. 2 shift fork shaft (**Figure 55**).

13. Position the No. 2 shift fork shaft and shift fork assembly with the cam pin follower on the No. 3 shift fork (**Figure 56**) facing *up* away from the right-hand crankcase.

14. Mesh the No. 3 shift fork pin with the shift drum (A, **Figure 57**), then push the shift fork shaft (B, **Figure 57**) all the way down and into the receptacle in the right-hand crankcase.

15. Install the reverse idle shaft (**Figure 58**).

16. Install the spacer (**Figure 59**) onto the reverse idle shaft.

7

NOTE
*Some models may have a flange on one side of the bushing (**Figure 60**). On these models, position the bushing with the flange side going on last or toward the reverse idle gear that will be installed in Step 18.*

17. Install the bushing (**Figure 61**) onto the reverse idle shaft.

18. Position the reverse idle gear with the long shoulder side (**Figure 62**) going on first and install the reverse idle gear (**Figure 63**) onto the reverse idle shaft.

19. Install the washer (**Figure 64**) onto the reverse idle shaft.

20. Spin the transmission shafts and shift through all gears using the shift drum. Make sure you can shift into all gears. This is the time to find that something may be installed incorrectly—not after the crankcase is completely assembled.

NOTE
This procedure is best done with the aid of a helper as the assemblies are loose and won't spin very easily. Have the helper spin the transmission shaft while you turn the shift drum through all the gears.

21. Make sure the washer (**Figure 64**) is still in place on the reverse idle gear.

22. Assemble the crankcase as described in Chapter Five.

23. Install the reverse cam detent (**Figure 65**) and new gasket into the right-hand crankcase half and tighten securely.

24. Install the engine in the frame as described in Chapter Five.

**Transmission
Preliminary Inspection**

After the transmission shaft assemblies have been removed from the crankcase, clean and inspect the assemblies prior to disassembling them. Place the assembled shaft into a large can or plastic bucket and thoroughly clean with a petroleum based solvent such as kerosene and a stiff brush. Dry with compressed air or let it sit on rags to drip dry. Repeat for the other shaft assembly.

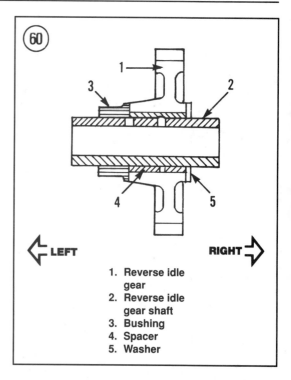

LEFT   RIGHT

1. Reverse idle gear
2. Reverse idle gear shaft
3. Bushing
4. Spacer
5. Washer

1. After they have been cleaned, visually inspect the components of the assemblies for excessive wear. Any burrs, pitting or roughness on the teeth of a gear will cause wear on the mating gear. Minor roughness can be cleaned up with an oilstone but there's little point in attempting to remove deep scars.

NOTE
Defective gears should be replaced. It's a good idea to replace the mating gear on the other shaft even though it may not show as much wear or damage.

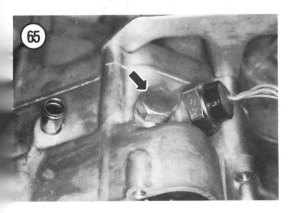

2. Carefully check the engagement dogs. If any are chipped, worn, rounded or missing, the affected gear must be replaced.

3. Rotate the transmission and shift drum bearings (**Figure 66**) in both crankcases by hand. Check for roughness, noise and radial play. Any bearing that is suspect should be replaced as described in Chapter Five.

4. If the transmission shafts are satisfactory and are not going to be disassembled, apply assembly oil or engine oil to all components and reinstall them in the crankcase as described in this chapter.

NOTE
If disassembling a used, well run-in (high mileage) transmission for the first time by yourself, pay particular attention to any additional shims that may have been added by a previous owner. Additional shims may have been added to take up the tolerance of worn components and must be reinstalled in the same position since the shims have developed a wear pattern. If new parts are going to be installed, these shims may be eliminated. This is something you will have to determine upon reassembly.

**Transmission
Service Notes**

1. A divided container, such as a restaurant type egg carton can be used to help maintain correct alignment and positioning of the parts. As you remove a part from the shaft, set it in one of the depressions in the same position from which it was removed as

7

shown in **Figure 67**. This is an easy way to remember the correct relationship of all parts.

2. The circlips are a tight fit on the transmission shafts. It is recommended to replace all circlips during reassembly.

3. Circlips will turn and fold over making removal and installation difficult. To ease replacement, open the circlips with a pair of circlip pliers while at the same time holding the back of the circlip with a pair of pliers and remove them. Repeat for installation.

Countershaft
Inspection

Inspect the clutch nut threads (A, **Figure 68**) and the clutch hub splines (B, **Figure 68**). If the threads have burrs or have minor damage, clean with a proper size metric thread die.

If any of the splines are damaged, the shaft must be replaced.

Countershaft
Disassembly/Assembly

The 2nd gear (**Figure 69**) is pressed onto the shaft. Replacing the gears on the countershaft requires a hydraulic press and special skills; therefore, this task should be entrusted to a Suzuki dealer or competent machine shop. If the shaft assembly has been serviced make sure the 5th gear (**Figure 70**) will spin freely after the 2nd gear has been pressed into place. There must be no binding that would hinder the rotation of either gear.

> *CAUTION*
> *The 2nd gear can be removed from the countershaft only **2 times**. If the 2nd gear must be removed for the third time, the countershaft shaft must be replaced as it can no longer retain the 2nd gear in the correct location on the shaft. Do not replace the 2nd gear as it is not the part that has worn from the gear installation procedure. The outer surface of the shaft, made of a softer grade of steel than the inner surface of the gear, has been worn down from the repeated pressing on and off of the gear, therefore the shaft must be replaced—not the gear.*

Main Shaft
Disassembly/Inspection

Refer to **Figure 71** for this procedure.

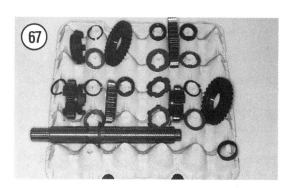

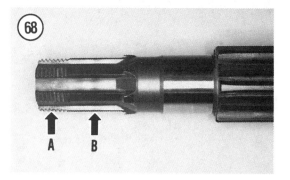

(71)

TRANSMISSION

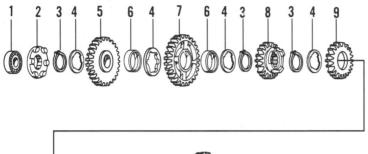

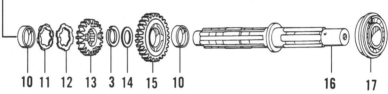

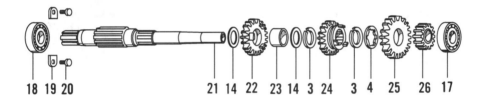

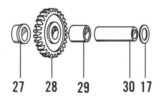

1. Bearing
2. Reverse shift dog
3. Circlip
4. Splined washer
5. Reverse driven gear
6. Bushing
7. Mainshaft 1st gear
8. Mainshaft 4th gear
9. Mainshaft 3rd gear
10. Mainshaft 3rd gear
    bushing
11. Splined lockwasher
12. Lockwasher
13. Mainshaft 5th gear
14. Washer
15. Mainshaft 2nd gear
16. Mainshaft

17. Bearing
18. Bearing
19. Bearing retainer
20. Bolt
21. Countershaft
22. Countershaft 4th gear
23. Countershaft 4th gear
    bushing
24. Countershaft 3rd gear
25. Countershaft 5th gear
26. Countershaft 2nd gear
27. Bearing
28. Reverse idle gear
29. Reverse idle gear
    bushing
30. Reverse idle gear shaft

1. If not cleaned in the *Preliminary Inspection* sequence, place the assembled shaft into a large can or plastic bucket and thoroughly clean with solvent and a stiff brush. Dry with compressed air or let it sit on rags to dry.

2. Slide off the reverse shift dog.

3. Remove the circlip and slide off the splined washer.

4. Slide off the reverse driven gear and gear bushing.

5. Rotate the splined washer in either direction to disengage the tangs from the grooves on the transmission shaft. Slide off the splined washer, 1st gear and 1st gear bushing.

6. Slide off the splined washer and remove the circlip.

7. Slide off the 4th gear.

8. Remove the circlip and splined washer.

9. Slide off the 3rd gear and 3rd gear bushing.

10. Rotate the splined lockwasher in either direction to disengage the tangs from the grooves on the transmission shaft. Slide off the splined lockwasher, then remove the splined washer.

11. Slide off the 5th gear.

12. Remove the circlip and washer.

13. Slide off the 2nd gear and 2nd gear bushing.

14. Check each gear for excessive wear, burrs, pitting, or chipped or missing teeth (**Figure 72**). Make sure the lugs on the gears (**Figure 73**) and on the reverse shift dog (A, **Figure 74**) are in good condition. Replace if necessary.

15. Check the outer surface (A, **Figure 75**) of each gear bushing for excessive wear, pitting or damage. Replace if necessary.

16. Check the inner surface (**Figure 76**) of each gear equipped with a bushing (A, **Figure 75**), for excessive wear, pitting or damage. Replace if necessary.

17. Check the inner splines of gears and gear bushings (B, **Figure 75**) and on the reverse shift dog (B, **Figure 74**) for wear or damage. Replace if necessary.

18. Inspect the splined washers for bending wear or damage. Replace if necessary.

19. Inspect the splined lockwashers and splined washers (**Figure 77**) for wear, cracks or damage. Replace if necessary.

20. Inspect the shift fork-to-gear clearance as described under *Internal Gearshift Mechanism* in this chapter.

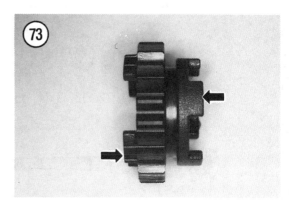

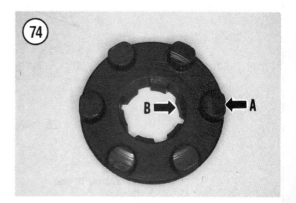

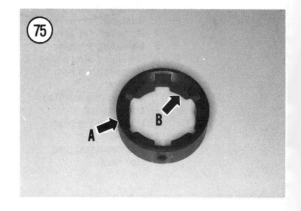

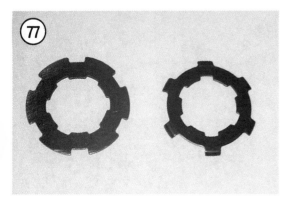

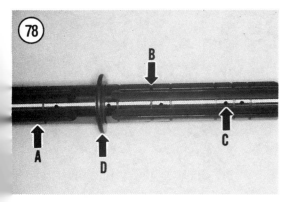

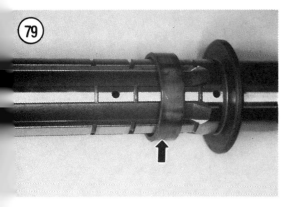

NOTE
Defective gears should be replaced. It is a good idea to replace the mating gear on the countershaft even though it may not show as much wear or damage.

21. Make sure that all gears slide smoothly on the main shaft splines.

NOTE
*Suzuki recommends that all circlips **be replaced every time** the transmission is disassembled to ensure proper gear alignment. Do not expand a circlip more than necessary to slide it over the shaft.*

22. Inspect the splines (A, **Figure 78**) and circlip grooves (B, **Figure 78**) on the countershaft. If any are damaged, the shaft must be replaced.

23. Make sure *all* oil control holes (C, **Figure 78**) are clear. If necessary, clean out with a piece of wire, then thoroughly clean with solvent. Blow each hole clear with compressed air.

24. Inspect the flange (D, **Figure 78**) for cracks, wear or damage. If damaged, the shaft must be replaced.

Main Shaft Assembly

1. Apply a light coat of clean engine oil to all sliding surfaces prior to installing any parts.

2. Slide on the 2nd gear bushing (**Figure 79**) and the 2nd gear (**Figure 80**).

3. Slide on the thrust washer (A, **Figure 81**) and install the circlip (B, **Figure 81**). Make sure the circlip is correctly seated (**Figure 82**).

4. Position the 5th gear with the shift fork groove going on last and slide on the 5th gear (**Figure 83**).

5. Slide on the splined washer and rotate it until the tangs go into the grooves on the transmission shaft splines (**Figure 84**).

6. Slide on the splined lockwasher (**Figure 85**). Push the lockwasher on until the tangs go into the open areas of the splined washer and lock the washer into place (**Figure 86**).

7. Align the oil hole (A, **Figure 87**) in the 3rd gear bushing with the oil hole (B, **Figure 87**) in the shaft and slide the bushing into place making sure the oil hole is aligned properly (**Figure 88**).

8. Position the 3rd gear with the chamfered surface on the teeth going on first (**Figure 89**) and slide on the 3rd gear (**Figure 90**).

9. Slide on the splined washer (A, **Figure 91**) and install the circlip (B, **Figure 91**). Make sure the circlip is correctly seated (**Figure 92**).

10. Position the 4th gear with the shift fork groove going on first and slide on the 4th gear (A, **Figure 93**).

11. Install the circlip (B, **Figure 93**). Make sure the circlip is correctly seated.

7

12. Slide on the splined washer (**Figure 94**).

13. Align the oil hole (A, **Figure 95**) in the 1st gear bushing with the oil hole (B, **Figure 95**) in the shaft and slide the bushing into place.

14. Position the 1st gear with the flush side going on last and install the 1st gear (**Figure 96**).

15. Slide on the splined washer (**Figure 97**) and rotate it until the tangs go into the grooves on the transmission shaft splines (**Figure 98**).

16. Align the oil hole (A, **Figure 99**) in the reverse driven gear bushing with the oil hole (B, **Figure 99**) in the shaft.

17. Slide the reverse driven gear bushing onto the shaft. Push the bushing on until the tangs (A, **Figure 100**) go into the open areas of the splined washer (B, **Figure 100**) (installed in Step 15) and lock the splined washer into place (**Figure 101**).

18. Position the reverse driven gear with the flush side on first (**Figure 102**) and install the reverse driven gear (**Figure 103**).

19. Slide the splined washer (**Figure 104**) onto the shaft and install the circlip (**Figure 105**). Make sure the circlip is correctly seated (**Figure 106**).

20. Slide on the reverse engagement dog (**Figure 107**) and push it all the way into the reverse driven gear (**Figure 108**).

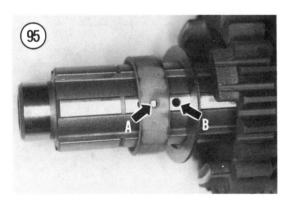

7

21. Refer to **Figure 109** for correct placement of all gears. Make sure all circlips are correctly seated in the countershaft grooves.

22. After both transmission shafts have been assembled, mesh the 2 assemblies together in the correct position (**Figure 110**). Check that the gear engages properly to the adjoining gear where applicable. This is your last check prior to installing the shaft assemblies into the crankcase; make sure they are correctly assembled.

Reverse Idle Gear Inspection

1. Clean all parts with solvent and a stiff brush. Dry with compressed air or let it sit on rags to dry (**Figure 111**).

2. Check the gear for excessive wear, burrs, pitting, or chipped or missing teeth (**Figure 112**). Replace if necessary.

3. Make sure the oil control holes (**Figure 113**) in the gear bushing and the reverse idle shaft are clear. Clean out with a piece of wire, then clean with solvent and blow out with compressed air.

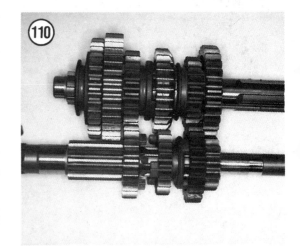

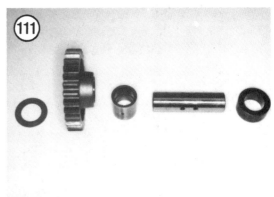

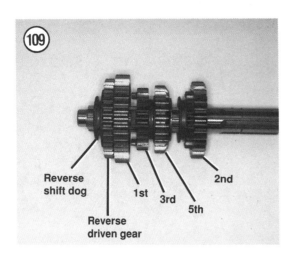

Reverse
shift dog   2nd
          1st
          3rd
          5th
Reverse
driven gear

4. Check the inner surface (**Figure 114**) of the gear for excessive wear, pitting or damage. Replace if necessary.

5. Check the outer surface of the gear bushing and the reverse idle shaft for excessive wear, pitting or damage. Replace if necessary.

6. Insert the gear bushing into the gear and rotate it by hand (**Figure 115**). It should rotate freely with no binding or looseness. Replace the worn part(s) if necessary.

7. Insert the reverse idle shaft into the gear bushing and rotate it by hand. It should rotate freely with no binding or looseness. Replace the worn part(s) if necessary.

MAIN TRANSMISSION
INTERNAL SHIFT MECHANISM
INSPECTION

Refer to **Figure 116** for this procedure.

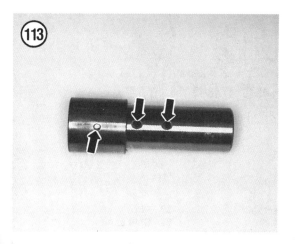

1. Inspect each shift fork for signs of wear or cracking. Check for bending and make sure each fork slides smoothly on the shaft. Replace any worn or damaged forks.

2. Check for any arc-shaped wear or burn marks on the shift fork fingers (**Figure 117**). This indicates that the shift fork has come in contact with the gear with excessive force. The fork fingers have become excessively worn and the fork(s) must be replaced.

3. Check the shift fork shift dowel pins (A, **Figure 118**) for wear or damage; replace as necessary.

4. Inspect the inner surface (B, **Figure 118**) of the shift fork where it rides on the shift fork shaft for excessive wear. Replace if necessary.

6. Roll each shift fork shaft on a flat surface such as a piece of plate glass and check for any bends. If the shaft is bent, it must be replaced.

7. Measure the width of the gearshift fork fingers with a micrometer (**Figure 119**). Replace the ones worn to the service limit (or less) listed in **Table 1**.

8. Install the shift forks onto their respective shafts. Refer to **Figure 120** and **Figure 121**. Move the forks back and forth and make sure they move freely with no binding. Replace any worn or damaged parts.

9. Install each shift fork into its respective gear. Use a flat feeler gauge and measure the clearance between the shift fork fingers and groove in the gear or shift dog (**Figure 122**). The specified clearance is listed in **Table 1**. Replace the worn part(s).

CAUTION
It is recommended that marginal shift forks be replaced. Worn forks can cause the transmission to slip out of gear, leading to more serious and expensive damage.

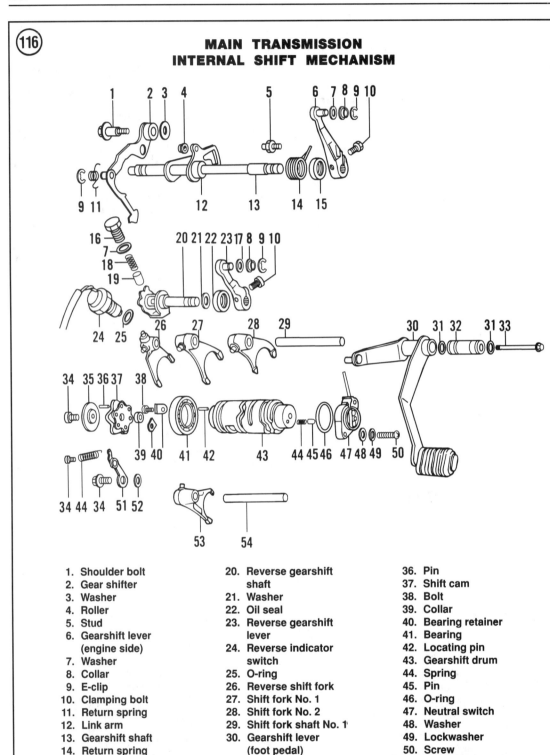

MAIN TRANSMISSION INTERNAL SHIFT MECHANISM

1. Shoulder bolt	20. Reverse gearshift shaft	36. Pin
2. Gear shifter	21. Washer	37. Shift cam
3. Washer	22. Oil seal	38. Bolt
4. Roller	23. Reverse gearshift lever	39. Collar
5. Stud	24. Reverse indicator switch	40. Bearing retainer
6. Gearshift lever (engine side)	25. O-ring	41. Bearing
7. Washer	26. Reverse shift fork	42. Locating pin
8. Collar	27. Shift fork No. 1	43. Gearshift drum
9. E-clip	28. Shift fork No. 2	44. Spring
10. Clamping bolt	29. Shift fork shaft No. 1	45. Pin
11. Return spring	30. Gearshift lever (foot pedal)	46. O-ring
12. Link arm	31. O-ring	47. Neutral switch
13. Gearshift shaft	32. Collar	48. Washer
14. Return spring	33. Bolt	49. Lockwasher
15. Oil seal	34. Bolt	50. Screw
16. Reverse cam stopper	35. Shift cam plate	51. Cam stopper arm
17. Gasket		52. Washer
18. Spring		53. Shift fork No. 3
19. Stopper pin		54. Shift fork shaft No. 2

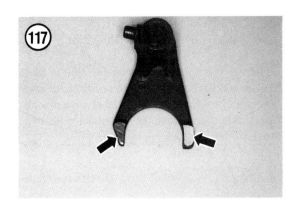

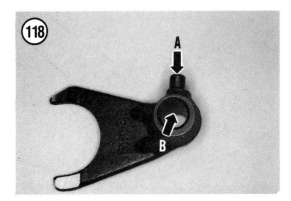

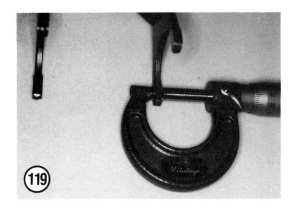

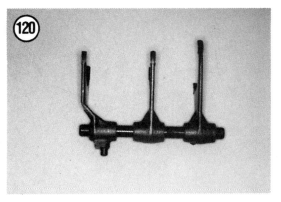

10. If the width of the shift fork fingers are within tolerance, but the clearance between the fork fingers and the gear groove is excessive, use a vernier caliper and measure the gear groove width (**Figure 123**). If the gear groove width exceeds the dimension listed in **Table 1**, the gear(s) must be replaced.

7

11. Check the grooves in the shift drum (**Figure 124**) for wear or roughness. If any of the groove profiles have excessive wear or damage, replace the shift drum.

12. Remove the pin and spring (**Figure 125**) from the left-hand end of the shift drum. Inspect the pin for wear and make sure the spring has not sagged. Replace any part(s) that is worn or damaged. If the parts are okay, reinstall them in the end of the shift drum.

13. Inspect the locating pin (**Figure 126**) in the right-hand end of the shift drum for wear or damage. Replace the pin if necessary.

14. Inspect the engagement groove (A, **Figure 127**) in the sub-transmission gearshift cam. Check the shaft portion (B, **Figure 127**) for bending or other damage. Also check the splines (C, **Figure 127**) for the shift lever for wear or damage. Replace if necessary.

15. Check the cam stopper ramps (**Figure 128**) for wear or damage. Replace the gearshift cam if necessary.

16. Apply a light coat of oil to the shift fork shafts and the inside bores of the shift forks prior to installation.

SUB-TRANSMISSION AND SHIFT MECHANISM

The sub-transmission components are the same on all models with the exception of the additional driven gear assembly for the 4-wheel drive models. Where differences occur, they are noted in the text.

Refer to the following illustrations for this procedure:

a. Figure 129: 2-wheel drive models sub-transmission.

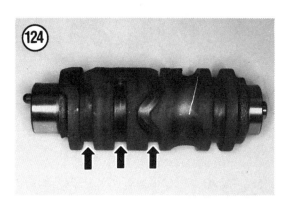

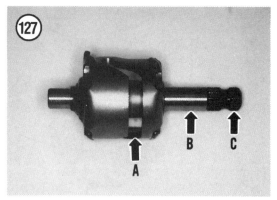

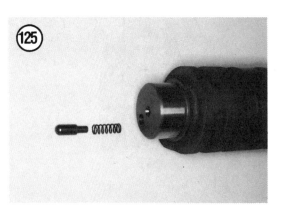

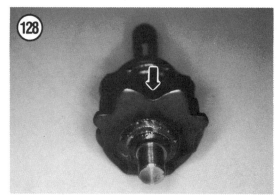

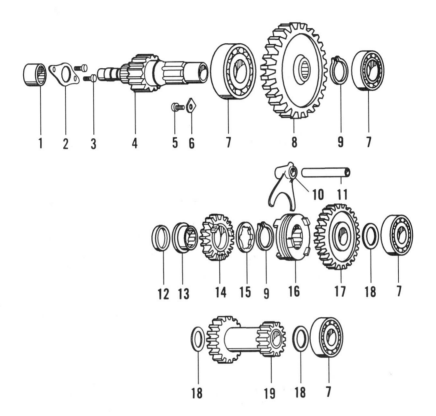

SUB-TRANSMISSION AND SHIFT MECHANISM (2-WHEEL DRIVE MODELS)

1. Needle bearing
2. Bearing retainer
3. Bolt
4. Output shaft
5. Screw
6. Bearing retainer
7. Ball bearing
8. Driven gear No. 1
9. Circlip
10. Shift fork No. 2
11. Shift fork shaft No. 2
12. Spacer
13. Drive gear No. 1 bushing
14. Drive gear No. 1
15. Splined washer
16. Drive gear shift dog
17. Drive gear No. 2
18. Washer
19. Idle gear

7

b. Figure 130: 4-wheel drive models sub-transmission.

c. Figure 131: sub-transmission shifter mechanism.

Removal

1. Remove the engine from the frame as described in Chapter Five.

2. On the left-hand side of the engine, remove the bolt (A, **Figure 132**) and remove the sub-transmission gearshift lever (B, **Figure 132**).

3. Remove the left-hand crankcase cover as described under *Right-hand Crankcase Cover Removal* in Chapter Five.

4. On 4-wheel drive models, perform the following:

    a. Remove the washer (**Figure 133**) from the end of the output shaft.

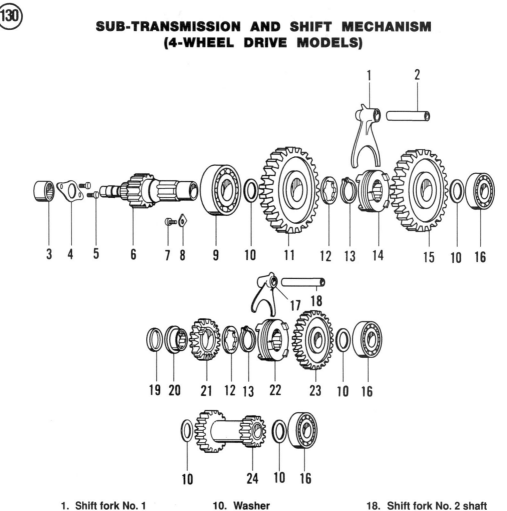

(130)

SUB-TRANSMISSION AND SHIFT MECHANISM (4-WHEEL DRIVE MODELS)

1. Shift fork No. 1
2. Shift fork No. 1 shaft
3. Needle bearing
4. Bearing retainer
5. Bolt
6. Output shaft
7. Screw
8. Bearing retainer
9. Ball bearing
10. Washer
11. Driven gear No. 1
12. Splined washer
13. Circlip
14. Driven gear shift dog
15. Driven gear No. 2
16. Ball bearing
17. Shift fork No. 2
18. Shift fork No. 2 shaft
19. Spacer
20. Drive gear No. 1 bushing
21. Drive gear No. 1
22. Drive gear shift dog
23. Drive gear No. 2
24. Idle gear

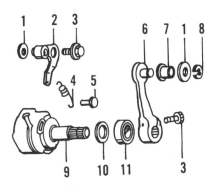

SUB-TRANSMISSION SHIFTER MECHANISM

1. Washer
2. Shift cam stopper arm
3. Bolt
4. Spring
5. Post
6. Gearshift lever
7. Bushing
8. E-clip
9. Gearshift cam
10. Washer
11. Oil seal

b. Slide off the driven gear No. 2 (**Figure 134**).

5. Remove the washer from the end of the transmission main shaft.

6. Slide off the drive gear No. 2 (**Figure 135**).

7. Remove the washer (**Figure 136**) from the end of the idle gear.

8. Remove the idle gear (**Figure 137**) and the thick washer (**Figure 138**) from the transmission countershaft.

9. On all models, withdraw the No. 1 shift fork shaft (A, **Figure 139**), then remove the No. 1 shift fork (B, **Figure 139**).

10. On 4-wheel drive models, withdraw the No. 2 shift fork shaft (A, **Figure 140**), then remove the No. 2 shift fork (B, **Figure 140**) and the driven gear shift dog (C, **Figure 140**).

11. Remove the circlip and washer (**Figure 141**), then slide off the drive gear No. 1 (**Figure 142**).

12. Slide off the bushing (A, **Figure 143**) and the spacer (B, **Figure 143**).

13. Remove the circlip and washer (**Figure 144**), then slide off the driven gear No. 1 (**Figure 145**).

14. Slide off the washer (**Figure 146**).

15. Disengage the gearshift cam stopper arm (A, **Figure 147**) from the gearshift cam and remove the gearshift cam (B, **Figure 147**) from the crankcase.

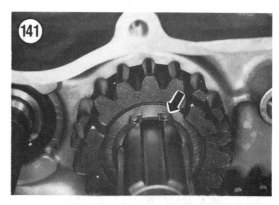

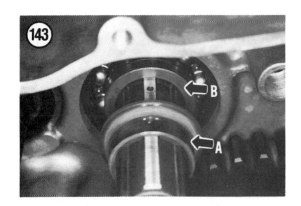

16. Unhook the return spring (A, **Figure 148**), then remove the bolt (B, **Figure 148**) and remove the gearshift stopper arm and washer (C, **Figure 148**).

Sub-transmission
Gear Inspection

1. Clean all parts with solvent and a stiff brush. Dry with compressed air or let it sit on rags to dry.
2. Check each gear for excessive wear, burrs, pitting, or chipped or missing teeth (**Figure 149**). Replace if necessary.

7

3. Check the bushing surface (**Figure 150**) of the gears for wear or damage.

4. Inspect the drive gear No. 1 as follows:

   a. Check the inner surface (A, **Figure 151**) of the gear where the bushing rides for excessive wear, pitting or damage. Replace if necessary.

   b. Check the outer surface of the bushing (B, **Figure 151**) for excessive wear, pitting or damage. Replace if necessary.

   c. Insert the gear bushing into the gear and rotate it by hand (**Figure 152**). It should rotate freely with no binding or looseness. Replace the worn part(s) if necessary.

5. Check the lugs on the gears (C, **Figure 151**) and the dog engagement receptacles (**Figure 153**) for excessive wear or damage. Replace if necessary.

6. Inspect the idle gear as follows:

   a. Check each gear for excessive wear, burrs, pitting, or chipped or missing teeth (**Figure 154**). Replace if necessary.

   b. Check the bushing surfaces of the gear for wear or damage. Refer to **Figure 155** and **Figure 156**.

Sub-transmission
Shift Mechanism Inspection

1. Inspect each shift fork for signs of wear or cracking. Check for bending and make sure each fork slides smoothly on the shaft. Replace any worn or damaged forks.

2. Check for any arc-shaped wear or burned marks on the shift fork fingers (**Figure 157**). This indicates that the shift fork has come in contact with the gear with excessive force. The fork fingers have become excessively worn and the fork(s) must be replaced.

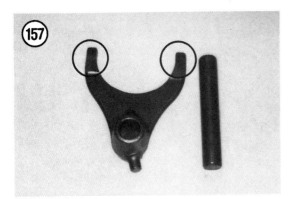

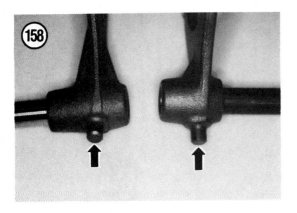

3. Check the shift fork shift dowel pins (**Figure 158**) for wear or damage; replace as necessary.

4. Inspect the inner surface (A, **Figure 159**) of the shift fork where it rides on the shift fork shaft for excessive wear. Replace if necessary.

5. Roll each shift fork shaft (B, **Figure 159**) on a flat surface such as a piece of plate glass and check for any bends. If the shaft is bent, it must be replaced.

6. Measure the width of the gearshift fork fingers with a micrometer (**Figure 160**). Replace the ones worn to the service limit listed in **Table 1** (or less).

7. Install the shift forks onto their respective shafts (**Figure 161**). Move the forks back and forth to make

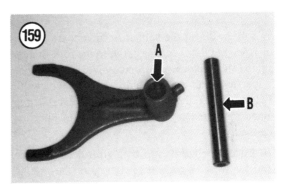

7

sure they move freely with no binding. Replace any worn or damaged parts.

8. Install each shift fork into its respective shift dog. Use a flat feeler gauge and measure the clearance between the shift fork fingers and the groove in the gear or shift dog (**Figure 162**). The specified clearance is listed in **Table 1**. Replace the worn part(s).

> *CAUTION*
> *It is recommended that marginal shift forks be replaced. Worn forks can cause the sub-transmission to slip out of gear, leading to more serious and expensive damage.*

9. If the width of the shift fork fingers are within tolerance but the clearance between the fork fingers and the shift dog groove is excessive, use a vernier caliper and measure the shift dog groove width (**Figure 163**). If the gear groove width exceeds the dimension listed in **Table 1**, the gear(s) must be replaced.

10. Check the grooves in both shift dogs (**Figure 164**) for wear or roughness. If any of the groove

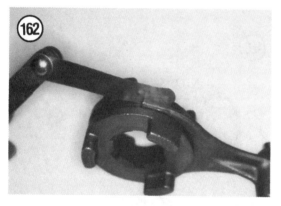

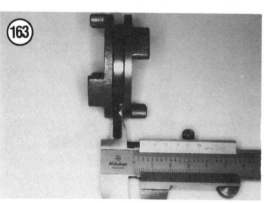

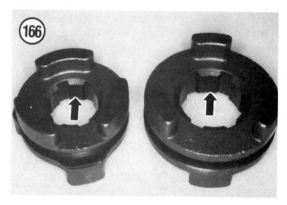

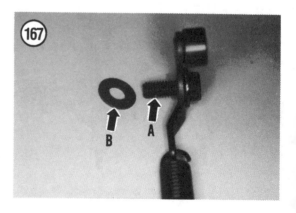

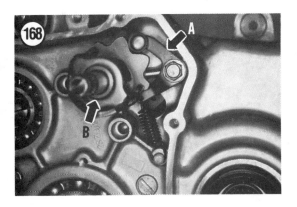

profiles have excessive wear or damage, replace the shift dog(s).

11. Check that the engagement lugs (**Figure 165**) on the shift dogs are in good condition. If any are damaged, replace the shift dog(s) if necessary.

12. Inspect the inner splines (**Figure 166**) of the shift dogs for wear or damage. Replace the shift dog(s) if necessary.

13. Apply a light coat of oil to the shift fork shafts and the inside bores of the shift forks prior to installation.

Installation

1. Insert the bolt (A, **Figure 167**) through the gearshift stopper arm and install the washer (B, **Figure 167**) onto the bolt. Apply a light coat of blue Loctite (No. 242) to the bolt threads prior to installation.

2. Install the gearshift stopper arm assembly (C, **Figure 148**) onto the crankcase. Make sure the washer is still in place on the bolt. Tighten the bolt (B, **Figure 148**) securely, then hook the return spring (A, **Figure 148**) onto the post.

3. Move the gearshift cam stopper arm (A, **Figure 168**) up out of the way and install the gearshift cam (B, **Figure 168**) onto the crankcase. Release the arm onto the gearshift cam.

4. Slide on the washer (**Figure 146**).

5. Position the driven gear No. 1 with the shoulder side (**Figure 169**) going on first and install the driven gear No. 1 (**Figure 145**).

6. Install the washer (**Figure 170**) and the circlip (**Figure 171**). Make sure the circlip is seated correctly (**Figure 144**) in the shaft groove.

7. Slide on the spacer (**Figure 172**).

8. Align the oil hole (**Figure 173**) in the bushing with the shaft oil hole (**Figure 174**) and slide the bushing on all the way.

9. Slide the drive gear No. 1 (**Figure 175**) onto the bushing and push the gear and bushing on all the way.

10. Slide on the washer (A, **Figure 176**) and install the circlip (B, **Figure 176**). Make sure the circlip is seated correctly (**Figure 141**) in the shaft groove.

11. On 4-wheel drive models, perform the following:

  a. Slide the driven gear shift dog (A, **Figure 177**) onto the shaft.

  b. Position the No. 2 shift fork with the long shoulder (A, **Figure 178**) side facing away from the crankcase and insert the No. 2 shift fork shaft (B, **Figure 178**) into the No. 2 shift fork.

  c. Install the No. 2 shift fork (B, **Figure 177**) onto the driven gear shift dog groove.

  d. Move the No. 2 shift fork and shaft (C, **Figure 177**) up and into position in the gearshift cam. Make sure the cam pin follower is inserted correctly into the gearshift cam (A, **Figure 179**).

  e. Push the shaft (B, **Figure 179**) into the receptacle in the crankcase (C, **Figure 179**) until it stops.

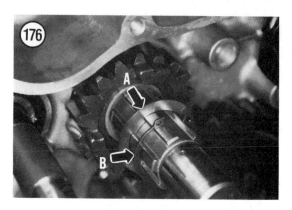

NOTE
*The drive gear shift dog is **not** symmetrical and must be installed as described in Step 12. If installed backward, the shift dog will not operate correctly.*

12. Position the drive gear shift dog with the thinner portion (shift fork groove-to-edge of dog) going on first toward the driven gear No. 1 (A, **Figure 180**).

13. Position the No. 1 shift fork with the long shoulder side going on first toward the crankcase and insert the No. 1 shift fork (B, **Figure 180**) onto the drive gear shift dog.

14. Insert the No. 1 shift fork shaft (C, **Figure 180**) into the No. 1 shift fork (B, **Figure 180**).

15. Slide the drive gear shift dog assembly (A, **Figure 181**) onto the shaft (B, **Figure 181**) and into position in the gearshift cam (C, **Figure 181**). Make sure the cam pin follower is inserted correctly into the gearshift cam (A, **Figure 182**).

16. Push the shaft (B, **Figure 182**) into the receptacle in the crankcase until it stops.

17. Install the thick washer (**Figure 183**) onto the transmission countershaft. Push the washer all the way on (**Figure 184**).

18. Position the idle gear with the larger diameter gear end going on first and install the idle gear (**Figure 185**).

19. Install the washer (**Figure 186**) onto the end of the idle gear shaft.

20. Position the drive gear No. 2 with the shift dog receptacle side (**Figure 187**) going on first and install the drive gear No. 2 (**Figure 188**).

21. Install the washer (**Figure 189**) onto the end of the transmission main shaft.

22. On 4-wheel drive models, perform the following:

   a. Position the driven gear No. 2 with the shift dog receptacle side (**Figure 190**) going on first and install the driven gear No. 2 (**Figure 191**).

NOTE
*At this time, both the drive gear No. 2 (A, **Figure 192**) and the driven gear No. 2 (B, **Figure 192**) should be flush with each other where both gears mesh (C, **Figure 192**). If they are not flush, one of the gears is installed backward. Correct the problem at this time.*

   b. Install the washer (**Figure 193**) onto the end of the output shaft.

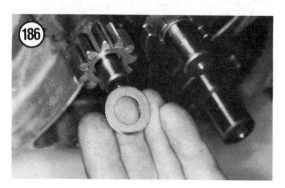

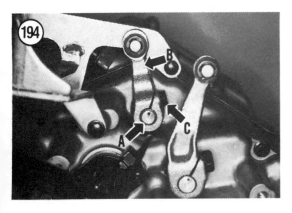

23. Install the left-hand crankcase cover as described under *Right-hand Crankcase Cover Removal* in Chapter Five.

24. On the left-hand side of the engine, align the split on the sub-transmission gearshift lever with the index mark on the end of the shaft (A, **Figure 194**) and install the sub-transmission gearshift lever (B, **Figure 194**). Install the bolt (C, **Figure 194**) and tighten securely.

25. Install the engine into the frame as described in Chapter Five.

GEARSHIFT LEVER CONTROL MECHANISM

Refer to the following illustrations for this procedure:

a. Figure 195: 2-wheel drive models.

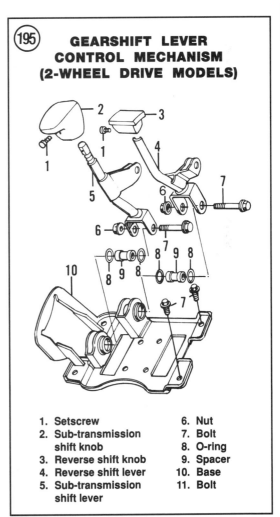

GEARSHIFT LEVER CONTROL MECHANISM (2-WHEEL DRIVE MODELS)

1. Setscrew	6. Nut
2. Sub-transmission shift knob	7. Bolt
3. Reverse shift knob	8. O-ring
4. Reverse shift lever	9. Spacer
5. Sub-transmission shift lever	10. Base
	11. Bolt

7

b. Figure 196: 4-wheel drive models.

Gearshift Lever Assembly Removal/Installation

1. Remove the seat as described under *Seat Removal/Installation* in Chapter Fourteen.
2. Remove the setscrew (**Figure 197**) securing each shift knob.
3. Remove the sub-transmission shift knob (A, **Figure 198**), the reverse shift knob (B, **Figure 198**) and

on 4-wheel drive models, the range selection lever knob (C, **Figure 198**) from the shift levers.

4. Remove the screws (**Figure 199**) at the rear securing the shift lever cover.

NOTE
Move the handlebar from full lock side-to-side to expose the front screws.

5. Remove the screws at the front securing the shift lever cover. Refer to **Figure 200** and A, **Figure 201**.
6. Unscrew the fuel filler cap (B, **Figure 201**).

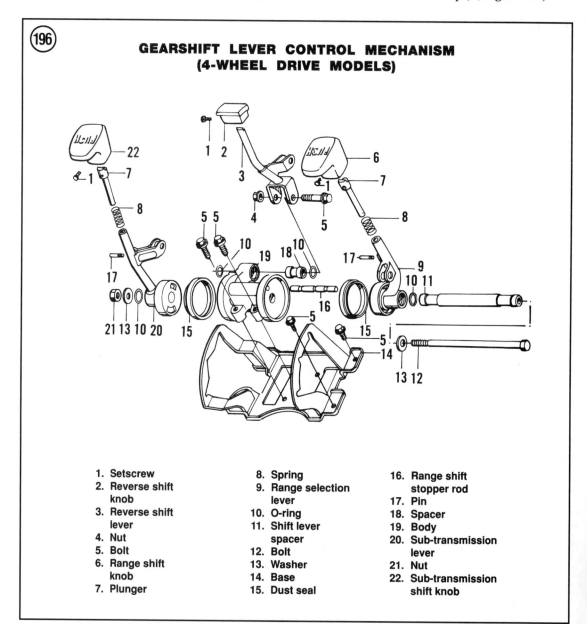

GEARSHIFT LEVER CONTROL MECHANISM (4-WHEEL DRIVE MODELS)

1. Setscrew
2. Reverse shift knob
3. Reverse shift lever
4. Nut
5. Bolt
6. Range shift knob
7. Plunger
8. Spring
9. Range selection lever
10. O-ring
11. Shift lever spacer
12. Bolt
13. Washer
14. Base
15. Dust seal
16. Range shift stopper rod
17. Pin
18. Spacer
19. Body
20. Sub-transmission lever
21. Nut
22. Sub-transmission shift knob

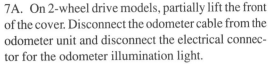

7A. On 2-wheel drive models, partially lift the front of the cover. Disconnect the odometer cable from the odometer unit and disconnect the electrical connector for the odometer illumination light.

7B. On 4-wheel drive models, remove the shift lever cover (**Figure 202**).

8. Reinstall the fuel filler cap and tighten securely.

9. Remove the screw, cable clamp and washer (A, **Figure 203**) securing the air filter air intake tube to the frame rail.

10. Loosen the clamp screw and move the front clamp back onto the rubber connector, away from the tube.

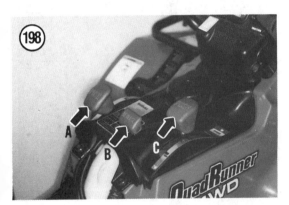

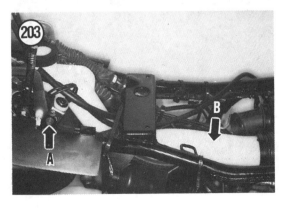

11. Remove the air filter air intake tube (B, **Figure 203**) from the frame rail.

12. Disconnect the upper end of the control cables (A, **Figure 204**) from the shift levers as described in this chapter.

13. Remove the bolts (B, **Figure 204**) securing the gearshift lever base to the frame and remove the base assembly from the frame.

14. Install by reversing these removal steps. Tighten the mounting bolts securely.

Control Cable
Removal/Installation

1. Perform Steps 1-7 of *Gearshift Lever Assembly Removal/Installation* in this chapter.

2. At the upper end of the control cable, perform the following:

   a. Remove the E-clip from the pivot pin(s).

   b. Withdraw the pivot pin and disconnect the control cable(s) from the gearshift lever(s) (**Figure 205**).

   c. Reinstall the pivot pin and E-clip onto the end of the control cable(s) to avoid misplacing them.

3. Remove the E-clip and washer (A, **Figure 206**) from the sub-transmission lever pivot post.

4. Remove the cable (B, **Figure 206**) from the pivot pin. Don't lose the collar on the pivot pin.

5. Reinstall the washer and E-clip onto the pivot pin to avoid misplacing them.

6. Remove the retaining clip (**Figure 207**) securing the control cable to the mounting bracket on the crankcase.

7. Move the control cable up and out of the mounting bracket, then reinstall the retaining clip back onto the control cable to avoid misplacing it.

8. Disconnect the cable from any retaining brackets on the frame (**Figure 208**).

NOTE
The piece of string attached in the next step is used to pull the new control ca-

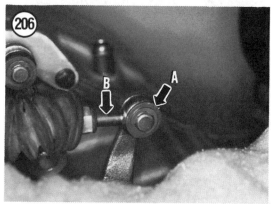

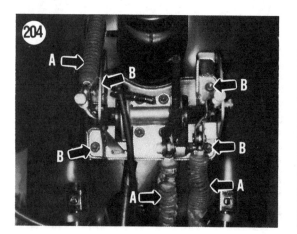

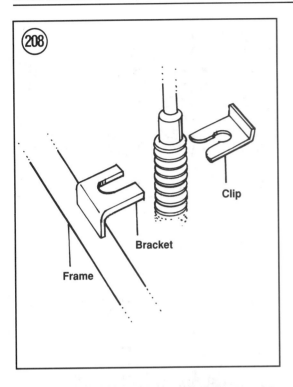

Frame

Bracket

Clip

ble(s) back through the frame so they will be routed in exactly the same position as the old ones.

9. Tie a piece of heavy string or cord (approximately 6 ft. [2 m long]) to the crankcase shift lever end of the control cable. Wrap this end with masking or duct tape. Tie the other end of the string to the frame in the adjacent area.

10. At the upper end of the control cable, carefully pull the cable (and attached string) out through the frame. Make sure the attached string follows the same path as the cable through the frame.

11. Remove the tape and untie the string from the old cable.

12. Tie the string to the new control cable and wrap it with tape.

13. Carefully pull the string back through the frame routing the new cable through the same path as the old cable.

14. Remove the tape and untie the string from the cable and the frame.

15. Transfer the pivot pin and E-clip to the upper end of the new cable(s).

16. Install the retaining clip (**Figure 209**) securing the control cable to the mounting bracket on the crankcase. Push the clip all the way down until it locks in place (**Figure 207**).

17. If removed install the bushing into the control cable pivot end, then apply a light coat of molybdenum disulfide grease to the inner surface of the gearshift cable pivot bushing (**Figure 210**).

18. Connect the control cable (A, **Figure 211**) onto the lever pivot post. Install the bushing onto the

7

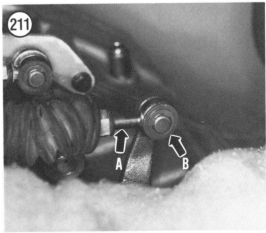

A   B

control cable as shown in **Figure 212**. The bushing flange must face toward the gearshift lever.

19. Install the washer and E-clip (B, **Figure 211**) securing the gearshift cable to the gearshift lever. Make sure the E-clip is properly installed in the pivot post groove.

20. At the upper end of the control cable, perform the following:

   a. Apply a light coat of molybdenum disulfide grease to the inner surface of the control cable pivot bushing.

   b. Remove the E-clip from the pivot pin(s) from the cable.

   c. Connect the control cable(s) onto the gearshift lever(s) (**Figure 205**).

   d. Install the pivot pin through the bracket on the lever and the cable and install the E-clip. Make sure the E-clip is seated correctly in the pivot pin groove.

21. Repeat for the transmission shift control cable and on 4-wheel drive models and the range selection control cable attached to the front differential shift lever (**Figure 213**).

22. Adjust the cable(s) as described in this chapter.

23. Install all components removed.

Control Cable Adjustment

2-wheel drive models

1. To adjust the RANGE control cable, perform the following:

   a. Move the RANGE shift lever on the crankcase to the high-range position (**Figure 214**).

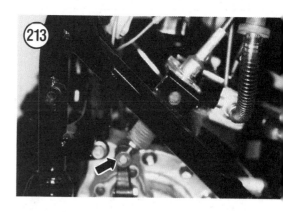

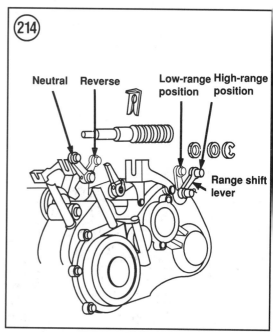

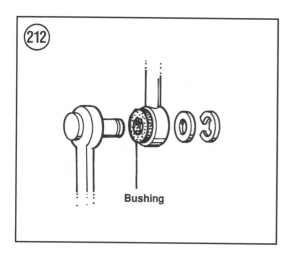

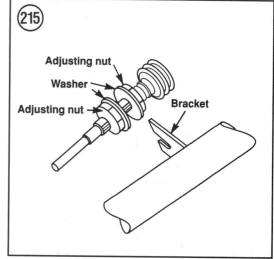

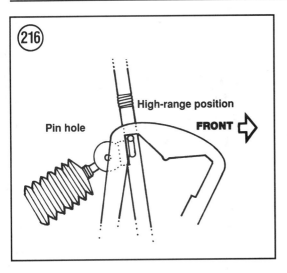

High-range position

Pin hole

FRONT

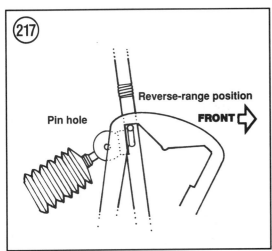

Reverse-range position

Pin hole

FRONT

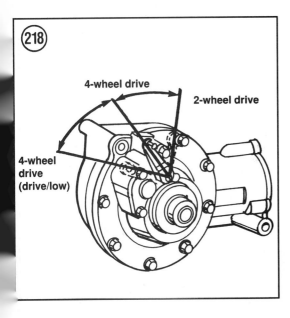

4-wheel drive

2-wheel drive

4-wheel drive (drive/low)

b. Loosen the adjusting nuts on the cable (**Figure 215**) at the frame bracket.

c. Turn the adjust nuts in either direction to align the control cable pin hole with the notch in the shift lever bracket (**Figure 216**).

d. Tighten the adjusting nuts against the frame bracket.

2. To adjust the REVERSE control cable, perform the following:

a. Move the REVERSE shift lever on the crankcase to the reverse-range position (**Figure 214**).

b. Loosen the adjusting nuts on the cable (**Figure 215**) at the frame bracket.

c. Turn the adjust nuts in either direction to align the control cable pin hole with the notch in the shift lever bracket (**Figure 217**).

d. Tighten the adjusting nuts against the frame bracket.

4-wheel drive models

1. To adjust the SELECTION control cable, perform the following:

a. Move the SELECTION shift lever on the differential case to the "4-wheel drive" range position (**Figure 218**).

b. Move the SELECTION shift lever to the "4-wheel drive" range position (**Figure 219**).

7

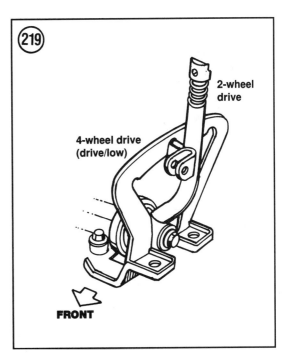

2-wheel drive

4-wheel drive (drive/low)

FRONT

c. Loosen the adjusting nuts on the cable (**Figure 220**) at the frame bracket.

d. Turn the adjust nuts in either direction to align the control cable pin hole with the "4-wheel drive" notch in the shift lever bracket (**Figure 221**).

e. Tighten the adjusting nuts against the frame bracket.

2. To adjust the RANGE control cable, perform the following:

a. Move the RANGE shift lever on the crankcase to the low-range position (**Figure 222**).

b. Move the RANGE shift lever to the low-range position (**Figure 223**).

c. Loosen the adjusting nuts on the cable (**Figure 220**) at the crankcase bracket.

d. Turn the adjust nuts in either direction to align the control cable pin hole with the low-range notch in the shift lever bracket.

e. Tighten the adjusting nuts against the frame bracket.

3. To adjust the REVERSE control cable, perform the following:

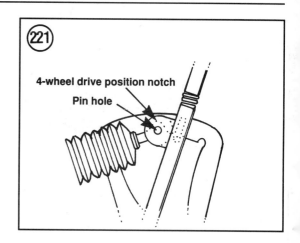

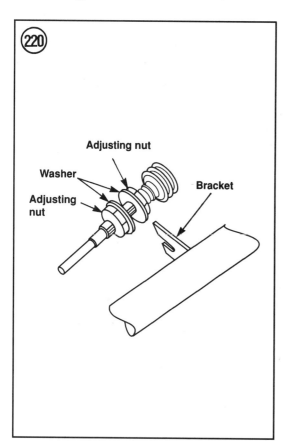

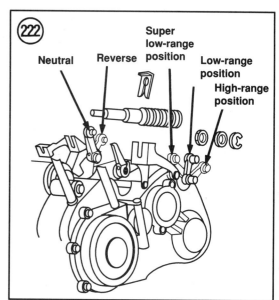

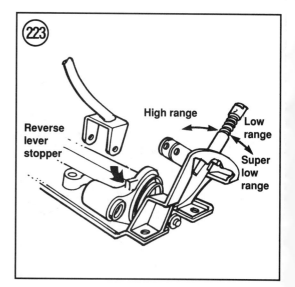

a. Move the REVERSE shift lever on the crankcase to the reverse-range position (**Figure 222**).

NOTE
*The shift lever is in the neutral position when the lever is pushed all the way forward until the U-shaped bracket contacts the reverse lever stopper (**Figure 223**).*

b. Move the REVERSE shift lever to the neutral-range position.

c. Loosen the adjusting nuts on the cable (**Figure 215**) to the crankcase bracket.

d. Turn the adjust nuts in either direction until the cable maintains the shift lever on the crankcase in the reverse position and the shift lever in the neutral position.

e. Tighten the adjusting nuts against the crankcase bracket.

Table 1 INTERNAL SHIFT MECHANISM SERVICE SPECIFICATIONS

Item	Specifications	Wear limit
Main transmission		
Shift fork finger thickness		
No. 1, 2 and 3	4.30-4.40 mm (0.169-0.173 in.)	—
Reverse	3.80-3.90 mm (0.150-0.154 in.)	—
Shift fork groove width in gears		
No. 1, 2 and 3	4.50-4.60 mm (0.177-0.181 in.)	—
Reverse	4.00-4.10 mm (0.157-0.161 in.)	—
Shift fork to gear		
groove clearance	0.10-0.30 mm (0.004-0.012 in.)	0.50 mm (0.020 in.)
Sub-transmission		
Shift fork finger thickness		
No. 1 and 2	5.30-5.40 mm (0.209-0.213 in.)	—
Shift fork groove width in gears		
No. 1 and 2	5.45-5.55 mm (0.215-0.219 in.)	—
Shift fork to gear		
groove clearance	0.05-0.25 mm (0.002-0.010 in.)	0.05 mm (0.002 in.)

7

FUEL AND EXHAUST SYSTEMS

The fuel system consists of the fuel tank, the shutoff valve, a single carburetor, a fuel pump and an air filter. The exhaust system consists of an exhaust pipe and a muffler.

This chapter includes service procedures for all parts of the fuel system and exhaust system. Air filter service is covered in Chapter Three.

Carburetor specifications are covered in **Table 1**. **Table 1** and **Table 2** are located at the end of this chapter.

CARBURETOR OPERATION

For proper operation a gasoline engine must be supplied with fuel and air mixed in proper proportions by weight. A mixture in which there is an excess of fuel is said to be rich. A lean mixture is one which contains insufficient fuel. A properly adjusted carburetor supplies the proper mixture to the engine under all operating conditions.

Each carburetor consists of several major systems. A float and float valve mechanism maintain a constant fuel level in the float bowl. The pilot system supplies fuel at low speeds. The main fuel system supplies fuel at medium and high speeds. A starter (choke) system supplies the very rich mixture needed to start a cold engine.

CARBURETOR SERVICE

Major carburetor service (removal and cleaning) should be performed at the intervals indicated in **Table 1** in Chapter Three or when poor engine performance, hesitation and little or no response to mixture adjustment is observed. Alterations in jet size, throttle slide cutaway, and changes in jet needle position, etc., should be attempted only if you're experienced in this type of "tuning" work; a bad guess could result in costly engine damage or, at least, poor performance. If, after servicing the carburetor and making the adjustments described in this chapter, the ATV does not perform correctly (and assuming that other factors affecting performance are correct, such as the condition of the ignition components, etc.), the vehicle should be checked by a dealer or a qualified performance tuning specialist.

Carburetor specifications are covered in **Table 1** at the end of this chapter.

CARBURETOR
(1987-1989 MODELS)

Removal/Installation

1. Place the ATV on level ground and set the parking brake. Block the wheels so the vehicle will not roll in either direction.

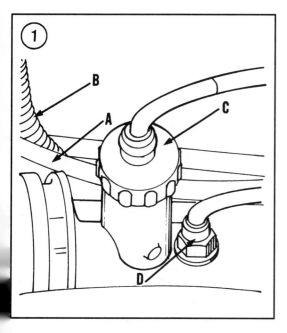

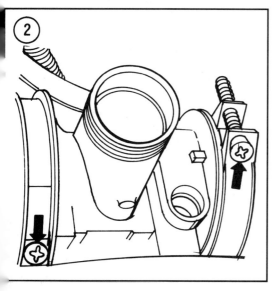

2. Remove the seat as described in Chapter Fourteen.

3. Disconnect the carburetor breather hose vent line (A, **Figure 1**) and the fuel line (B, **Figure 1**) from the carburetor. Plug the ends of both the breather hose and fuel line to prevent the discharge of fuel and the entry of foreign matter.

NOTE
Prior to removing the top cap, thoroughly clean the area around it so no dirt will fall into the carburetor.

4. Unscrew the carburetor top cap (C, **Figure 1**) and pull the throttle valve assembly up and out of the carburetor.

NOTE
If the top cap and throttle valve assembly are not going to be removed from the throttle cable for cleaning, place them in a reclosable plastic bag to help keep them clean.

5. Unscrew the nut (D, **Figure 1**) and remove the starter valve assembly from the carburetor.

6. Loosen the screws (**Figure 2**) on the clamping bands on each side of the carburetor. Slide the clamping bands away from the carburetor.

7. Note the routing of the carburetor drain tube through the frame. Carefully pull the tube free from the frame and leave it attached to the carburetor.

8. Carefully remove the carburetor from the rubber mounting tubes on the engine and the air filter air box.

9. Take the carburetor to a workbench for disassembly and cleaning.

10. To remove the throttle valve from the throttle cable, depress the throttle spring away from the throttle valve. Push the throttle cable end down and out along the groove in the side of the throttle valve and remove the throttle valve and needle jet assembly.

NOTE
Do not lose the spring clip that will come out when the needle is removed.

11. Install by reversing these removal steps while noting the following:
   a. Align the groove in the throttle slide with the pin in the carburetor body.

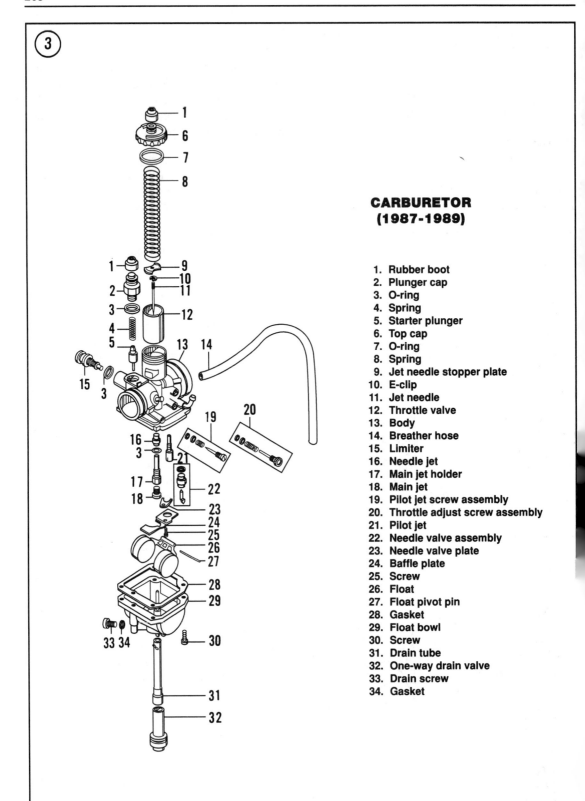

③

CARBURETOR
(1987-1989)

1. Rubber boot
2. Plunger cap
3. O-ring
4. Spring
5. Starter plunger
6. Top cap
7. O-ring
8. Spring
9. Jet needle stopper plate
10. E-clip
11. Jet needle
12. Throttle valve
13. Body
14. Breather hose
15. Limiter
16. Needle jet
17. Main jet holder
18. Main jet
19. Pilot jet screw assembly
20. Throttle adjust screw assembly
21. Pilot jet
22. Needle valve assembly
23. Needle valve plate
24. Baffle plate
25. Screw
26. Float
27. Float pivot pin
28. Gasket
29. Float bowl
30. Screw
31. Drain tube
32. One-way drain valve
33. Drain screw
34. Gasket

b. Make sure the screws on the clamping bands are tight to avoid a vacuum loss and possible valve damage.

Disassembly/Assembly

Refer to **Figure 3** for this procedure.

1. Remove the screws (**Figure 4**) securing the float bowl and remove the float bowl.

2. Remove the float pivot pin (**Figure 5**) and remove the float.

3. Remove the float valve from the float arm.

4. Remove the pilot jet (**Figure 6**).

5. Remove the screw (A, **Figure 7**) securing the baffle plate and the needle valve plate.

6. Remove the baffle plate (B, **Figure 7**).

7. Remove the needle valve plate (**Figure 8**).

8. Remove the needle valve and O-ring (**Figure 9**).

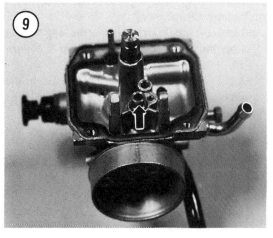

8

9. Remove the main jet and the needle jet holder (**Figure 10**).

10. Turn the carburetor over and gently tap the side of the body. Catch the needle jet as it falls out into your hand. If the needle jet does not fall out, use a plastic or fiber tool and gently push the needle jet out. Do not use any metal tool for this purpose.

NOTE
*Prior to removing the pilot screw, carefully screw it in until it **lightly** seats. Count and record the number of turns so it can be installed in the same position.*

11. Unscrew the pilot screw and spring (A, **Figure 11**).

12. Unscrew the idle adjust screw and spring (B, **Figure 11**).

13. Unscrew and remove the choke assembly from the carburetor body (A, **Figure 12**).

14. Remove the float bowl gasket (B, **Figure 12**) from the carburetor body or float bowl. The gasket may stick to either part.

15. If not already removed, push the jet needle from the throttle slide. Do not lose the jet needle retaining clip.

NOTE
Further disassembly is neither necessary nor recommended. If throttle or choke shafts or butterflies are damaged, take the carburetor body to a Suzuki dealer for replacement.

16. Clean and inspect all parts as described in this chapter.

17. Assemble by reversing these disassembly steps while noting the following:

   a. Install the needle jet by placing the long portion from the shoulder in first as shown in **Figure 13**.

   b. Make sure the O-ring seal is in place on the needle jet holder (**Figure 14**) and the needle jet (**Figure 15**) prior to installation.

   c. Install the needle jet clip in the correct groove; refer to **Table 1** at the end of this chapter.

   d. Check the float height and adjust if necessary as described in this chapter.

   e. After the carburetor has been disassembled the idle speed should be adjusted as described in Chapter Three.

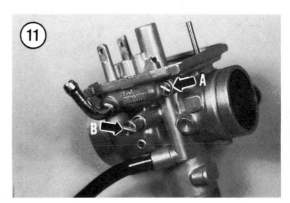

CARBURETOR
(1990-ON MODELS)

Removal/Installation

1. Place the ATV on level ground and set the parking brake. Block the wheels so the vehicle will not roll in either direction.

2. Remove the seat as described in Chapter Fourteen.

3. Remove the fuel line from the right-hand side of the carburetor. Plug the end of the fuel line to prevent the discharge of fuel.

4. Disconnect the vent tube from the carburetor body.

5. Loosen the screws (**Figure 16**) on the clamping bands on each side of the carburetor. Slide the clamping bands away from the carburetor.

NOTE
Prior to removing the carburetor assembly, thoroughly clean the area around it so no dirt will fall into the engine or air box.

6. Note the routing of the carburetor drain tube through the frame. Carefully pull the tube free from the frame and leave it attached to the carburetor.

7. Carefully remove the carburetor from the rubber mounting tubes on the engine and the air filter air box and pull the carburetor part way out toward the left-hand side of the frame.

NOTE
Prior to removing the side cover, thoroughly clean the area around it so no dirt will fall into the carburetor body.

8. Remove the screws securing the side cover (**Figure 17**) and remove the side cover from the carburetor body.

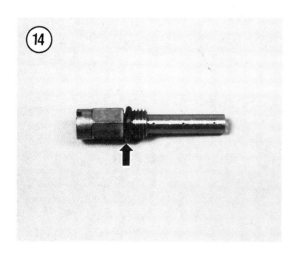

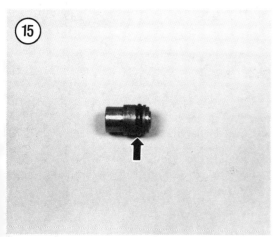

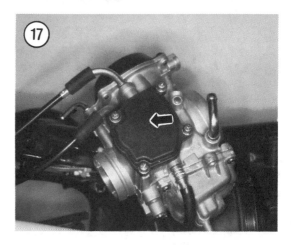

9. Unscrew the starter plunger (**Figure 18**) from the carburetor body.

10. Rotate the throttle shaft assembly plate (A, **Figure 19**) toward the top of the carburetor body.

11. Disengage the throttle cable guide (B, **Figure 19**) from the throttle shaft plate.

12. Disengage the throttle cable guide (A, **Figure 20**) from the throttle cable (B, **Figure 20**).

13. Withdraw the throttle cable from the carburetor body and remove the O-ring seal (**Figure 21**) from the throttle cable.

14. Install by reversing these removal steps while noting the following:

   a. Be sure to install the O-ring seal (**Figure 21**) onto the throttle cable prior to installing the throttle cable into the carburetor body. This is necessary to keep moisture out of the carburetor body.

   b. Make sure the gasket is in place on the side cover and install the side cover (**Figure 17**) and screws. Tighten the screws securely.

   c. If removed, make sure the fine screen sleeve (**Figure 22**) is in place in the intake tube on the cylinder head.

   d. Make sure the screws (**Figure 16**) on the clamping bands are tight to avoid a vacuum loss and possible valve damage.

Disassembly

Refer to **Figure 23** for this procedure.

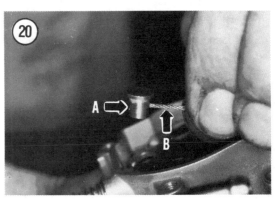

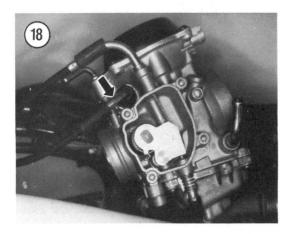

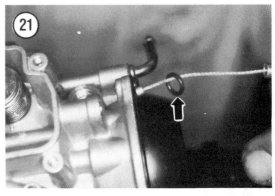

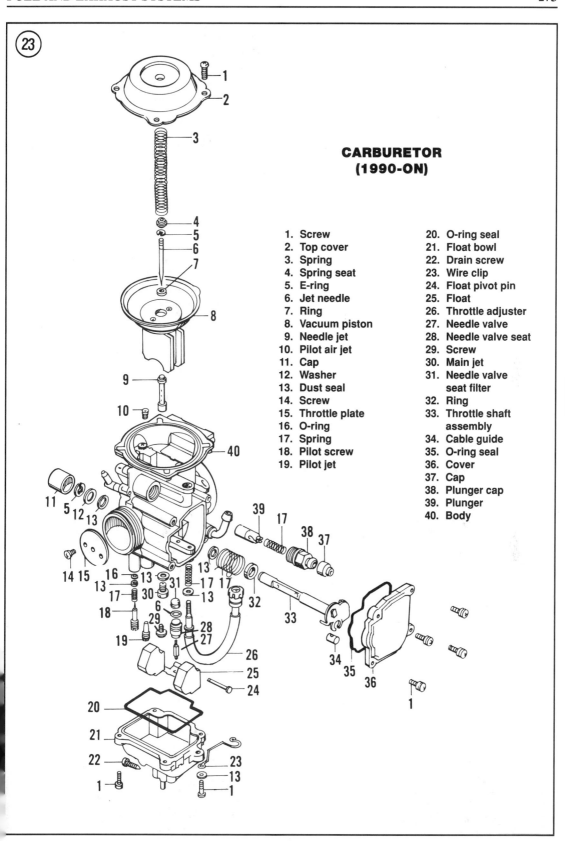

**CARBURETOR
(1990-ON)**

1. Screw
2. Top cover
3. Spring
4. Spring seat
5. E-ring
6. Jet needle
7. Ring
8. Vacuum piston
9. Needle jet
10. Pilot air jet
11. Cap
12. Washer
13. Dust seal
14. Screw
15. Throttle plate
16. O-ring
17. Spring
18. Pilot screw
19. Pilot jet
20. O-ring seal
21. Float bowl
22. Drain screw
23. Wire clip
24. Float pivot pin
25. Float
26. Throttle adjuster
27. Needle valve
28. Needle valve seat
29. Screw
30. Main jet
31. Needle valve
    seat filter
32. Ring
33. Throttle shaft
    assembly
34. Cable guide
35. O-ring seal
36. Cover
37. Cap
38. Plunger cap
39. Plunger
40. Body

1. To disassemble the starter choke plunger assembly from the cable perform the following:

    a. Hold onto the cable end and compress the spring (A, **Figure 24**) with one hand.

    b. Unhook the cable end (B, **Figure 24**) from the plunger and remove the plunger (C, **Figure 24**).

    c. Remove the spring (**Figure 25**) from the end of the cable.

    d. Remove the starter holder (A, **Figure 26**) and cap (B, **Figure 26**) from the starter cable (C, **Figure 26**).

2. Remove the screws (**Figure 27**) securing the top cover and remove the cover.

3. Remove the spring, spring seat and the vacuum piston/diaphragm assembly (**Figure 28**) from the carburetor body.

4. Remove the spring from the vacuum piston/diaphragm assembly.

5. Turn the vacuum piston/diaphragm assembly over and remove the spring seat and jet needle.

NOTE
*Prior to removing the pilot screw, screw the pilot jet in (**Figure 29**) and record the number of turns necessary until the*

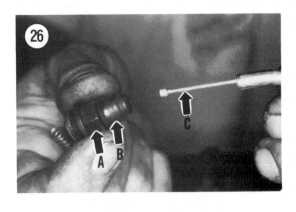

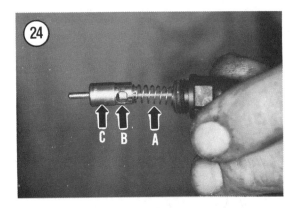

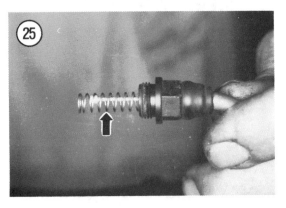

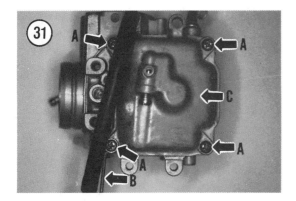

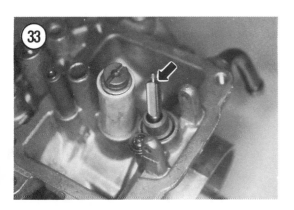

*screw **lightly** seats. Record the number of turns as the pilot screw must be reinstalled at the exact same setting.*

6. Unscrew the pilot screw assembly (**Figure 30**) and remove it from the carburetor body.

7. Remove the screws (A, **Figure 31**) securing the float bowl. Note the location of the throttle adjuster wire clip (B, **Figure 31**) and remove the float bowl (C, **Figure 31**) and O-ring seal.

8. Withdraw the float pin (A, **Figure 32**) from the mounting boss and remove the float (B, **Figure 32**).

9. Remove the needle valve (**Figure 33**).

10. Unscrew the pilot jet (**Figure 34**).

11. Unscrew the main jet (**Figure 35**) and the washer (**Figure 36**).

8

12. Remove the screw (A, **Figure 37**) and the needle valve seat assembly (B, **Figure 37**).

13. Turn the carburetor body over and tap in on the palm of your hand to dislodge the needle jet holder from the body. Turn the body back over and remove the needle jet holder (**Figure 38**).

14. Remove the pilot air jet (**Figure 39**).

15. Remove the O-ring seal (**Figure 40**) from the float bowl.

16. Remove the drain screw (**Figure 41**) from the float bowl.

NOTE
*Further disassembly is neither necessary nor recommended. If the throttle shaft assembly (**Figure 42**) or throttle plate (**Figure 43**) is damaged, take the carburetor body to a dealer for replacement.*

17. Clean and inspect all parts as described under *Cleaning and Inspection* in this chapter.

Assembly

1. Install the drain screw (**Figure 41**) into the float bowl and tighten securely.

2. Install the O-ring seal (**Figure 40**) into the float bowl.

3. Install the pilot air jet (**Figure 39**).

4. Install the needle jet holder (**Figure 38**) into the body. Push it until it bottoms out (C, **Figure 37**).

5. Install the needle valve seat assembly (B, **Figure 37**) and the screw (A, **Figure 37**). Tighten the screw securely.

6. Install the needle jet as follows:

   a. Position the needle jet as shown in **Figure 44**.

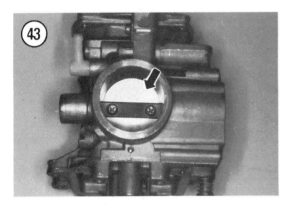

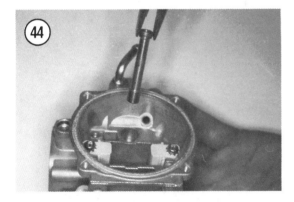

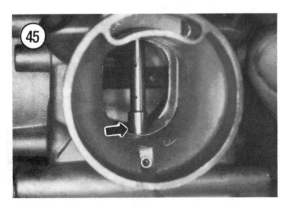

b. Install the needle jet part way into the holder.

c. Look through the venturi area and guide the needle jet into the receptacle in the carburetor body (**Figure 45**).

d. Align the flat on the needle jet with the flat on the needle jet holder and push the needle jet the rest of the way until it stops (C, **Figure 37**).

e. Make sure the flats on both parts are aligned correctly (**Figure 46**).

7. Install the washer (**Figure 36**) and the main jet (**Figure 35**). Tighten the main jet securely.

8. Install the pilot jet (**Figure 47**) and tighten securely (**Figure 34**).

9. Install the needle valve (**Figure 33**) into the receptacle in the carburetor body.

10. Install the float (B, **Figure 32**) between the mounting bosses.

11. Install the float pin (A, **Figure 32**) into the mounting boss and push it in until it bottoms out

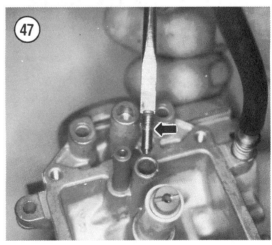

8

(**Figure 48**). After the pivot pin is installed, make sure the float pivots freely on the pin to ensure proper fuel flow.

12. Inspect the float height and adjust if necessary. Refer to *Float Adjustment* in this chapter.

13. Make sure the O-ring seal is in place, then install the float bowl (C, **Figure 31**).

14. Move the throttle adjuster wire clip (B, **Figure 31**) into position, then install the screws (A, **Figure 31**) securing the float bowl. Tighten the screws securely.

15. Install the pilot screw assembly (**Figure 49**) into the carburetor body. Screw the pilot screw (**Figure 50**) into the exact same position (same number of turns) as recorded during Step 6 of *Disassembly*.

> *NOTE*
> *If a new pilot screw is being installed, turn it out the number of turns indicated in **Table 1**, from the **lightly seated** position.*

16. Install the ring (**Figure 51**) onto the lower end of the jet needle, then install this assembly (**Figure 52**) into the vacuum piston/diaphragm assembly.

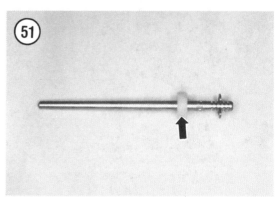

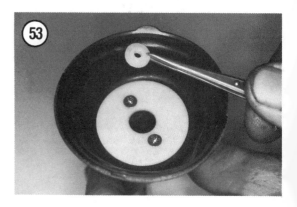

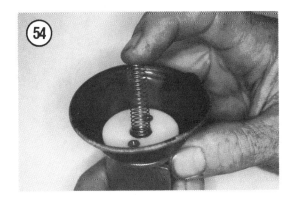

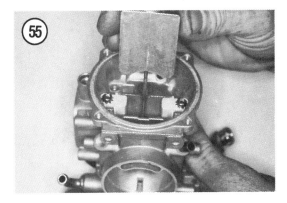

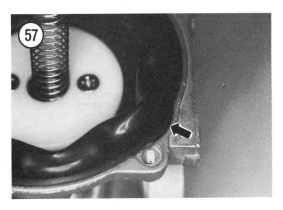

17. Install the spring seat (**Figure 53**) into the vacuum piston/diaphragm assembly on top of the jet needle.

18. Install the spring (**Figure 54**) into the vacuum piston/diaphragm assembly.

19. Install the piston/diaphragm assembly (**Figure 55**) into the carburetor body. Guide the jet needle into the needle jet (**Figure 56**) and align the tab on the diaphragm with the cutout in the carburetor body (**Figure 57**).

20. Install the spring onto the spring seat (**Figure 58**) in the top cover.

21. Install the top cover and tighten the screws (**Figure 59**) securely.

22. Insert your finger into the carburetor venturi and slowly push the vacuum piston/diaphragm assembly up in the carburetor body. It should move up freely and the spring should push the assembly back down.

23. To assemble the starter choke plunger assembly onto the cable, perform the following:

8

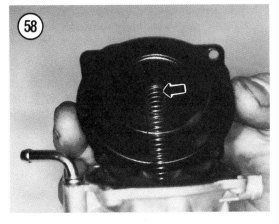

a. Install the starter cable (A, **Figure 60**) through the cap (B, **Figure 60**) and the starter holder (C, **Figure 60**).

b. Install the spring (**Figure 61**) on the end of the cable. Push it all the way on.

c. Hold onto the cable end and compress the spring (A, **Figure 62**) with one hand.

d. Hook the cable end (B, **Figure 62**) into the plunger (C, **Figure 62**).

24. After the carburetor has been disassembled, the idle speed should be adjusted as described in Chapter Three.

CLEANING AND INSPECTION (ALL MODELS)

1. Thoroughly clean and dry all parts. Suzuki does not recommend the use of a caustic carburetor cleaning solvent. Instead, clean carburetor parts in a petroleum based solvent. Then rinse in clean water.

> *CAUTION*
> *If compressed air is not available, allow the parts to air dry or use a clean lint-free cloth. Do **not** use a paper towel to dry carburetor parts, as small paper particles may plug openings in the carburetor body or jets.*

2. Allow the carburetor to dry thoroughly before assembly and blow dry with compressed air. Blow out the jets and needle jet holder with compressed air.

3A. On 1987-1989 models, inspect the float bowl gasket for hardness. Replace if necessary.

3B. On 1990-on models, inspect the float chamber O-ring seal (**Figure 63**). O-ring seals tend to become

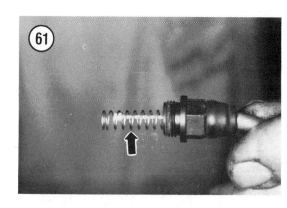

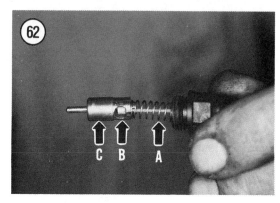

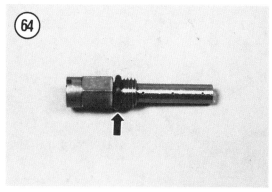

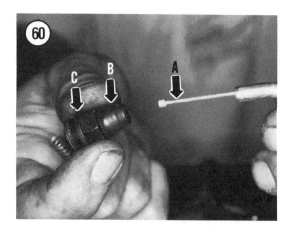

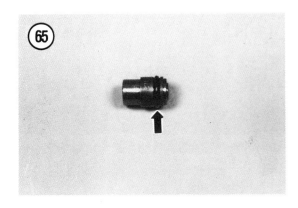

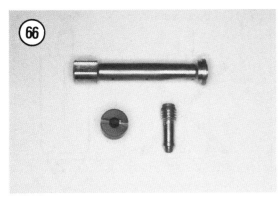

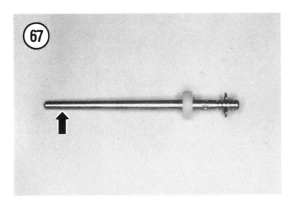

hardened after prolonged use and exposure to high temperatures and therefore lose their ability to seal properly.

4. On 1987-1989 models, inspect the O-ring seal on the needle jet holder (**Figure 64**) and on the needle jet (**Figure 65**). O-ring seals tend to become hardened after prolonged use and exposure to high temperatures and therefore lose their ability to seal properly.

> *CAUTION*
> *If compressed air is not available, allow the parts to air dry or use a clean lint-free cloth. Do **not** use a paper towel to dry carburetor parts, as small paper particles may plug openings in the carburetor body or jets.*

> *CAUTION*
> *Do **not** use a piece of wire to clean them as minor gouges in the jet can alter flow rate and upset the fuel/air mixture.*

5. Make sure the holes in the needle jet, pilot jet and main jet are clear (**Figure 66**). Clean out if they are plugged in any way. Replace the needle jet and/or jets if you cannot unplug the holes.

6. Examine the jet needle (**Figure 67**), spring and spring seat for wear or damage.

7. On 1990-on models, inspect the following:
   a. Make sure the diaphragm (**Figure 68**) is not torn or cracked. Replace any damaged or worn parts.
   b. Inspect the piston valve (**Figure 69**) portion of the vacuum piston/diaphragm assembly for wear or damage. Replace the assembly if necessary.

8

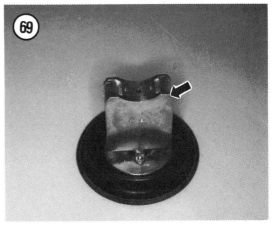

c. Inspect the piston valve grooves (**Figure 70**) section of the carburetor body for wear or damage. If damaged, replace the carburetor assembly.

8. Inspect the float (**Figure 71**) for deterioration or damage. If the float is suspected of leakage, place it in a container of non-caustic solution and push it down. If the float sinks or if bubbles appear (indicating a leak), replace the float assembly.

9. Inspect the end of the float valve (**Figure 72**) and seat in the float chamber for wear or damage. Refer to **Figure 73** and replace either or both parts if necessary.

10. On 1990-on models, inspect the filter (**Figure 74**) on the end of the needle valve seat for holes or damage. Replace if necessary. Inspect the O-ring seal (**Figure 75**) on the needle valve seat for hardness. Replace if necessary.

11. Inspect the pilot screw assembly (**Figure 76**) for wear or damage. Replace any faulty parts of the assembly, or the entire assembly, if necessary.

12. Make sure all openings in the carburetor body are clear. Refer to **Figure 77** and **Figure 78**. Clean

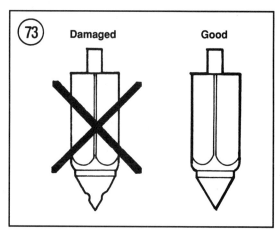

Damaged   Good

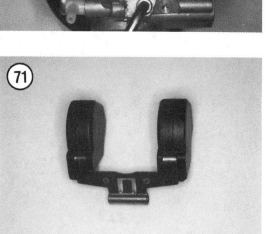

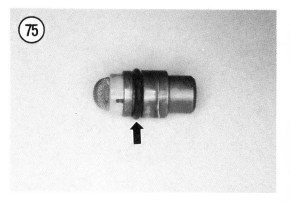

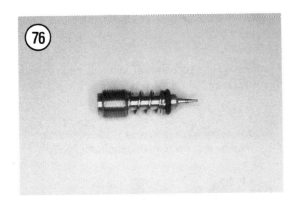

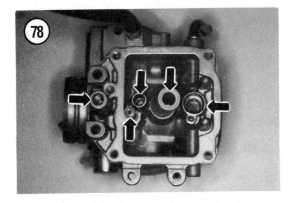

out with compressed air if they are plugged in any way.

13. Inspect the carburetor body (**Figure 79**) for any internal or external damage. If damaged, replace the carburetor assembly as the body cannot be replaced individually.

14. Inspect the choke plunger (A, **Figure 80**) and spring (B, **Figure 80**) for wear or damage. Replace if necessary.

15. Make sure the idle adjust screw and cable assembly (**Figure 81**) rotate smoothly. Replace the cable assembly if necessary.

CARBURETOR ADJUSTMENTS

Float Adjustment

The carburetor assembly has to be removed and partially disassembled for this adjustment.

1. Remove the carburetor as described in this chapter.

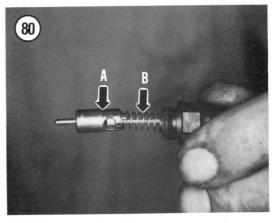

2. Remove the screws securing the float bowl and remove float bowl. Refer to **Figure 82** for 1987-1989 models or **Figure 83** for 1990-on models.

3. Hold the carburetor so the float arm is just touching the float needle—not pushing it down. Use a float level gauge, vernier caliper or small ruler and measure the distance from the carburetor body to the float (**Figure 84**). The correct height is listed in **Table 1**.

4. Adjust by carefully bending the tang on the float arm (**Figure 85**). If the float level is set too high, fuel will run from the float bowl overflow tube and cause the engine to flood. Also, it will cause a rich fuel/air mixture. If it is set too low, the mixture will be too lean and the engine will stumble on acceleration and run too lean to develop peak efficiency and power.

5. Reassemble and install the carburetor.

FUEL SYSTEM CLEANLINESS INSPECTION

1. Place the ATV on level ground and set the parking brake. Block the wheels so the vehicle will not roll in either direction.

NOTE
Figure 86 is shown with the carburetor removed for clarity. Do not remove the carburetor for this procedure.

2. Locate the drain tube from the drain outlet fitting (A, **Figure 86**) on the carburetor float bowl.

3. Place the loose end in a *clean* transparent container.

4. Loosen the carburetor float bowl drain screw (B, **Figure 86**) several turns and drain the fuel from the carburetor float bowl.

5. Tighten the carburetor drain screw securely.

6. Inspect the spent fuel for water, rust and other contaminates. If water is present in the fuel, it will be in a layer by itself *below* the fuel. Dispose of this fuel properly.

7. Water in the fuel usually is a result of water contaminated gasoline or from a leaking fuel filler cap that has allowed moisture to enter the fuel tank.

8. Rust particles also may have come from a contaminated gasoline container.

9. If water and/or rust is present in the fuel system, it must be corrected as soon as possible.

10. Remove the carburetor, disassemble and clean it to remove all contaminates. Make sure all jets are clear.

11. Remove the fuel shutoff valve as described in this chapter and clean the integral fuel filter.

NOTE
Even though the fuel tank is plastic, rust may be present from contaminated fuel.

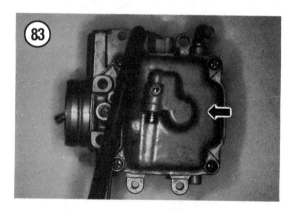

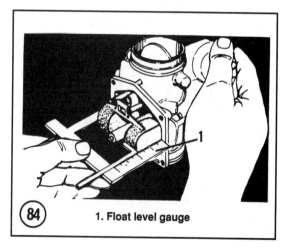

1. Float level gauge

12. Remove the fuel tank and the fuel filler cap as described in this chapter. Inspect the fuel tank for rust accumulation and check the filler cap for any possible leaks. Have the fuel tank cleaned to remove the rust and correct any possible fuel filler cap leaks.

THROTTLE CABLE

Removal

1. Place the ATV on level ground and set the parking brake. Block the wheels so the vehicle will not roll in either direction.

2. Remove the seat, the front fender and rear fender as described in Chapter Fourteen.

> *NOTE*
> *Step 3 is necessary to disconnect the lower end of the throttle cable from the carburetor.*

3A. On 1987-1989 models, perform Steps 3, 4 and 10 of *Carburetor Removal/Installation* in this chapter.

3B. On 1990-on models, remove the carburetor as described in this chapter.

4. Disassemble the throttle lever assembly as follows:

   a. Slide the rubber boot (A, **Figure 87**) away from the throttle lever assembly.

   b. Remove the screws securing the throttle cover (B, **Figure 87**) and separate the 2 halves of the throttle lever assembly.

   c. Remove the throttle cable end from the throttle lever.

5. Disconnect the throttle cable from any clips holding the cable to the frame.

> *NOTE*
> *The piece of string attached in the next step is used to pull the new throttle cable back through the frame so it will be routed in the exact same position as the old one.*

6. Tie a piece of heavy string or cord (approximately 6-8 ft. [1.8-2.4 m long]) to the carburetor end of the throttle cable. Wrap this end with masking or duct tape. Do not use an excessive amount of tape as it will be pulled through the frame, and on some models a rubber grommet, during removal. Tie the other end of the string to the frame.

7. At the throttle lever end of the cable, carefully pull the cable (and attached string) out through the frame. Make sure the attached string follows the same path of the cable through the frame.

8. Remove the tape and untie the string from the old cable.

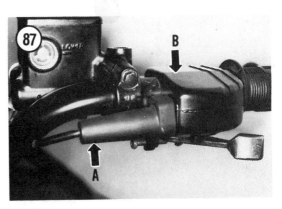

Installation

1. Lubricate the new cable as described in Chapter Three.

2. Tie the string (used during removal) to the new throttle cable and wrap it with tape.

3. Carefully pull the string back through the frame routing the new cable through the same path as the old cable.

4. Remove the tape and untie the string from the cable and the frame.

5. Reverse Steps 2-5 of *Removal* while noting the following:

    a. Apply grease to the pivot bushing in the throttle lever cover and to the throttle lever.

    b. Operate the throttle lever and make sure the carburetor throttle linkage is operating correctly without binding. If operation is incorrect or there is binding, carefully check that the cable is attached correctly and there are no tight bends in the cable.

    c. Adjust the throttle cable as described in Chapter Three.

    d. Test ride the ATV to make sure the throttle is operating correctly.

CHOKE CABLE (1990-ON MODELS)

Removal

1. Place the ATV on level ground and set the parking brake. Block the wheels so the vehicle will not roll in either direction.

2. Remove the seat, the front fender and rear fender as described in Chapter Fourteen.

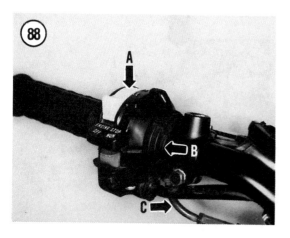

3. Remove the screws securing the left-hand switch (A, **Figure 88**) and separate the 2 halves of the switch.

4. Move the ring cover (B, **Figure 88**) off the choke lever.

5. Remove the choke cable (C, **Figure 88**) end from the choke lever.

6. Disconnect the choke cable from any clips holding the cable to the frame.

7. Unscrew the choke plunger assembly from the carburetor body.

8. To disconnect the starter choke plunger assembly from the cable perform the following:

    a. Hold onto the cable end and compress the spring (A, **Figure 89**) with one hand.

    b. Unhook the cable end (B, **Figure 89**) from the plunger and remove the plunger (C, **Figure 89**).

    c. Remove the spring (**Figure 90**) from the end of the cable.

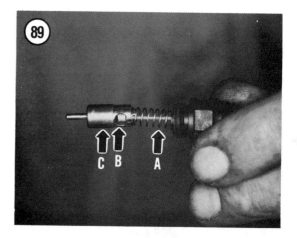

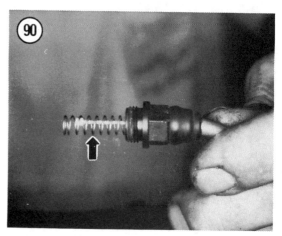

d. Remove the starter holder (A, **Figure 91**) and cap (B, **Figure 91**) from the starter cable (C, **Figure 91**).

NOTE
The piece of string attached in the next step is used to pull the new choke cable back through the frame so it will be routed in the same position as the old cable.

9. Tie a piece of heavy string or cord (approximately 6-8 ft./1.8-2.4 m long) to the carburetor end of the choke cable. Wrap this end with masking or duct tape. Do not use an excessive amount of tape as it will be pulled through the frame during removal. Tie the other end of the string to the frame.

10. Carefully pull the cable (and attached string) out through the frame. Make sure the attached string follows the same path that the cable does through the frame.

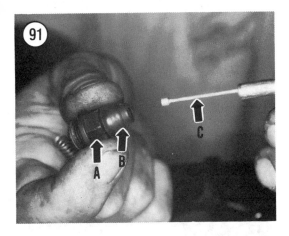

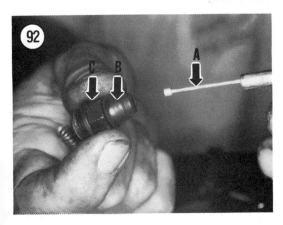

11. Remove the tape and untie the string from the old cable.

Installation

1. Lubricate the new cable as described in Chapter Three.
2. Tie the string to the new choke cable and wrap it with tape.
3. Carefully pull the string back through the frame routing the new cable through the same path as the old cable.
4. Remove the tape and untie the string from the cable and the frame.
5. To assemble the starter choke plunger assembly onto the cable, perform the following:
   a. Install the starter cable (A, **Figure 92**) through the cap (B, **Figure 92**) and the starter holder (C, **Figure 92**).
   b. Install the spring (**Figure 90**) on the end of the cable. Push it all the way on.
   c. Hold onto the cable end and compress the spring (A, **Figure 89**) with one hand.
   d. Hook the cable end (B, **Figure 89**) into the plunger (C, **Figure 89**).
6. Install and screw the choke plunger into the carburetor body.
7. Install the choke cable end onto the choke lever.
8. Install the ring cover back onto the choke lever and cable. Make sure it is correctly seated.
9. Assemble the 2 halves of the left-hand switch together and install the screws. Tighten the screws securely.
10. Operate the choke lever and make sure the carburetor choke plunger is operating correctly without binding. If operation is incorrect or there is binding, carefully check that the cable is attached correctly and there are no tight bends in the cable.
11. Install the rear and front fenders and the seat.

FUEL SHUTOFF VALVE

Removal/Installation

1. Place the ATV on level ground and set the parking brake. Block the wheels so the vehicle will not roll in either direction.
2. Disconnect the battery negative lead as described in Chapter Three.

3. Remove the seat and the front fender as described in Chapter Fourteen.

4. Turn the fuel shutoff valve to the OFF position.

5. Disconnect the fuel pump-to-shutoff valve fuel line (A, **Figure 93**) from the fuel pump. Disconnect tie-wraps (B, **Figure 93**) securing the fuel line to the frame.

6. Place the loose end in a clean container suitable for gasoline storage.

7. Turn the shutoff valve to the RES position and drain the fuel from the fuel tank. Raise the right-hand side of the vehicle to drain as much fuel as possible from the fuel tank. The fuel tank must be empty to perform this procedure.

8. Turn the fuel shutoff valve to the OFF position, remove the fuel line from the container and plug the fuel line to prevent any residual fuel from draining out.

9. Raise the left-hand side of the vehicle and place blocks under the wheels. This will place any residual fuel in the tank away from the shutoff valve location on the tank.

10. On models so equipped, disconnect the hose (**Figure 94**) from the backside of the shutoff valve. Plug the hose to prevent the entry of foreign matter.

11. Remove the screws (A, **Figure 95**) securing the fuel shutoff valve to the fuel tank.

12. Carefully pull the fuel shutoff valve (B, **Figure 95**) from the fuel tank.

13. Install by reversing these removal steps while noting the following:

   a. Inspect the O-ring seal and replace if necessary. Make sure the O-ring seal is in place prior to installing the shutoff valve on the tank.

   b. Refill the fuel tank and check for fuel leakage after installation is completed.

FUEL TANK

Removal/Installation

Refer to **Figure 96** for this procedure.

1. Place the ATV on level ground and set the parking brake. Block the wheels so the vehicle will not roll in either direction.

2. Perform Steps 4-9 of *Fuel Shutoff Valve Removal/Installation* in this chapter and drain the fuel from the tank prior to removal.

3. Remove the engine as described under *Engine Removal/Installation* in Chapter Five.

4. Remove the CDI unit (A, **Figure 97**) from the right-hand side of the fuel tank as described under *CDI Unit Removal/Installation* in Chapter Nine.

5. Remove the fuel filler cap (B, **Figure 97**) and cover the opening with duct tape to prevent the entry of foreign matter.

6. Remove the 4 bolts securing the gearshift lever assembly base (**Figure 98**) to the frame. Do not disconnect any of the gearshift lever control cables, just move the assembly toward the rear to expose the rear mounting bolts.

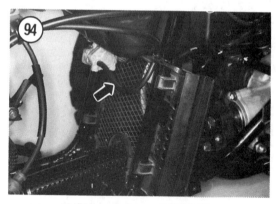

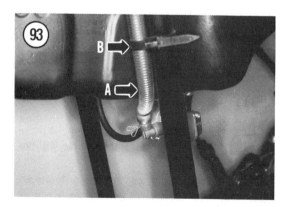

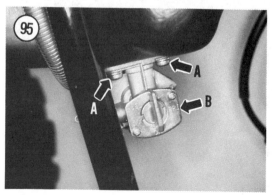

96

FUEL TANK

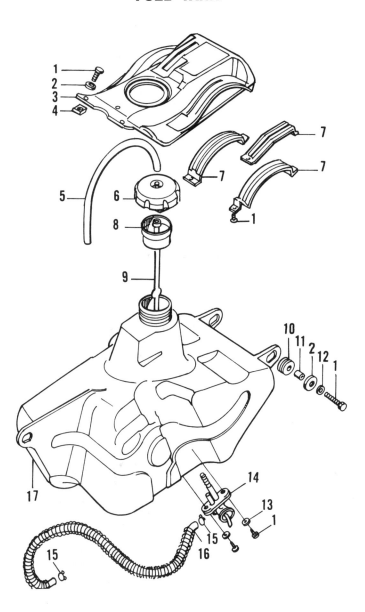

1. Screw
2. Washer
3. Top cover
4. Special nut
5. Breather hose
6. Filler cap
7. Shift lever
   seal plate
8. Inlet tube

9. Fuel gauge
   (dipstick)
10. Rubber bushing
11. Collar
12. Lockwasher
13. Lockwasher
14. Fuel shutoff valve
15. Hose clamp
16. Fuel hose
17. Fuel tank

8

7. Remove the fuel pump from the left-hand side of the fuel tank as described in this chapter.

8. Remove the front bolt, lockwasher and washer (**Figure 99**) securing the front mounting tab of the fuel tank to the frame mounting flange.

9. Remove the rear bolt, lockwasher and washer on each side securing the rear mounting tabs of the fuel tank to the frame. Remove the rear bolt on the right-hand side that screws into the ignition coil mounting bracket (**Figure 100**). After the bolt has been removed, secure the ignition coil and bracket to the frame with a piece of wire.

10. Lower the fuel tank (C, **Figure 97**), pull it toward the rear and remove it from the frame.

11. Install by reversing these removal steps while noting the following:

   a. Inspect the rubber cushions in the mounting tabs on the fuel tank. Replace as a set if any are damaged or starting to deteriorate.

   b. During assembly, be careful not to damage or kink any of the fuel lines.

   c. Be sure to install a collar and rubber cushion in each fuel tank mounting tab. Tighten the bolts securely.

   d. Check for fuel leakage after installation is completed.

FUEL PUMP

The fuel pump is operated by engine vacuum when the engine is running. The pump *cannot* be serviced and if defective, must be replaced.

Removal/Installation

1. Place the ATV on level ground and set the parking brake. Block the wheels so the vehicle will not roll in either direction.

2. Remove the front fender as described in Chapter Fourteen.

3. Disconnect the vacuum line from the backside of the fuel pump.

4. Slide the hose clamps back off the fittings on the fuel pump.

5. Disconnect the inlet hose (A, **Figure 101**) and the outlet hose (B, **Figure 101**) from the fuel pump. Plug the end of both fuel lines to prevent any residual fuel from draining out.

6. Remove the bolts securing the fuel pump (C, **Figure 101**) to the mounting tabs on the frame and remove the fuel pump.

7. Install by reversing these removal steps while noting the following:

   a. Be sure to route the fuel lines to the correct fittings otherwise the fuel pump will not operate correctly.

   b. Check for fuel leakage after installation is completed.

AIR FILTER HOUSING

Removal/Installation

Refer to **Figure 102** for this procedure.

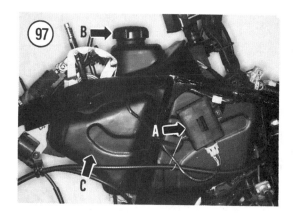

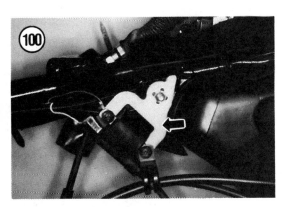

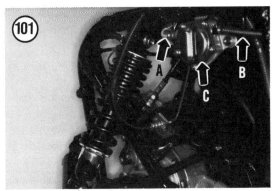

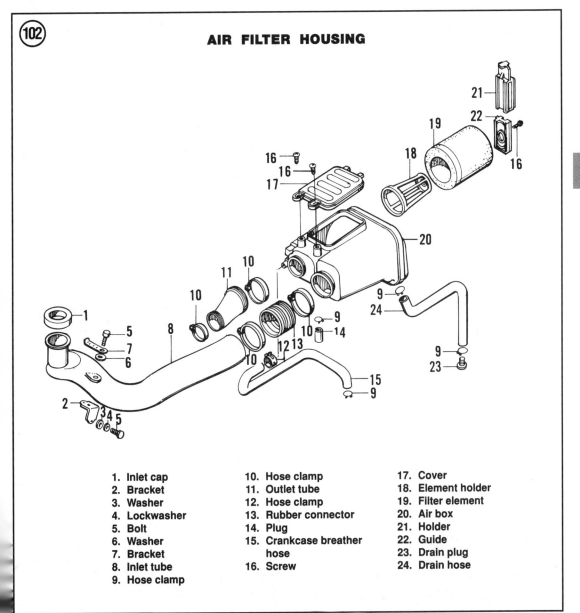

AIR FILTER HOUSING

1. Inlet cap
2. Bracket
3. Washer
4. Lockwasher
5. Bolt
6. Washer
7. Bracket
8. Inlet tube
9. Hose clamp
10. Hose clamp
11. Outlet tube
12. Hose clamp
13. Rubber connector
14. Plug
15. Crankcase breather hose
16. Screw
17. Cover
18. Element holder
19. Filter element
20. Air box
21. Holder
22. Guide
23. Drain plug
24. Drain hose

1. Place the ATV on level ground and set the parking brake. Block the wheels so the vehicle will not roll in either direction.

2. Remove the seat, front fender and rear fender as described in Chapter Fourteen.

3. Remove the carburetor as described in this chapter.

4. Remove the screw, cable clamp and washer (A, **Figure 103**) securing the air filter air intake tube to the frame rail.

5. Loosen the clamp screw and move the front clamp (**Figure 104**) back onto the rubber connector, away from the tube.

6. Remove the air filter air intake tube (B, **Figure 103**) from the frame rail.

7. On the right-hand side, slide the hose clamp off the air box fitting on the bottom of the air box. Remove the blow-by/drain hose(s) off the fitting(s) and remove it(them) from the air box.

8. On the left-hand side, perform the following:

   a. Slide the hose clamp (A, **Figure 105**) off the air box fitting and remove the crankcase breather hose from the fitting.

   b. Slide the hose clamp (**Figure 106**) off the crankcase fitting and remove the crankcase breather hose from the fitting.

   c. Remove the crankcase breather hose (**Figure 107**).

9. Remove the front bolt (B, **Figure 105**) and both rear bolts (**Figure 108**) securing the air box to the frame.

10. Remove the air filter air box from the frame.

11. Install by reversing these removal steps while noting the following:

   a. Make sure all fittings are tight to avoid an air leak that would allow unfiltered air to enter the engine.

   b. Refer to Chapter Three and clean the air filter element prior to installing it in the housing.

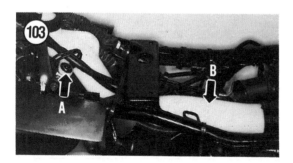

EXHAUST SYSTEM

The exhaust system is a vital performance component and frequently, because of its design, it is a vulnerable piece of equipment.

If the exhaust system is damaged or if the muffler becomes clogged with carbon, the performance of

the engine can be greatly affected. Check the exhaust system for deep dents and fractures and repair them or replace parts immediately. Check the muffler frame mounting flanges for fractures and loose bolts or nuts. Check the cylinder head mounting flange for tightness. A loose exhaust pipe connection will cause excessive exhaust noise and rob the engine of power.

Refer to the following illustrations for this procedure:

    a. **Figure 109**: 1987-1989 models.

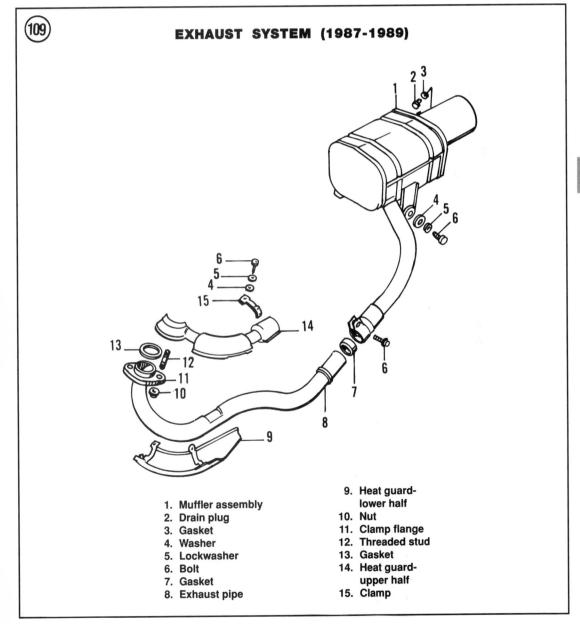

EXHAUST SYSTEM (1987-1989)

1. Muffler assembly
2. Drain plug
3. Gasket
4. Washer
5. Lockwasher
6. Bolt
7. Gasket
8. Exhaust pipe
9. Heat guard- lower half
10. Nut
11. Clamp flange
12. Threaded stud
13. Gasket
14. Heat guard- upper half
15. Clamp

b. **Figure 110**: 1990 models.

c. **Figure 111**: 1991-on models.

Removal/Installation

1. Place the ATV on level ground and set the parking brake. Block the wheel so the vehicle will not roll in either direction.

2. Remove the seat and the front and rear fenders as described in Chapter Fourteen.

3. Remove the left-hand rear wheel as described under *Rear Wheel Removal/Installation* in Chapter Twelve.

4. Remove the left-hand rear shock absorber as described under *Rear Shock Absorber Removal/Installation* in Chapter Twelve.

5. Remove the nut (A, **Figure 112**) from the engine front lower mounting through bolt. It is not necessary to remove the bolt unless the bolt has been installed from the left-hand side; if so, remove the bolt as well as the spacer (**Figure 113**) and nut.

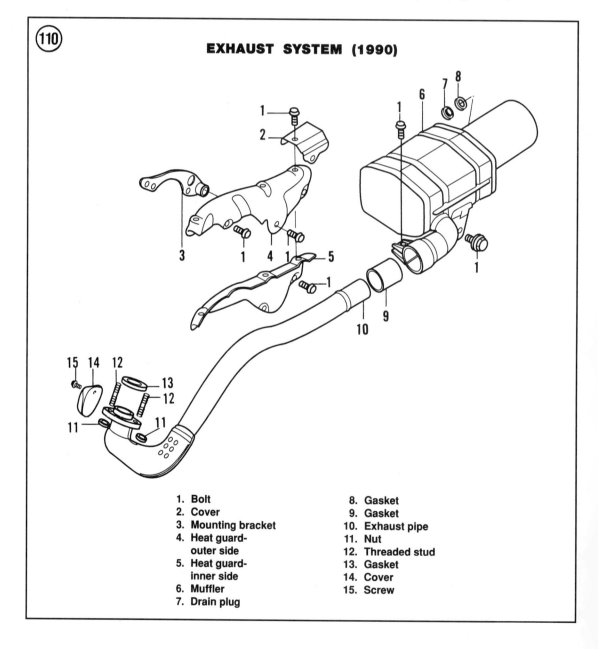

110

EXHAUST SYSTEM (1990)

1. Bolt
2. Cover
3. Mounting bracket
4. Heat guard-
   outer side
5. Heat guard-
   inner side
6. Muffler
7. Drain plug
8. Gasket
9. Gasket
10. Exhaust pipe
11. Nut
12. Threaded stud
13. Gasket
14. Cover
15. Screw

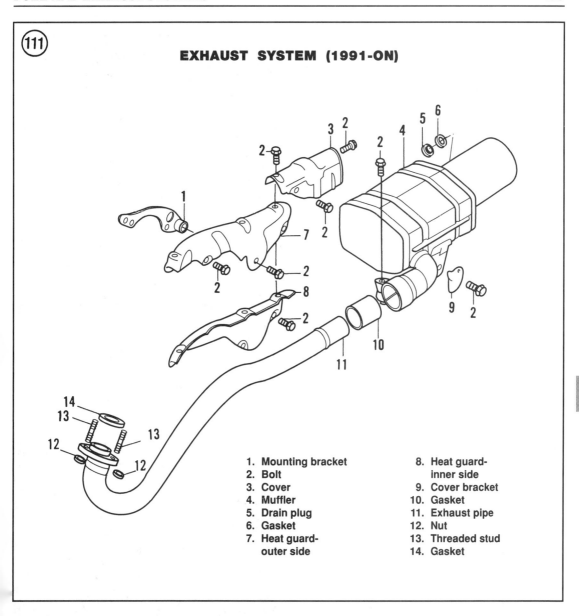

EXHAUST SYSTEM (1991-ON)

1. Mounting bracket
2. Bolt
3. Cover
4. Muffler
5. Drain plug
6. Gasket
7. Heat guard-
   outer side
8. Heat guard-
   inner side
9. Cover bracket
10. Gasket
11. Exhaust pipe
12. Nut
13. Threaded stud
14. Gasket

8

6. Disconnect the sub-transmission gearshift control cable (**Figure 114**) from the shift lever on the crankcase. Refer to *Gearshift Lever Control Mechanism, Control Cable Replacement* in Chapter Seven.

7. Loosen the center mounting bolts (**Figure 115**).

8. Loosen, then remove the upper and lower bolts (B, **Figure 112**) securing the frame left-hand side bridge to the frame.

9. It is not necessary to disconnect the rear brake cable (C, **Figure 112**) from the left-hand side bridge.

10. Remove the bolts loosened in Step 7.

11. Move the frame left-hand side bridge away from the frame. Move it, along with the rear brake cable, forward and let it set on the foot rest assembly.

12. On 1990-on models, remove the bolt(s) securing the rear cover (**Figure 116**) and remove the cover.

13. Remove the bolts securing the sub-transmission control cable bracket (**Figure 117**) to the crankcase and remove the bracket.

14. Remove the bolts securing the outer heat shield and remove the outer heat shield.

15. On models so equipped, remove the bolt (**Figure 118**) securing the front heat shield (**Figure 119**) and remove the front head shield.

16. Loosen the clamp bolt (**Figure 120**) securing the muffler to the exhaust pipe.

17. Remove the flange bolt (**Figure 121**) securing the muffler to the crankcase.

18. Carefully pull the muffler straight back and disengage it from the exhaust pipe, then remove the muffler (**Figure 122**).

NOTE
*In **Figure 123**, only 1 nut is visible. Be sure to remove both nuts securing the exhaust pipe to the cylinder head.*

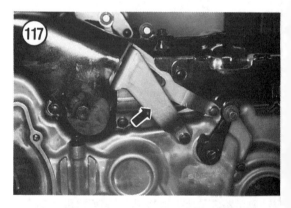

19. Remove the 2 nuts (**Figure 123**) securing the exhaust pipe to the cylinder head.

20. Move the exhaust pipe toward the front of the vehicle to clear the mounting studs on the cylinder head and remove the assembly from the frame.

21. If the exhaust system is being removed for engine removal, perform the following:

   a. Remove the bolts securing the mounting bracket (A, **Figure 124**) and remove the bracket.

   b. Remove the bolts securing the side inner heat shield (B, **Figure 124**) and remove the heat shield.

22. Install by reversing these removal steps while noting the following:

   a. Make sure the gasket is in place in the cylinder head exhaust port and where the exhaust pipe and muffler connect.

   b. Tighten the nuts on the cylinder head first, then the bolts securing the muffler to the frame. This will minimize the chances of an exhaust leak at the cylinder head. Tighten the nuts and bolts to the torque specifications listed in **Table 2**.

   c. After installation is complete, start the engine and make sure there are no exhaust leaks.

8

Table 1 CARBURETOR SPECIFICATIONS

Item	1987-1989 U.S. Models 1987, 1988 Canadian Models (LT-F250, LT-4WD)
Model No.	Mikuni VM24SS
Identification No.	
1987	19AB0
1988, 1989	19B02
Bore size	24 mm (0.94 in.)
Main jet No.	100
Main air jet	1.0 mm (0.04 in.)
Jet needle	5L21
Jet needle clip position	3rd groove
Needle jet	0-1
Pilot jet No.	22.5
Pilot air jet	1.5 mm (0.06 in.)
Starter jet No.	30
Pilot screw opening	
1987	2 turns out
1988, 1989	1 3/4 turns out
Float level	23.5-25.5 mm (0.92-1.00 in.)
Idle speed	1,350-1,450 rpm

Item	1989 Canadian Models (LT-F250, LT-4WD)
Model No.	Mikuni BST31SS
Identification No.	19B50
Bore size	31 mm (1.22 in.)
Main jet No.	120
Main air jet	0.6 mm (0.02 in.)
Jet needle	5D40
Jet needle clip position	3rd groove
Needle jet	P-4
Pilot jet No.	42.5
Pilot air jet No.	160
Starter jet No.	50
Pilot screw opening	2 turns out
Float level	12.5-13.5 mm (0.49-0.53 in.)
Idle speed	1,350-1,450 rpm

Item	1990-1995 U.S. and Canadian (LT-F250) 1990-1991 U.S. and Canadian (LT-4WD)
Model No.	Mikuni BST31SS
Identification No.	19B60
Bore size	31 mm (1.22 in.)
Main jet No.	122.5
Main air jet	0.6 mm (0.02 in.)
Jet needle	5D40
Jet needle clip position	4th groove
Needle jet	P-4
Pilot jet No.	40
Pilot air jet No.	160
Starter jet No.	50
Pilot screw opening	
1990-1991 (LT-F250, LF-4WD)	2 turns out
1992-1995 (LT-F250)	2 3/4 turns out
Float level	12.5-13.5 mm (0.49-0.53 in.)
Idle speed	1,400-1,600 rpm

(continued)

Table 1 CARBURETOR SPECIFICATIONS (continued)

Item	1992-1995 U.S. and Canadian (LT-4WD)
Model No.	Mikuni BST31SS
Identification No.	
1992-1994	19B6
1995	19BA
Bore size	31 mm (1.22 in.)
Main jet No.	122.5
Main air jet	0.6 mm (0.02 in.)
Jet needle	5D40
Jet needle clip position	4th groove
Needle jet	P-4
Pilot jet No.	40
Pilot air jet No.	160
Starter jet No.	42.5
Pilot screw opening	2 7/8 turns out
Float level	12.5-13.5 mm (0.49-0.53 in.)
Idle speed	1,400-1,600 rpm

Item	1991-1995 U.S. and Canadian (LT-4WDX)
Model No.	Mikuni BST31SS
Identification No.	
1991-1993	19B8
1994-1995	19B9
Bore size	31 mm (1.22 in.)
Main jet No.	120
Main air jet	1.1 mm (0.04 in.)
Jet needle	5D40
Jet needle clip position	4th groove
Needle jet	P-2
Pilot jet No.	37.5
Pilot air jet No.	155
Starter jet No.	42.5
Pilot screw opening	2 5/8 turns out
Float level	12.5-13.5 mm (0.49-0.53 in.)
Idle speed	1,400-1,600 rpm

8

Table 2 EXHAUST SYSTEM TIGHTENING TORQUE

Item	N·m	ft.-lb.
Exhaust pipe-to-cylinder head nuts	9-12	6.5-8.5
Muffler-to-exhaust pipe bolt	18-23	13-16.5
Muffler mounting bolts	18-28	13-20
Frame left-hand side bridge bolts	60-70	43.5-50.5

CHAPTER NINE

ELECTRICAL SYSTEM

This chapter contains operating principles and service and test procedures for all electrical and ignition components. Information regarding the battery and spark plugs are covered in Chapter Three.

The electrical system includes the following systems:

a. Charging system.
b. Ignition system.
c. Lighting system.

Tables 1-4 are at the end of this chapter.

ELECTRICAL CONNECTORS

The Suzuki ATV is equipped with many electrical components, connectors and wires. Since this type of ATV is used in many construction and agricultural applications, the vehicle may be subjected to a high moisture environment. Corrosion-causing moisture can enter these many electrical connectors and cause poor electrical connections leading to component failure. Troubleshooting an electrical circuit with one or more corroded electrical connectors can be very time consuming and frustrating.

When reconnecting electrical connectors, pack them in a dielectric grease compound. Dielectric grease is especially formulated for sealing and waterproofing electrical connectors and will not interfere with the current flow through the electrical connectors. Use only this compound or an equivalent designed for this specific purpose. Do *not* use a substitute that may interfere with the current flow within the electrical connector. Do *not* use silicone sealant as this may lock the two connectors together making it almost impossible to separate the electrical connectors.

After cleaning both the male and female connectors, make sure they are thoroughly dry. Make sure there are no bent pins on the male side of the connector (**Figure 1**) and that the metal terminal on each end of the wire (**Figure 2**) is pushed all the way into the connector. If not, push it in with a narrow-blade screwdriver.

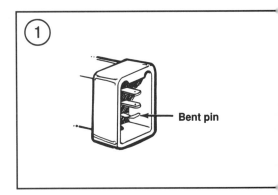

Bent pin

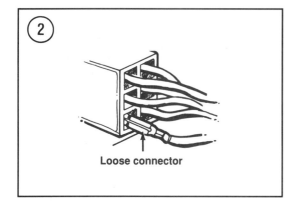

Loose connector

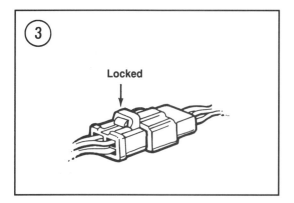

Locked

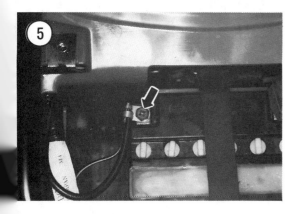

Using the dielectric compound, pack the interior of one of the connectors prior to connecting the 2 connector halves. On multi-pin connectors, pack the male side and on single-wire connectors, pack the female side. Use a good-size glob so that it will squish out when the two halves are pushed together. For best results, the compound should fill the entire inner area of the connector. Push the connectors together and make sure they are fully engaged and locked together (**Figure 3**). On multi-pin connectors, also pack the backside of both the male and female connectors with the compound to prevent moisture from entering the backside of the connector and causing corrosion. After the connector is fully packed, wipe the exterior of all excessive dielectric compound.

Get into the practice of cleaning and sealing all electrical connectors every time they are unplugged. This may prevent a breakdown on the trail, or job site, and also save you time when troubleshooting a circuit.

Always make sure all ground connections are free of corrosion and are tight at various locations on the vehicle.

BATTERY NEGATIVE TERMINAL

Some of the component replacement procedures and some of the test procedures in this chapter require disconnecting the battery negative (–) lead as a safety precaution.

1. Place the ATV on level ground and set the parking brake. Block the rear wheels so the vehicle will not roll in either direction.

2. Remove the screws securing the front cover (**Figure 4**) and remove the front cover.

3. Remove the bolt and disconnect the battery negative (**Figure 5**) cable from the terminal.

4. Move the negative lead out of the way so it will not accidentally make contact with the battery negative terminal.

5. After the procedure is completed, make sure the battery terminal and the cable connector are free of corrosion. Thoroughly clean if necessary; refer to *Battery* in Chapter Three.

6. Reconnect the battery negative cable to the terminal and tighten the bolt securely.

7. Install the front cover and tighten the screws securely.

CHARGING SYSTEM

The charging system consists of the battery, AC generator and a solid-state voltage regulator/rectifier. **Figure 6** shows the charging system.

Alternating current generated by the AC generator is rectified to direct current. The voltage regulator maintains the voltage to the electrical load (lights, ignition, etc.) at a constant rate regardless of variations in engine speed and load.

A malfunction in the charging system generally causes the battery to remain undercharged. To prevent damage to the AC generator and the regulator/rectifier when testing and repairing the charging system, note the following precautions:

1. Always disconnect the negative battery cable, as described in this chapter, before removing a component in the charging system.

2. If necessary to charge the battery, remove the battery from the vehicle and recharge it as described in Chapter Three.

3. Inspect the physical condition of the battery. Look for bulges or cracks in the case, leaking electrolyte or corrosion buildup.

4. Check the wiring in the charging system for signs of chafing, deterioration or other damage.

5. Check the wiring for corroded or loose connections. Clean, tighten or reconnect as required.

Leakage Test

Perform this test prior to performing the output test.

1. Turn the ignition switch OFF.

2. Disconnect the battery negative (–) lead (**Figure 5**) as described in this chapter.

CAUTION
Before connecting the ammeter into the circuit in Step 3, set the meter to its highest amperage scale. This will prevent a large current flow from damaging the meter or blowing the meter's fuse, if so equipped.

3. Connect an ammeter between the battery negative (–) lead and the negative (–) terminal of the battery (**Figure 7**).

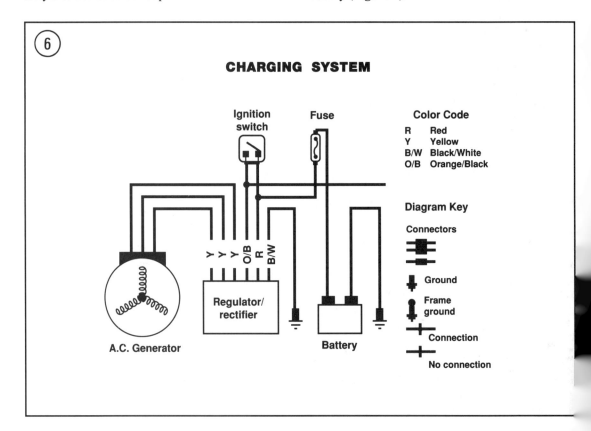

CHARGING SYSTEM

Ignition switch   Fuse

Color Code
R   Red
Y   Yellow
B/W   Black/White
O/B   Orange/Black

Diagram Key

Connectors

Regulator/ rectifier

A.C. Generator

Battery

Ground

Frame ground

Connection

No connection

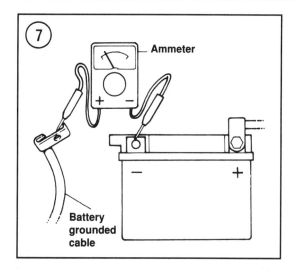

Ammeter

Battery grounded cable

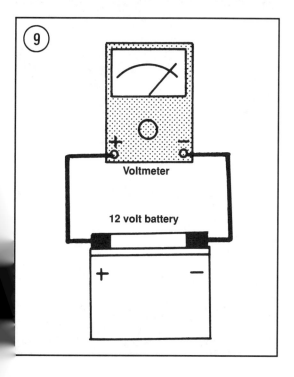

Voltmeter

12 volt battery

4. Switch the ammeter from its highest to lowest amperage scale while reading the meter scale. The ammeter should read less than 1.2 mA. If the amperage is greater, this indicates there is a voltage drain in the system that will discharge the battery.

5. If the current rate is excessive, the probable causes are:

   a. Damaged battery.

   b. Short circuit in the system.

   c. Loose, dirty or faulty electrical connectors in the charging system wiring harness system.

6. Disconnect the ammeter and reconnect the battery negative lead.

Charging System Output Test (Voltage Regulator Test)

Whenever charging system trouble is suspected, make sure the battery is fully charged and in good condition before going any further. Clean and test the battery as described in Chapter Three. Make sure all electrical connectors are tight and free of corrosion.

1. Place the ATV on level ground and set the parking brake. Block the wheels so the vehicle will not roll in either direction.

2. Remove the screws securing the front cover (**Figure 4**) and remove the front cover.

3. Start the engine and let it reach normal operating temperature; shut off the engine.

4. Connect a portable tachometer following its manufacturer's instructions.

5. Start the engine and let it idle.

6. Leave the battery wires connected to the battery and connect a 0-15 *DC* voltmeter between the battery positive and negative terminals (**Figure 8**) as shown in **Figure 9**.

7. Increase engine speed to 5,000 rpm. At this engine speed, the voltmeter should read between 14 and 15.5 volts. If the charging voltage is under 14 volts or over 15.5 volts, perform the *AC Generator No-load Performance Test* in this chapter.

8. If the AC generator passes the no-load test, then the voltage regulator/rectifier is faulty and must be replaced as described in this chapter.

9. After the test is completed, disconnect the voltmeter and portable tachometer.

10. Install all items removed.

AC Generator No-load Performance Test

1. Place the ATV on level ground and set the parking brake. Block the wheels so the vehicle will not roll in either direction.
2. Start the engine and let it reach normal operating temperature; shut off the engine.
3. Remove the seat and the front fender as described in Chapter Fourteen.
4. Connect a portable tachometer following its manufacturer's instructions.
5. Disconnect the electrical connector (**Figure 10**) containing 3 wires (3 yellow).
6. Start the engine and increase and maintain engine speed at 5,000 rpm.
7. Connect a *AC* voltmeter between each of the 3 yellow terminals in the AC generator side of the electrical connector.
8. At this engine speed the voltmeter should read above 55 volts. If the charging voltage is under 55 volts, the AC generator is faulty and must be replaced.
9. After the test is completed, disconnect the voltmeter and portable tachometer.
10. Connect the AC generator electrical connector.
11. Install all items removed.

VOLTAGE REGULATOR/RECTIFIER

Testing

Complete testing of the voltage regulator/rectifier unit requires the use of a special Suzuki Pocket Tester (part No. 09900-25002) and should be tested by a Suzuki dealer service department. This test procedure is provided if you are able to procure this piece of test equipment and choose to perform this test yourself.

NOTE
Do not perform this test procedure with an ohmmeter other than that specified in this procedure. As transistors, capacitors, zener diodes, etc, are used inside the voltage regulator/rectifier unit, the resistance readings will differ when an ohmmeter other than the Suzuki Pocket Tester is used. This may lead to the wrong diagnosis of a problem that may or may not exist within the voltage regulator/rectifier unit.

A Suzuki dealer will either test the voltage regulator/rectifier unit with the special tool or perform a "remove and replace" test to see if the voltage regulator/rectifier unit is faulty. This type of "R/R" test is expensive if performed by yourself. Remember if you purchase a new voltage regulator/rectifier unit and it does *not* solve your particular charging system problem, you *cannot* return the voltage regulator/rectifier unit for refund. Most motorcycle dealers will *not* accept returns on any electrical component since they could be damaged internally even though they look okay externally.

Make sure all connections between the various components are clean and tight. Be sure that the wiring connectors are pushed together firmly and packed with a dielectric compound to help keep out moisture.

Resistance Value Inspection

If the voltage regulator/rectifier fails either the output voltage and/or output current test, then the voltage regulator/rectifier should be tested for an internal short or open.

1. Place the ATV on level ground and set the parking brake. Block the wheels so the vehicle will not roll in either direction.

2. Start the engine and let it reach normal operating temperature. Shut off the engine.

3. Remove the seat and the front fender as described in Chapter Fourteen.

NOTE
During front fender removal, the battery is disconnected and removed from the chassis. Do not reconnect the battery since it must be removed from the circuit for this test procedure.

4A. *1987-1989 models*—Disconnect the 6-pin connector (**Figure 11**) from the voltage regulator/recti-

fier. The connector contains 3 yellow wires, 1 red wire, 1 orange/black wire and 1 black/white wire.

4B. *1990-on models*—Disconnect the 5-pin connector from the voltage regulator/rectifier. The connector contains 3 yellow wires, 1 red wire and 1 black/white wire.

NOTE
In Step 5 connect the Pocket Tester ohm-meter test leads to the voltage regulator/rectifier electrical connector terminals.

5. Use the Suzuki Pocket Tester, set at R × K, and check continuity between each of the voltage regulator/rectifier terminals. Refer to **Figure 12** for 1987-1989 models or **Figure 13** for 1990-on models

VOLTAGE REGULATOR TEST POINTS (1987-1989)

Unit: Approx. kΩ

Positive probe of tester to:

Negative probe of tester to:	R	O/B	B/W	Y (A)	Y (B)	Y (C)
R		∞	∞	∞	∞	∞
O/B	6 – 20		0.1 – 1	2 – 7	2 – 7	2 – 7
B/W	6 – 20	0.1 – 1		1 – 6	1 – 6	1 – 6
Y (A)	1 – 6	∞	∞		∞	∞
Y (B)	1 – 6	∞	∞	∞		∞
Y (C)	1 – 6	∞	∞	∞	∞	

for terminal identification and for test lead placement and specified resistance readings. For terminal location within the electrical connector, refer to **Figure 14** for 1987-1989 or **Figure 15** for 1990-on models.

6. If any of the resistance readings are higher than specified, there is an open in the unit. If any of the resistance readings are lower than specified, there is a short in the unit.

7. If the voltage regulator/rectifier fails any portion of this test, the unit is faulty and must be replaced as described in this chapter.

Removal/Installation

1. Place the ATV on level ground and set the parking brake. Block the wheels so the vehicle will not roll in either direction.

2. Remove the seat and the front fender as described in Chapter Fourteen.

NOTE
During front fender removal, the battery is disconnected and removed from the chassis. Do not reconnect the battery since it must be removed from the circuit for this test procedure.

3A. *1987-1989 models*—Disconnect the 6-pin connector (**Figure 11**) from the voltage regulator/rectifier. The connector contains 3 yellow wires, 1 red wire, 1 orange/black wire and 1 black/white wire.

3B. *1990-on models*—Disconnect the 5-pin connector from the voltage regulator/rectifier. The connector contains 3 yellow wires, 1 red wire and 1 black/white wire.

4. Remove the bolts securing the voltage regulator (**Figure 16**) to the frame and remove the voltage regulator.

5. Install by reversing these removal steps while noting the following:

   a. Tighten the mounting bolts securely.

⑬ **VOLTAGE REGULATOR TEST POINTS (1990-ON)**

Unit: kΩ

		R	Y_1	Y_2	Y_3	B/W
Positive probe of tester to:						
Negative probe of tester to:	R		20 – 100	20 – 100	20 – 100	15 – 60
	Y_1	1 – 8		20 – 200	20 – 200	20 – 100
	Y_2	1 – 8	20 – 200		20 – 200	20 – 100
	Y_3	1 – 8	20 – 200	20 – 200		20 – 100
	B/W	1.5 – 10	1 – 8	1 – 8	1 – 8	

b. Make sure all electrical connections are tight and free of corrosion.

c. Connect the battery negative (–) lead.

AC GENERATOR

The AC generator is a form of electrical generator in which a magnetized field called a rotor revolves around a set of stationary coils called a stator assembly. As the rotor revolves, alternating current is induced in the stator coils. The current is then rectified to direct current and is used to operate the electrical systems on the vehicle and to keep the

battery charged. The rotor is permanently magnetized.

Rotor Testing

The rotor is permanently magnetized and cannot be tested except by replacing it with a known good one. The rotor can lose magnetism from old age or a sharp hit. If defective, the rotor must be replaced; it cannot be re-magnetized.

Stator Testing

1. Remove the seat as described in Chapter Fourteen.

2. Start the engine and let it reach normal operating temperature. Shut off the engine.

3. Follow the electrical wiring harness from the AC generator to where it connects to the main wiring harness on the left-hand side of the vehicle.

4. Disconnect the alternator stator coil 3-pin electrical connector containing 3 yellow wires.

5. Use an ohmmeter set at R × 1 and check continuity between each yellow terminal on the alternator stator side of the connector. The specified resistance is listed in **Table 1**.

6. Replace the stator assembly if any yellow terminal shows no continuity (infinite resistance) to any other yellow terminal. This would indicate an open in the stator coil winding.

7. Use an ohmmeter set at R × 1 and check continuity from each yellow terminal on the alternator stator side of the connector to ground.

> *NOTE*
> *The CDI pickup coil and stator are one assembly and cannot be replaced sepa-*

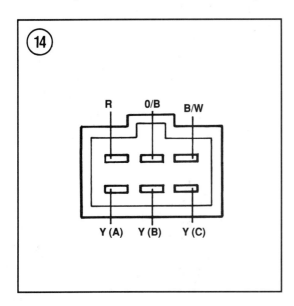

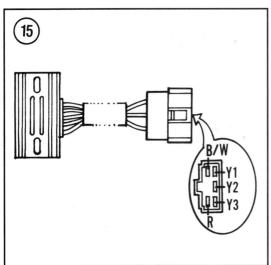

rately. If either of the components fail, the entire assembly must be replaced.

8. Replace the pickup coil/stator assembly if any yellow terminal shows continuity (indicated resistance) to ground. This would indicate a short within the stator coil winding.

NOTE
Prior to replacing the pickup coil/stator assembly, check the electrical wires to and within the electrical connector for any opens or poor connections.

9. If the stator assembly fails either of these tests, it must be replaced as described in this chapter.
10. If the stator checks okay, reconnect the 3-pin electrical connector. Make sure it is free of corrosion and is tight.
11. Install the seat.

**Stator Assembly
Removal/Installation**

1. Remove the left-hand crankcase cover as described under *Left-hand Crankcase Cover Removal/Installation* in Chapter Five.
2. If necessary, remove the bolts (**Figure 17**) securing the stator assembly to the left-hand crankcase cover.
3. Remove the screws (A, **Figure 18**) securing the CDI pickup coil to the left-hand crankcase cover.
4. Pull the electrical harness and rubber grommet (B, **Figure 18**) from the left-hand crankcase cover and remove the stator and CDI pickup coil assembly.
5. Install the stator and CDI pickup coil assembly into the left-hand crankcase cover.
6. Apply blue Loctite (No. 242) to the stator assembly bolt threads prior to installation. Install the bolts (**Figure 17**) and tighten securely.
7. Apply a light coat of gasket sealer to the groove in the electrical harness rubber grommet prior to installation. Make sure the rubber grommet is positioned correctly and pushed all the way down into the cover to prevent an oil leak.
8. Install the screws (A, **Figure 18**) securing the CDI pickup coil to the left-hand crankcase cover and tighten securely.
9. Apply a light coat of silicone sealant to the top surface of the electrical harness rubber grommet and to the crankcase sealing surface on each side of the

grommet (**Figure 19**). This is necessary to prevent an oil leak.
10. Install the left-hand crankcase cover as described in Chapter Five.
11. Route the electrical harness the same way it was before removal. Make sure the electrical connector is free of corrosion and is tight.

Rotor Removal/Inspection

Refer to **Figure 20** for this procedure.

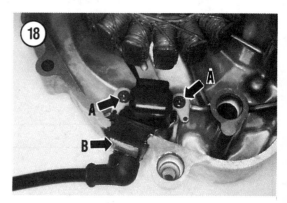

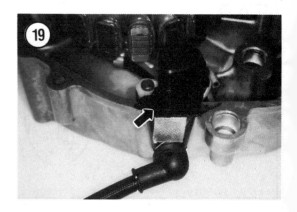

AC GENERATOR

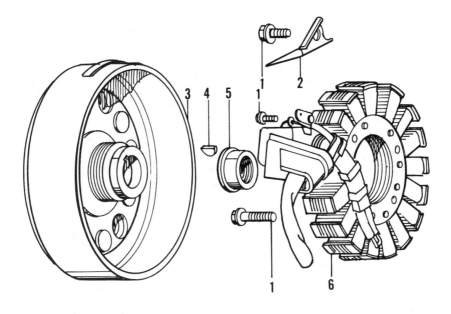

1. Bolt
2. Oil baffle
3. Rotor
4. Woodruff key
5. Nut
6. Stator/pickup
   coil assembly

9

1. Remove the left-hand crankcase cover as described under *Left-hand Crankcase Cover Removal/Installation* in Chapter Five.

2. Remove the starter idle gear assembly as described under *Starter Reduction Gears Removal/Installation* in Chapter Five.

3. Secure the rotor with a 29 mm box wrench (A, **Figure 21**) and loosen the nut with a 22 mm long socket (B, **Figure 21**).

4. Remove the nut (**Figure 22**) securing the A.C. generator rotor.

CAUTION
The rotor has fine threads that are easily damaged if the puller is installed incorrectly. When attaching the flywheel puller be careful to not cross-thread it during installation to avoid thread damage.

5. Screw on a flywheel puller until it stops (**Figure 23**). Use the Suzuki flywheel puller (part No. 09930-31920), or equivalent.

CAUTION
Don't try to remove the rotor without a puller; any attempt to do so will ultimately lead to some form of damage to the engine and/or rotor. Many aftermarket pullers are available from motorcycle dealers or mail order houses. The cost of one of these pullers is low and it makes an excellent addition to any mechanic's tool box. If you can't buy or borrow one, have the dealer remove the rotor.

6. Hold the puller with an adjustable wrench and gradually tighten the center bolt until the rotor disengages from the crankshaft.

NOTE
If the rotor is difficult to remove, strike the puller center bolt with a hammer a few times. This will usually break it loose.

CAUTION
Never strike the rotor with a hammer as this could destroy the magnetism in the rotor. If destroyed, the rotor must be replaced.

7. Reach behind the rotor and grab onto the starter
clutch gear. Remove the starter clutch gear, rotor,
needle bearing and the puller from the crankshaft.
After removal, unscrew the puller from the rotor.

8. If necessary, remove the Woodruff key from the
crankshaft then remove the starter clutch assembly
and the needle bearing.

9. If necessary, remove the starter clutch gear and
needle bearing (**Figure 24**) from the backside of the
rotor.

10. Inspect the inside of the rotor (**Figure 25**) for
small bolts, washers or other metal "trash" that may
have been picked up by the magnets. These small
metal bits can cause severe damage to the AC generator stator plate components.

11. Inspect the rotor keyway (**Figure 26**) for wear
or damage. If damage is severe, replace the rotor.

Rotor Installation

1. Use an aerosol, electrical contact cleaner and
clean all oil residue from the crankshaft taper where
the rotor slides onto it and the matching inside
tapered surface in the rotor. This is to assure a good
tight fit of the rotor onto the crankshaft.

2. If removed, install the Woodruff key (**Figure 27**)
in the crankshaft slot and center it.

3. Make sure the camshaft drive chain is properly
meshed with the crankshaft sprocket (**Figure 28**).

4. Install the starter clutch gear, rotor and needle
bearing onto the crankshaft. Push the rotor assembly
(A, **Figure 29**) all the way on until it bottoms out
(**Figure 30**).

5. Apply blue Loctite (No. 242) to the nut threads prior to installation. Screw the nut (**Figure 22**) all the way on until it stops.

6. Secure the rotor with a 29 mm box wrench and tighten the nut with a 22 mm long socket (**Figure 31**). Tighten the nut to the torque specification listed in **Table 2**.

7. Install the starter idle gear assembly (B, **Figure 29**) as described in Chapter Five.

8. Install the left-hand crankcase cover as described in Chapter Five.

CAPACITOR DISCHARGE IGNITION

All models are equipped with a capacitor discharge ignition (CDI) system, a solid-state system that uses no mechanical parts such as cams or breaker points and no routine maintenance is required. The CDI ignition circuit is shown in **Figure 32**.

As the rotor is turned by the crankshaft, the permanent magnets within the rotor cause an electronic pulse to develop in the primary coil of the stator assembly. This pulse is then routed to the CDI unit where it is amplified. A pulse from the pickup coil in the stator assembly is used to trigger the output of the CDI unit which in turn triggers the output of the ignition coil and fires the spark plug.

CDI Precautions

Certain measures must be taken to protect the ignition system. Damage to the semiconductors in the system will occur if the following precautions are not observed.

1. Never connect the battery backward. If the battery polarity is wrong, damage will occur to the voltage regulator/rectifier, CDI unit and alternator stator assembly.

2. Do not disconnect the battery when the engine is running. A voltage surge will occur which will damage the voltage regulator/rectifier and possibly burn out light bulbs.

3. Never disconnect any of the electrical connections while the engine is running.

4. Keep all connections between the various ignition system units clean and tight. Be sure that the wiring connectors are pushed together firmly to help keep out moisture. Also pack the connectors with

dielectric compound as described at the beginning of this chapter.

5. Do not substitute another type of ignition coil.

6. Most components are mounted within a rubber vibration isolator. Always be sure that the isolator is in place when installing the units in the system.

7. Prior to inspection or troubleshooting the ignition system, check the battery charge as described under *Battery* in Chapter Three. For best test results, the battery must be fully charged (12.0 volts or higher). A lower voltage reading will result with different and inaccurate test readings.

8. Do *not* crank the engine unless the spark plug is installed in the cylinder head or grounded against the engine.

CDI Troubleshooting

Problems with the CDI ignition system are indicated by either a weak spark or no spark at all. Refer to **Table 1** for ignition component specifications.

CDI Testing

Complete testing of the CDI unit requires a special Suzuki Pocket Tester (part No. 09900-25002) and

should be tested by a Suzuki dealer service department. This test procedure is provided if you are able to procure this piece of test equipment and choose to perform this test yourself.

NOTE
Do not perform this test procedure with an ohmmeter other than that specified in this procedure. As transistors, capacitors, zener diodes, etc, are used inside the CDI unit, the resistance readings will differ when an ohmmeter other than the Suzuki pocket tester is used. This may lead to the wrong diagnosis of a problem that may or may not exist within the CDI unit.

A Suzuki dealer will either test the CDI unit with the special tool or perform a "remove and replace" test to see if the CDI unit is faulty. This type of "R/R" test is expensive to perform on your own. Remember if you purchase a new CDI unit and it does *not* solve your particular ignition system problem, you *cannot* return the CDI unit for refund. Most motorcycle dealers will *not* accept returns on any electrical component since they could be damaged internally even though they look okay externally.

Make sure all connections between the various components are clean and tight. Be sure that the wiring connectors within the circuit are pushed together firmly and packed with a dielectric compound to help keep out moisture.

Performance Test

1. Place the ATV on level ground and set the parking brake. Block the wheels so the vehicle will not roll in either direction.

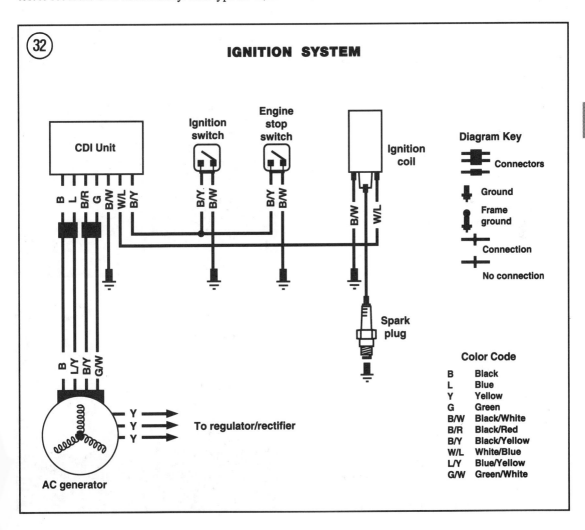

2. Disconnect the high voltage lead (**Figure 33**) from the spark plug. Remove the spark plug from the cylinder head as described under *Spark Plug* in Chapter Three.

> *NOTE*
> *The spark plug must ground out against a piece of bare metal on the engine or frame. If necessary, carefully scrape away some of the paint to reach bare metal.*

3. Connect a new or known good spark plug to the high voltage lead and place the spark plug base on a good ground like the engine cylinder head. Position the spark plug so you can see the electrodes.

> *WARNING*
> *If it is necessary to hold the high voltage lead, do so with an insulated pair of pliers. The high voltage generated by the ignitor unit could produce serious or fatal shocks.*

4. Turn the engine over rapidly with the starter motor or recoil starter and check for a spark. If there is a fat blue spark, the CDI unit is working properly.
5. If a weak spark or no spark is obtained and the pickup coil and ignition coil are okay, test the CDI unit yourself or have it tested by a Suzuki dealer.
6. Reinstall the spark plug and connect the high voltage lead onto the spark plug.
7. If all of the ignition components are okay, then check the following:
   a. Check for an open or short in the wire harness between each component in the ignition system.
   b. Again, make sure all connections between the various components are clean and tight. Be sure that the wiring connectors are pushed together firmly to help keep out moisture.

Resistance Test

1. Place the ATV on level ground and set the parking brake. Block the wheels so the vehicle will not roll in either direction.
2. Remove the seat and the front fender as described in Chapter Fourteen.

> *NOTE*
> *During front fender removal, the battery is disconnected and removed from the chassis. Do not reconnect the battery*

since it must be removed from the circuit for this test procedure.

> *NOTE*
> *The number of CDI electrical connectors varies among the different model years.*

3. Disconnect the electrical connector(s) from the CDI unit (**Figure 34**).
4. Use the Suzuki Pocket Tester, set at R × K, and check continuity between each of the CDI terminals. Refer to **Figure 35** for 1987-1989 models or **Figure 36** for 1990-on models for terminal identification and for test lead placement and specified resistance readings.
5. Connect the Pocket Tester to the CDI unit side of the electrical connector(s). If any of the resistance readings are higher than specified, there is an open in the unit. If any of the resistance readings are lower than specified, there is a short in the unit.

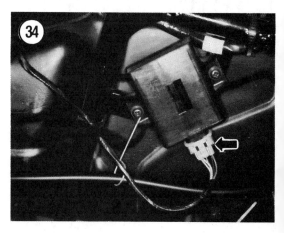

6. If the CDI unit fails any portion of this test, the unit is faulty and must be replaced as described in this chapter.

7. If the CDI unit checks out okay, reconnect the electrical connector(s). Make sure the electrical connector(s) is free of corrosion and is tight.

Replacement

1. Place the ATV on level ground and set the parking brake. Block the wheels so the vehicle will not roll in either direction.

2. Remove the seat and front fender as described in Chapter Fourteen.

3. Disconnect the electrical connector(s) from the CDI unit (A, **Figure 37**).

4. Remove the screws (B, **Figure 37**) securing the CDI unit to the frame.

5. Install a new CDI unit onto the frame. On models so equipped, install the wire guide (C, **Figure 37**) to the mounting screw.

6. Connect the electrical connector(s) to the CDI unit. Make sure the electrical connector(s) are free of corrosion and are tight.

---

(35) CDI TEST POINTS (1987-1989)

Unit: Approx. kΩ

Positive probe of tester:

Negative probe of tester:	B	BL	G	B/R	W/BL	B/W	B/Y
B		10 – 80	10 – 60	10 – 60	∞	10 – 60	2 – 10
Bl	5 – 40		5 – 30	4 – 20	∞	4 – 20	20 – 100
G	3 – 20	3 – 20		1 – 6	∞	1 – 6	8 – 40
B/R	2 – 10	2 – 10	1 – 6		∞	0	5 – 30
W/Bl	∞	∞	∞	∞		∞	∞
B/W	2 – 10	2 – 10	1 – 6	0			5 – 30
B/Y	∞	∞	∞	∞	∞	∞	

9

7. Install the front fender and seat as described in Chapter Fourteen.

PICKUP COIL

Resistance Check

1. Place the ATV on level ground and set the parking brake. Block the wheels so the vehicle will not roll in either direction.

2. Remove the seat as described in Chapter Fourteen.

3. Start the engine and let it reach normal operating temperature. Shut off the engine.

NOTE
The number of electrical connectors differs between the models and years. Refer to the wiring diagrams at the end of this book for your specific model. There are either two 2-pin connectors or one 2-pin electrical connector for both the pickup coil and the alternator stator coil assembly.

(36)	CDI TEST POINTS (1990-ON)				
					Unit: kΩ

		Positive probe of tester to:			
		0	B/W	G	B/BL	W/BL
Negative probe of tester to:	0		2 – 12	3 – 20	2 – 12	∞
	B/W	∞		1 – 6	0	∞
	G	∞	1 – 6		1 – 6	∞
	B/Bl	∞	0	1 – 6		∞
	W/Bl	∞	1 – 6	3 – 15	1 – 6	

4. Follow the electrical wiring harness from the AC generator to where it connects to the main wiring harness on the left-hand side of the vehicle.

5. Disconnect the pickup and alternator stator coil electrical connector(s).

6. Use an ohmmeter set at R × 1 and check continuity between the black/yellow and the green/white terminals on the AC generator stator side of the connector. The specified resistance is listed in **Table 1**.

NOTE
The CDI pickup coil and stator are one assembly and cannot be replaced separately. If either of the components fail, the entire assembly must be replaced.

7. If the pickup coil resistance does not meet (or come close to) the specifications, the pickup coil and AC generator stator assembly must be replaced as an assembly as described in this chapter.

NOTE
Prior to replacing the pickup coil/stator assembly, check the electrical wires to and within the electrical connector for any opens or poor connections.

8. If the pickup coil checks okay, reconnect the electrical connector(s). Make sure they are free of corrosion and are tight.

9. Install the seat as described in Chapter Fourteen.

IGNITION COIL

Performance Test

NOTE
The spark plug must ground out against a piece of bare metal on the engine or frame.

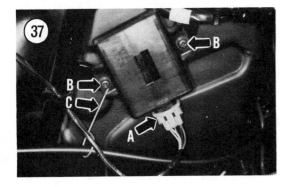

First as a quick check of ignition coil condition, disconnect the high voltage lead from the spark plug. Remove the spark plug (**Figure 33**) from the cylinder heads as described under *Spark Plug* in Chapter Three. Connect a new or known good spark plug to the high voltage lead and place the spark plug base on a good ground like the engine cylinder head. Position the spark plug so you can see the electrodes.

WARNING
If it is necessary to hold the high voltage lead, do so with an insulated pair of pliers. The high voltage generated by the signal generator could produce serious or fatal shocks.

Crank the engine with the starter motor or recoil starter. If a fat blue spark occurs, the coil is in good condition; if not, proceed as follows. Make sure that you are using a known good spark plug for this test. If the spark plug used is defective, the test results will be incorrect.

Reinstall the spark plug in the cylinder head and connect the high voltage lead.

Resistance Test

NOTE
In order to get accurate resistance measurements, the coil must be warm (minimum temperature is 20°C [68° F]). If necessary, start the engine and let it warm up to normal operating temperature. If the engine will not start, warm the ignition coil with a portable hair dryer.

1. Place the ATV on level ground and set the parking brake. Block the wheels so the vehicle will not roll in either direction.

2. Remove the front fender as described in Chapter Fourteen.

NOTE
During front fender removal, the battery is disconnected and removed from the chassis. Do not reconnect the battery since it must be removed from the circuit for this test procedure.

3. Disconnect all ignition coil wires (including the spark plug lead from the spark plug) before testing.

4. Set the ohmmeter to R × 1 and zero the test leads.

5. Measure the primary coil resistance between the primary wire terminals (positive + and negative -) on top of the ignition coil (**Figure 38**). The specified resistance value is listed in **Table 1**.

6. Set the ohmmeter to R × K and zero the test leads.

7. Measure the secondary coil resistance between the spark plug lead cap and the negative (-) terminal (**Figure 38**). The specified resistance value is listed in **Table 1**.

8. If the coil resistance does not meet (or come close to) either of these specifications, the coil must be replaced. If the coil exhibits visible damage, it should be replaced as described in this chapter.

9. If the coil checks out okay, reconnect all ignition coil wires to the ignition coil.

10. Install the front fender as described in Chapter Fourteen.

Removal/Installation

1. Place the ATV on level ground and set the parking brake. Block the wheels so the vehicle will not roll in either direction.

2. Remove the seat and the front fender as described in Chapter Fourteen.

> *NOTE*
> *During front fender removal, the battery is disconnected and removed from the chassis. Do not reconnect the battery since it must be removed from the circuit for this procedure.*

3. Disconnect the high voltage lead (**Figure 33**) from the spark plug.

4. Disconnect the primary electrical wires (A, **Figure 39**) from the ignition coil.

5. Remove the bolts (B, **Figure 39**) securing the ignition coil to the frame and remove the coil.

6. Install by reversing these removal steps while noting the following:

  a. Be sure to install the primary ground wire (C, **Figure 39**) under the upper mounting bolt. Tighten both bolts securely.

  b. Make sure all electrical connections are free of corrosion and are tight.

STARTING SYSTEM

The starter system includes an ignition switch, a starter switch, reverse switch, neutral switch, starter

relay, battery and starter motor as shown in **Figure 40**. Each component of this system is covered separately in this chapter except for the battery that is covered in Chapter Three and the starter clutch and gears that are covered in Chapter Five.

The recoil starter is a backup system that can be used in case the electric starter will not operate. The recoil starter is covered in Chapter Five.

Table 3, at the end of the chapter, lists possible starter problems, probable causes and most common remedies.

> *CAUTION*
> *Do not operate the starter for more than 5 seconds at a time. Let it rest approximately 10 seconds, then use it again.*

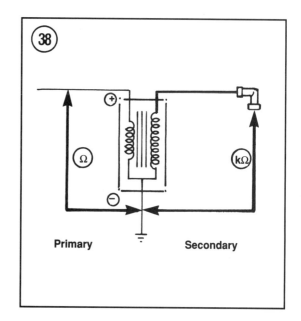

Primary   Secondary

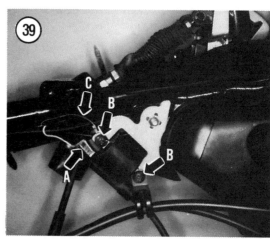

ELECTRIC STARTER

Removal/Installation

1. Place the ATV on level ground and set the parking brake. Block the wheels so the vehicle will not roll in either direction.

2. Remove the seat and the front fender as described in Chapter Fourteen.

NOTE
During front fender removal, the battery is disconnected and removed from the chassis. Do not reconnect the battery

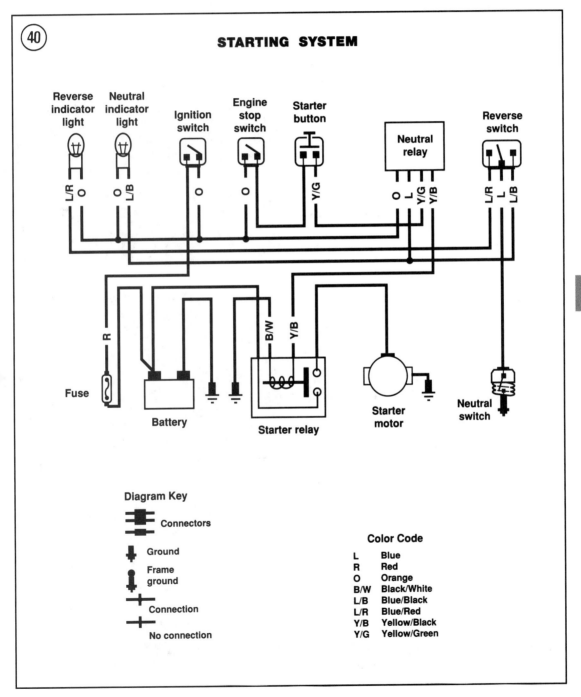

40

STARTING SYSTEM

Diagram Key

Connectors

Ground

Frame ground

Connection

No connection

Color Code

L	Blue
R	Red
O	Orange
B/W	Black/White
L/B	Blue/Black
L/R	Blue/Red
Y/B	Yellow/Black
Y/G	Yellow/Green

9

since it must be removed from the circuit for this procedure.

3. Remove the cotter pin, washer, pivot pin and washer, then disconnect the rear brake cable from the rear brake pedal (A, **Figure 41**).

4. Loosen the locknut, disconnect the rear brake cable from the bracket (B, **Figure 41**) and move the brake cable out of the way from the starter motor.

5. Slide back the rubber boot (A, **Figure 42**) on the electrical cable connector.

6. Remove the nut and disconnect the starter electrical motor cable (B, **Figure 42**) from the starter motor.

7. Remove the 2 bolts (C, **Figure 42**) securing the starter motor to the crankcase.

8. Remove the ground cable (D, **Figure 42**) from the front bolt.

9. Pull the starter motor toward the left-hand side to disengage it from the idle gears. Remove the starter motor (E, **Figure 42**) from the opening in the crankcase.

10. Inspect the starter motor as described in this chapter.

11. Install by reversing these removal steps while noting the following:

   a. Make sure the O-ring seal (A, **Figure 43**) is in place on the end of the end case and apply a light coat of clean engine oil to it prior to installing it in the crankcase.

   b. If the starter motor gear will not mesh properly, slightly rotate the gear and try again until alignment is correct.

   c. Push the starter motor all the way in until it bottoms out on the crankcase surface.

   d. Refill the engine with the recommended type and quantity of engine oil as described in Chapter Three.

   e. Start the engine and check for proper operation.

Preliminary Inspection

The overhaul of a starter motor is best left to an expert. This procedure shows how to detect a defective starter.

Inspect the O-ring seal (A, **Figure 43**). O-ring seals tend to harden after prolonged use and heat and therefore lose their ability to seal properly. Replace as necessary.

Inspect the gear (B, **Figure 43**) for chipped or missing teeth. If damaged, the starter assembly must be replaced.

Disassembly

Refer to **Figure 44** for this procedure.

1. Remove the case through bolts, special washers and O-rings (**Figure 45**).

2. Remove the left-hand end cap (**Figure 46**) from the case.

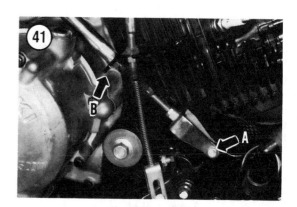

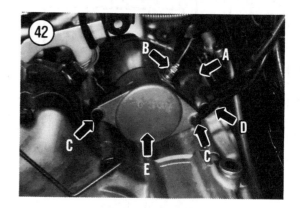

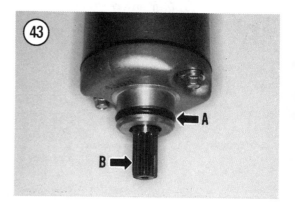

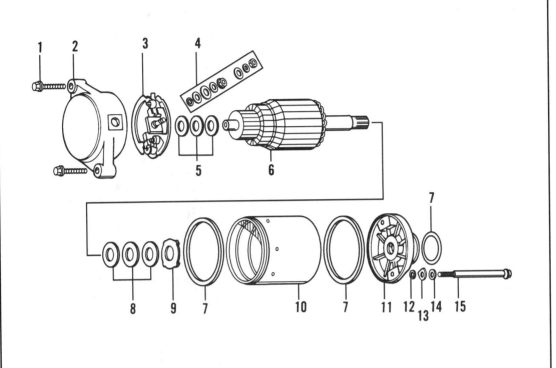

STARTING SYSTEM

1. Mounting bolt
2. Right-hand end cap
3. Brush holder assembly
4. Positive terminal assembly
5. Shim set
6. Armature
7. O-ring
8. Shim set
9. Lockwasher
10. Case
11. Left-hand end cap
12. O-ring
13. Special washer
14. Washer
15. Through bolt

9

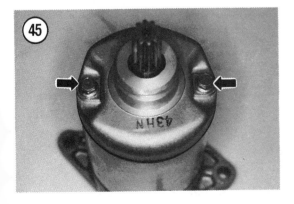

NOTE
*Write down the number of shims (**Figure 47**) used on the shaft next to the left-hand end cap.*

3. Slide off the lockwasher (A, **Figure 48**) and shims (B, **Figure 48**) from the armature shaft.

4. Remove the right-hand end cap (A, **Figure 49**) and brush holder set from the case.

NOTE
*Write down the number of shims (A, **Figure 50**) used on the shaft next to the commutator and next to the left-hand end cap.*

5. Slide off the shims (**Figure 51**) from the armature shaft.

6. Withdraw the armature coil assembly (B, **Figure 50**) from the case.

NOTE
*Before removing the nut, washers and O-ring (**Figure 52**), write down their description and order (**Figure 53**). They must be reinstalled in the same order to insulate this set of brushes from the case.*

7. If necessary, remove the nut, washers and O-ring (**Figure 52**) securing the brush positive (+) and negative (–) brush assembly and remove the brush assembly from the right-hand end cover.

CAUTION
Do not immerse the wire windings in the case or the armature coil in solvent as the insulation may be damaged. Wipe the windings with a cloth lightly moistened with solvent and thoroughly dry.

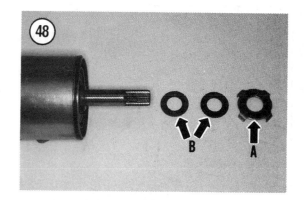

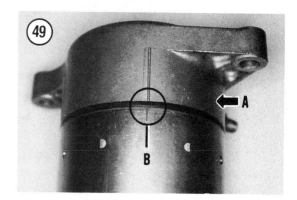

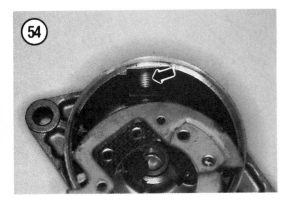

8. Clean all grease, dirt and carbon from all components.

9. Inspect the starter motor components as described in this chapter.

Assembly

Refer to **Figure 44** for this procedure.

> *NOTE*
> *In the next step, install all parts in the same order as noted during disassembly. This is essential in order to insulate the positive (+) set of brushes from the case.*

1. If removed, install the positive (+) and negative (−) brush assembly into the right-hand end cap as follows:

    a. Insert the threaded stud through the hole in the end cap (**Figure 54**).

    b. Align the grooves (A, **Figure 55**) with the tabs (B, **Figure 55**) on the end cap and install the brush assembly into place in the end cap.

    c. Install the O-ring seal (**Figure 56**) onto the threaded stud and push it all the way down into the recess in the end cap (**Figure 57**).

9

    d. Install the washers and nut in the exact same order as removal (**Figure 53**). Tighten the nut securely (**Figure 52**).

2. Install a new O-ring seal (A, **Figure 58**) onto each end of the case. Apply a light coat of clean engine oil to the O-rings.

3. Position the armature coil assembly so the commutator end will be adjacent to the depressions (B, **Figure 58**) in the outer surface of the case.

4. Insert the armature coil assembly (B, **Figure 50**) into the end of the case.

> *NOTE*
> *In the next step, install the exact same number of shims (**Figure 51**) as noted during disassembly. This is necessary to maintain the correct amount of commutator end play.*

5. Slide the shims (A, **Figure 50**) onto the armature shaft.

6. Apply a light coat of molybdenum disulfide grease to the armature shaft (C, **Figure 50**) where it rides in the right-hand cap.

7. Slowly install the right-hand end cap onto the case (**Figure 59**). Carefully slide the armature past both brushes in the end cap, then slide the end cap on all the way. Align the alignment marks on the end cap and case (B, **Figure 49**).

> *NOTE*
> *In the next step, install the exact same number of shims (**Figure 47**) as noted during disassembly. This is necessary to main the correct amount of commutator end play.*

8. Slide the shims (**Figure 47**) onto the armature shaft.

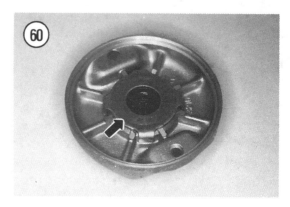

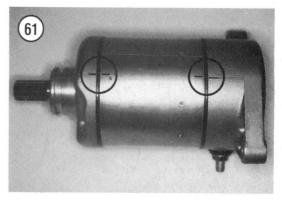

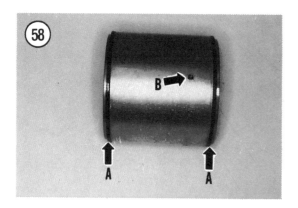

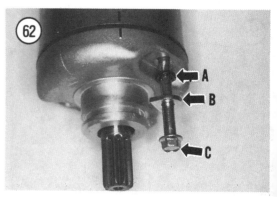

9. Install the lockwasher (**Figure 60**) onto the left-hand end cap. Make sure it is properly located within the end cap.

10. Install the left-hand end cap (**Figure 46**).

11. Slightly rotate it back and forth to make sure the alignment marks on the end caps with the case are aligned properly (**Figure 61**).

12. Apply a small amount of blue Loctite (No. 242) to the case through bolt threads prior to installation.

13. Install a new O-ring seal (A, **Figure 62**) and the special washer (B, **Figure 62**) onto the through bolts.

14. Install the through bolts (C, **Figure 62**) and tighten securely.

Inspection

1. Measure the length of each brush with a vernier caliper (**Figure 63**). If the length is worn the service limit listed in **Table 1** or less, replace the brush assembly.

2. Inspect the armature assembly (A, **Figure 64**) for damage or wear. Replace if necessary.

3. Inspect the commutator (B, **Figure 64**). The mica in a good commutator is below the surface of the copper bars. On a worn commutator, the mica and copper bars may be worn to the same level (**Figure 65**). If necessary, have the commutator serviced by a dealer or electrical repair shop.

4. Inspect the commutator copper bars (**Figure 66**) for discoloration. If a pair of bars are discolored, grounded armature coils are indicated.

5. Use an ohmmeter and perform the following:

    a. Check for continuity between the commutator bars (**Figure 67**); there should be continuity (indicated resistance) between pairs of bars.

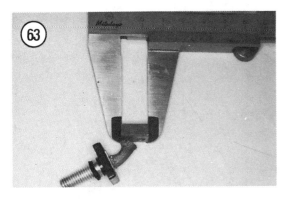

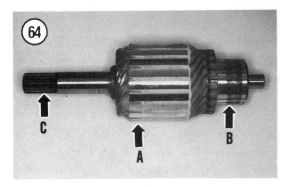

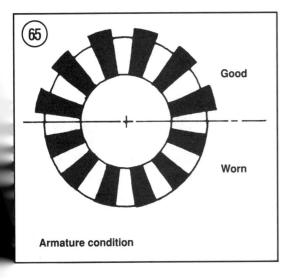

Armature condition

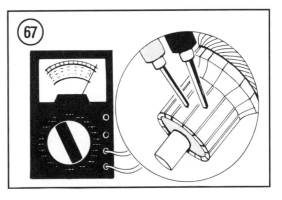

b. Check for continuity between the commutator bars and the shaft (**Figure 68**); there should be *no* continuity (infinite resistance).

c. If the unit fails either of these tests, the starter assembly must be replaced. The armature cannot be replaced individually.

6. Use an ohmmeter and perform the following:

a. Check for continuity between the starter cable terminal (A, **Figure 69**) and the right-hand end cap (B, **Figure 69**); there should be continuity (indicated resistance).

b. Check for continuity between the starter cable terminal and the brush wire terminal; there should be *no* continuity (infinite resistance).

7. Inspect the oil seal (**Figure 70**) and needle bearings (**Figure 71**) in the left-hand end cap for wear, damage or deterioration. Neither part is available as a replacement part. If either is damaged, replace the left-hand end cap.

8. Inspect the right-hand end cap and bushing (**Figure 72**) for wear or damage. The bushing is not available as a replacement part. If either is damaged, replace the right-hand end cap.

9. Inspect the case assembly for wear or damage. Make sure the field coils (**Figure 73**) are bonded securely in place. If damaged, or if any field coils are loose, replace the case assembly.

10. Inspect the brush holder assembly (**Figure 74**) for wear or damage. Inspect the brush springs for wear or damage. The springs are the only replacement parts available for this assembly.

11. Inspect the threads on the positive brush portion for wear or damage. Clean the threads with an appropriate size metric die if necessary.

12. Inspect the gear splines (C, **Figure 64**) on the armature coil assembly for wear or damage. If damage is severe, replace the starter motor assembly.

STARTER RELAY

Testing

1. Remove the front fender as described in Chapter Fourteen.

2. Shift the transmission into neutral.

> *CAUTION*
> *Because the battery positive (+) lead at the starter relay is connected directly to the battery, even when the ignition switch is OFF, do **not** allow the end of*

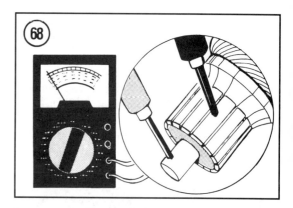

the lead to touch any part of the vehicle during the following procedure—this would result in a short.

3. Move the rubber boot (**Figure 75**) back off the electrical connectors on top of the starter relay.

4. Remove the nuts and washers and disconnect the starter motor lead and the battery positive (+) cable (A, **Figure 76**) from the starter relay.

5. Position the switches in the following positions to run this test correctly:

   a. Ignition switch: ON.

   b. Engine stop switch: RUN.

   c. Neutral switch: ON (transmission in neutral).

   d. Starter button: ON.

6. Set the ohmmeter to R × 1 and zero the test leads.

7. Connect the ohmmeter between the large relay positive (A, **Figure 76**) and negative (B, **Figure 76**) terminals, press the start button. There should be continuity (indicated resistance) indicating the relay is operating correctly. If there is no continuity (infinity), the relay is faulty and must be replaced.

8. Disconnect the primary wires (from the neutral relay) (C, **Figure 76**) from the starter relay.

9. Set the ohmmeter to R × 10 and zero the test leads.

10. Connect the ohmmeter between the 2 primary terminals. There should be indicated resistance. Refer to the standard resistance listed in **Table 1**. If the resistance does not fall within these specifications, the relay is faulty and must be replaced.

11. If the relay checks out okay, install all electrical wires to the relay and tighten the nuts securely. Make sure the electrical connectors are on tight and that the rubber boot is properly installed to keep out moisture.

12. If the relay is faulty, replace it as described in this chapter.

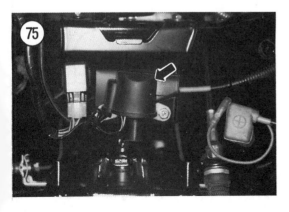

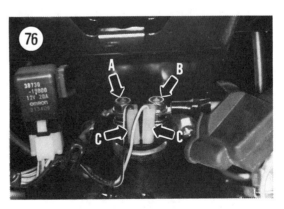

13. Install the front fender.

Removal/Installation

1. Remove the front fender as described in Chapter Fourteen.

> *NOTE*
> *During front fender removal, the battery is disconnected and removed from the chassis. Do not reconnect the battery since it must be removed from the circuit for this procedure.*

2. Shift the transmission into neutral.

> *CAUTION*
> *Because the battery positive (+) lead at the starter relay is connected directly to the battery, even when the ignition switch is OFF, do **not** allow the end of the lead to touch any part of the vehicle during the following procedure—this would result in a short.*

3. Move the rubber boot (**Figure 75**) back off the electrical connectors on top of the starter relay.

4. Remove the nuts and washers and disconnect the starter motor lead and the battery positive (+) cable (A, **Figure 76**) and the negative (B, **Figure 76**) from the starter relay.

5. Disconnect the primary wires (from the neutral relay) (C, **Figure 76**) from the starter relay.

6. Pull the rubber isolator from the mounting tab on the frame.

7. Withdraw the relay from the rubber isolator and install a new one.

8. Replace by reversing these removal steps while noting the following:

   a. Install all electrical wires to the relay. Tighten the nuts securely.

   b. Make sure the electrical connectors are on tight and that the rubber boot is properly installed (**Figure 75**) to keep out moisture.

NEUTRAL RELAY

Removal/Testing/Installation

1. Remove the front fender as described in Chapter Fourteen.

> *NOTE*
> *During front fender removal, the battery is disconnected and removed from the chassis. Do not reconnect the battery since it must be removed from the circuit for this procedure.*

2. Remove the neutral relay from the rubber mount (A, **Figure 77**).

3. Disconnect the electrical connector (B, **Figure 77**) from the neutral relay.

4. Connect a fully charged 12-volt battery to terminals A, **Figure 78** on the relay. Connect the positive (+) cable to the upper "A" terminal and the negative (–) to the lower "A" terminal.

5. With the battery connected to the "A" terminals, use an ohmmeter and check for continuity.

6. Set the ohmmeter to R × 1 and zero the test leads.

7. Connect the ohmmeter between the 2 "B" terminals of the relay. There should be continuity (low resistance).

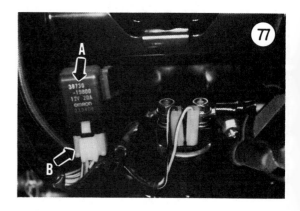

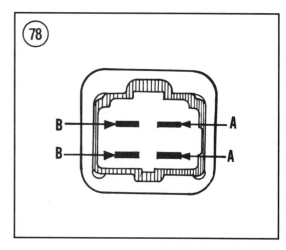

8. If there is no continuity (infinite resistance), the relay is defective and must be replaced.

9. If the old relay checks out okay, reinstall the old relay. If the relay is defective, install a new relay.

10. Reconnect the electrical connector to the relay and install the relay in the rubber mount.

11. Make sure the electrical connector is tight and free of corrosion.

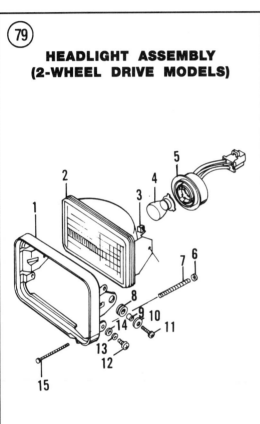

(79)

HEADLIGHT ASSEMBLY (2-WHEEL DRIVE MODELS)

1. Trim ring
2. Lens unit
3. Nut
4. Bulb
5. Electrical connector/ socket assembly
6. Nut
7. Spring
8. Rubber grommet
9. Collar
10. Washer
11. Screw
12. Screw
13. Lockwasher
14. Washer
15. Adjust bolt

12. Install the front fender as described in Chapter Fourteen.

LIGHTING SYSTEM

The lighting system consists of a headlight and taillight. All models are equipped with a neutral and reverse indicator lights housed in the odometer housing (LT-4WD) or indicator panel (LT-F250). **Table 4** lists replacement bulbs for these components.

Always use the correct wattage bulb as indicated in this section. The use of a larger wattage bulb will give a dim light and a smaller wattage bulb will burn out prematurely.

Headlight Bulb Replacement (2-Wheel Drive Models)

Refer to **Figure 79** for this procedure.

1. Remove the screws and washers securing the headlight assembly in the headlight housing.

2. Carefully pull the headlight lens unit out of the housing.

3. Disconnect the electrical connector/socket from the headlight lens unit.

4. Remove the bulb from the electrical connector/socket and replace with a new bulb.

5. Install by reversing these removal steps.

Headlight Housing Removal/Installation (2-Wheel Drive Models)

Refer to **Figure 80** for this procedure.

1. Disconnect the electrical connector from the housing on the left-hand side.

2. Pull up on the release bar to release the headlight assembly from the mounting bracket.

3. Remove the headlight housing from the mounting bracket and remove the headlight assembly.

4. To remove the mounting bracket, remove the screws and lockwashers securing the bracket to the plate at the top of the steering column.

5. Install by reversing these removal steps. Make sure the electrical connection is free of corrosion and is tight.

9

**Headlight Bulb Replacement
(4-Wheel Drive Models)**

Refer to **Figure 81** for this procedure.

1. Remove the screws securing the front cover (**Figure 82**) and remove the cover.

2. Remove the rubber cover (**Figure 83**) from the back of the headlight lens unit.

3. Push in on the socket (**Figure 84**), rotate the socket *counterclockwise* and remove it from the back of the headlight lens unit.

CAUTION
Carefully read all instructions shipped with the replacement quartz halogen bulb. Do not touch the bulb glass with your fingers because of the oil on your skin. Any traces of oil on the glass will drastically reduce bulb life. Clean any traces of oil from the bulb with a cloth moistened in alcohol or lacquer thinner.

4. Remove the light bulb (**Figure 85**).

5. Replace with a new bulb assembly—do not touch the bulb with your fingers.

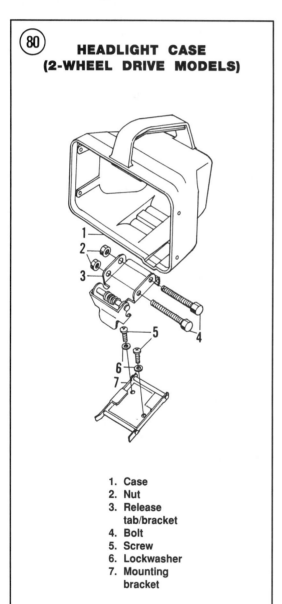

**HEADLIGHT CASE
(2-WHEEL DRIVE MODELS)**

1. Case
2. Nut
3. Release tab/bracket
4. Bolt
5. Screw
6. Lockwasher
7. Mounting bracket

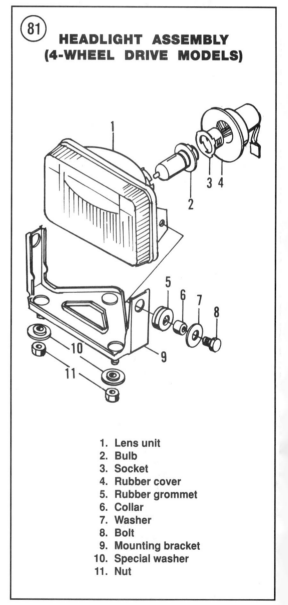

**HEADLIGHT ASSEMBLY
(4-WHEEL DRIVE MODELS)**

1. Lens unit
2. Bulb
3. Socket
4. Rubber cover
5. Rubber grommet
6. Collar
7. Washer
8. Bolt
9. Mounting bracket
10. Special washer
11. Nut

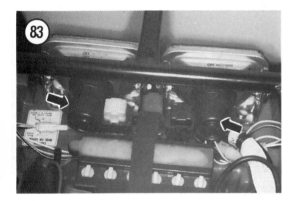

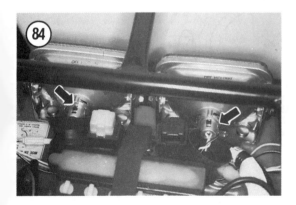

6. Install by reversing these removal steps while noting the following:

    a. Install the rubber cover with the TOP mark facing up.

    b. Make sure all electrical connections are free of corrosion and are tight.

Headlight Housing Removal/Installation (4-Wheel Drive Models)

Refer to **Figure 81** for this procedure.

1. Remove the screws securing the front cover (**Figure 82**) and remove the cover.

2. Remove the rubber cover(s) (A, **Figure 86**) from the back of the headlight lens unit(s).

3. Push in on the socket (**Figure 84**), rotate the socket *counterclockwise* and remove it from the back of the headlight lens unit.

4. Remove the light bulb(s) (**Figure 85**)—do not touch the bulbs with your fingers. Place the bulb(s) in a reclosable plastic bag to keep them clean.

5. Working under the front fender, remove the nuts and washers securing the mounting bracket to the front fender assembly.

6. Remove the headlight housing and mounting bracket (B, **Figure 86**) from the front fender assembly.

7. Install by reversing these removal steps while noting the following:

    a. Install the rubber cover with the TOP mark facing up.

    b. Make sure all electrical connections are free of corrosion and are tight.

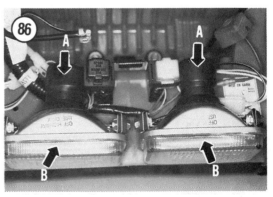

Taillight Replacement

Refer to **Figure 87** for this procedure.

1. Remove the screws (A, **Figure 88**) and washers securing the lens (B, **Figure 88**) and remove the lens.

2. Wash out the inside and outside of the lens with a mild detergent and wipe dry.

3. Inspect the lens gasket and replace it if damaged or deteriorated.

4. Carefully wipe off the reflective portion of the housing.

5. Replace the bulb and install the lens; do not over tighten the screws as the lens may crack.

Taillight Housing Removal/Installation

Refer to **Figure 87** for this procedure.

1. Disconnect the electrical connector from the wiring harness.

2. Remove the nuts, clamps and washers securing the housing to the mounting bracket on the frame.

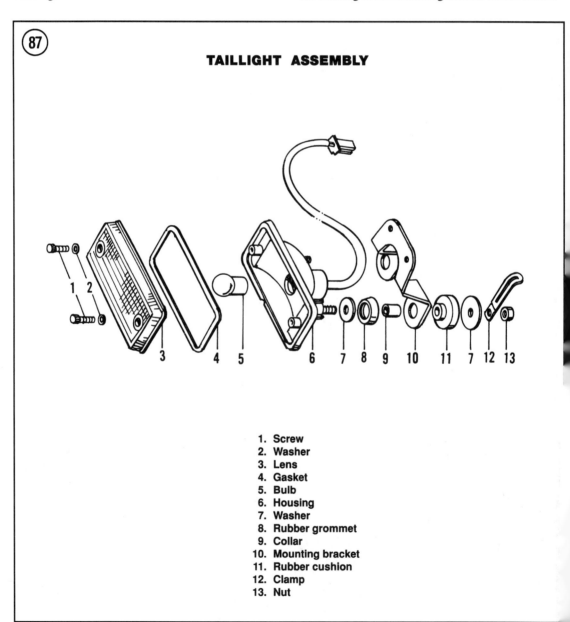

TAILLIGHT ASSEMBLY

1. Screw
2. Washer
3. Lens
4. Gasket
5. Bulb
6. Housing
7. Washer
8. Rubber grommet
9. Collar
10. Mounting bracket
11. Rubber cushion
12. Clamp
13. Nut

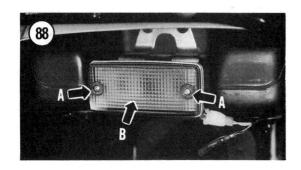

88

A A

B

IGNITION AND LIGHTING SWITCH

89

Position	Color				
	R	O	GR	B/Y	B/W
Off				•——•	
On	•——•				
Light	•——•——•				

ENGINE STOP AND START SWITCH

90

Position	Color				
	B/W	B/Y	O	O/W	Y/G
Off	•——•				
Run			•——•		
Start (push)				•——•	

DIMMER SWITCH

91

Position	Color		
	GR	Y	W
Hi	•——•——•		
Lo	•———————•		

REVERSE SWITCH

92

Position	Color		
	BL/B	BL/R	BL
Neutral	•———————•		
Reverse		•——•	

3. The rubber cushions may stay on the mounting bracket or stick to the housing and washer.

4. Remove the housing from the frame. Don't lose the collar located within each rubber cushion.

5. Install by reversing these removal steps. Make sure the electrical connection is free of corrosion and is tight.

SWITCHES

Switches can be tested for continuity with an ohmmeter (see Chapter One) or a test light at the switch connector plug by operating the switch in each of its operating positions and comparing results with the switch operation. For example, **Figure 89** shows a continuity diagram for the ignition and lighting switch. It shows which terminals should show continuity when the ignition switch is in a given position.

When the ignition switch is in the ON position, there should be continuity between terminals red and orange. This is indicated by the line on the continuity diagram. An ohmmeter connected between these 2 terminals should indicate little or no resistance and a test lamp should light. When the ignition switch is OFF, there should be continuity between the black/yellow and black/white terminals. In the OFF position, the vehicle cannot be started even with the recoil starter.

Testing

If the switch or button doesn't perform properly, replace it. Refer to the following figures when testing the switches:

   a. Ignition and lighting switch: **Figure 89**.
   b. Engine stop switch and start switch: **Figure 90**.
   c. Headlight dimmer switch: **Figure 91**.
   d. Reverse switch: **Figure 92**.
   e. Neutral switch: **Figure 93**.
When testing switches, note the following:

9

NEUTRAL SWITCH

93

Position	Color	
	BL	Ground
On	•——•	
Off		

a. First check the fuses as described under *Fuses* in this chapter.

b. Check the battery as described under *Battery* in Chapter Three; charge the battery to the correct state of charge, if required.

c. Disconnect the negative (–) cable from the battery, as described in this chapter, if the switch connectors are not disconnected in the circuit.

> *CAUTION*
> *Do not attempt to start the engine with the battery negative (–) cable disconnected or you will damage the wiring harness.*

d. When separating 2 electrical connectors, depress the retaining clip and pull on the electrical connector housings, *not* the wires (**Figure 94**).

> *NOTE*
> *Electrical connectors can be serviced by disconnecting them and cleaning with aerosol electrical contact cleaner. Multiple pin connectors should be packed with a dielectric compound (available at most automotive and motorcycle supply stores).*

e. After locating a defective circuit, check the electrical connectors to make sure they are clean and properly connected. Make sure there are no bent metal pins on the male side of the connector (**Figure 95**). Check all wires going into the electrical connector housing to make sure each wire is properly positioned and that the wire end is not loose (**Figure 96**).

f. To connect electrical connectors properly, push them together until they click and are locked into place (**Figure 97**).

g. When replacing the handlebar switch assembly, make sure the wiring is routed correctly so that it is not crimped when the handlebar is turned from side to side. Also secure the wiring to the handlebar with the plastic tie wraps at the proper location(s).

Ignition and Lighting Switch
Removal/Installation

1. Remove the front fender as described in Chapter Fourteen.

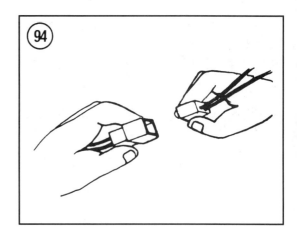

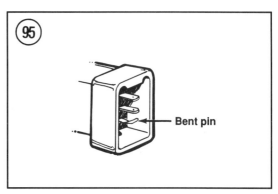
Bent pin

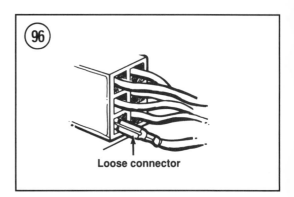
Loose connector

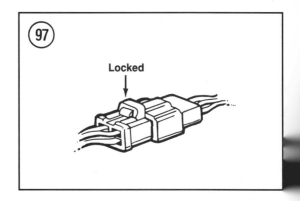
Locked

NOTE
During front fender removal, the battery is disconnected and removed from the chassis. Do not reconnect the battery since it must be removed from the circuit for this procedure.

2A. On 2-wheel drive models, remove the indicator panel and ignition switch assembly from the handlebar.

2B. On 4-wheel drive models, perform the following:

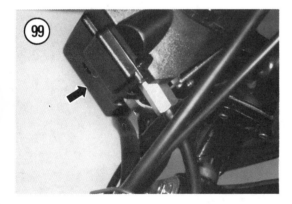

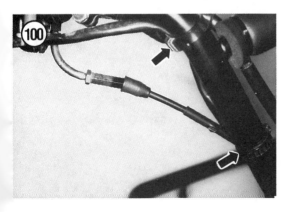

a. Loosen the locking ring at the top of the ignition switch (A, **Figure 98**).

b. Remove the meter assembly (B, **Figure 98**) as described in this chapter.

3. Follow the wiring harness from the ignition switch to the wiring harness.

4. Disconnect the ignition switch 4-pin electrical connector containing 4 wires (1 red, 1 orange, 1 gray and 1 black/white). Also disconnect the single individual wire connector (1 black/yellow).

5. Remove the switch assembly from the indicator panel (2-wheel drive models) or meter assembly (4-wheel drive models).

6. Install the new ignition switch securely.

7. Reconnect the 4-pin electrical connector and the single individual connector. Make sure the electrical connectors are free of corrosion and are tight.

8. Remove the front fender as described in Chapter Fourteen.

9. Connect the battery negative (–) lead as described in this chapter.

10. Install the indicator panel (2-wheel drive models) or meter assembly (4-wheel drive models) as described in this chapter.

**Left-hand Combination Switch
(Start Switch, Engine Stop Switch
and Headlight Dimmer Switch)
Removal/Installation**

The left-hand combination switch assembly contains the start switch, engine stop switch and headlight dimmer switch. If any portion of the switch is faulty, the entire switch assembly must be replaced.

1. Disconnect the battery negative (–) lead as described in this chapter.

2A. On 2-wheel drive models, remove the front fender as described in Chapter Fourteen.

2B. On 4-wheel drive models, remove the screws securing the meter assembly lower cover (**Figure 99**) and remove the lower cover.

3. Remove the tie-wraps (**Figure 100**) securing the wire harness to the handlebar.

4. Remove the wire harness from any clips on the frame.

5. Follow the left-hand switch electrical wiring harness on the handlebar to the frame area.

6. Locate and disconnect the electrical connectors.

7. Remove the screws securing the left-hand combination switch together and remove the switch assembly (A, **Figure 101**) from the handlebar.

8. Disconnect the choke lever assembly (B, **Figure 101**) from the left-hand switch assembly.

9. Install a new switch and tighten the screws securely. Do not over-tighten the screws or the plastic switch housing may crack.

10. Reconnect the electrical connectors.

11. Make sure the electrical connectors are free of corrosion and are tight.

12. Install the tie warps to hold the electrical wires to the handlebar or frame.

13A. On 2-wheel drive models, install the front fender as described in Chapter Fourteen.

13B. On 4-wheel drive models, install the meter assembly lower cover (**Figure 99**) and tighten the screws.

14. Connect the battery negative (–) lead as described in this chapter.

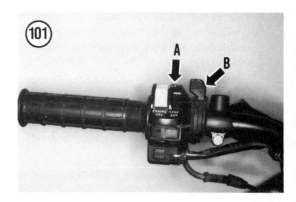

Neutral Switch
Removal/Installation

The neutral switch is located on the upper left-hand surface of the crankcase behind the exhaust system inner heat shield (**Figure 102**).

1. Place the ATV on level ground and set the parking brake. Block the wheels so the vehicle will not roll in either direction.

2. Remove the seat as described in Chapter Fourteen.

3. Remove the exhaust system as described under *Exhaust System Removal/Installation* in Chapter Eight.

NOTE
The following Steps are shown with the engine removed from the frame and partially disassembled for clarity. It is not necessary to remove the engine from the frame for this procedure.

4. Remove the screws (A, **Figure 103**) securing the neutral switch to the crankcase.

5. Remove the neutral switch (B, **Figure 103**) from crankcase. Follow the wiring harness up through the frame and disconnect the 2-pin electrical connector from the main wiring harness.

6. Remove the pin (**Figure 104**) and spring (**Figure 105**) from the end of the gearshift drum.

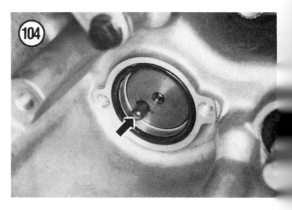

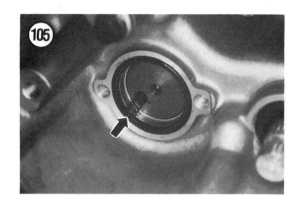

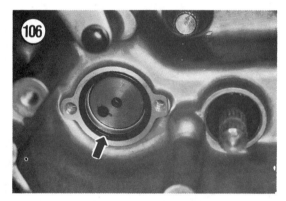

7. Remove the O-ring seal (**Figure 106**) from the crankcase.

8. Install by reversing these removal steps while noting the following:

   a. Install a new O-ring seal (**Figure 106**) and apply clean engine oil to it.

   b. Be sure to install the spring and pin.

   c. Tighten the neutral switch mounting screws securely but do not over tighten as the plastic mounting tabs may fracture.

   d. Make sure the electrical connector is free of corrosion and is tight.

Reverse Switch

The reverse switch is located on the upper right-hand surface of the crankcase behind the starter motor (**Figure 107**).

1. Place the ATV on level ground and set the parking brake. Block the wheels so the vehicle will not roll in either direction.

2. Remove the seat and the front fender as described in Chapter Fourteen.

3. Remove the cotter pin, washer, pivot pin and washer, then disconnect the rear brake cable from the rear brake pedal (A, **Figure 108**).

4. Loosen the locknut, disconnect the rear brake cable from the bracket (B, **Figure 108**) and move the brake cable out of the way.

5. Unscrew the reverse switch (**Figure 109**) from the crankcase. Follow the wiring harness up through the frame and disconnect the 2-pin electrical connector from the main wiring harness.

6. Apply gasket sealer to the switch threads prior to installation and install the switch. Tighten the switch securely.

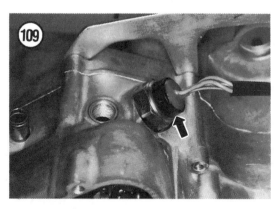

7. Make sure the electrical connector is free of corrosion and is tight.

8. Install all items removed.

ODOMETER HOUSING
(2-WHEEL DRIVE MODELS)

Removal/Installation

Refer to **Figure 110** for this procedure.

1. Set the ATV on level ground and set the parking brake. Block the wheels so the vehicle will not roll in either direction.

2. Remove the seat as described in Chapter Fourteen.

3. Remove the set screw securing each shift knob.

4. Remove the sub-transmission shift knob and the reverse shift knob from the shift levers.

5. Remove the screws at the rear securing the shift lever cover.

NOTE
Move the handlebar from full lock side-to-side to expose the front screws.

6. Remove the screws securing the shift lever cover.

7. Unscrew the fuel filler cap.

8. Partially lift the front of the cover. Disconnect the odometer drive cable from the odometer unit and disconnect the electrical connector for the odometer illumination light.

9. If disassembly is necessary, turn the cover over on the work bench. Remove the screws securing the odometer case mounting bracket and remove the odometer case assembly from the backside of the cover.

10. Install by reversing these removal steps while noting the following:

   a. Make sure the electrical connector is free of corrosion and is tight.

   b. Install all items removed.

SPEEDOMETER HOUSING
(4-WHEEL DRIVE MODELS)

Removal/Installation

Refer to **Figure 111** for this procedure.

1. Set the ATV on level ground and set the parking brake. Block the wheels so the vehicle will not roll in either direction.

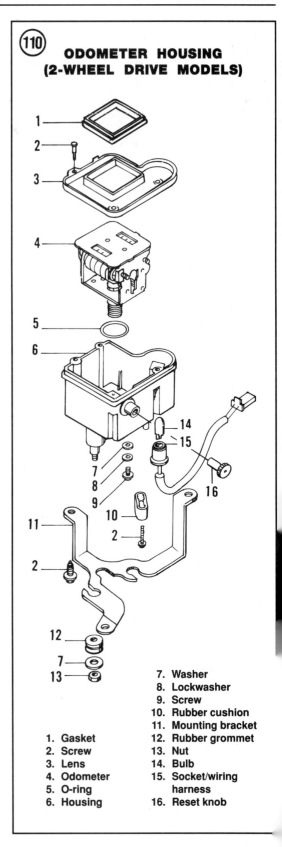

**ODOMETER HOUSING
(2-WHEEL DRIVE MODELS)**

1. Gasket	7. Washer
2. Screw	8. Lockwasher
3. Lens	9. Screw
4. Odometer	10. Rubber cushion
5. O-ring	11. Mounting bracket
6. Housing	12. Rubber grommet
	13. Nut
	14. Bulb
	15. Socket/wiring harness
	16. Reset knob

(111)

SPEEDOMETER HOUSING
(4-WHEEL DRIVE MODELS)

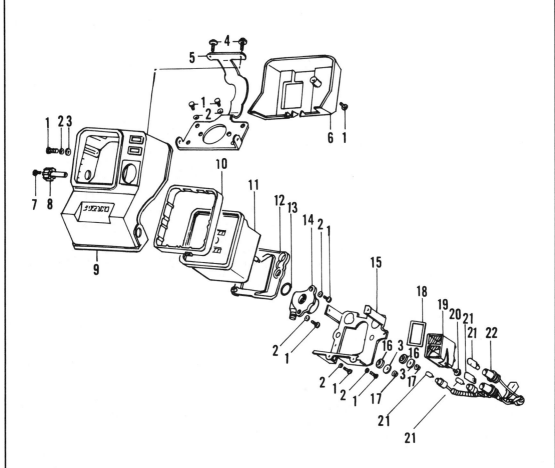

9

1. Screw	12. Rubber cushion
2. Lockwasher	13. O-ring
3. Washer	14. Speedometer gear box
4. Screw	15. Mounting bracket
5. Mounting bracket	16. Rubber grommet
6. Lower cover	17. Nut
7. Set screw	18. Gasket
8. Reset knob	19. Case
9. Upper cover	20. Screw
10. Gasket	21. Bulb
11. Speedometer/odometer	22. Socket/wiring harness

2. Remove the seat and front fender as described in Chapter Fourteen.

3. Disconnect the speedometer drive cable (**Figure 112**) from the speedometer housing.

4. Remove the screws (**Figure 113**) securing the lower cover and remove the lower cover (A, **Figure 114**).

5. Disconnect the electrical connectors from the wiring harness.

6. Remove the screw, lockwasher and washer (B, **Figure 114**) on each side securing the speedometer housing to the mounting bracket attached to the steering column.

7. Carefully pull the speedometer housing (C, **Figure 114**) straight up and off the mounting bracket.

8. Install by reversing these removal steps while noting the following:

    a. Make sure the electrical connector is free of corrosion and is tight.

    b. Install all items removed.

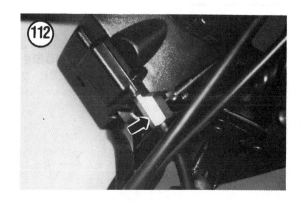

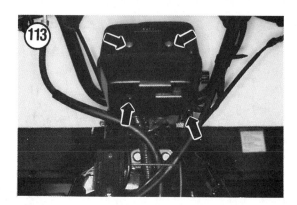

OUTPUT TERMINAL

An electrical output terminal (**Figure 115**) for use with electrical accessories is located at the right-hand rear corner of the vehicle next to the taillight.

This output terminal is rated for 180 watts and can be used with electrical accessories rated at or below this wattage rating. If the accessory exceeds 180 watts, damage will occur to the electrical system and the wiring harness. This circuit is protected by a 15 amp fuse described in the following procedure.

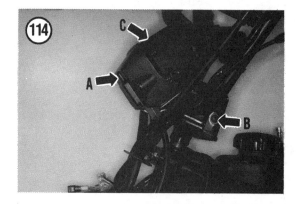

FUSES

There is one 20 amp main fuse and one 15 amp output terminal fuse in the electrical system. Both fuses are located under the front cover, in front of the battery.

NOTE
Always carry spare fuses.

Whenever the fuse blows, find out the reason for the failure before replacing the fuse. Usually, the trouble is a short circuit in the wiring. This may be caused by worn-through insulation or a disconnected wire shorted to ground.

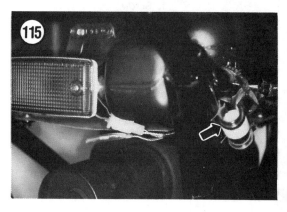

Fuse Replacement

1. Remove the screws securing the front cover (**Figure 116**) and remove the front cover.

NOTE
*The main (20A) fuse is located on the right-hand side (A, **Figure 117**) and the output terminal fuse (15A) is located on the left-hand side (B, **Figure 117**).*

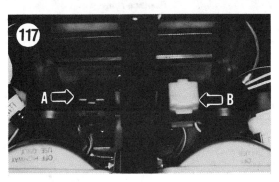

2. Remove the fuse cover(s) (A and B, **Figure 117**).
3. Remove the fuse(s) with your fingers or needlenose pliers and inspect it. If the fuse is blown, there will be a break in the element (**Figure 118**). There are spare fuses in each fuse housing.

NOTE
If one of the spare fuses was used, install a new spare fuse as soon as possible to avoid being stranded on the trail or job site at some future time.

4. Install the new fuse and push it all the way down until it seats completely. Install the cover and push it down until it locks in place.
5. Install the front cover and tighten the screws securely.

WIRING DIAGRAMS

Wiring diagrams for all models are located at the end of this book.

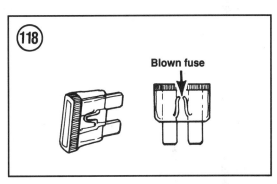

Blown fuse

Table 1 ELECTRICAL SYSTEM SPECIFICATIONS

Item	Test connections	Resistance
AC generator		
Pickup coil resistance	black/yellow to green/white	100-200 ohms
Source coil resistance	black to blue/yellow	105-160 ohms
Charge coil resistance	yellow to yellow	0.1-1.0 ohms
Ignition coil		
Primary resistance		0-0.5 ohms
Secondary resistance		
LT-F250, LT-4WD (1987-1989)		10,000-16,000 ohms
LT-F250, LT-4WD (1990-on),		
LT-4WDX		12,000-20,000 ohms
Starter motor brush length		
service limit		6 mm (0.24 in.)

Table 2 ELECTRICAL SYSTEM TIGHTENING TORQUE

Item	N·m	ft.-lb.
AC generator nut	145-175	105-126.5

Table 3 STARTER TROUBLESHOOTING

Symptom	Probable cause	Remedy
Starter does not work	Low battery	Recharge battery
	Worn brushes	Replace brushes
	Defective relay	Repair or replace
	Defective switch	Repair or replace
	Defective wiring or connection	Repair wire or clean connection
	Internal short circuit	Repair or replace defective component
Starter action is weak	Low battery	Recharge battery
	Pitted relay contacts	Clean or replace
	Worn brushes	Replace brushes
	Defective connection	Clean and tighten
	Short circuit in commutator	Replace armature
Starter runs continuously	Stuck relay	Replace relay
Starter turns; does not turn engine	Defective starter clutch	Replace starter clutch

Table 4 REPLACEMENT BULBS

Item and Model	Voltage/Wattage
Headlight	
LT-250	12V 45/45W
LT-4WD, LT-4WDX	12V 30/30W
Taillight	12V 5W
Speedometer and odometer	12V 3.4W
Indicator light	
LT-250	12V 2W
LT-4WD, LT-4WDX	12V 3.4W

CHAPTER TEN

FRONT SUSPENSION AND STEERING

This chapter describes repair and maintenance of the front wheels, hubs, front suspension arms and steering components.

On 4-wheel drive models, the front drive axles and drive mechanism components are covered in Chapter Eleven.

Refer to **Table 1** for torque specifications for the front suspension components. **Table 1** and **Table 2** are located at the end of this chapter.

> *CAUTION*
> *Self-locking nuts are used to secure some of the front suspension components. Suzuki recommends that all self-locking nuts must be discarded once they have been removed. The self-locking portion of the nut is damaged once it has been removed and will no longer properly lock onto the lower holder threads. Always install **new** self-locking nuts. **Never** reinstall a used nut once it has been removed.*

FRONT WHEEL

Removal/Installation

Refer to **Figure 1** for this procedure.

> *NOTE*
> *The front and rear tire tread on the factory equipped tires is directional and must rotate in the correct direction. These tires have a direction arrow (**Figure 2**) on the side wall to indicate the correct direction of wheel rotation. Prior to removing the wheel, mark the rim with a piece of masking tape. Mark it as to which side of the vehicle the tire was mounted and the direction of forward rotation. This is necessary for tire installation as described in this chapter.*

1. Place the ATV on level ground and set the parking brake. Block the rear wheels so the vehicle will not roll in either direction.

2. Loosen, do not remove, the lug nuts (**Figure 3**) securing the wheel to the hub/brake drum.

3. Jack up the front of the vehicle with a small hydraulic or scissor jack. Place the jack under the frame with a piece of wood between the jack and the frame.

4. Place wooden block(s) under the frame to support the ATV securely with the front wheels off the ground.

5. Remove the lug nuts and washers (**Figure 3**) securing the wheel to the hub/brake drum. Remove the front wheel.

6. Repeat Steps 2-5 for the other wheel if necessary.

NOTE
Install the tire and wheel onto the same side of the vehicle from which it was removed. See Note at the beginning of this procedure. Also refer to the direction arrow on the tire side wall.

7. Install the front wheel, then install the washers and the lug nuts securely—but not to the final torque.

8. After the wheel is installed completely, rotate it in the normal forward rotation (**Figure 4**); apply the

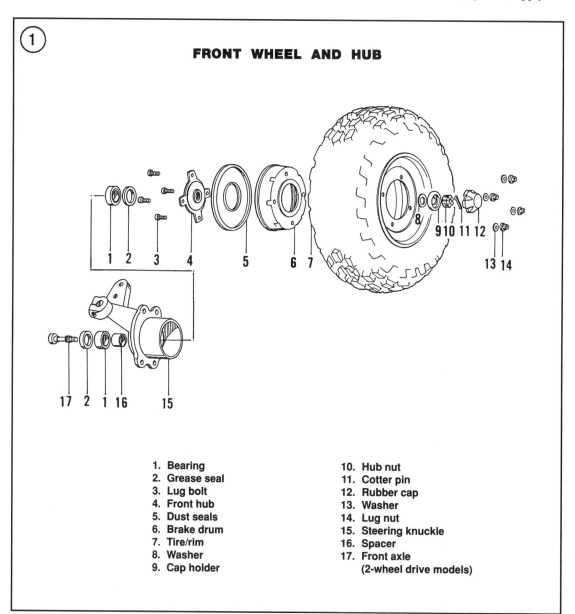

① **FRONT WHEEL AND HUB**

1. Bearing	10. Hub nut
2. Grease seal	11. Cotter pin
3. Lug bolt	12. Rubber cap
4. Front hub	13. Washer
5. Dust seals	14. Lug nut
6. Brake drum	15. Steering knuckle
7. Tire/rim	16. Spacer
8. Washer	17. Front axle
9. Cap holder	(2-wheel drive models)

brake several times to make sure that the wheel rotates freely and that the brake is operating correctly.

9. Jack the front of the vehicle up a little and remove the wooden block(s).

10. Let the jack down and remove the jack and wooden block(s).

WARNING
Always tighten the lug nuts to the correct torque specification or the lug nuts may work loose and the wheel could fall off.

11. Use a torque wrench and tighten the lug nuts, in a crisscross pattern, to the torque specification listed in **Table 1**.

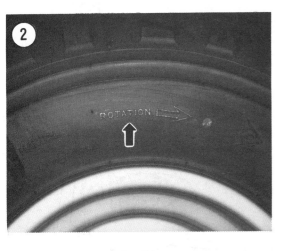

TIRES AND WHEELS

All models are equipped with tubeless, low pressure tires designed specifically for off-road use only. Rapid tire wear will occur if the vehicle is ridden on paved surfaces. Due to their low pressure requirements, they should be inflated only with a hand-operated air pump instead of using an air compressor or the air available at service stations.

CAUTION
*Do not overinflate the stock tires as they will be permanently distorted and damaged. If overinflated, they will bulge out similar to an inner tube that is not within the constraints of a tire and **will not** return to their original contour.*

NOTE
Additional inflation pressure in the stock tires will not improve the ride or the handling characteristics of the machine.

CAUTION
Do not use conventional motorcycle tire irons for tire removal as the tire sealing bead will be damaged when forced away from the rim flange.

Tire Changing

The rims used on these models are of the 1-piece type and have a built-in ridge to keep the tire bead seated on the rim under severe riding conditions. Unfortunately, it also tends to keep the tire on the rim during tire removal as well.

10

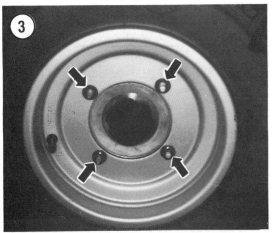

A special type of tool *is required* for tire changing on these models. There are various models available from dealers and mail order houses (**Figure 5**). When purchasing the tire tool, get the type that exerts all of the applied pressure to a very small section of the tire bead at a time. Many aftermarket bead breakers spread out the applied pressure over a larger section of the tire bead and therefore are unable to break the bead loose from this type of rim.

The tool shown in this procedure is the one suggested by Suzuki.

1. Remove the valve stem cap and deflate the tire.

2. Lubricate the tire bead and rim flanges with a liquid dish detergent or any rubber lubricant. Press the tire sidewall/bead down to allow the liquid to run into and around the bead area. Also apply lubricant to the area where the bead breaker arm will come in contact with the tire sidewall.

CAUTION
If you are using aftermarket aluminum wheels, special care must be taken when changing tires to avoid scratches and gouges to the outer rim surface.

3. Position the wheel into the tire removal tool as shown in **Figure 6**.

4. Slowly pull down on the lever making sure the tool is up against the rim and break the tire bead away from the rim.

5. Using your hands, press down on the tire on either side of the tool and try to break the rest of the bead free from the rim.

6. If the rest of the tire bead cannot be broken loose, raise the tool, rotate the tire/rim assembly and repeat Step 4 and Step 5 until the entire bead is broken loose from the rim (**Figure 7**).

7. Remove the tire/rim assembly from the tool assembly.

8. Turn the wheel over and repeat Steps 2-6 for the tire rim flange on the other side.

9. Remove the tire from the rim using tire irons and rim protectors (**Figure 8**).

10. Inspect the rim sealing surface of the rim. If the rim has been severely hit, it will probably cause an air leak. Either repair or replace any damaged rim.

11. Inspect the tire for cuts, tears, abrasions or any other defects.

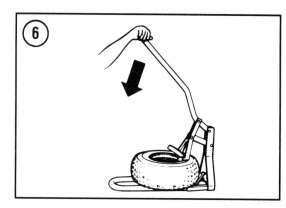

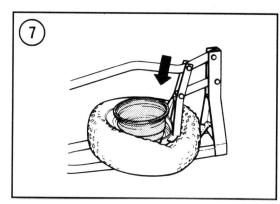

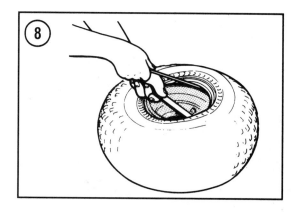

12. Wipe the tire beads and rims free from any lubricating agent used in Step 2.

13. Apply clean water to the rim flanges, tire rim beads and onto the outer rim. Make sure the rim flange is clean. Wipe with a lint-free cloth.

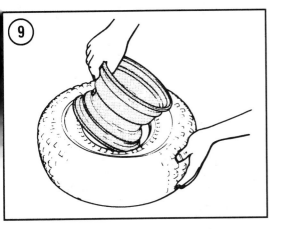

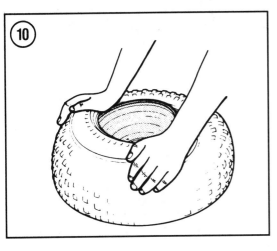

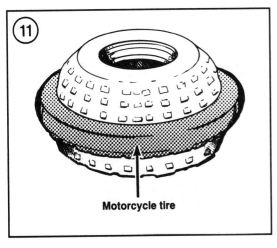

Motorcycle tire

CAUTION
Never use engine oil or gasoline as a mounting lubricant as they will deteriorate the tire.

14. Apply tire mounting lubricant, Armor-All or a liquid dish detergent to both tire beads.

15. Position the tire so the arrow on the sidewall is pointing in the correct direction of rotation (**Figure 2**).

16. Position the rim with the outer side facing up.

17. Install the rim into the tire as shown in **Figure 9**.

18. Press the tire onto the rim with your hands as shown in **Figure 10**.

19. Repeat Step 18 for the other side of the tire.

CAUTION
Do not inflate the tire past the maximum inflation pressure of 0.7 kg/cm^2 (10 psi).

NOTE
*If it is difficult to seat the beads of the tire against the rim, try this procedure. Place an old motorcycle tire (of the appropriate size) over the ATV tire so it is positioned in the middle of the ATV tire tread (**Figure 11**). The motorcycle tire will support the middle of the ATV tire and push the beads against the rim flanges to help make an air-tight seal.*

20. Inflate the tire to the recommended tire pressure (A, **Figure 12**) listed in **Table 2**.

21. Inspect the "rim line" of the tire in relation to the rim. It must be equally spaced from the rim all around the circumference (B, **Figure 12**). If the distance varies, this indicates that the bead is not properly seated and the tire must be reinstalled correctly on the rim. Repeat Steps 16-21.

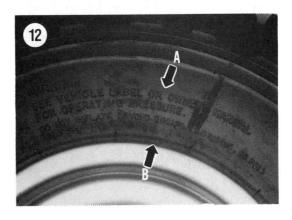

10

22. Deflate the tire and let it sit for about one hour.
23. Inflate the tire to the recommended air pressure, refer to **Table 2**.
24. Check for air leaks and install the valve cap.

SHOCK ABSORBER

Removal/Installation

1. Remove the front wheel(s) as described in this chapter.
2. Remove the front fender as described in Chapter Fourteen.
3. Remove the upper and lower bolts and nuts (**Figure 13**) securing the shock absorber to the frame and upper wishbone and remove the shock absorber.
4. Repeat for the other side if necessary.
5. Install by reversing of these steps while noting the following:
   a. Apply a light coat of multipurpose grease to the pivot points on the frame and upper wishbone where the shock absorber is attached and to the upper and lower pivot points on the shock absorber (A, **Figure 14**).
   b. Tighten the bolts and nuts to the torque specification listed in **Table 2**.
   c. Push down on the front of the ATV and make sure the front suspension is operating properly.

Inspection

Replacement parts for the factory installed shock absorber are not available from Suzuki. If the unit is leaking fluid or any part is damaged, the entire unit must be replaced.

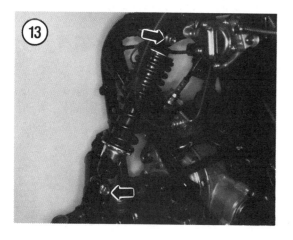

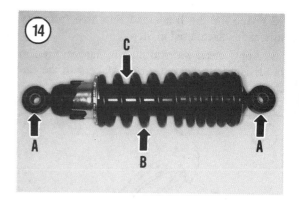

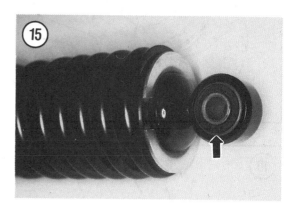

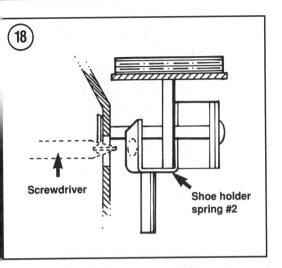

1. Inspect the rubber bushing at the upper (**Figure 15**) and at the lower (**Figure 16**) joints for wear or damage.
2. Inspect the spring (B, **Figure 14**) for weakness or damage.
3. Check the damper unit (C, **Figure 14**) for leakage and make sure the damper rod is straight.
4. If the shock absorber fails any of these inspection steps, replace the shock absorber.

FRONT HUB AND BRAKE DRUM

Removal

Refer to **Figure 1** for this procedure.
1. Remove the front wheel(s) as described in this chapter.
2. Remove the cotter pin from the front axle and discard it.
3. Have an assistant apply the front brake, then loosen and remove the axle nut (A, **Figure 17**).

NOTE
*If the brake drum is difficult to remove in the next step, insert a screwdriver into the hole in the brake backing plate and push on the shoe holder spring No. 2 (**Figure 18**). This will relax the brake shoe self-adjuster and the spring will back the shoes away from the drum.*

4. Slide the brake drum (B, **Figure 17**) off the brake shoes and remove the brake drum.
5. Remove the axle nut (**Figure 19**), the cap holder (**Figure 20**) and the washer (**Figure 21**) from the front axle.
6. Attach a section of heavy duty chain onto two of the opposite front hub threaded studs (A, **Figure 22**).

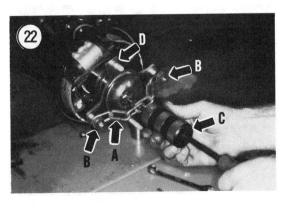

7. Install 2 of the lug nuts (B, **Figure 22**) to hold the chain in place. Screw the lug nuts on far enough so the stud threads are exposed past the screwed on nuts. This will ensure that the nuts have a good grip on the threaded studs to avoid thread damage.

8. Attach a body shop slide hammer (C, **Figure 22**) to the center of the chain. Slide the weight on the hammer and withdraw the front hub (D, **Figure 22**) from the front axle.

9. Remove the front hub from the front axle (**Figure 23**).

10. Remove the hub nuts and chain from the front hub.

11. Inspect the front hub as described in this chapter.

Inspection

The front hub is not equipped with front axle bearings. The front axle bearings are located in the front steering knuckle and service for these bearings is covered in that section of this chapter.

1. Inspect the front hub for cracks, fractures or damage. Replace the front hub if damaged in any way.

2. Inspect the threaded studs (**Figure 24**) for wear or damage. Minor damage can be cleaned up with the appropriate size metric die. If damage is severe, a damaged stud can be pressed out and a new one installed.

3. Inspect the inner splines (**Figure 25**) for wear or damage. If damaged, the front hub should be replaced. If damage is severe, inspect the outer splines (**Figure 26**) on the front axle as it may also be damaged and require replacement.

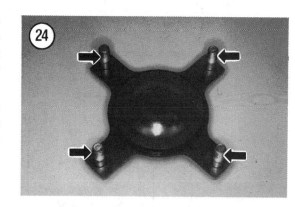

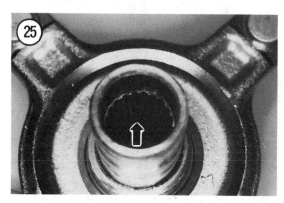

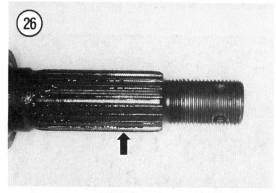

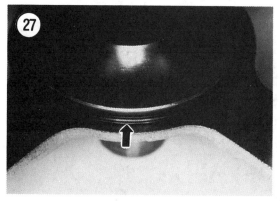

NOTE
Figure 26 is shown on a 4-wheel drive front axle. The 2-wheel drive model is basically the same only shorter.

CAUTION
Both dust seals are very important as they not only keep out dust and dirt but also moisture. If the condition of these seals is questionable, replace them as

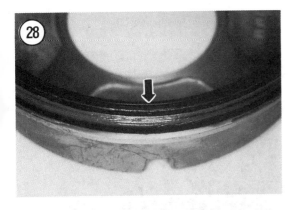

they will prevent damage to the front drum brake components and the steering knuckle bearings.

4. Inspect the rubber dust seal on the front hub (**Figure 27**) and on the back of the brake drum (**Figure 28**) for wear, hardness or deterioration. Replace if necessary.

Installation

NOTE
During removal of the brake drum the brake shoes will usually move out to their maximum extension making it impossible to install the brake drum.

1. The brake shoes are positioned out to their maximum extension making it impossible to install the brake drum. Therefore, to install the brake drum, the brake shoes must be retraced to allow sufficient clearance. To retract the brake shoes, perform the following:

   a. Using a narrow blade screwdriver (**Figure 29**), insert the screwdriver (A, **Figure 30**) between the strut (B, **Figure 30**) and the ratchet (C, **Figure 30**).

   b. Carefully push down on the screwdriver (A, **Figure 30**). The ratchet (A, **Figure 31**) will now move down enabling the strut (B, **Figure 31**) to also move thus retracting the brake shoes.

2. Apply wheel bearing grease to the inner splines of the front hub and to the outer splines of the front axle.

3. Partially install the front hub onto the front axle splines.

10

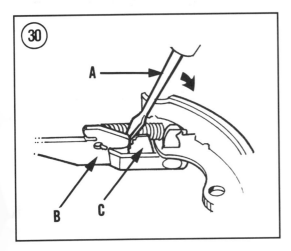

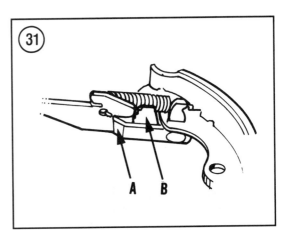

4A. On 2-wheel drive models, place a heavy backup hammer behind the short front axle to hold the front axle in place in the steering knuckle.

> *CAUTION*
> *On 4-wheel drive models it is very important to hold onto the front axle securely during the next step. Damage may occur to the front differential while driving the front hub onto the front axle if the front axle is not held securely. Do not allow the driving force of the mallet to be transferred from the front axle to the front differential.*

4B. On 4-wheel drive models, hold onto the front axle with one hand (A, **Figure 32**).

5. Use a soft-faced or plastic mallet (B, **Figure 32**) and drive the front hub onto the front axle. Drive the front hub on until it bottoms out.

6. Install the washer (**Figure 21**), the cap holder (**Figure 20**) and the axle nut (**Figure 19**) onto the front axle. Tighten the axle nut only finger-tight at this time.

7. Slide the brake drum (B, **Figure 17**) onto the brake shoes. Push it on until it stops.

8. Have an assistant apply the front brake and use a torque wrench to tighten the axle nut (A, **Figure 17**) to the torque specification listed in **Table 1**.

9. Align one of the castillations on the nut with the cotter pin hole in the front axle. If not aligned, tighten the nut—do *not* loosen the nut to achieve alignment.

> *NOTE*
> *Always install a new cotter pin. Never reuse an old one as it may break and fall off.*

10. Install a new cotter pin and bend the ends over completely (**Figure 33**).

11. Install the front wheel(s) as described in this chapter.

STEERING SYSTEM

Handlebar Assembly
Removal/Installation

> *NOTE*
> *If it is not necessary to remove the components from each end of the handlebar for service, perform this procedure. If component removal is necessary, refer to the **Disassembly/Assembly** in the following procedure.*

1A. On 2-wheel drive models, remove the odometer housing from the center top of the handlebar as described under *Odometer Housing Removal/Installation* in Chapter Nine.

1B. On 4-wheel drive models, remove the speedometer housing from the center top of the handlebar as described under *Speedometer Housing Removal/Installation* in Chapter Nine.

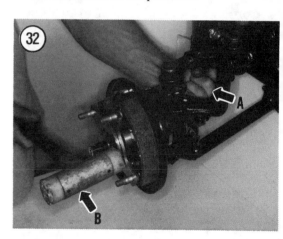

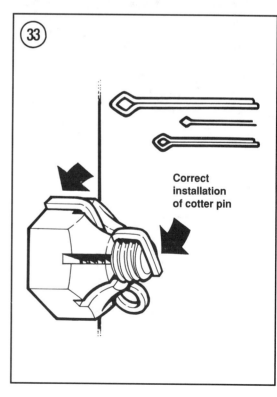

Correct installation of cotter pin

CAUTION
Cover the surrounding area with a heavy cloth or plastic tarp to protect it from accidental spilling of clutch and brake fluid. Wash any spilled clutch or brake fluid off any painted or plated surface immediately, as it will destroy the finish. Use soapy water and rinse thoroughly.

2. Remove the tie wraps (**Figure 34**) securing the left-hand switch electrical harness to the handlebar.

3. Remove the bolts and lockwashers securing the handlebar upper holders.

NOTE
On 1990-on 2-wheel drive models, the odometer bracket is a loose part, not attached to the top surface of the steer-ing stem as on all other models. Be prepared to catch this part after the handlebar is removed.

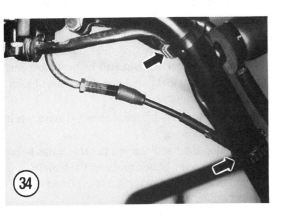

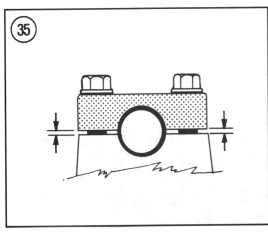

4. Remove the upper holders, the handlebar assem-bly and the lower holders.

NOTE
On all models, the handlebar lower holders are not permanently attached to the top surface of the steering stem. They are held in place by the bolts re-moved in Step 3.

5. Move the handlebar assembly back and rest it on the gearshift lever cover or the frame.

6. Reinstall the handlebar lower and upper holders and on models so equipped, the odometer bracket, onto the steering stem. Then install the bolts to avoid misplacing these parts.

7. Secure the handlebar assembly so the brake mas-ter cylinder reservoir remains in the upright position. This is to minimize loss of hydraulic fluid and to keep air from entering into the brake system. It is not necessary to remove the hydraulic line.

8. Install by reversing these removal steps while noting the following:

   a. Position the handlebar on the lower handlebar holders so the punch mark on the handlebar is aligned with the top surface of the lower handle-bar holders.

   b. Tighten the handlebar bolts to the torque speci-fication listed in **Table 1**. Tighten them so there is an equal gap at the front and rear between the handlebar upper and lower holders (**Figure 35**).

   c. Check the throttle operation. If necessary, adjust the throttle operation as described in Chapter Three.

WARNING
*After installation is completed, make sure the brake lever does not come in contact with the right-hand grip when it is pulled on fully. If it touches, the brake fluid may be low in the reservoir and must be refilled. Refer to **Front Brakes** in Chapter Thirteen.*

Handlebar and Component Removal/Installation

NOTE
If it is necessary to remove the compo-nents from the handlebar for service, perform this procedure. If component removal is not necessary, only the re-

moval of the handlebar assembly, refer to the preceding procedure.

CAUTION
Cover the seat and front fender with a heavy cloth or plastic tarp to protect it from the accidental spilling of brake fluid. Wash any spilled brake fluid off any painted or plastic surface immediately as it will destroy the finish. Use soapy water and rinse thoroughly.

1A. On 2-wheel drive models, remove the odometer housing from the center top of the handlebar as described under *Odometer Housing Removal/Installation* in Chapter Nine.

1B. On 4-wheel drive models, remove the speedometer housing from the center top of the handlebar as described under *Speedometer Housing Removal/Installation* in Chapter Nine.

2. Remove the screws securing the throttle case assembly (A, **Figure 36**) together. Separate the throttle case and remove the assembly. Reassemble the case and tighten the screws. Lay the assembly over the front fender or fuel tank. Be careful that the cable does not get crimped or damaged.

3. Remove the bolts securing the front master cylinder (B, **Figure 36**) to the handlebar and lay it over the front fender or fuel tank. Keep the reservoir in the upright position to minimize loss of brake fluid and to keep air from entering the brake system. It is not necessary to remove the hydraulic brake line from the master cylinder.

4. Remove the plastic tie wraps (**Figure 34**) holding the electrical cables to each side of the handlebar.

5. Remove the left-hand grip (A, **Figure 37**) from the end of the handlebar.

6. Remove the screws securing the left-hand switch (B, **Figure 37**). Separate the 2 halves of the switch and remove the assembly. Reassemble the switch and tighten the screws.

7. Slide the ring cover off the choke lever then slide the choke lever assembly (C, **Figure 37**) off the handlebar.

8. Remove the bolt (D, **Figure 37**) securing the parking brake assembly to the handlebar and slide off the assembly. Lay the assembly over the front fender or fuel tank. Be careful that the cable does not get crimped or damaged.

9. Remove the bolts and lockwashers securing the handlebar upper holders.

NOTE
On 1990-on 2-wheel drive models, the odometer bracket is a loose part, not attached to the top surface of the steering stem as on all other models. Be prepared to catch this part after the handlebar is removed.

10. Remove the upper holders, the handlebar and the lower holders.

NOTE
On all models, the handlebar lower holders are not permanently attached to the top surface of the steering stem. They are held in place by the bolts removed in Step 3.

11. Remove the handlebar.

12. Reinstall the handlebar lower and upper holders and on models so equipped, the odometer bracket, onto the steering stem. Then install the bolts to avoid misplacing these parts.

13. To maintain a good grip on the handlebar and to prevent it from slipping down, clean the knurled section of the handlebar with a wire brush. It should be kept rough so it will be held securely by the holders. The holders should also be kept clean and free of any metal that may have been gouged loose by handlebar slippage.

14. Install by reversing these removal steps while noting the following:

   a. Position the handlebar on the lower handlebar holders so the punch mark on the handlebar is aligned with the top surface of the lower handlebar holders.

   b. Tighten the handlebar bolts to the torque specification listed in **Table 1**. Tighten them so there

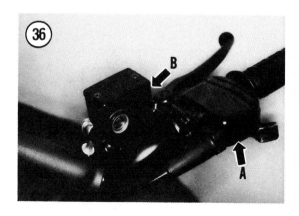

is an equal gap at the front and rear between the handlebar upper and lower holders (**Figure 35**).

c. Tighten the master cylinder upper bolt first and then the lower. Tighten the bolts to the torque specification listed in **Table 1**.

d. Check the throttle operation. If necessary, adjust the throttle operation as described in Chapter Three.

> *WARNING*
> *After installation is completed, make sure the brake lever does not contact the right-hand grip when it is pulled on fully. If it touches, the brake fluid may be low in the reservoir and must be refilled. Refer to **Front Brakes** in Chapter Thirteen.*

Steering Shaft Removal

Refer to the following illustrations for this procedure:

a. Figure 38: 2-wheel drive models.

b. Figure 39: 4-wheel drive models.

1. Place the ATV on level ground and set the parking brake. Block the rear wheels so the vehicle will not roll in either direction.

2. Remove the seat and front fender as described in Chapter Fourteen.

3. Remove both front wheels as described in this chapter.

4. Disconnect both tie rods from the steering shaft end as described in this chapter.

5. Remove the handlebar as described in this chapter.

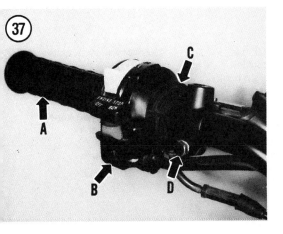

6. On 2-wheel drive models, remove the headlight housing as described under *Headlight Housing Removal/Installation* in Chapter Nine.

7. Remove the 4 bolts securing the gearshift lever assembly base (**Figure 40**) to the frame. Do not disconnect any of the gearshift lever control cables, just move the assembly toward the rear to expose the rear mounting bolts.

8. Remove the front bolt, lockwasher and washer (**Figure 41**) securing the front mounting tab of the fuel tank to the frame mounting flange.

9. Remove the rear bolt, lockwasher and washer on each side securing the rear mounting tabs of the fuel tank to the frame. The rear bolt on the right-hand side screws into the ignition coil mounting bracket (**Figure 42**). After the bolt has been removed, secure the ignition coil and bracket to the frame with a piece of wire.

10. Pull the fuel tank toward the rear. It is not necessary to remove it, just move it back.

11. Remove the cotter pin, nut, lockwasher and washer (**Figure 43**) securing the lower end of the steering shaft to the frame. Discard the cotter pin.

12. Remove the lower dust seal and O-ring seal from the end of the steering shaft.

13. Remove the cotter pins from the steering shaft holder bolts. Discard the cotter pins.

14. Remove the bolts (A, **Figure 44**) securing the steering shaft inner and outer holders (B, **Figure 44**). Remove the inner and outer holders. On 4-wheel drive models, remove the cable guide (C, **Figure 44**).

15. Carefully pull the steering shaft straight up and out of the bushing in the frame. Be careful not to snag any electrical wiring or hoses with the tie-rod mounting flange during removal.

16. Remove the upper dust seal from the lower end of the steering column.

Steering Shaft Inspection

1. Carefully inspect the entire steering shaft assembly, especially if the vehicle has been involved in a collision or spill. If the shaft is bent or twisted in any way, it must be replaced. If a damaged shaft is installed in the vehicle, it will cause rapid and excessive wear to the bushings as well as place undue stress on other components in the frame and steering system.

10

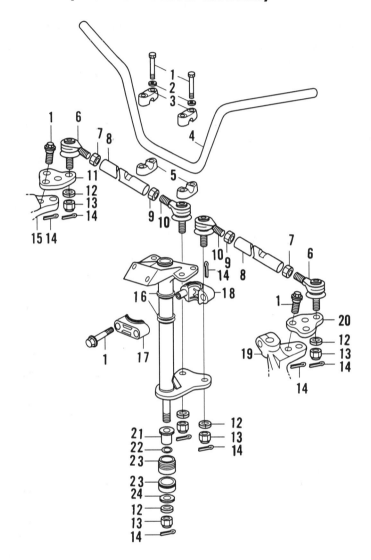

STEERING SHAFT
(2-WHEEL DRIVE MODELS)

1. Bolts
2. Washers
3. Handlebar upper holders
4. Handlebar
5. Handlebar lower holders
6. Tie rod end (outer)
7. Nut (outer)
8. Tie rod
9. Nut (inner left-hand thread)
10. Tie rod end (inner)
11. Steering knuckle arm plate (right-hand)
12. Lockwasher
13. Nut
14. Cotter pin
15. Steering knuckle arm (right-hand)
16. Steering shaft and dust seals
17. Steering shaft holder (front)
18. Steering shaft holder (rear)
19. Steering knuckle arm (left-hand)
20. Steering knuckle arm plate (left-hand)
21. Frame bushing
22. O-ring
23. Dust seals
24. Washer

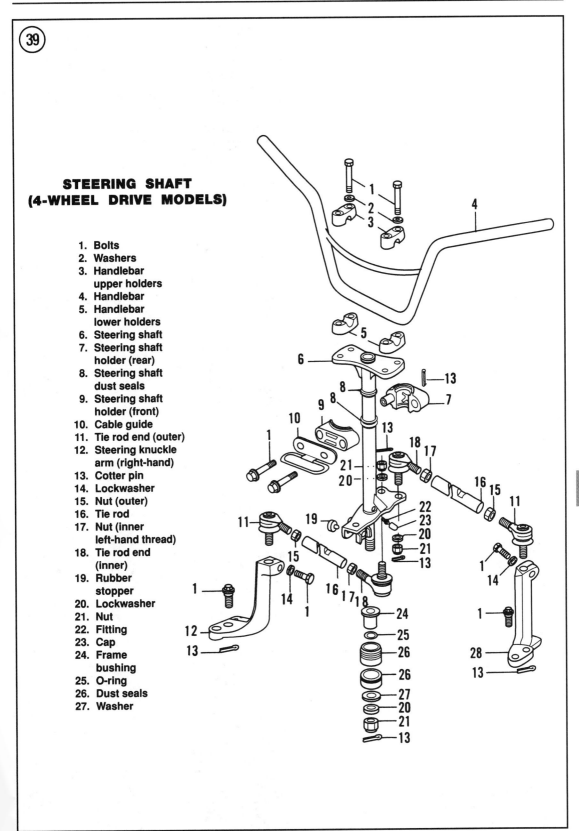

**STEERING SHAFT
(4-WHEEL DRIVE MODELS)**

1. Bolts
2. Washers
3. Handlebar
   upper holders
4. Handlebar
5. Handlebar
   lower holders
6. Steering shaft
7. Steering shaft
   holder (rear)
8. Steering shaft
   dust seals
9. Steering shaft
   holder (front)
10. Cable guide
11. Tie rod end (outer)
12. Steering knuckle
    arm (right-hand)
13. Cotter pin
14. Lockwasher
15. Nut (outer)
16. Tie rod
17. Nut (inner
    left-hand thread)
18. Tie rod end
    (inner)
19. Rubber
    stopper
20. Lockwasher
21. Nut
22. Fitting
23. Cap
24. Frame
    bushing
25. O-ring
26. Dust seals
27. Washer

10

2. Inspect the dust seals on the upper end of the steering shaft. If the seals are damaged in any way, they should be replaced in pairs.

3. Inspect the steering column lower bushing in the frame. If the bushing is worn or shows signs of galling due to lack of lubrication, it must be replaced.

4. Inspect the frame dust seals. If the seals are damaged in any way, they should be replaced in pairs. A damaged dust seal will allow grit and moisture to enter the lower bushing.

5. Examine the steering shaft holders for wear or damage. Replace if necessary.

Steering Shaft Installation

Refer to the following illustrations for this procedure:

    a. Figure 38: 2-wheel drive models.

    b. Figure 39: 4-wheel drive models.

1. If removed, install new dust seals on the upper end of the steering shaft where they ride in the steering stem holders.

2. Apply a coat of waterproof grease to the bushing in the frame where the lower end of the steering shaft rides.

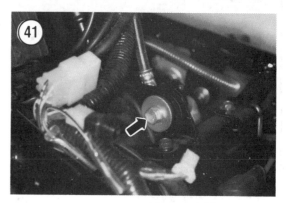

3. Apply a coat of waterproof grease to the upper dust seal and install it onto the lower end of the steering column.

4. Apply a coat of waterproof grease to the lower end of the steering column where it rides in the bushing.

5. Install the steering shaft into the frame. Carefully guide the lower end into the frame bushing being careful not to damage the bushing.

6. Correctly position the steering shaft in the frame and install the steering shaft inner and outer holders. On 4-wheel drive models, install the cable guide.

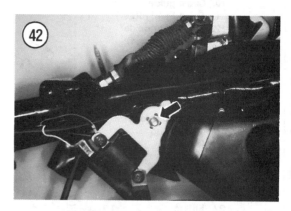

7. Install the bolts and tighten to the torque specification listed in **Table 1**. Install new cotter pins and bend the ends over completely (**Figure 33**).

8. Apply a coat of waterproof grease to the lower dust seal and O-ring seal. Install the dust seal over the end of the steering shaft and install the O-ring.

9. Install the washer, lockwasher and nut. Tighten the locknut to the torque specification listed in **Table 1** and install a new cotter pin. Bend the ends over completely (**Figure 33**).

10. Push the fuel tank toward the front and into position. Install the rear bolt, lockwasher and washer on each side of the fuel tank. Move the ignition coil

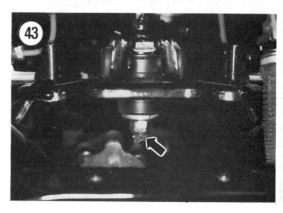

into position and install the rear bolt on the right-hand side (**Figure 42**).

11. Move the gearshift lever assembly back into position and install the 4 bolts securely.

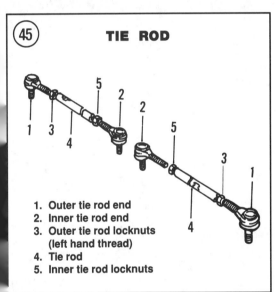

TIE ROD

1. Outer tie rod end
2. Inner tie rod end
3. Outer tie rod locknuts (left hand thread)
4. Tie rod
5. Inner tie rod locknuts

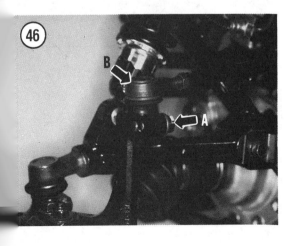

12. On 2-wheel drive models, install the headlight housing as described in Chapter Nine.

13. Install the handlebar as described in this chapter.

14. Connect both tie rods to the steering shaft end as described in this chapter.

15. Install both front wheels as described in this chapter.

16. Install the seat and front fender as described in Chapter Fourteen,

Tie Rod Removal

Both tie rod assemblies are the same as shown in **Figure 45**.

Refer to the following illustrations for this procedure:

a. Figure 38: 2-wheel drive models.
b. Figure 39: 4-wheel drive models.

1. Place the ATV on level ground and set the parking brake. Block the rear wheels so the vehicle will not roll in either direction.

2. Remove the seat and front fender as described in Chapter Fourteen.

3. Remove both front wheels as described in this chapter.

4A. On 2-wheel drive models, remove the cotter pin, nut and lockwasher securing the outer end of the tie rod end to the steering knuckle arm plate. Discard the cotter pin.

4B. On 4-wheel drive models, remove the clamping bolt (A, **Figure 46**) and lockwasher securing the outer end of the tie rod to the steering knuckle arm.

CAUTION
If the tie rod is difficult to remove from the steering knuckle plate or arm, do not attempt to pry it out as the tie rod seal may be damaged.

5A. On 2-wheel drive models, carefully disconnect the tie rod from the steering knuckle plate. If the tie rod end is difficult to remove, install the nut just enough to cover the threads on the tie rod end and tap the tie rod end out of the steering knuckle plate with a soft-faced mallet. Remove the nut.

5B. On 4-wheel drive models, carefully disconnect the tie rod (B, **Figure 46**) from the steering knuckle arm. If the tie rod end is difficult to remove, use a large flat-bladed screwdriver and carefully pry open the clamping portion of the steering knuckle arm to

10

release the tie rod end. Reinstall the clamp bolt and lockwasher to avoid misplacing them.

> *NOTE*
> *Figure 47 is shown with the steering knuckle and wishbones removed for clarity. Do not remove these items for this procedure.*

6. Remove the cotter pin, nut and lockwasher (**Figure 47**) securing the tie rod end to the lower end of the steering shaft. Discard the cotter pin.
7. Carefully disconnect the tie rod (**Figure 48**) from the steering shaft end and remove the tie rod assembly.
8. Repeat Step 4-7 for the other tie rod.

Tie Rod Inspection/Disassembly/Assembly

1. Inspect the rubber boot at each end of the tie rod end swivel joint. The swivel joints are permanently packed with grease. If the rubber boot is damaged, dirt and moisture can enter the swivel joint and destroy it. If the boot is damaged in any way, disassemble the tie rod assembly and replace the rod end(s) as they can be replaced separately.
2. If the tie rod ends (swivel joint) are to be replaced, refer to **Figure 45** and perform the following:
   a. Carefully measure and write down the overall length of the tie rod assembly before removing the worn tie rod ends.
   b. Loosen the locknuts securing the tie rod ends. The locknuts securing the tie rod ends that are colored yellow, have *left-hand* threads.
   c. Unscrew the damaged tie rod end(s).
   d. Install the new tie rod end and turn it in or out until the overall length of the tie rod assembly is the same as that measured in Sub-step a. Leave the locknuts loose at this time. They will be tightened after the wheel alignment is adjusted.

Tie Rod Installation

1A. On 2-wheel drive models, position the tie rod so the short end is positioned toward the *outside* and is attached to the steering knuckle arm plate.
1B. On 4-wheel drive models, position the tie rod so the short end is positioned toward the *inside* (**Figure 49**) and is attached to the steering knuckle arm.

2. Attach the tie rod assembly to the lower end of the steering shaft (**Figure 48**). Install the lockwasher and nut (**Figure 47**). Tighten the nut to the torque specification listed in **Table 1**.
3A. On 2-wheel drive models, install the outer end of the tie rod end to the steering knuckle arm plate. Install the lockwasher and nut. Tighten the nut to the torque specification listed in **Table 1**. Install a new cotter pin and bend the ends over completely (**Figure 33**).
3B. On 4-wheel drive models, install the outer end of the tie rod into the steering knuckle arm. Install

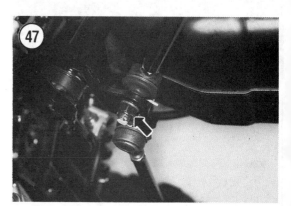

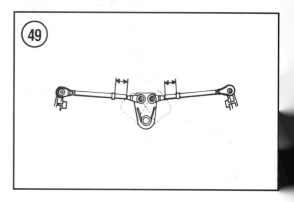

and tighten the clamping bolt (A, **Figure 46**) to the torque specification listed in **Table 1**.

4. Install a new cotter pin at each location and bend the ends over completely (**Figure 33**).

5. Install both front wheels as described in this chapter.

6. Adjust the toe-in of the front wheels as described in Chapter Three.

7. Tighten the tie rod end locknuts to the torque specification listed in **Table 1**.

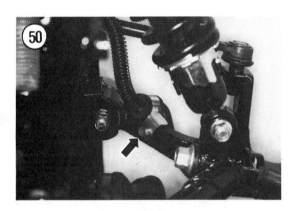

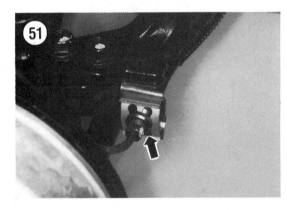

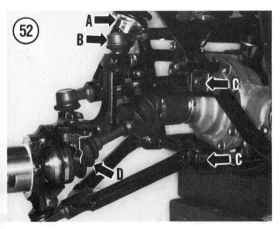

8. Install the seat and front fender as described in Chapter Fourteen.

FRONT SUSPENSION

Front Wishbones and Steering Knuckle Removal/Installation

NOTE
The steering knuckle is the only part that varies slightly between the 2-wheel drive and the 4-wheel drive models. On 2-wheel drive models, a short front axle attached to the backside surface of the steering knuckle. On 4-wheel drive models, the front drive axle goes through the steering knuckle.

1. Place the ATV on level ground and set the parking brake. Block the rear wheels so the vehicle will not roll in either direction.

2. Remove the seat and front fender as described in Chapter Fourteen.

3. Remove both front wheels as described in this chapter.

4. Remove the front drum brake assemblies as described in Chapter Thirteen.

5. Disconnect the hydraulic brake line from the lower wishbone (**Figure 50**) and the steering knuckle arm (**Figure 51**).

6. Remove the bolt securing the lower portion of the shock absorber (A, **Figure 52**) to the upper wishbone. Move the shock absorber up and out of the way; there is no need to remove it.

7. Remove the outer end of the tie rod assembly (B, **Figure 52**) from the steering knuckle as described in this chapter.

8A. On 2-wheel drive models, remove the bolts and nuts securing the wishbone and steering knuckle assembly to the frame and remove the assembly.

8B. On 4-wheel drive models, remove the bolts and nuts (C, **Figure 52**) securing the wishbone and steering knuckle assembly to the frame and remove the assembly. Carefully guide the front drive axle (D, **Figure 52**) out of the steering knuckle.

9. Install by reversing these removal steps while noting the following:
   a. Apply a coat of waterproof grease to all pivot areas prior to installing any components.
   b. Install the shock absorber first then tighten the wishbone arm mounting bolts. This will prop-

10

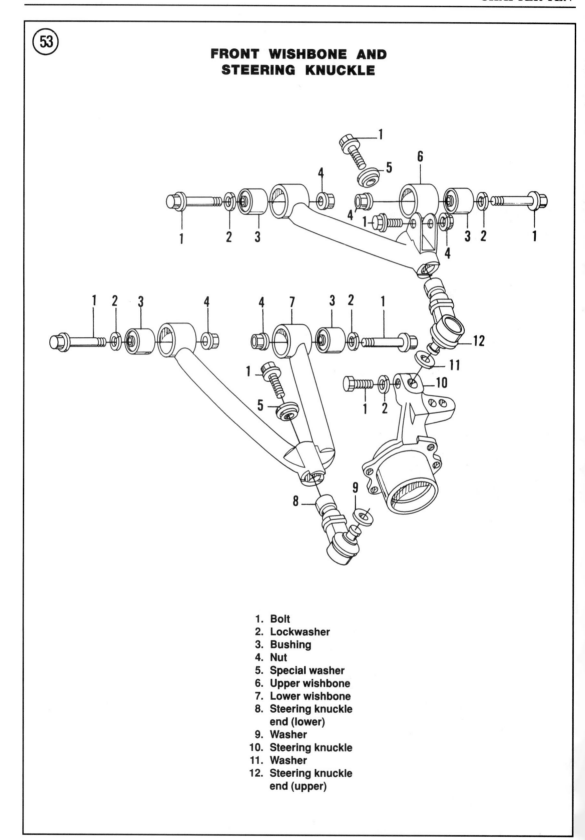

**FRONT WISHBONE AND
STEERING KNUCKLE**

1. Bolt
2. Lockwasher
3. Bushing
4. Nut
5. Special washer
6. Upper wishbone
7. Lower wishbone
8. Steering knuckle
   end (lower)
9. Washer
10. Steering knuckle
11. Washer
12. Steering knuckle
    end (upper)

erly locate the wishbones in the frame prior to tightening the mounting bolts.

c. Tighten all bolts and nuts to the torque specification listed in **Table 1**.

d. Be sure to route the brake line properly onto the lower wishbone (**Figure 50**) and the steering knuckle arm (**Figure 51**).

Front Wishbone and Steering Knuckle Inspection

Refer to **Figure 53** for all models for this procedure.

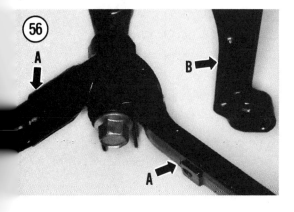

1. Inspect the rubber bushings (**Figure 54**) where the wishbones attach to the frame. Replace the bushings as a set, as described in this chapter, if any are worn or damaged.

2. Inspect the rubber bladder (**Figure 55**) of the steering knuckle end for cracks or leakage of lubrication. Replace if damaged or starting to deteriorate.

3. Inspect the wishbones (A, **Figure 56**) and the steering knuckle arm (B, **Figure 56**) for damage, rust and fractures. Replace as necessary.

4. Inspect the pivot bolts and nuts (**Figure 57**) for wear or damage. Check the threads for damage and repair if necessary.

5. Inspect the shock absorber lower mounting brackets (**Figure 58**) on the upper wishbone for wear or damage. Make sure the mounting holes are not elongated or damaged. If necessary, replace the upper wishbone.

10

6. Turn each steering knuckle bearing (**Figure 59**) by hand. Make sure each bearing turns smoothly. Replace the bearing(s) as described in this chapter if they are noisy or have excessive play (**Figure 60**).

7. Check the tightness of all of the bolts and nuts securing the steering knuckle to the wishbones as follows:

   a. Steering knuckle end-to-wishbone bolt: **Figure 61**.

   b. Steering knuckle-to-wishbone bolts: **Figure 62**.

   c. Steering knuckle-to-steering arm bolts: **Figure 63**.

Refer to **Table 1** for torque specifications.

Front Wishbone and Steering Knuckle Disassembly/Assembly

1. To separate the steering knuckle from the wishbones, perform the following:

   a. Remove the clamping bolts (**Figure 62**) and lockwashers securing the steering knuckle to the upper and lower wishbone.

   b. Separate the steering knuckle from the wishbones.

2. To separate the steering knuckle arm from the steering knuckle, perform the following:

   a. Remove the cotter pins (**Figure 64**) from the ends of the bolts. Discard the cotter pins.

   b. Remove the bolts (**Figure 63**) securing the steering knuckle arm to the steering knuckle.

   c. Separate the steering knuckle arm from the steering knuckle.

3. To remove the steering knuckle end from the wishbone, perform the following:

a. Separate the steering knuckle from the wishbone as described Step 1.

b. Place the sides of the steering knuckle end in a vise with soft jaws.

c. Use a metric socket and loosen the bolt securing the steering knuckle to the wishbone.

d. Remove the steering knuckle end from the vise.

e. Completely unscrew the bolt and remove the bolt, collar and steering knuckle end from the wishbone.

4. Assemble by reversing these removal steps while noting the following:

   a. Apply red Loctite (No. 271) to all bolt threads prior to installation.

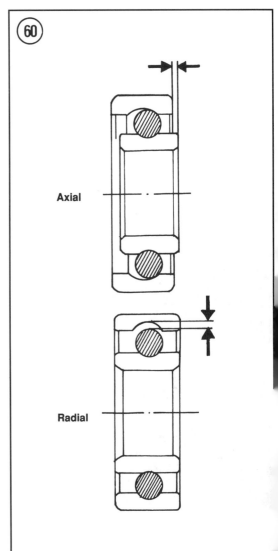

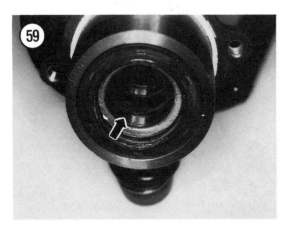

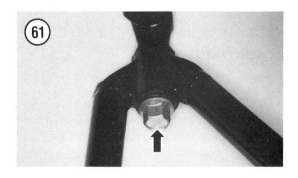

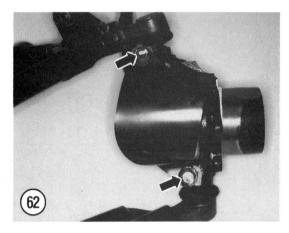

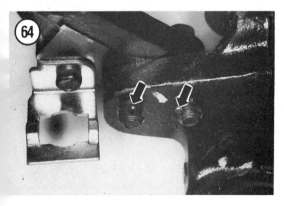

b. Tighten all bolts to the torque specification listed in **Table 1**.

c. After correctly tightening the steering knuckle arm-to-steering knuckle bolts, install a new cotter pin in each bolt end. Bend the cotter pin ends over completely. See **Figure 65**.

Front Wishbone Bushing Replacement

> *NOTE*
> *Replace the bushings as a pair even though only one may be damaged. This will ensure an even amount of load on the front wishbones during use.*

1. Use a hydraulic press and press the old bushing (**Figure 66**) out of the wishbone. Discard the old bushing.

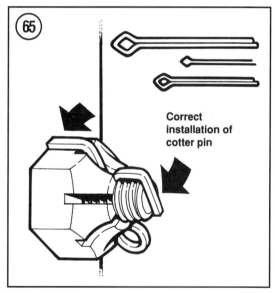

Correct installation of cotter pin

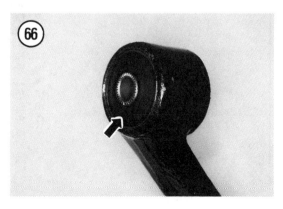

10

FRONT WHEEL AND HUB

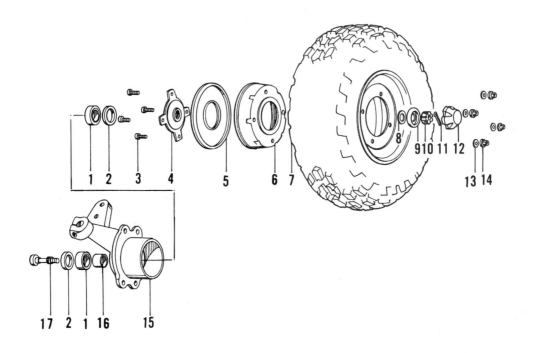

1. Bearing
2. Grease seal
3. Lug bolt
4. Front hub
5. Dust seals
6. Brake drum
7. Tire/rim
8. Washer
9. Cap holder
10. Hub nut
11. Cotter pin
12. Rubber cap
13. Washer
14. Lug nut
15. Steering knuckle
16. Spacer
17. Front axle (2-wheel drive models)

2. Remove any rust or corrosion from the bushing receptacle in the wishbone. Clean out with solvent and thoroughly dry.

3. Clean the outer surface of the new bushing with an aerosol electrical contact cleaner to remove all traces of oil.

4. Apply red Loctite (No. 271) to the outer surface of the new bushing.

5. Press the new bushing into the wishbone. Press the bushing in until it is flush with each side of the wishbone pivot point.

6. Repeat Steps 1-5 for the other bushing.

Steering Knuckle Bearing

Inspection

Inspect each bearing prior to removing it from the steering knuckle.

CAUTION
Do not remove the bearings for inspection purposes as they will be damaged

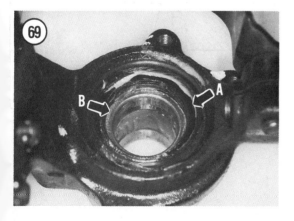

during the removal process. Remove the bearings only if they are to be replaced.

1. Separate the steering knuckle from the wishbones as described in this chapter.

2. Turn each bearing by hand. Make sure each bearing turns smoothly. Replace the bearing(s) if they are noisy or have excessive play (**Figure 60**).

NOTE
Some axial play is normal, but radial play should be negligible. The bearing should turn smoothly.

3. On non-sealed bearings, check the balls for evidence of wear, pitting or excessive heat (bluish tint). Replace bearings if necessary; always replace as a complete set. When replacing, be sure to take your old bearings along to ensure a perfect matchup.

NOTE
Fully sealed bearings are available from many good bearing specialty shops. Fully sealed bearings provide better protection from dirt and moisture that may get into the hub.

4. Inspect the grease seals and O-ring seals. Replace if they are deteriorating or starting to harden.

Bearing removal

Refer to **Figure 67** for this procedure.

Special tools are required for the removal and installation of the steering knuckle bearings. For bearing removal, use Suzuki special tool, Bearing Remover (part No. 09923-74510) and Slide Shaft (part No. 09930-30102). For installation, use Suzuki Bearing Installer Set (part No. 09930-84510). If alternate tools are used for this purpose, the steering knuckle may be damaged.

1. Remove the outer grease seal (A, **Figure 68**) from the steering knuckle.

2. Remove the inner grease seal (A, **Figure 69**) from the steering knuckle.

3. Install the bearing puller behind one of the bearings (B, **Figure 68**), then attach the slide shaft to the bearing puller. Slide the weight on the shaft back, using hard strokes and withdraw the bearing from that side. Remove the special tools.

4. Remove the spacer that fits between the bearings.

10

5. Repeat Step 3 for the other bearing (B, **Figure 69**).

6. Thoroughly clean out the inside of the steering knuckle bearing area with solvent and dry with compressed air or a shop cloth.

Bearing installation

1. On non-sealed bearings, pack the bearings with a good quality bearing grease. Work the grease in between the balls thoroughly. Turn the bearing by hand a couple of times to make sure the grease is distributed evenly inside the bearing.

2. Apply a coat of multipurpose grease to the inside surface of the steering knuckle bearing area and to the outer surface of both bearings and the spacer.

3. Install the outer bearing into the steering knuckle first.

4. Position the bearing (A, **Figure 70**) with the sealed side facing out and install the bearing installer as shown in B, **Figure 70**. Tighten the bearing in-

staller until the bearing is completely seated. Remove the bearing installer.

5. Turn the steering knuckle over and install the spacer (A, **Figure 71**).

NOTE
Suzuki does not specify an exact clearance dimension between the spacer and the inner race of both bearings. The important thing is that the bearings are not pressed tightly against the spacer.

6. Position the bearing (B, **Figure 71**) with the sealed side facing out and install the bearing installer as shown in C, **Figure 71**. Tighten the bearing installer until the bearing almost seats against the collar.

7. Remove the bearing installer and make sure the collar is aligned correctly with the inner race of both bearings. This alignment is necessary so the front axle can be inserted through all 3 parts.

8. Apply a coat of multipurpose grease to both grease seals and install both seals. Push the grease seals in until they are completely seated.

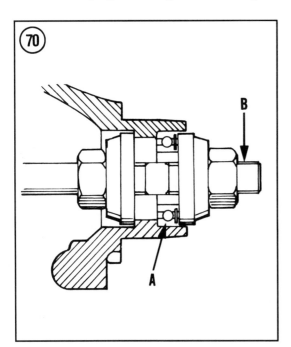

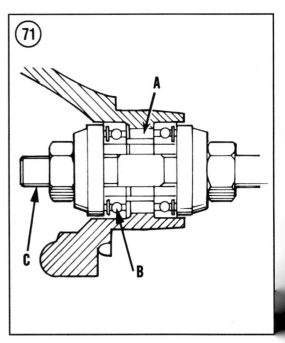

FRONT SUSPENSION AND STEERING

369

Table 1 FRONT SUSPENSION TIGHTENING TORQUES

Item and Model	N·m	ft.-lb.
Front wheel hub nut	85-115	61.5-83
Front wheel lug nuts	45-65	32.5-47
Handlebar holder bolts	18-28	13-20
Steering shaft		
Holder bolts	18-28	13-20
Lower nut	38-60	27.5-43.5
Steering knuckle		
End-to-suspension arm bolt	120-170	87.5-123
Knuckle-to-lower		
wishbone clamping bolt	44-66	32-48
Knuckle-to-arm bolt	40-60	29-43.5
Wishbone-to-frame bolts and nuts	50-70	36-51
Tie rods		
End-to-steering shaft nuts	22-35	16-25.5
Outer end pinch bolt	40-60	29-44
Shock absorber bolts and nuts	40-60	29-44
Front master cylinder clamp bolts	40-50	29-36

Table 2 TIRE INFLATION PRESSURE (COLD)*

| | Tire pressure | | | |
| | Front tires | | Rear tires | |
Load capacity	kPa	psi	kPa	psi
LT-F250 models				
All loads	25	3.6	25	3.6
LT-4WD models				
Up to 80 kg (175 lb.)	30	4.4	20	2.9
80-172 kg (175-380 lb.)	35	5.1	20	2.9
LT-4WDX models				
All loads up to 177 kg				
(90 lb.) maximum	30	4.4	27.5	4.0

* Tire inflation pressure for factory equipped tires. Aftermarket tires may require different inflation pressure.

10

CHAPTER ELEVEN

FRONT DRIVE MECHANISM FOUR-WHEEL DRIVE

This chapter contains repair and replacement procedures for the front drive mechanism. Service to the front drive mechanism consists of periodically checking the rubber boots on the front drive axles. If the boot(s) gets torn or damaged, the pivot bearings may get damaged from dirt and water. The lubrication level check and service procedures for the front differential is covered in Chapter Three.

The secondary bevel gear and output shaft assemblies are located within the crankcase and are covered in Chapter Five.

Front drive mechanism torque specifications are listed in **Table 1** located at the end of this chapter.

FRONT DRIVE AXLES

There are two different front axles used among the different years. The front axle used on 1987 models is equipped with nonserviceable outboard and inboard universal joints. The only portion of this front axle that can be serviced is the replacement of the rubber boots.

On 1988-on models, the front axle has a constant velocity (CV) joint at both the outboard and inboard joints. The inboard CV joint can be disassembled for service, the outboard joint cannot be serviced.

Removal

1. Place the vehicle on level ground and set the parking brake. Block the rear wheels so the vehicle will not roll in either direction.

2. Remove the front wheels as described in Chapter Ten.

3. Remove the front brake drum and backing plate as described in Chapter Thirteen.

4. Drain the front differential oil as described in Chapter Three.

5. Remove the front wishbone and steering knuckle assembly as described in Chapter Ten.

CAUTION
To avoid damage to the front differential oil seal, hold the front drive axle hori-

zontal and straight out from the front differential during removal.

6A. On 1987 models, perform the following:

  a. Reinstall the front hub onto the front axle and install the nut. Tighten the nut securely.

  b. Hold the drive axle *straight out.*

  c. Use a rubber or soft-faced mallet and tap on the backside of the front hub until the drive axle stopper ring is free from the front differential side gear spline groove.

  d. Hold onto the inboard joint of the drive axle and pull the drive axle *straight out* of the front differential and remove the front drive axle shaft from the differential splines.

NOTE
If you are unsuccessful in removing the front axle, attach a hook onto the end of a slide hammer. Attach the hook onto the universal joint, move the weight back and forth on the slide hammer and withdraw the universal joint from the front differential splines.

  e. Remove the front hub from the front axle.

6B. On 1988-on models, perform the following:

CAUTION
*In the next step, do not install the bearing splitter insert behind the bronze colored cover (A, **Figure 1**) located between the inboard joint and the front differential. If the insert is positioned on the cover, the cover will be damaged as it will be forced over the inner end of the inboard joint during axle removal.*

  a. Install a bearing splitter (**Figure 2**) behind the back surface on the inboard joint (B, **Figure 1**).

  b. Hold the drive axle *straight out.*

  c. Attach a hook onto the end of a slide hammer. Attach the hook onto one side of the bearing puller insert, move the weight back and forth on the slide hammer and withdraw the inboard joint from the front differential splines.

External Inspection

NOTE
The boots are subjected to a lot of abuse if the vehicle is ridden in rough terrain. If the boots are damaged and left un-repaired, the axle shaft joints will fail prematurely by allowing the joint to be exposed to dirt, mud and moisture. This also allows the loss of critical lubrication.

NOTE
Figure 3 shows on a 1988-on model. The rubber boots on the 1987 model are in the same basic location but have a different appearance.

11

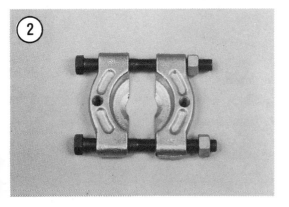

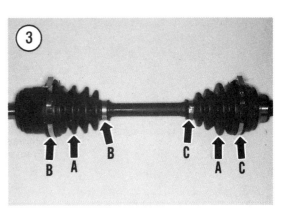

1. Check the rubber boots (A, **Figure 3**) for wear, cuts or damage and replace if necessary as described under the *Disassembly/Assembly* procedure in this chapter.

2. Move each end of the drive axle in a circular motion and check the drive shaft joints for excessive wear or play.

3A. On 1987 models, neither the outboard pivot joint nor the inboard universal joint can be serviced. If either is worn or damaged, the front axle must be replaced. The universal joint assembly can be removed from the front axle and replaced separately from the axle.

3B. On 1988-on models, the inboard pivot joint can be serviced if there is wear or play. The outboard pivot joint *cannot* be serviced if worn or damaged. If damaged, replace the drive axle assembly.

Installation

1. Make sure the stopper ring is in place on the front differential output shaft where the front axle rides.

2. Apply a light coat of molybdenum disulfide grease to the front differential output shaft splines

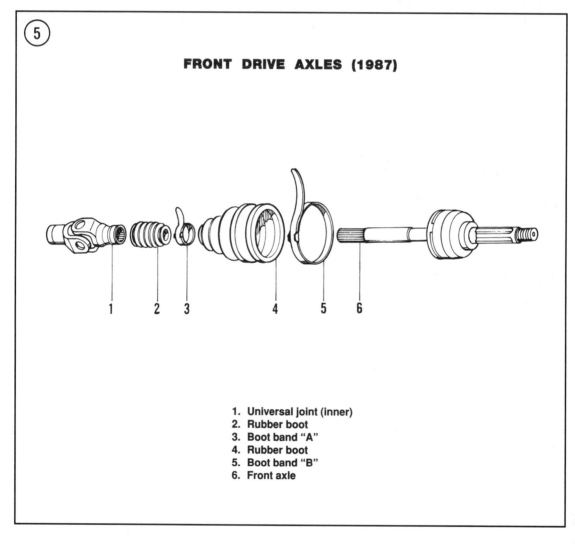

FRONT DRIVE AXLES (1987)

1. Universal joint (inner)
2. Rubber boot
3. Boot band "A"
4. Rubber boot
5. Boot band "B"
6. Front axle

and to the lips of the grease seal. Also apply the grease to the inner splines of the inboard pivot joint on the front axle.

CAUTION
To avoid damage to the front differential oil seal, hold the front drive shaft horizontal and straight into the front differential during installation.

3. Hold the drive axle *straight onto* the front differential output shaft splines.

4. Push the drive axle *straight onto* the front differential and push it in all the way until it bottoms out and the stopper rings snap into place. If necessary, carefully tap on the outer end of the front axle with a rubber mallet or soft-faced mallet.

5. After the drive axle is installed, pull the inboard joint a little to make sure the output shaft stopper ring has locked into the front axle inboard pivot joint groove.

6. Shift the transmission into neutral.

7. Rotate the front axle (**Figure 4**) and make sure it rotates smoothly prior to installing the remaining components.

8. Install the front wishbone and steering knuckle assembly as described in Chapter Ten.

9. Install the front brake drum and backing plate as described in Chapter Thirteen.

10. Install the front wheels as described in Chapter Nine.

11. Refill the front differential with the specified oil as described in Chapter Three.

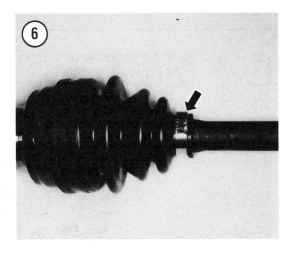

Disassembly/Assembly
(1987 Models)

Refer to **Figure 5** for this procedure.

1. To remove the universal joint portion of the front axle, perform the following:
   a. Slide the universal joint and the rubber boot off the front drive axle.
   b. Remove the boot from the universal joint.

2. To remove the rubber boot on the front axle shaft and joint, perform the following:
   a. Open the clamps on both boot bands "A" and "B" on the outboard joint, then remove both boot bands. Discard both boot bands; they cannot be reused.
   b. Slide the boot off the outboard joint and discard it.
   c. Install the new boot onto the outboard joint.
   d. Position the large end into the correct position on the outboard joint.

NOTE
*Position the new boot bands with their tabs facing toward the **rear** of the vehicle.*

   e. Install 2 new boot bands onto the drive axle boot.
   f. Bend down the tab on the boot bands and secure the tab with the locking clips and tap them with a plastic hammer. Make sure they are locked in place (**Figure 6**).

NOTE
There is no set in and out position for the universal joint on the front axle during assembly. It will position itself correctly when the front axle assembly is installed on the vehicle.

3. To install the universal joint onto the front axle, perform the following:
   a. Slide the rubber boot onto the front axle. Move it past its normal position so the front axle end splines are exposed.
   b. Apply molybdenum disulfide grease to the front axle end splines and to the inner splines of the universal joint.
   c. Slide the universal joint onto the front drive axle. Move it back and forth to make sure it moves freely.
   d. Move the boot into position on the universal joint.

11

Disassembly
(1988-on Models)

Refer to **Figure 7** for this procedure.

NOTE
The outboard joint cannot be disassembled or repaired. If damaged or faulty, the drive axle assembly must be replaced.

1. Thoroughly clean all road dirt and grease from the outer surface of the rubber boot and the front axle with solvent and thoroughly dry.

2. Open the clamps on both boot bands "A" and "B" (B, **Figure 3**) on the inboard joint, then remove boot band "B." Discard the boot band, it cannot be reused.

3. Carefully slide the boot (A, **Figure 8**) onto the front axle and off the inboard joint.

4. Wipe out all of the molybdenum disulfide grease within the inboard joint cavity (B, **Figure 8**).

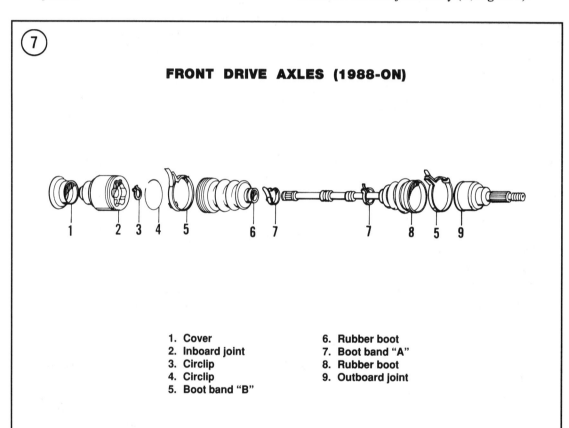

FRONT DRIVE AXLES (1988-ON)

1. Cover
2. Inboard joint
3. Circlip
4. Circlip
5. Boot band "B"
6. Rubber boot
7. Boot band "A"
8. Rubber boot
9. Outboard joint

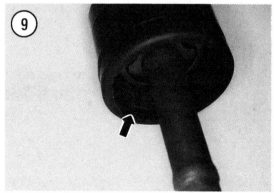

5. Remove the stopper ring (**Figure 9**) from the inboard joint.

6. Remove the inboard joint (**Figure 10**) from the front axle.

7. Remove the circlip (**Figure 11**) and slide off the bearing assembly (**Figure 12**).

8. Slide the inboard boot off the drive axle and discard boot band "A." It cannot be reused.

9. If the outboard boot requires replacement, perform the following:

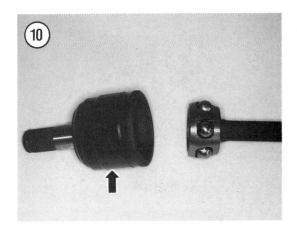

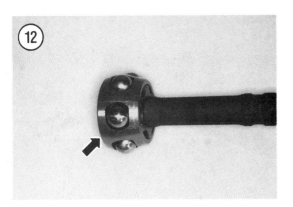

a. Open the clamps on both boot bands "A" and "B" (C, **Figure 3**) on the outboard joint, then remove boot band "B." Discard the boot band; it cannot be reused.

b. Slide the outboard boot off the drive axle and discard boot band "A." It cannot be reused.

10. Inspect the drive axle as described in this chapter.

**Internal Inspection
(1988-on Models)**

Refer to **Figure 7** for this procedure.

1. Wipe off the grease from the exterior of the bearing assembly, then clean in solvent and thoroughly dry. Make sure the balls are thoroughly clean so they can be inspected.

2. Inspect the steel balls (**Figure 13**), bearing case (A, **Figure 14**) and the bearing race (B, **Figure 14**) for wear or damage.

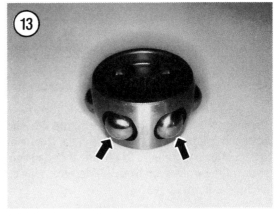

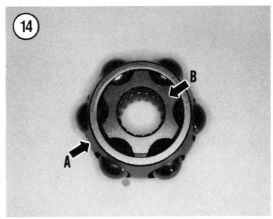

11

3. Check for wear or damage to the inner splines (**Figure 15**) of the bearing race.

4. If any of the components of the bearing assembly are damaged, replace the entire assembly as no replacement parts are available.

5. Wipe off the grease from the exterior and interior of the inboard joint, then clean in solvent and thoroughly dry.

6. Inspect the interior of the inboard joint where the steel balls ride (A, **Figure 16**). Check for wear or damage and replace the joint if necessary.

7. Inspect the snap ring groove (B, **Figure 16**) on the inboard joint for wear or damage.

8. Inspect the splines (A, **Figure 17**) on the inboard joint for wear or damage.

9. Check the stopper ring (B, **Figure 17**) in the end of the inboard joint. Make sure it seats in the groove correctly, if damaged the ring must be replaced.

10. Inspect the exterior of the inboard joint (**Figure 18**) for cracks or damage. Replace if necessary.

11. Check the outboard joint (**Figure 19**) for excessive play or noise by moving the drive axle in a circular direction. If movement is difficult or limited, replace the front axle assembly.

12. Inspect the drive axle for bending, wear or damage.

13. Inspect the inner end splines (**Figure 20**), the outer end splines (A, **Figure 21**) and the front hub cotter pin hole (B, **Figure 21**) for wear or damage. If any of these areas are worn or damaged, replace the front axle.

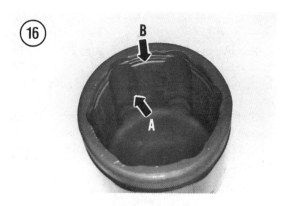

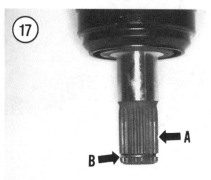

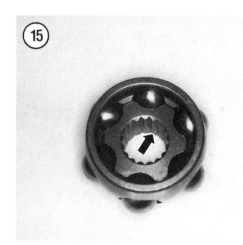

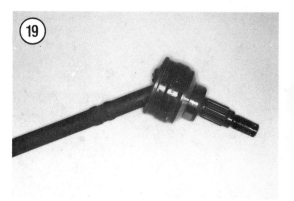

Assembly
(1988-on Models)

Refer to **Figure 7** for this procedure.
1. If the outboard boot was removed, install a new boot onto the drive axle at this time.

NOTE
*Position the new boot bands with their tabs facing toward the **rear** of the vehicle.*

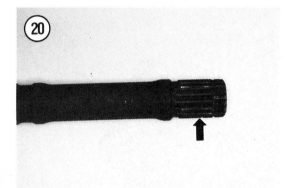

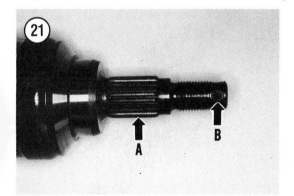

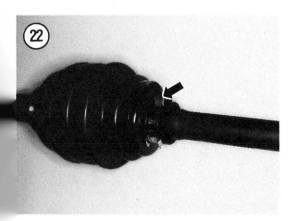

2. Install 2 new small boot bands "A" onto the front axle.

3. Install the inboard boot and move the small boot band "A" onto the boot (**Figure 22**). Bend down the tab on the boot band and secure the tab with the locking clips and tap them with a plastic hammer. Make sure they are locked in place (**Figure 23**).

4. Thoroughly pack the bearing assembly with molybdenum disulfide grease. Work the grease in between the balls, the race and the case. Make sure all voids are filled with grease.

5. Position the bearing assembly with the *small end* of the bearing going on first and install the bearing onto the drive axle (**Figure 12**).

6. Push the bearing assembly on until it stops, then install the circlip (**Figure 24**). Make sure the circlip seats correctly in the drive axle groove.

7. Apply a liberal amount of molybdenum disulfide grease to the exterior of the bearing assembly (**Fig-**

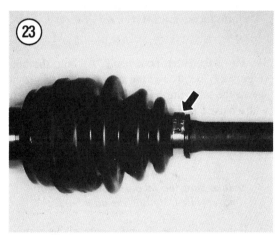

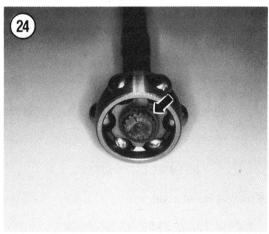

11

ure 25). Work the grease in between the balls, the race and the case. Make sure all voids are filled with grease.

8. Apply a liberal amount of molybdenum disulfide grease to the inner surfaces of the inboard joint.

9. Install the inboard joint over the bearing assembly (**Figure 26**) and install the stopper ring (**Figure 27**). Make sure it is seated correctly in the inboard joint groove.

10. After the stopper ring is in place, fill the inboard joint cavity behind the bearing assembly with additional molybdenum disulfide grease (B, **Figure 8**).

11. Pack each boot with 1-2 oz. of molybdenum disulfide grease.

12. Move the inboard boot onto the inboard joint (**Figure 28**).

13. Move the inboard joint on the drive axle until the recess for the boot band is aligned with the boot.

NOTE
*Position the new boot bands with their tabs facing toward the **rear** of the vehicle.*

14. Move the small boot band "A" onto the boot (**Figure 29**). Bend down the tab on the boot band and secure the tab with the locking clips and tap them with a plastic hammer. Make sure they are locked in place (**Figure 23**).

15. Install the large boot bands "B" onto each boot.

CAUTION
Make sure the inboard joint does not move while installing the boot bands.

16. Refer to **Figure 30** and secure all large boot bands. Bend down the tab (**Figure 31**) on the boot band and secure the tab with the locking clips and tap them with a plastic hammer. Make sure they are locked in place (**Figure 32**).

17. If removed, install the stopper ring (B, **Figure 17**) and make sure it is seated correctly in the drive axle groove.

18. Apply molybdenum disulfide grease to the end splines.

PROPELLER SHAFT

Removal/Installation

Refer to **Figure 33** for this procedure.

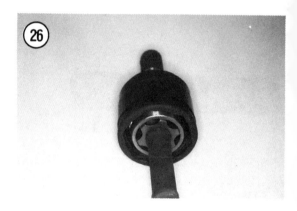

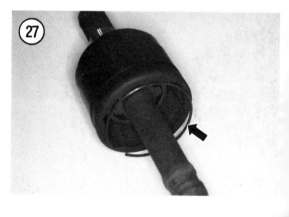

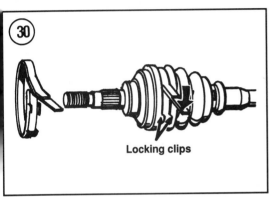

Locking clips

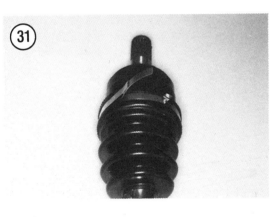

1. Drain the oil from the front differential as described in Chapter Three.

2. Remove the front fender as described in Chapter Fourteen.

3. Remove the front portion of the exhaust system as described in Chapter Eight.

4. Remove both front drive axles as described in this chapter.

5. Remove the front bolt, lockwasher and washer (A, **Figure 34**) and the rear nut, lockwasher and washer (B, **Figure 34**) securing the propeller shaft cover.

6. Pull the propeller shaft cover (C, **Figure 34**) up and forward and remove it from the frame.

7. Place a box wrench on the nut (A, **Figure 35**) and a socket wrench on the bolt (B, **Figure 35**). Remove the 3 bolts and nuts (**Figure 36**) securing the propeller shaft to the front differential via the rubber coupling. Leave the rubber coupling attached to the front differential.

8. Lift the front of the propeller shaft up to clear the rubber coupling, pull the propeller shaft forward and remove it from the secondary driven output shaft universal joint and rubber boot in the front of the engine crankcase. Remove the propeller shaft from the frame.

9. Inspect the components as described in this chapter.

10. Install by reversing these removal steps while noting the following:

    a. Make sure the rubber boot (**Figure 37**) is in place on the crankcase.

    b. Apply molybdenum disulfide grease to the propeller shaft outer splines and to the inner splines of the output shaft universal joint in the crankcase.

    c. Apply red Loctite (No. 271) to the rubber coupling bolt threads prior to installing them. Tighten the bolts and nuts to the torque specification listed in **Table 1**.

    d. After the propeller shaft (**Figure 38**) is installed, and prior to installing the cover, rotate it by hand to make sure it rotates freely with no binding. Make sure the rubber boot (**Figure 39**) is in place on the drive shaft.

    e. Refill the front differential with the recommended type of oil as described in Chapter Three.

11

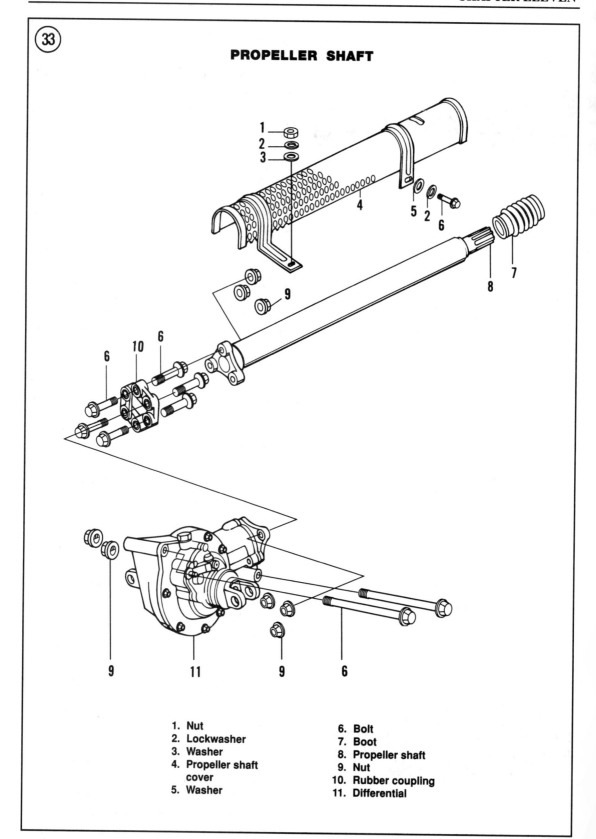

PROPELLER SHAFT

1. Nut
2. Lockwasher
3. Washer
4. Propeller shaft
   cover
5. Washer
6. Bolt
7. Boot
8. Propeller shaft
9. Nut
10. Rubber coupling
11. Differential

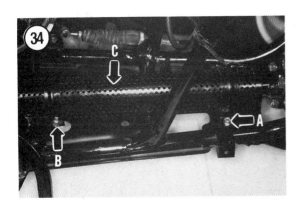

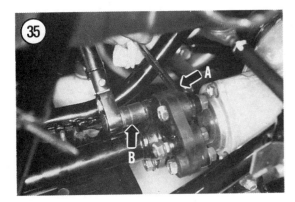

Inspection

1. Inspect the propeller shaft (**Figure 40**) for external damage or wear. If damaged, replace the propeller shaft.

11

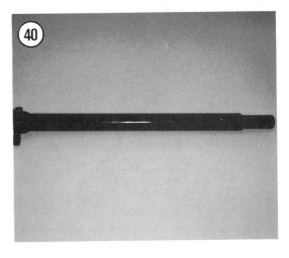

2. Inspect the front mounting flange (**Figure 41**) for wear, fractures or damage. Make sure the bolt holes are not elongated. If damaged, replace the propeller shaft.

3. Inspect the rear splines (**Figure 42**) for wear or damage. If damage is severe, also check the inner splines of the secondary driven output shaft universal joint.

4. Inspect the rubber coupling (**Figure 43**) for wear, damage or deterioration. Replace if necessary.

5. Inspect the rubber boot (**Figure 37**) on the crankcase for wear, damage or deterioration. Replace if necessary.

FRONT DIFFERENTIAL

Removal/Installation

Refer to **Figure 33** for this procedure.

1. Remove the E-clip and washer (A, **Figure 44**) securing the differential lock cable to the shift arm. Remove the cable from the shift arm. Don't lose the flanged bushing on the shift arm pivot pin. Reinstall the flanged bushing (if removed), washer and E-clip onto the shift arm pivot pin to avoid misplacing them.

2. Remove the cable clip (**Figure 45**) securing the shift cable to the frame bracket and move the cable out of the way.

3. On the right-hand side, disconnect the breather hose from the front differential.

4. Remove both front axles (B, **Figure 44**) as described in this chapter.

5. Remove the propeller shaft as described in this chapter.

6. Remove the front differential rear mounting bolt (C, **Figure 44**) and nut.

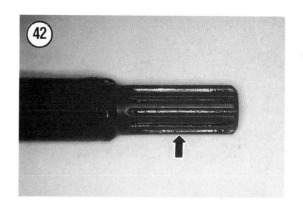

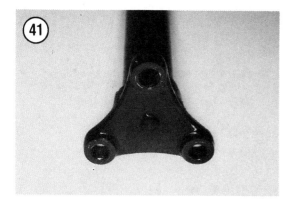

7. Remove the front differential front mounting bolt (D, **Figure 44**) and nut.

8. Carefully pull the front differential toward the rear and remove it from the left-hand side of the frame.

9. Inspect the front differential as described in this chapter.

10. Installation is the reverse of these removal steps, noting the following:

   a. Apply molybdenum disulfide grease to the splines of each end of the propeller shaft and to the oil seal of the front differential.

   b. Correctly position the front differential in the chassis.

   c. Tighten the mounting bolts and nuts to the torque specification listed in **Table 1**.

   d. Refill the front differential with the recommended type of oil as described in Chapter Three.

Disassembly/Inspection/Assembly

The front differential requires a considerable number of special Suzuki tools for disassembly and assembly. The dollar cost of all of these tools could be more than the price of most repairs or the seal replacement by a dealer.

1. Check the entire front differential unit for oil leakage.
2. Inspect the splines of the pinion gear for wear or damage. If damaged, repair should be entrusted to a dealer as disassembly is required.

NOTE
If these splines are damaged, also inspect the splines on the propeller shaft, it may require replacement also.

3. Inspect the grease seal on the right-hand side and the left-hand side for damage and replace if necessary.
4. Rotate the drive pinion by hand. It should turn smoothly and quietly. If the rotation is rough or noisy, have the unit serviced by a Suzuki dealer.

Table 1 FRONT DRIVE MECHANISM TIGHTENING TORQUES

Item and Model	N·m	ft.-lb.
Propeller shaft-to-rubber coupling bolts	40-50	29-36
Front differential mounting bolts	40-50	29-36

11

CHAPTER TWELVE

REAR SUSPENSION, REAR AXLE AND FINAL DRIVE

This chapter contains repair and replacement procedures for the rear wheel, rear axles and the rear suspension. Service to the rear suspension consists of periodically checking bolt tightness and checking the condition of the rear shock absorbers and replacing them as necessary. Tire removal and repair are covered in Chapter Ten.

The rear final drive gears are located within the crankcase and are covered in Chapter Five.

Refer to **Table 1**, located at the end of this chapter, for rear suspension torque specifications.

> *CAUTION*
> *Self-locking nuts are used to secure some of the rear suspension components. Suzuki recommends that all self-locking nuts must be discarded once they have been removed. The self-locking portion of the nut is damaged once it has been removed and will no longer properly lock onto the lower holder threads. Always install **new** self-locking nuts. **Never** reinstall a used nut once it has been removed.*

REAR WHEEL

Removal/Installation

Refer to **Figure 1** for this procedure.

> *NOTE*
> *The front and rear tire tread on the factory equipped tires is directional and must rotate in the correct direction. These tires have a direction arrow (**Figure 2**) on the side wall to indicate the correct direction of wheel rotation. Prior to removing for wheel, mark the rim with a piece of masking tape. Mark it as to which side of the vehicle the tire was mounted and the direction of forward rotation. This is necessary for tire installation as described in this chapter.*

1. Place the ATV on level ground and set the parking brake. Block the front wheels so the vehicle will not roll in either direction.

> *NOTE*
> *The LT-4WDX 4-wheel drive model (280 cc), is equipped with 5 lug nuts. All other models are equipped with 4 lug nuts as shown in **Figure 3**.*

2. Loosen, do not remove, the lug nuts (**Figure 3**) securing the wheel to the hub/brake drum.

3. Jack up the rear of the vehicle with a small hydraulic or scissor jack. Place the jack under the frame with a piece of wood between the jack and the frame.

①

REAR WHEEL AND HUB

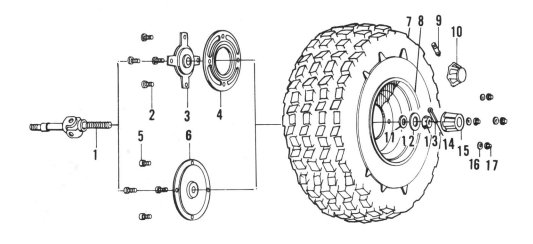

1. Rear axle
2. Lug bolts
3. Rear hub
4. Spacer (left-hand
   side only)
5. Lug bolts
6. Rear hub (LT-4WDX
   [280 cc] models)
7. Tire
8. Wheel

9. Valve stem
10. Rubber cap
11. Washer
12. Cap holder
13. Hub nut
14. Cotter pin
15. Rubber cap (LT-4WDX
    [280 cc] models)
16. Washer
17. Lug nut

12

4. Place wooden block(s) under the frame to support the ATV securely with the rear wheels off the ground.

5. Remove the lug nuts and washers (**Figure 3**) securing the wheel to the hub/brake drum. Remove the rear wheel.

6. Repeat Steps 2-5 for the other wheel if necessary.

NOTE
Install the tire and wheel onto the same side of the vehicle from which it was removed. See NOTE at the beginning of this procedure. Also refer to the direction arrow on the tire side wall.

7. Install the rear wheel, then install the lug nuts securely, but not the final torque.

8. Shift the transmission into neutral.

9. After the wheel is installed completely, rotate it in the normal forward rotation; apply the brake several times to make sure that the wheel rotates freely and that the brake is operating correctly.

10. Jack the rear of the vehicle up a little and remove the wooden block(s).

11. Let the jack down and remove the jack and wooden block(s).

WARNING
Always tighten the lug nuts to the correct torque specification or the lug nuts may work loose and the wheel could fall off.

12. Use a torque wrench and tighten the lug nuts (**Figure 3**), in a crisscross pattern, to the torque specification listed in **Table 1**.

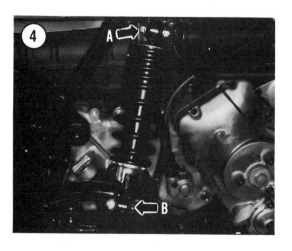

SHOCK ABSORBER

Removal

1. Place the ATV on level ground and set the parking brake. Block the front wheels so the vehicle will not roll in either direction.

2. Place wooden block(s) under the frame to support the ATV securely with the rear wheels off of the ground.

3. Remove the seat and rear fender as described in Chapter Fourteen.

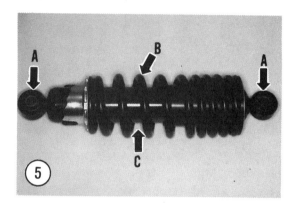

4. Remove both rear wheels as described in this chapter. It is not necessary to remove the wheels, but it makes shock absorber removal a lot easier with the additional working area.

5. Remove the bolt and nut (A, **Figure 4**) securing the upper portion of the shock absorber to the frame.

6. Remove the bolt and nut (B, **Figure 4**) securing the lower portion of the shock absorber to the rear suspension arm.

7. Remove the shock absorber assembly from the frame.

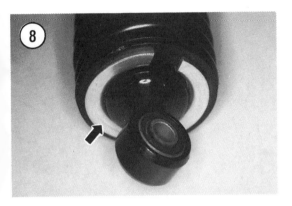

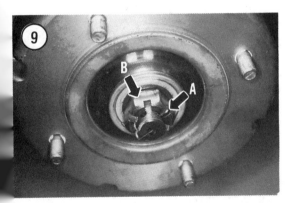

8. Install by reversing these steps while noting the following:

  a. Apply a light coat of multipurpose grease to the pivot points on the frame, upper wishbone where the shock absorber is attached and the pivot points on the shock absorber (A, **Figure 5**).

  b. Tighten the bolts and nuts to the torque specification listed in **Table 1**.

  c. Push down on the rear of the ATV and make sure the rear suspension is operating properly.

Inspection

Replacement parts for the factory installed shock absorber are not available from Suzuki. If the unit is leaking fluid or any part is damaged, the entire unit must be replaced.

1. Inspect the rubber bushing at the upper (**Figure 6**) and at the lower (**Figure 7**) joints for wear or damage. If either is worn or damaged, replace the shock absorber.

2. Inspect the spring (B, **Figure 5**) for weakness or damage.

3. Check the spring upper seat (**Figure 8**) for damage. Make sure it is properly seated.

4. Check the damper unit (C, **Figure 5**) for leakage and make sure the damper rod is straight.

5. If the shock absorber fails any of these inspection steps, replace the shock absorber.

REAR HUB AND BRAKE DRUM

There is only one rear brake assembly, and it is located only on the right-hand side of the vehicle.

Removal

Refer to **Figure 1** for this procedure.

1. Remove the rear wheel(s) as described in this chapter.

2A. On the right-hand side of the vehicle, perform the following:

  a. Remove the cotter pin (A, **Figure 9**) from the rear axle and discard it.

  b. Shift the transmission into gear, then loosen and remove the axle nut (B, **Figure 9**).

  c. Remove the washer (A, **Figure 10**) and the cap holder (B, **Figure 10**).

12

d. Slide the brake drum (**Figure 11**) off the brake shoes and remove the brake drum.

2B. On the left-hand side of the vehicle, perform the following:

  a. Remove the spacer (A, **Figure 12**) and cap (B, **Figure 12**) from the hub.

  b. Remove the cotter pin (**Figure 13**) from the rear axle and discard it.

  c. Shift the transmission into gear, then loosen and remove the axle nut (**Figure 14**).

  d. Remove the washer (A, **Figure 15**) and the cap holder (B, **Figure 15**).

NOTE
Step 3 is shown removing the front hub from the front axle. The procedure is exactly the same for both the front and rear hubs.

3. Remove the rear hub (**Figure 16**) from the rear axle. If the rear hub will not slide off the rear axle, perform the following:

  a. Attach a section of heavy duty chain to two of the opposite rear hub threaded studs (A, **Figure 17**).

  b. Install 2 of the lug nuts (B, **Figure 17**) to hold the chain in place. Screw the lug nuts on far enough so the stud threads are exposed past the screwed on nuts. This will ensure that the nuts have a good grip on the threaded studs to avoid thread damage.

  c. Attach a body shop slide hammer (C, **Figure 17**) to the center of the chain. Slide the weight on the hammer and withdraw the rear hub (D, **Figure 17**) from the rear axle.

  d. Remove the rear hub from the rear axle (**Figure 18**).

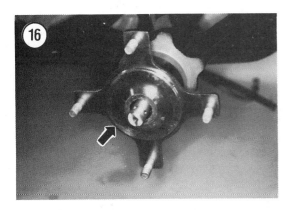

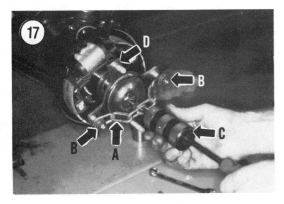

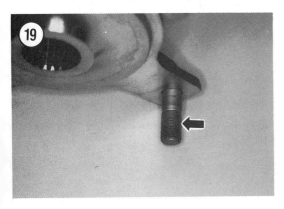

e. Remove the hub nuts and chain from the rear hub.

4. Inspect the rear hub as described in this chapter.

Inspection

The rear hub is not equipped with rear axle bearings. The rear axle bearings are located in the rear suspension arm and service for these bearings is covered in that section of this chapter.

1. Inspect the rear hub for cracks, fractures or damage. Replace the rear hub if damaged in any way.

2. Inspect the threaded studs (**Figure 19**) for wear or damage. Minor damage can be cleaned up with the appropriate size metric die. If damage is severe, a damaged stud can be pressed out and a new one installed. Refer this to a Suzuki dealer service department.

3. Inspect the inner splines for wear or damage. If damaged, the rear hub should be replaced. Refer to **Figure 20** and **Figure 21**. If damage is severe,

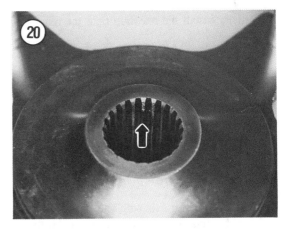

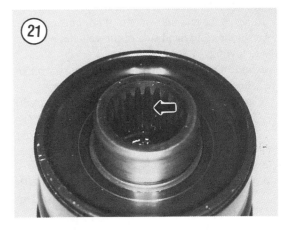

12

inspect the outer splines (**Figure 22**) on the rear axle as it may also be damaged and require replacement.

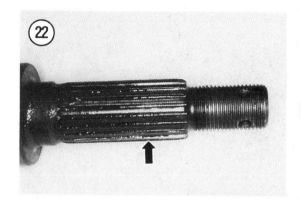

> *CAUTION*
> *Both dust seals are very important as they not only keep out dust and dirt but also moisture. If the condition of these seals is questionable, replace them as they will prevent damage to the rear drum brake components and the steering knuckle bearings.*

4. Inspect the rubber dust seal on the rear hub (**Figure 23**) and on the rear brake backing plate (**Figure 24**) for wear, hardness or deterioration. Replace if necessary.

5. Inspect the left-hand side spacer (**Figure 25**) for wear or damage. Replace if necessary.

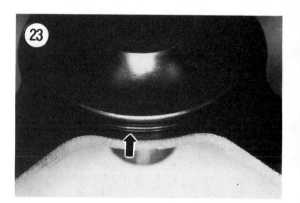

Installation

1. Apply wheel bearing grease to the inner splines of the rear hub and to the outer splines of the rear axle.

2. Partially install the rear hub onto the rear axle splines.

> *CAUTION*
> *It is very important to hold onto the rear axle securely during the next step. Damage may occur to the rear final drive gear while driving the rear hub onto the rear axle if the rear axle is not held securely. Do not allow the driving force of the mallet to be transferred from the rear axle to the rear final drive gear.*

3. Hold onto the rear axle with one hand.

4. While holding onto the rear axle, use a soft-faced or plastic mallet, and drive the rear hub onto the rear axle. Drive the rear hub on until it bottoms out.

5A. On the right-hand side of the vehicle, perform the following:

   a. Slide the brake drum (**Figure 10**) onto the brake shoes and rear hub. Push it on until it stops.
   b. Install the washer and the cap holder (**Figure 9**) on the rear axle, then install the axle nut (B, **Figure 9**). Tighten the axle nut only finger-tight at this time.
   c. Make sure the transmission is still in gear.
   d. Use a torque wrench and tighten the axle nut (B, **Figure 9**) to the torque specification listed in **Table 1**.

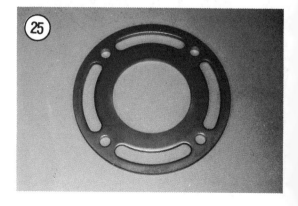

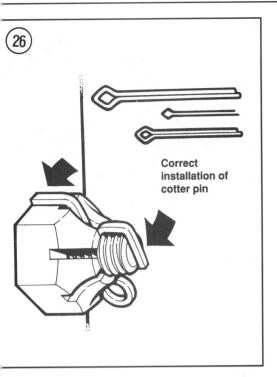

Correct installation of cotter pin

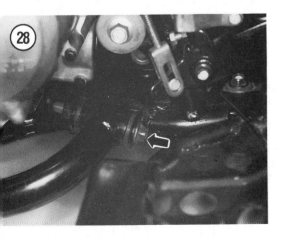

5B. On the left-hand side of the vehicle, perform the following:
  a. Install the washer (B, **Figure 15**) and the cap holder (A, **Figure 15**), then install the axle nut (**Figure 14**). Tighten the axle nut only finger-tight at this time.
  b. Make sure the transmission is still in gear.
  c. Use a torque wrench and tighten the axle nut (**Figure 14**) to the torque specification listed in **Table 1**.
  d. Install the spacer (A, **Figure 12**) and cap (B, **Figure 12**) onto the hub.
6. Align one of the castillations on the nut with the cotter pin hole in the rear axle. If not aligned, tighten the nut. Do *not* loosen the nut to achieve alignment.

> *NOTE*
> *Always install a new cotter pin. Never reuse an old one as it may break and fall off.*

7. Install a new cotter pin and bend the ends over completely (**Figure 26**).
8. Install the rear wheel(s) as described in this chapter.

REAR SUSPENSION ARM

Removal/Installation

1. Place the ATV on level ground and set the parking brake. Block the front wheels so the vehicle will not roll in either direction. Release the parking brake.
2. Remove the seat and rear fender as described in Chapter Fourteen.
3. Remove both rear wheels as described in this chapter.
4. Remove the rear drum brake assembly as described in Chapter Thirteen.
5. Remove the bolt securing the lower portion of the shock absorber (**Figure 27**) to the suspension arm. Move the shock absorber up and out of the way. There is no need to remove it.
6. Remove the front bolt and nut (**Figure 28**) and the rear bolt and nut (**Figure 29**) securing the suspension arm to the frame and remove the suspension arm from the frame. Carefully guide the suspension arm out past the rear drive axle.
7. Carefully lower the rear drive axle until it stops. There is no need to tie up or support the rear axle.

12

8. Install by reversing these removal steps while noting the following:

a. Apply a coat of waterproof grease to all pivot areas prior to installing any components.

b. Install the suspension arm onto the frame mounting bosses. Install the bolts and nuts only finger-tight at this time.

c. Install the shock absorber, then tighten the suspension arm mounting bolts and nuts. This will properly locate the suspension arm's mounting bushings in the frame prior to tightening the mounting bolts.

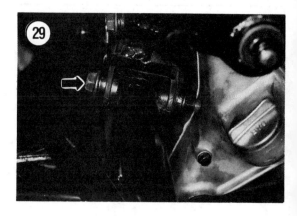

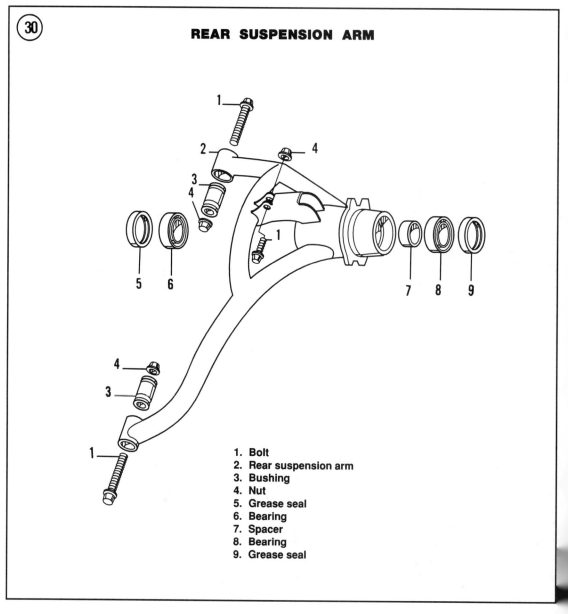

REAR SUSPENSION ARM

1. Bolt
2. Rear suspension arm
3. Bushing
4. Nut
5. Grease seal
6. Bearing
7. Spacer
8. Bearing
9. Grease seal

d. Tighten all bolts and nuts to the torque specification listed in **Table 1**.

Inspection

Refer to **Figure 30** for all models for this procedure.

1. Inspect the rubber bushings (**Figure 31**) where the suspension arm attaches to the frame. Replace the bushings as a set, as described in this chapter, if either are worn or damaged.

2. Inspect the suspension arm (**Figure 32**) for damage, rust and fractures. Replace as necessary.

3. Inspect the pivot bolts and nuts (**Figure 33**) for wear or damage. Check the threads for damage and repair if necessary.

4. Inspect the shock absorber lower mounting brackets for wear or damage. Make sure the mounting holes are not elongated or damaged. If necessary, replace the upper wishbone.

5. Inspect the suspension arm bearings and grease seals as described in this chapter.

Bushing Replacement

NOTE
Replace the bushings as a pair even though only one may be damaged. This will ensure an even amount of load on the suspension arm during use.

1. Use a hydraulic press and suitable size socket and press the old bushing (**Figure 31**) out of the suspension arm. Discard the old bushing.

2. Remove any rust or corrosion from the bushing receptacle in the wishbone. Clean out with solvent and thoroughly dry.

3. Clean the outer surface of the new bushing with an aerosol electrical contact cleaner to remove all traces of oil.

4. Apply red Loctite (No. 271) to the outer surface of the new bushing.

5. Press the new bushing into the suspension arm. Press the bushing in until it is flush with each side of the wishbone pivot point.

6. Repeat Steps 1-5 for the other bushing.

Bearing

Inspection

Inspect each bearing prior to removing it from the steering knuckle.

CAUTION
Do not remove the bearings for inspection purposes as they will be damaged during the removal process. Remove the bearings only if they are to be replaced.

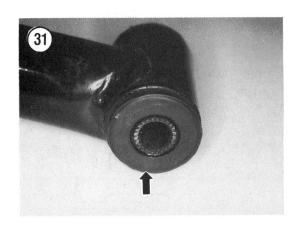

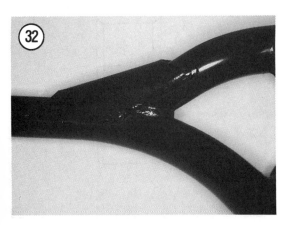

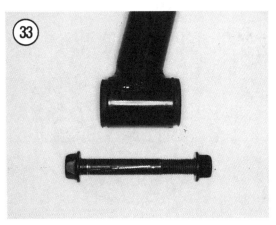

12

1. Turn each bearing (A, **Figure 34**) by hand. Make sure each bearing turns smoothly. Replace the bearing(s) if it is noisy or has excessive play (**Figure 35**).

> *NOTE*
> *Some axial play is normal, but radial play should be negligible. The bearing should turn smoothly.*

2. On non-sealed bearings, check the balls for evidence of wear, pitting or excessive heat (bluish tint). Replace bearings if necessary; always replace as a complete set. When replacing the bearings, be sure to take your old bearings along to ensure a perfect matchup.

> *NOTE*
> *Fully sealed bearings are available from many good bearing specialty shops. Fully sealed bearings provide better protection from dirt and moisture that may get into the hub.*

3. Inspect the grease seals (B, **Figure 34**). Replace if they are deteriorating or starting to harden.

Bearing removal

Refer to **Figure 30** for this procedure.

Special tools are required for the removal and installation of the steering knuckle bearings. For bearing removal, use Suzuki special tools, Bearing Remover (part No. 09913-60710) and Slide Shaft (part No. 09930-30102). For installation, use Suzuki Bearing Installer Set (part No. 09930-84510). If alternate tools are used for this purpose, the steering knuckle may be damaged.

1. Remove the grease seal (**Figure 36**) from each side of the suspension arm.

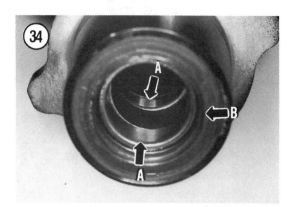

2. Install the bearing puller behind one of the bearings, then attach the slide shaft to the bearing puller. Slide the weight on the shaft back, using hard strokes and withdraw the bearing from that side. Remove the special tools.

3. Remove the spacer that fits between the bearings.

4. Repeat Step 2 for the other bearing.

5. Thoroughly clean out the inside of the suspension arm bearing area with solvent and dry with compressed air or a shop cloth.

Bearing installation

1. On non-sealed bearings, pack the bearings with a good quality bearing grease. Work the grease in

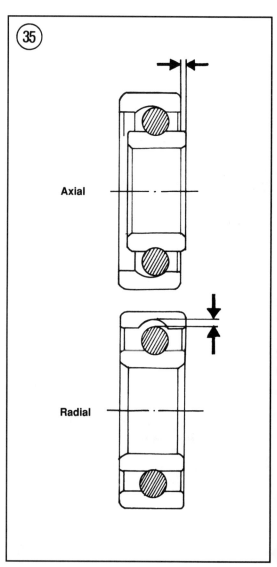

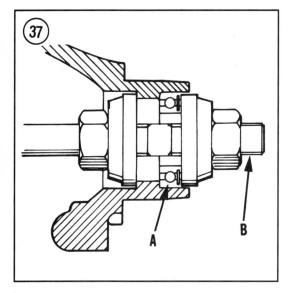

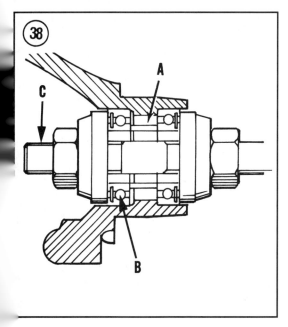

between the balls thoroughly. Turn the bearing by hand a couple of times to make sure the grease is distributed evenly inside the bearing.

2. Apply a coat of multipurpose grease to the inside surface of the suspension arm bearing area and to the outer surface of both bearings and the spacer.

3. Install the outer bearing into the steering knuckle first.

4. Position the bearing (A, **Figure 37**) with the sealed side facing out and install the bearing installer as shown in B, **Figure 37**. Tighten the bearing installer until the bearing is completely seated. Remove the bearing installer.

5. Turn the steering knuckle over and install the spacer (A, **Figure 38**).

NOTE
Suzuki does not specify an exact clearance dimension between the spacer and the inner race of both bearings. The important thing is that the bearings are not pressed tightly against the spacer.

6. Position the bearing (B, **Figure 38**) with the sealed side facing out and install the bearing installer as shown in C, **Figure 38**. Tighten the bearing installer until the bearing almost seats against the collar.

7. Remove the bearing installer and make sure the collar (**Figure 39**) is aligned correctly with the inner race of both bearings. This alignment is necessary so the rear axle can be inserted through all 3 parts. Realign if necessary.

8. Apply a coat of multipurpose grease to both grease seals and install both seals. Push the grease seals in until they are completely seated.

REAR DRIVE AXLES

Removal/Installation

The rear drive axles are equipped with non-serviceable universal joints at each end. The only portion of this rear axle that can be serviced is the replacement of the rubber boot.

Removal

1. Place the vehicle on level ground and set the parking brake. Block the front wheels so the vehicle will not roll in either direction. Release the parking brake.

2. Remove the rear wheels as described in Chapter Ten.

3. Remove the rear brake drum and backing plate as described in Chapter Thirteen.

4. Drain the engine oil as described in Chapter Three.

5. Remove the rear suspension arm as described in this chapter.

NOTE
The size of the rubber boot varies among the different years. The boot on 1987-1993 models is smaller and covers only the spline area of the drive shaft and a small portion of the inboard universal joint. On 1994-on models, the boot is larger and completely covers the inboard universal joint. It is also secured to the universal joint cover next to the crankcase.

6A. On 1987-1993 models, perform the following:

a. Release the rubber boot from the shoulder on the inboard universal joint.

b. Pull the drive axle and rubber boot out of the inboard universal joint and remove it.

6B. On 1994-on models, perform the following:

a. Open the clamp on the boot band (**Figure 40**).

b. Slide the boot off the universal joint cover next to the crankcase.

7. Pull the rear drive axle assembly (**Figure 41**) out of the inboard universal joint and remove the axle assembly.

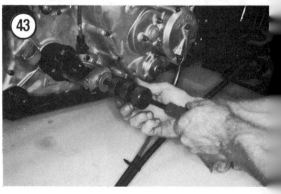

8. Attach a wheel puller to the outer yoke of the inboard universal joint (**Figure 42**).

CAUTION
To avoid damage to the rear drive axle oil seal in the crankcase, hold the inboard universal joint horizontal and straight out from the crankcase during removal.

9. Attach a slide hammer to the wheel puller, move the weight back and forth on the slide hammer (**Figure 43**) and withdraw the inboard universal joint from the output shaft splines in the crankcase.
10. Remove the tools from the inboard universal joint.
11. On 1994-on models, remove the boot band from the rubber boot and discard it.
12. Slide the rubber boot off the rear drive axle.

Inspection

Refer to **Figure 44** for this procedure.

NOTE
The size and shape of the cover on the inboard universal joint varies among the different models and years.

1. Remove the cover from the inboard universal joint.

NOTE
The boots are subjected to a lot of abuse if the vehicle is ridden in rough terrain. If the boots are damaged and left un-repaired, the axle shaft joints will fail prematurely by allowing the joint to be exposed to dirt, mud and moisture. This

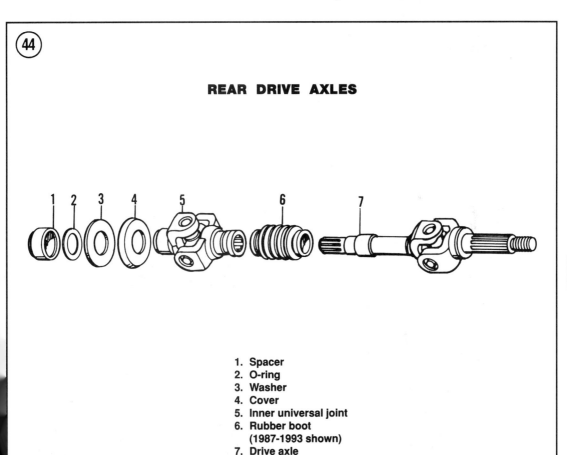

REAR DRIVE AXLES

1. Spacer
2. O-ring
3. Washer
4. Cover
5. Inner universal joint
6. Rubber boot
   (1987-1993 shown)
7. Drive axle

12

also allows the loss of critical lubrication.

NOTE
Figure 45 shows a 1994-on model. The rubber boot on prior models is smaller.

2. Check the rubber boot (**Figure 45**) for wear, cuts or damage and replace if necessary.

3. Inspect the exterior of both universal joints for cracks or damage and replace if necessary.

4. Move each universal joint in a circular motion and check for excessive wear or play. Refer to A, **Figure 46** and **Figure 47**. Neither universal joint can be serviced. If either is worn or damaged, either the universal joint or the drive axle must be replaced.

5. Inspect the drive axle (B, **Figure 46**) for bending, wear or damage.

6. Inspect the inner end splines of the inboard universal joint for wear or damage. Refer to **Figure 48** and **Figure 49**. If any of these areas are worn or damaged, replace the inboard universal joint.

7. Inspect the drive axle end splines for wear or damage. Refer to **Figure 50** and A, **Figure 51**. Inspect the rear hub cotter pin hole (B, **Figure 51**) for wear or damage. If any of these areas are worn or damaged, replace the rear drive axle.

8. Install the cover (**Figure 44**) onto the inboard universal joint. Push it on all the way until it stops.

Installation

1. Make sure the stopper ring (A, **Figure 52**) is in place on the output shaft where the axle rides.

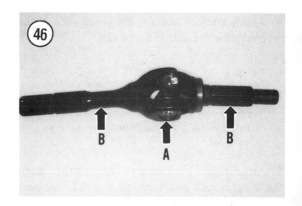

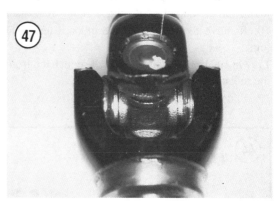

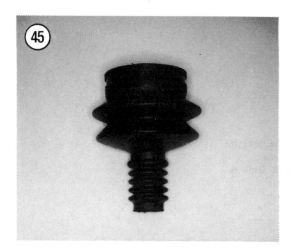

2. Apply a light coat of molybdenum disulfide grease to the output shaft splines and to the lips of the grease seal (B, **Figure 52**). Also apply the grease to the inner splines of the inboard universal joint (**Figure 49**).

CAUTION
To avoid damage to the rear output shaft oil seal, hold the inboard universal joint horizontal and straight into the crankcase during installation.

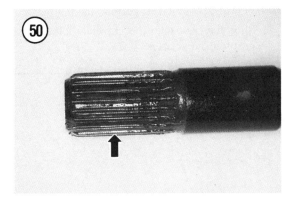

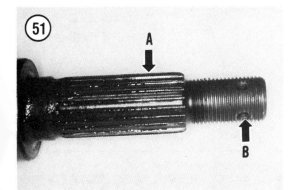

3. Hold the inboard universal joint *straight onto* the output shaft splines.

4. Push the inboard universal joint *straight onto* the output shaft splines and push it in all the way until it bottoms out and the stopper ring snaps into place (**Figure 53**). If necessary, carefully tap on the outer end of the inboard universal joint with a rubber mallet or soft-faced mallet.

5. After the inboard universal joint is installed, pull out on the inboard joint a little to make sure the output shaft stopper ring has locked into the inboard universal joint groove.

6. Slide the rubber boot onto the rear drive axle.

NOTE
*Position the new boot bands with their tabs facing toward the **rear** of the vehicle.*

7. On 1994-on models, install a new boot band (**Figure 54**) onto the rubber boot.

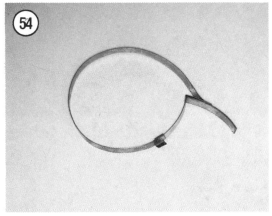

12

8. Apply a light coat of molybdenum disulfide grease to the rear drive axle outer splines (**Figure 50**).

> *CAUTION*
> *To prevent rear axle vibration, the yoke on the inboard universal joint and the yoke on the universal joint on the rear axle assembly must be synchronized with each other as shown in **Figure 55**. If they are not synchronized, a large fluctuation of the torque transmitted to the wheel during rear axle rotation will occur and produce a vibration. This vibration will place undo stress on all of the rear axle components leading to premature component failure.*

9. Pull back on the rubber boot and install the rear drive axle into the inboard universal joint (**Figure 56**). Push it on all the way.

10. Shift the transmission into neutral.

11. Rotate the rear axle (**Figure 41**) and make sure it rotates smoothly prior to installing the remaining components.

12A. On 1987-1993 models, move the rubber boot onto the shoulder on the inboard universal joint. Make sure the rubber boot is positioned correctly at both ends.

12B. On 1994-on models, perform the following:

   a. Slide the boot onto the universal joint cover next to the crankcase.

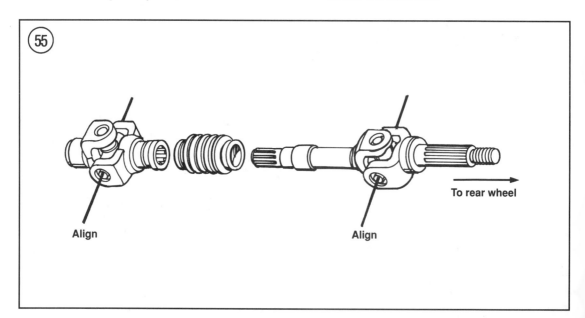

Align   Align

To rear wheel

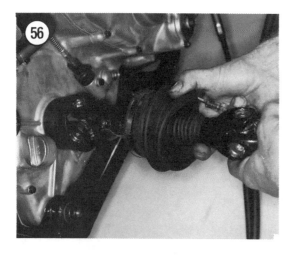

b. Move the boot band (**Figure 57**) into position on the boot.

c. Bend down the tab on the boot band and secure the tab with the locking clips and tap them with a plastic hammer. Make sure they are locked in place (**Figure 58**).

13. Install the rear suspension arm as described in this chapter.

14. Install the rear brake drum and backing plate as described in Chapter Thirteen.

15. Install the rear wheels as described in Chapter Nine.

16. Refill the crankcase with the specified oil as described in Chapter Three.

Table 1 REAR SUSPENSION TIGHTENING TORQUES

Item and Model	N·m	ft.-lb.
Rear hub nut	85-115	61.5-83
Wheel lug nuts	45-66	33-47
Shock absorber bolts and nuts	40-60	29-43.5
Suspension arm mounting bolts and nuts	50-70	36-50.5
Sub-transmission-to-final drive unit nuts	24-31	17-23

12

CHAPTER THIRTEEN

BRAKES

All models are equipped with self-adjusting dual front drum brakes and a single drum brake on the right-hand rear wheel.

The front drum brakes are operated by hydraulic brake fluid via two wheel cylinders and a master cylinder. The rear drum brake is cable operated by both the left-hand brake lever and the foot operated brake pedal on the right-hand side.

Rear brake lever and pedal free play must be maintained on the rear brake to minimize brake drag and premature brake wear and maximize braking effectiveness. Refer to Chapter Three for complete adjustment procedures.

Both rear brake cables must be inspected and replaced periodically as they will stretch with use until they can no longer be properly adjusted.

Table 1 contains the brake system specifications and **Table 2** contains brake system torque specifications. **Table 1** and **Table 2** are located at the end of this chapter.

FRONT DRUM BRAKES

Service Information

The front drum brakes are actuated by hydraulic fluid and are controlled by a hand lever that is attached to the front master cylinder on the right-hand side of the handlebar. As the brake linings wear, the brake fluid level drops in the reservoir and automatically adjusts for wear.

When working on hydraulic brake systems, it is necessary that the work area and all tools be absolutely clean. Any tiny particles of foreign matter and grit in the wheel cylinder or the master cylinder can damage the components. Also, sharp tools must not be used inside the master cylinder. If there is any doubt about your ability to correctly and safely carry out major service on the brake components, take the job to a Suzuki dealer or brake specialist.

> *NOTE*
> *If you recycle your old engine oil, **never** add used brake fluid to the old engine oil. Recyclers who accept old oil for recycling may not accept the oil if other fluids (brake fluid or any other type of petroleum based fluids) have been combined with it.*

Consider the following when servicing the drum brake system.

1. Drum brake components rarely require disassembly, except for brake shoe replacement, so do not disassemble them unless necessary.

> *WARNING*
> *Do not intermix silicone based (DOT 5) brake fluid as it can cause brake component damage leading to brake system failure.*

2. Use only DOT 3 or DOT 4 brake fluid from a sealed container.

3. Do not allow brake fluid to contact any plastic, painted or plated surfaces or surface damage will occur.

4. Always keep the master cylinder reservoir and spare cans of brake fluid closed to prevent dust or moisture from entering. If moisture enters the brake fluid it would result in brake fluid contamination and brake problems.

5. Use only DOT 3 or DOT 4 brake fluid to wash parts. Never clean any internal brake components with solvent or any other petroleum base cleaners.

6. Whenever *any* component has been removed from the brake system the system is considered "opened" and must be bled to remove air bubbles. Also, if the brake feels "spongy," this usually means there are air bubbles in the system and it must be bled. For safe brake operation, refer to *Bleeding the System* in this chapter.

CAUTION
Do not use solvents of any kind on the brake systems' internal components. Solvents will cause the seals to swell and distort. When disassembling and cleaning brake components (except brake linings) use new DOT 3 or DOT 4 brake fluid.

WARNING
*When working on the brake system, do **not** inhale brake dust. It may contain asbestos, which can cause lung injury and cancer. Wear a face mask that meets OSHA requirements for trapping asbestos particles, and wash your hands and forearms thoroughly after completing the work.*

Brake Shoe Replacement

Refer to **Figure 1** for this procedure.

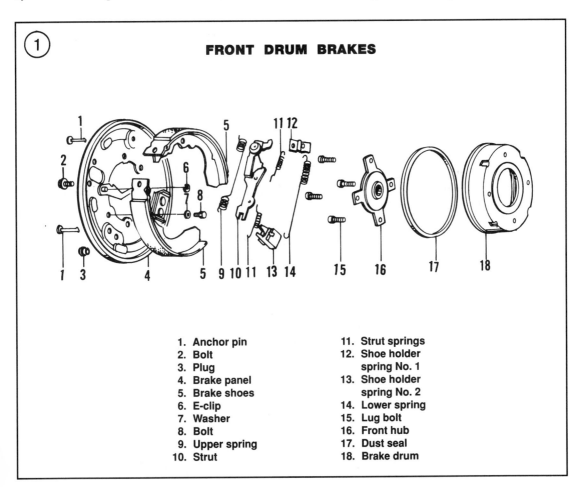

FRONT DRUM BRAKES

1. Anchor pin
2. Bolt
3. Plug
4. Brake panel
5. Brake shoes
6. E-clip
7. Washer
8. Bolt
9. Upper spring
10. Strut
11. Strut springs
12. Shoe holder spring No. 1
13. Shoe holder spring No. 2
14. Lower spring
15. Lug bolt
16. Front hub
17. Dust seal
18. Brake drum

13

There is no recommended mileage interval for changing the brake shoes in the drum brakes. Brake shoe wear depends greatly on riding habits and conditions. The shoes should be checked for wear at the interval listed in **Table 1**, *Maintenance Schedule* in Chapter Three. To maintain an even brake pressure on the drum, always replace both shoes in both front drum brake assemblies at the same time.

Disconnecting the hydraulic brake hose from the brake wheel cylinder is not necessary for brake shoe replacement. Disconnect the hose only if the brake panel or wheel cylinder assembly is going to be removed and serviced.

> *CAUTION*
> *Check the shoes more frequently when the shoes start to approach the limit dimension listed in **Table 1**. If shoe wear happens to be uneven for some reason, the backing plate may come in contact with the drum and cause damage.*

Removal

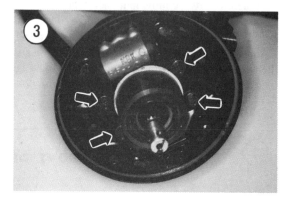

> *NOTE*
> *The front self-adjusting brake assembly is quite complicated. All components must be reinstalled in their original locations for the self-adjusting feature to operate correctly. It is suggested that only 1 brake assembly be disassembled at a time. This will enable the other brake assembly to be used for reference to make sure all components and springs are installed in their correct location.*

1. Remove the front wheels and the front hub/brake drum assembly as described in Chapter Ten.

2. Using a pair of pliers, rotate the brake shoe hold down spring pins 90°. Remove the No. 1 (A, **Figure 2**) and No. 2 (B, **Figure 2**) brake shoe hold down springs.

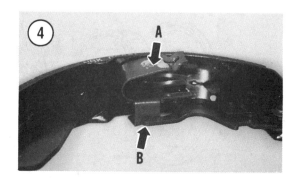

3. Pull the brake shoes out of the notches in the brake shoe retainer (C, **Figure 2**) and the wheel cylinder (D, **Figure 2**).

> *NOTE*
> *Place a clean shop rag on the linings to protect them from oil and grease during removal.*

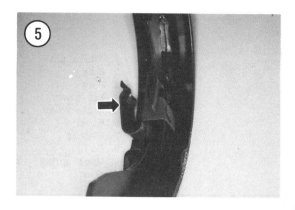

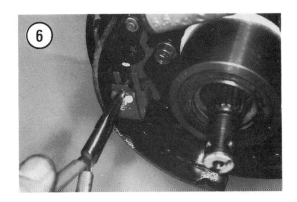

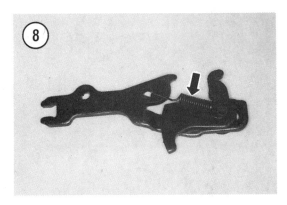

4. Remove the brake shoes, adjuster strut and springs from the backing plate by firmly pulling out and up on the center of each shoe.

5. Remove the return springs and separate the shoes.

6. Inspect the brake components as described in this chapter.

Installation

1. While the brake shoe assembly is removed, check the tightness of the brake panel mounting bolts (**Figure 3**). If loose, tighten to the torque specification listed in **Table 1**.

> *NOTE*
> *If new linings are being installed, file off the leading edge of each shoe a little so that the brake will not grab when applied.*

2. Apply a light coat of silicone grease to the brake shoe locating notches in the wheel cylinder and the brake shoe anchor.

3. Apply a light coat of silicone grease to the raised pads on the backside of the brake shoes metal plate where the brake shoes ride on the brake panel. Avoid getting any grease on the brake linings.

> *NOTE*
> *On the front brake shoe, make sure the shoe holder spring (A, **Figure 4**) is correctly indexed into the stopper arm (B, **Figure 4**). This is necessary for proper brake operation.*

4. If removed, make sure the shoe holder spring (**Figure 5**) is in place on each brake shoe.

5. Install the front brake shoe and spring holder into the locating notches in the wheel cylinder and the brake shoe anchor.

6. Using a pair of pliers, rotate the brake shoe hold down spring No. 2 pin 90° (**Figure 6**). Make sure it is seated correctly in the groove in the hold down spring (**Figure 7**).

7. If removed, make sure the strut rear return spring (**Figure 8**) is installed correctly on the strut.

8. Position the strut as shown in A, **Figure 9** and install the leading edge into the notch in the front brake shoe locating notch (**Figure 10**).

13

9. Correctly position the lower spring and install the end into the locating hole in the front brake shoe (B, **Figure 9**).

10. Correctly position the upper spring and install the end into the locating hole in the front brake shoe (**Figure 11**).

11. Install the upper spring end into the locating hole in the rear brake shoe (**Figure 12**).

12. Install the lower spring end into the locating hole in the rear brake shoe (**Figure 13**).

13. Pull the rear shoe toward the rear and correctly position the rear brake shoe into the locating notches in the wheel cylinder (**Figure 14**) and the brake shoe anchor (**Figure 15**). Push the rear brake shoe back against the brake panel and make sure it is firmly seated on the brake panel (**Figure 16**).

14. Push in on the brake shoe hold down spring (**Figure 17**) and using a pair of pliers, rotate the brake shoe hold down spring No. 2 pin 90° (**Figure 18**). Make sure it is seated correctly in the groove in the hold down spring.

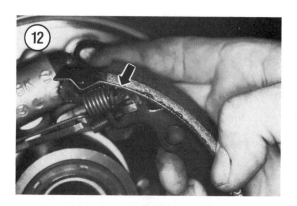

15. Correctly position the strut front spring and install the end into the locating hole in the strut (**Figure 19**).

16. Using a pair of pliers, pull the front end of the spring forward and install the end into the locating hole in the front brake shoe (A, **Figure 20**).

17. After all components have been installed, make sure the stopper (B, **Figure 20**) is correctly positioned on the hold down spring (C, **Figure 20**) of the front brake shoe.

18. After all components have been installed, the brake shoes are positioned out to their maximum extension making it impossible to install the brake drum. In order to install the brake drum, the brake shoes must be retraced to allow sufficient clearance. To retract the brake shoes, perform the following:

   a. Using a narrow blade screwdriver (**Figure 21**), insert the screwdriver (A, **Figure 22**) between

13

the strut (B, **Figure 22**) and the ratchet (C, **Figure 22**).

b. Carefully push down on the screwdriver (A, **Figure 22**). The ratchet (A, **Figure 23**) will now move down enabling the strut (B, **Figure 23**) to also move thus retracting the brake shoes.

NOTE
There is no adjustment procedure required after the front brake assembly is completed. After the vehicle is driven forward and the brakes applied, the brakes will automatically adjust.

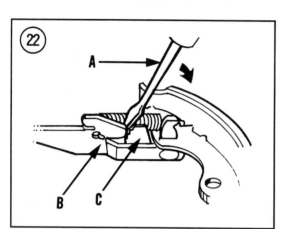

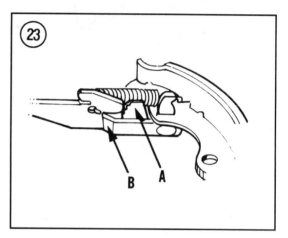

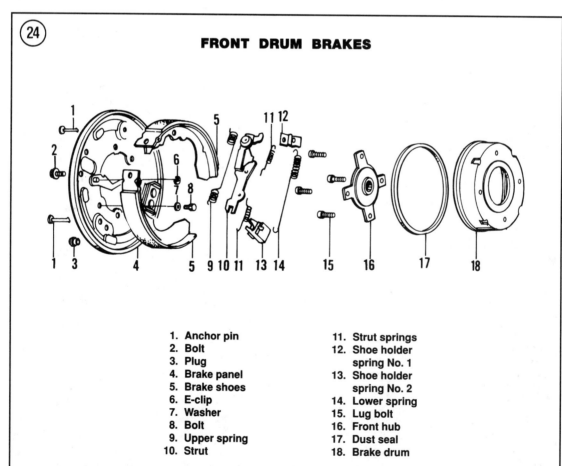

FRONT DRUM BRAKES

1. Anchor pin
2. Bolt
3. Plug
4. Brake panel
5. Brake shoes
6. E-clip
7. Washer
8. Bolt
9. Upper spring
10. Strut

11. Strut springs
12. Shoe holder
    spring No. 1
13. Shoe holder
    spring No. 2
14. Lower spring
15. Lug bolt
16. Front hub
17. Dust seal
18. Brake drum

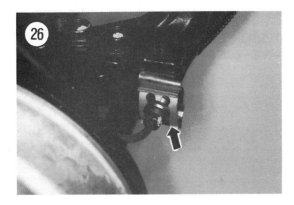

19. Install the front wheel and hub/brake drum assembly as described in Chapter Ten.

Brake Panel
Removal/Installation

Refer to **Figure 24** for this procedure.

1. Remove the front wheels and the front hub/brake drum (A, **Figure 25**) assembly as described in Chapter Ten.

2. Remove the brake shoes as described in this chapter.

3. Remove the clip (**Figure 26**) securing the hydraulic brake line and hose to the steering knuckle.

> *NOTE*
> *Removal of the bleed valve is necessary in order to fit an open-end wrench correctly on the brake line fitting in the Step 4.*

4. Unscrew the bleed valve (B, **Figure 25**) from the back of the wheel cylinder.

5. Use an open-end wrench, loosen then disconnect the hydraulic brake line fitting (**Figure 27**) from the backside of the wheel cylinder on the brake panel.

6. Carefully move the hydraulic brake line away from the brake panel. Plug the end of the brake hose with a golf tee then place the loose end in a reclosable plastic bag and close it.

7. Tie the loose end up to the shock absorber to prevent the loss of brake fluid.

8. Remove the bolts and lockwashers (**Figure 28**) securing the brake panel to the steering knuckle and remove the brake panel.

9. Install by reversing these removal steps while noting the following:

    a. Apply blue Loctite (No. 242) to the bolt threads prior to installation.

    b. Install the brake panel and install the mounting bolts. Tighten the bolts to the torque specification listed in **Table 2**.

    c. Align the hydraulic brake line with the threaded hole in the backside of the wheel cylinder and carefully screw the brake line fitting into the wheel cylinder. Be careful not to cross-thread it.

    d. Use an open-end wrench and tighten the brake line fitting to the torque specification listed in **Table 2**.

    e. Bleed the brakes as described in this chapter.

13

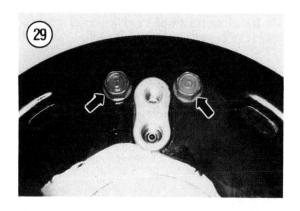

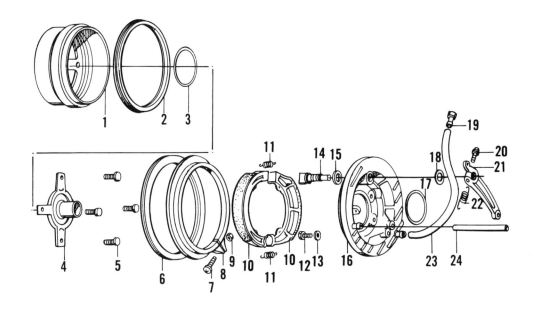

**REAR DRUM BRAKE
(LT-F250 AND LT-4WD [250 cc])**

1. Brake drum
2. Dust seal
3. O-ring
4. Rear hub
5. Lug bolt
6. Brake cover
7. Screw
8. Brake cover bracket
9. Nut
10. Brake shoes
11. Return springs
12. Bolt
13. Washer
14. Camshaft
15. O-ring
16. Brake panel
17. O-ring
18. Dust seal
19. Drain plug
20. Clamp bolt
21. Brake arm
22. Return spring
23. Drain hose
24. Breather hose

Wheel Cylinder
Removal/Installation

Some replacement parts are available for the wheel cylinder, but if the wheel cylinder is worn, leaking or damaged, replace the entire wheel cylinder assembly.

1. Remove the brake panel as described in this chapter.

2. Remove the bolts (**Figure 29**) securing the wheel cylinder to the brake panel.

3. Turn the brake panel over and remove the wheel cylinder and gasket (**Figure 30**). Discard the gasket as a new one must be installed every time the wheel cylinder is removed.

4. Clean off the area where the wheel cylinder attaches to the brake panel. If the existing wheel cylinder is going to be reinstalled, also clean off the backside of the wheel cylinder.

5. Install a new gasket onto the wheel cylinder and install the wheel cylinder and bolts. Tighten the bolts to the torque specification listed in **Table 1**.

6. Clean off the mounting surface of the steering knuckle where the brake panel attaches.

7. Install the brake panel as described in this chapter.

8. Bleed the brakes as described in this chapter.

REAR DRUM BRAKE

The single rear drum brake, located on the right-hand side of the rear axle, can be activated either by the cable-actuated foot pedal on the right-hand side of the vehicle or by the cable-operated hand lever on the left-hand side of the handlebar. Pushing down on the brake foot pedal, or applying the left-hand brake lever pulls the brake cable assembly which moves the brake arm that in turn rotates the camshaft. The rotating camshaft forces the brake shoes out into contact with the brake drum.

The rear brake is also used as a parking brake. The parking brake is set by applying the hand lever on the left-hand side of the handlebar and locked in place with the locking tab adjacent to the lever.

Pedal free play must be maintained to minimize brake drag and premature brake wear and maximize braking effectiveness. Refer to Chapter Three for complete rear drum brake adjustment procedures.

Brake Shoe Replacement

Refer to the following illustrations for this procedure:
  a. **Figure 31**: LT-F250 and LT-4WD (250 cc).
  b. **Figure 32**: LT-4WDX (280 cc).

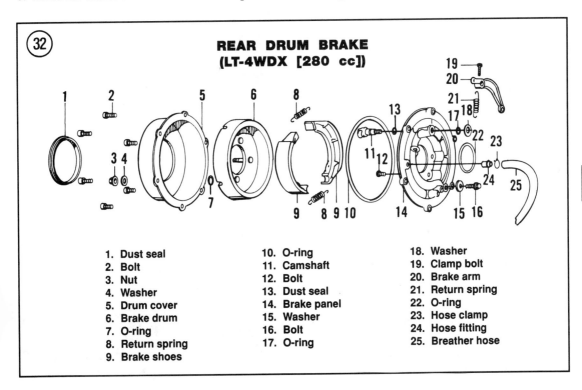

REAR DRUM BRAKE (LT-4WDX [280 cc])

1. Dust seal
2. Bolt
3. Nut
4. Washer
5. Drum cover
6. Brake drum
7. O-ring
8. Return spring
9. Brake shoes
10. O-ring
11. Camshaft
12. Bolt
13. Dust seal
14. Brake panel
15. Washer
16. Bolt
17. O-ring
18. Washer
19. Clamp bolt
20. Brake arm
21. Return spring
22. O-ring
23. Hose clamp
24. Hose fitting
25. Breather hose

13

1. Place the ATV on level ground and set the parking brake. Block the front wheel so the vehicle will not roll in either direction. Release the parking brake.

> *WARNING*
> *When working on the brake system, never blow off brake components or use compressed air. Do **not** inhale brake dust as it may contain asbestos, which can cause lung injury and cancer. Wear a face mask that meets OSHA requirements for trapping asbestos particles, and wash your hands and forearms thoroughly after completing the work.*

2. Remove the right-hand rear wheel and the rear hub/brake drum assembly as described in Chapter Ten.

3. On LT-4WDX (280 cc) models, remove the screws securing the brake drum cover and remove the cover.

4. Remove the brake shoes (**Figure 33**) from the rear brake panel by pulling up on the center of each shoe.

5. Remove the return springs and separate the shoes (**Figure 34**). If the brake shoes are going to be used again, place them in a plastic bag to avoid contamination with oil or grease.

6. Inspect the brake components as described in this chapter.

7. Apply a light coat of molybdenum disulfide grease to the brake camshaft and pivot post (**Figure 35**). Avoid getting any grease on the brake panel where the linings come in contact with it.

8. If removed, attach the return springs to the brake shoes.

9. Hold the brake shoes in a "V"-formation, install them onto the brake camshaft and pivot post (**Figure 36**), then snap them in place on the brake backing plate. Make sure they are firmly seated on the backing plate.

> *NOTE*
> *If new linings are being installed, file off the leading edge of each shoe a little (**Figure 37**) so that the brake will not grab when applied.*

10. On LT-4WDX (280 cc) models, perform the following:
   a. Apply a light coat of oil to the O-ring seal on the brake panel where the drum cover attaches.

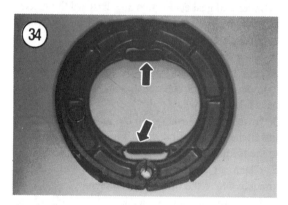

b. Install the brake drum cover and screws. Tighten the screws securely.

11. Install the right-hand rear hub/brake drum assembly and the right-hand rear wheel and as described in Chapter Ten.

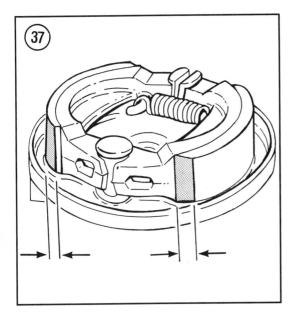

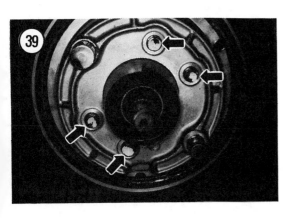

12. Adjust the rear brake as described in Chapter Three.

Brake Panel
Removal/Inspection/Installation

Refer to the following illustrations for this procedure:
   a. **Figure 31**: LT-F250 and LT-4WD (250 cc).
   b. **Figure 32**: LT-4WDX (280 cc).

1. Remove the brake shoes as described in this chapter.

2. On the backside of the brake panel, perform the following:
   a. Disconnect the breather hose and water drain hose from the fittings on the brake panel.
   b. Remove the cotter pin and washer, then remove the pivot pin (A, **Figure 38**) from the brake arm. Discard the cotter pin as a new one must be installed.
   c. Disconnect the brake cable (B, **Figure 38**) from the brake arm (C, **Figure 38**).

3. Remove the bolts (**Figure 39**) securing the rear brake panel to the rear hub.

4. Pull the brake panel off the hub and remove it.

5. Remove the O-ring seal from the hub where the brake panel attaches. This O-ring seal must be replaced every time the brake panel is removed.

6. To remove the brake arm from the brake panel, perform the following:
   a. Disconnect the return spring from the brake arm.
   b. Remove the bolt clamping the brake arm to the brake camshaft.
   c. Remove the brake arm from the brake camshaft.
   d. Remove the brake camshaft from the brake panel.
   e. Remove the O-ring seal and the dust seal from the recesses in the brake panel holes where the brake camshaft pivots. These parts must be replaced every time the camshaft is removed.

7. Inspect all brake components as described in this chapter.

8. To install the brake arm, perform the following:
   a. Install a new O-ring seal and dust seal into the recesses in the brake panel holes where the brake camshaft pivots.
   b. Apply a light coat of multipurpose grease to the O-ring seal, dust seal after installation.

13

c. Apply a light coat of multipurpose grease to the camshaft prior to installation.

d. Install the brake camshaft into the brake panel.

e. Align the punch marks on the brake arm with the alignment slit on the brake camshaft, then install the brake arm onto the brake camshaft.

f. Install the clamping bolt securing the brake arm to the brake camshaft. Tighten the bolt to the torque specification listed in **Table 2**.

9. Install a new O-ring seal on the hub where the brake panel fits, then apply a light coat of multi-purpose grease to it.

10. Apply a light coat of gasket sealer to the mounting pads on the rear hub where the mounting bolts attach.

11. Install the brake panel onto the hub and align the mounting bolt holes.

12. Install the bolts (**Figure 39**) securing the rear brake panel. Tighten the bolts to the torque specification listed in **Table 2**.

13. On the backside of the brake panel, perform the following:

a. Connect the brake cable (B, **Figure 38**) onto the brake arm (C, **Figure 38**) and align the pivot pin holes in both parts.

b. Install the pivot pin (A, **Figure 38**) through both parts, then install the washer and new cotter pin. Bend the ends over completely (**Figure 40**).

c. Connect the breather hose and water drain hose onto the fittings on the brake panel. Make sure

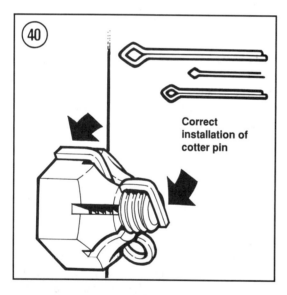

Correct
installation of
cotter pin

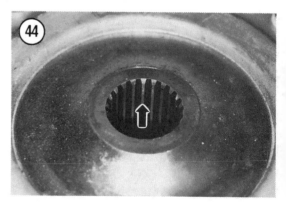

the hose clips are installed correctly to hold the hoses in place.

14. Install the brake shoes as described in this chapter.

DRUM BRAKE INSPECTION (FRONT AND REAR)

1. Thoroughly clean and dry all parts except the linings.

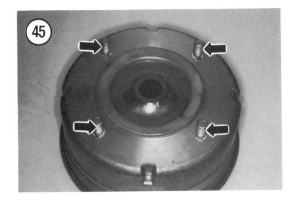

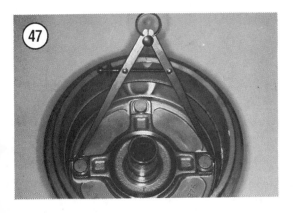

2. Check the contact surface of the drum for scoring. Refer to **Figure 41** for the front drums and **Figure 42** for the rear drum. If there are grooves deep enough to snag a fingernail, the drum should be reground and new shoes fitted. This type of wear can be avoided to a great extent if the brakes are disassembled and thoroughly cleaned after riding the vehicle in water, mud or deep sand.

NOTE
If oil or grease is on the drum surface, clean it off with a clean rag soaked in lacquer thinner—do not use any solvent that may leave an oil residue.

3. Inspect the external splines on the axles (**Figure 43**, typical) and internal splines on the brake drums (**Figure 44**, typical) for wear or damage. The drum and/or axle must be replaced if the splines are damaged.

4. Inspect the threaded studs (**Figure 45**) on the brake drum for wear or damage. Clean up with the appropriate size metric die if necessary.

5. Use a vernier caliper (**Figure 46**) or inside dividers (**Figure 47**) and measure the inside diameter of the drum for out-of-round or excessive wear. Turn the drum if it will still be within the service limit dimension. Replace the drum if it is worn to the service limit listed in **Table 1** or greater.

6. If the drum is turned, the linings will have to be replaced and the new linings arced to the new drum contour.

7. Inspect the linings (**Figure 48**) for imbedded foreign material. Dirt can be removed with a stiff wire brush. Check for traces of oil or grease. If they are contaminated, they must be replaced.

13

8. Measure the brake linings with a vernier caliper. Refer to **Figure 49** for front brakes or **Figure 50** for the rear brake. They should be replaced if worn to the service limit (distance from the metal backing plate) or less as listed in **Table 1**.

9. On the front brake, inspect the brake shoe linkage for wear and corrosion. Refer to **Figure 51** and **Figure 52**.

10. On the rear brake, inspect the camshaft lobe (**Figure 53**) and the pivot pin area of the shaft for wear and corrosion. Minor roughness can be removed with fine emery cloth.

11. On the rear brake, inspect the brake shoe return springs (**Figure 54**) for wear. If they are stretched, they will not fully retract the brake shoes from the drum, resulting in a power-robbing drag on the drums and premature wear of the linings. Replace as necessary and always replace as a pair.

12. Inspect the brake drum dust seal for wear, damage, hardness or deterioration. Replace if necessary.

REAR DRUM BRAKE CABLE AND FOOT PEDAL

Brake Pedal Cable Removal/Installation

1. Place the ATV on level ground and block the front wheels so the vehicle will not roll in either direction.

2. Remove the seat and front fender as described in Chapter Fourteen.

3. Remove the cotter pin and washer, then remove the pivot pin (A, **Figure 55**) from the brake pedal arm. Discard the cotter pin as a new one must be installed.

4. Disconnect the brake cable (B, **Figure 55**) from the brake pedal arm (C, **Figure 55**).

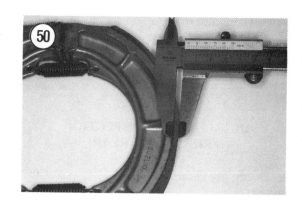

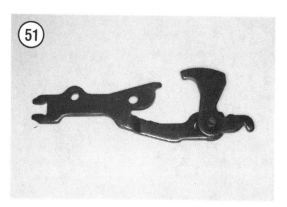

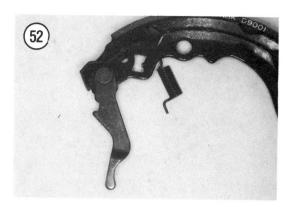

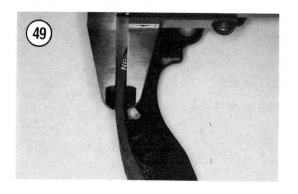

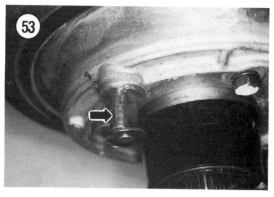

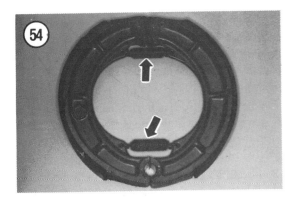

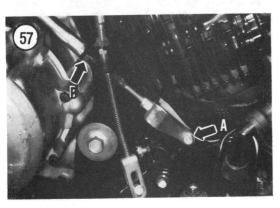

5. Remove the tie wrap (A, **Figure 56**) securing the brake cable to the hose.

6. Remove the E-clip (A, **Figure 57**) securing the brake cable to the brake pedal. Remove the pivot pin and disconnect the cable from the brake pedal.

7. Loosen the nut (B, **Figure 57**) securing the brake cable to the frame bracket and remove the cable from the bracket.

8. Remove the brake cable (B, **Figure 56**) from the cable guide (C, **Figure 56**) and remove the cable from the frame.

9. Install by reversing these removal steps while noting the following:

   a. Attach the plastic tie wraps to the new cable in the exact same position on the frame.

   b. At the brake arm, install a new cotter pin and bend the ends over completely.

   c. Adjust the rear brake as described in Chapter Three.

**Rear Drum Brake Parking Cable
(Left-hand Lever Cable)
Removal/Installation**

1. Place the ATV on level ground and set the parking brake. Block the front wheels so the vehicle will not roll in either direction. Release the parking brake.

2. Remove the seat and front fender as described in Chapter Fourteen.

3. Remove tie wraps securing the parking brake cable to the frame.

4. Loosen the nut (A, **Figure 58**) securing the parking brake cable to the frame bracket and remove the cable from the bracket.

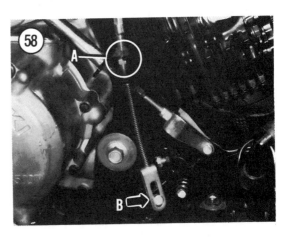

13

5. Remove the E-clip (B, **Figure 58**) securing the parking brake cable to the brake pedal. Remove the pivot pin and disconnect the parking brake cable from the brake pedal.

6. Slide the rubber boot (**Figure 59**) off the parking brake cable adjusters.

7. Loosen the locknut (A, **Figure 60**) and turn the adjuster (B, **Figure 60**) to allow maximum slack in the cable.

8. Pull the left-hand brake lever all the way to the grip, remove the cable nipple from the lever and remove the cable.

NOTE
The piece of string attached in the next step will be used to pull the new brake cable back through the frame so it will be routed in the exact same position.

9. Tie a piece of heavy string or cord (approximately 6 ft./1.8 m long) to the rear end of the brake cable. Wrap this end with masking or duct tape. Do not use an excessive amount of tape as it must be pulled through the frame during removal. Tie the other end of the string to the frame or rear brake pedal.

10. At the handlebar end of the cable, carefully pull the cable (and attached string) out from the frame. Make sure the attached string follows the same path of the cable through the frame.

11. Remove the tape and untie the string from the old cable.

12. Lubricate the new cable as described under *Control Cables* in Chapter Three.

13. Tie the string to the brake pedal end of the new brake cable and wrap it with tape.

14. Carefully pull the string back through the frame, routing the new cable through the same path as the old cable.

15. Remove the tape and untie the string from the cable and the frame.

16. Pull the left-hand brake lever all the way to the grip, install the cable nipple into the lever.

17. Turn the adjuster (B, **Figure 60**) sufficiently to hold the cable in place at the left-hand lever. Do not tighten the locknut at this time. It will be tightened when the brake is adjusted after the cable is completely installed.

18. Install the parking brake cable onto the brake pedal. Install the pivot pin and install the E-clip (B, **Figure 58**).

19. Install the parking brake cable to the frame bracket and temporarily tighten the nut (A, **Figure 58**).

20. Install all tie wraps securing the parking brake cable to the frame.

21. Install the front fender and seat as described in Chapter Fourteen.

22. Adjust the parking brake as described in Chapter Three.

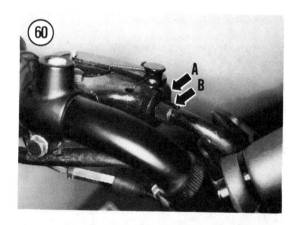

Brake Pedal
Removal/Installation

1. Place the ATV on level ground and block the front wheels so the vehicle will not roll in either direction.

2. Remove the seat and front fender as described in Chapter Fourteen.

3. Remove the E-clip securing the rear brake cable to the brake pedal (A, **Figure 61**). Remove the pivot pin and disconnect the rear brake cable from the brake pedal.

4. Remove the E-clip securing the parking brake cable to the brake pedal (B, **Figure 61**). Remove the pivot pin and disconnect the parking brake cable from the brake pedal.

5. Using vise-grip pliers, remove the return spring from the frame or brake pedal.

6. Remove the footrest assembly as described in Chapter Fourteen.

7. From the backside of the brake pedal, remove the cotter pin and discard it. Remove the pivot bolt nut and washer, then withdraw the pivot bolt (C, **Figure 61**) from the brake pedal.

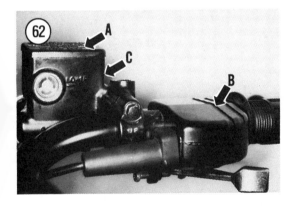

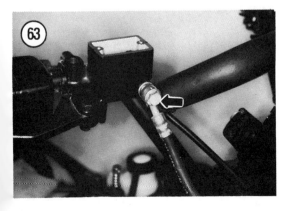

8. Remove the rear brake pedal assembly from the pivot receptacle in the frame.

9. Install by reversing these removal steps while noting the following:

    a. Apply multipurpose grease to the pedal pivot shaft and to the pivot receptacle in the frame prior to installing the pedal assembly in the frame.

    b. Install a new cotter pin and bend the ends over completely.

    c. Be sure that the return spring is properly attached.

    d. Adjust the rear brake as described in Chapter Three.

FRONT MASTER CYLINDER

Removal/Installation

1. Place the ATV on level ground and set the parking brake. Block the rear wheels so the vehicle will not roll in either direction.

> *CAUTION*
> *Cover the seat and front fender assembly with a heavy cloth or plastic tarp to protect them from accidental brake fluid spills. Wash any brake fluid off any painted or plastic surfaces immediately, as it will destroy the finish. Use soapy water and rinse completely.*

2. Clean the top of the master cylinder of all dirt and foreign matter.

3. Remove the screws securing the cover (A, **Figure 62**). Remove the cover and the diaphragm.

> *WARNING*
> *If a cooking baster is used for this purpose, DO NOT reuse it for cooking purposes due to brake fluid residue within it.*

4. If you have a shop syringe or a cooking baster, draw all of the brake fluid out of the master cylinder reservoir.

5. Place a shop cloth under the union bolt to catch any spilled brake fluid that will leak out.

6. Unscrew the union bolt (**Figure 63**) securing the brake hose to the master cylinder. Don't lose the sealing washer on each side of the hose fitting. Tie the loose end of the hose up to the handlebar and cover the end to prevent the entry of moisture and

13

foreign matter. Cover the loose end with a re-closable plastic bag.

7. Remove the screws securing the throttle case assembly (B, **Figure 62**) together. Separate the throttle case and remove the assembly. Reassemble the case and tighten the screws. Lay the assembly over the front fender or fuel tank. Be careful that the cable does not get crimped or damaged.

8. Remove the bolts and washers securing the front master cylinder (C, **Figure 62**) to the handlebar and remove the master cylinder.

9. Install by reversing these removal steps while noting the following:

NOTE
Figure 64 is shown with the master cylinder removed for clarity since the UP mark is hidden by the throttle cable that is already in place on the handlebar.

a. Install the master cylinder onto the handlebar. Position the clamp with the UP mark (**Figure 64**) facing up and install the clamp and bolts. Tighten the upper bolt first, then the lower bolt. Tighten the bolts to the torque specification listed in **Table 1**.

b. Place a sealing washer on each side of the brake hose fitting (**Figure 65**) and install the union bolt.

c. Tighten the union bolt to the torque specification listed in **Table 1**.

d. Bleed the front brakes as described under *Bleeding the System* in this chapter.

Disassembly

Refer to **Figure 66** for this procedure.

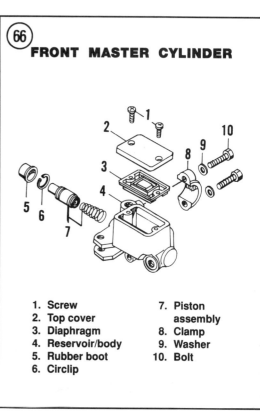

FRONT MASTER CYLINDER

1. Screw	7. Piston
2. Top cover	assembly
3. Diaphragm	8. Clamp
4. Reservoir/body	9. Washer
5. Rubber boot	10. Bolt
6. Circlip	

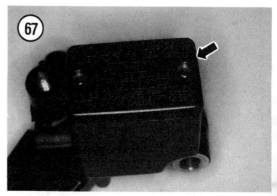

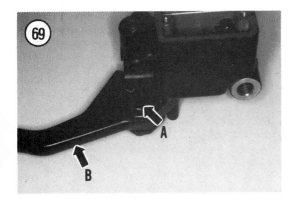

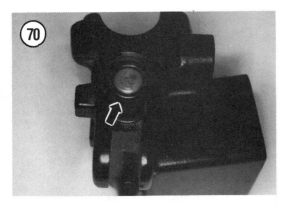

1. Remove the master cylinder as described in this chapter.

2. If not already removed, remove the screws securing the cover and remove the cover (**Figure 67**) and diaphragm (**Figure 68**); pour out any residual brake fluid and discard it. *Never reuse brake fluid.*

3. Remove the bolt (A, **Figure 69**) and nut securing the brake lever (B, **Figure 69**) and remove the brake lever.

4. Remove the rubber boot (**Figure 70**) from the area where the hand lever actuates the internal piston.

5. Using circlip pliers, remove the internal circlip (**Figure 71**) from the body.

6. Remove the piston/primary cup assembly (**Figure 72**).

7. Remove the spring (**Figure 73**).

Inspection

1. Clean all parts in denatured alcohol or fresh brake fluid. Inspect the cylinder bore and piston contact surfaces for signs of wear and damage. If either part is less than perfect, replace it.

13

2. Inspect the hand lever pivot hole (**Figure 74**). If worn or elongated the lever must be replaced.

3. Check the hand lever pivot lugs (**Figure 75**) on the master cylinder body for cracks or elongation. If damaged, replace the master cylinder assembly.

4. Make sure the passage (**Figure 76**) in the bottom of the body reservoir is clear. Clean out with brake fluid, then apply compressed air to make sure the passage is clear.

5. Check the reservoir cap and diaphragm (**Figure 77**) for damage and deterioration and replace as necessary.

6. Inspect the threads (**Figure 78**) for the union bolt in the body. If worn or damaged, clean out with a suitable size metric thread tap or replace the master cylinder assembly.

7. Inspect the viewing port (**Figure 79**) for signs of hydraulic fluid leakage. If leakage has occurred, replace the master cylinder assembly.

8. Inspect the piston contact surfaces (A, **Figure 80**) for signs of wear and damage. If less than perfect, replace the piston assembly.

9. Check the end of the piston (B, **Figure 80**) for wear caused by the hand lever. If worn, replace the piston assembly.

10. Inspect the piston cups (**Figure 81**) for any signs of wear or damage. Cups are not available separately and must be replaced along with the new piston and spring as an assembly.

11. Inspect the body cylinder bore surface for signs of wear and damage. If less than perfect, replace the master cylinder assembly. The body cannot be replaced separately.

12. Measure the cylinder bore with a small bore gauge (**Figure 82**). Measure the small bore gauge with a micrometer (**Figure 83**). Replace the master

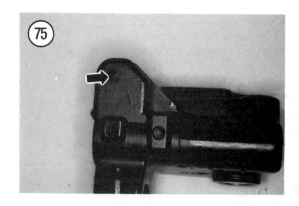

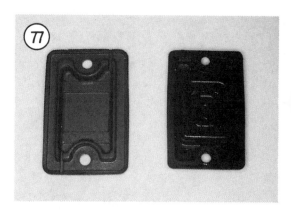

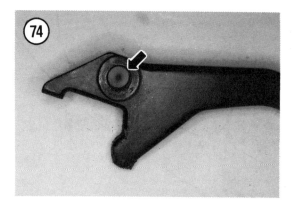

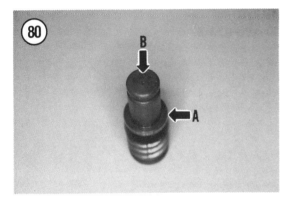

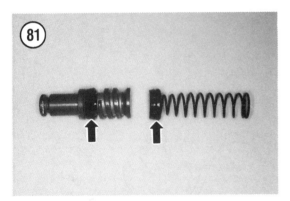

cylinder if the bore exceeds the service limit listed in **Table 1**.

13. Measure the outside diameter of the piston assembly (**Figure 84**) with a micrometer. Replace the piston assembly if it is worn to, or less than, the service limit listed in **Table 1**.

Assembly

1. Soak the new, or existing, piston assembly in fresh brake fluid for at least 15 minutes to makc the cups pliable. Coat the inside of the cylinder bore with fresh brake fluid prior to the assembly of parts.

> *CAUTION*
> *When installing the piston assembly, do not allow the cups to turn inside out as they will be damaged and allow brake fluid leakage within the cylinder bore.*

2. Position the spring as shown (**Figure 73**), then install the spring and the piston assembly (**Figure 72**) into the cylinder bore.

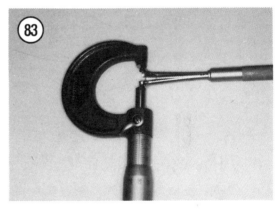

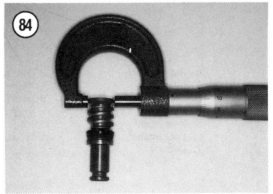

13

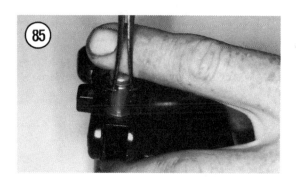

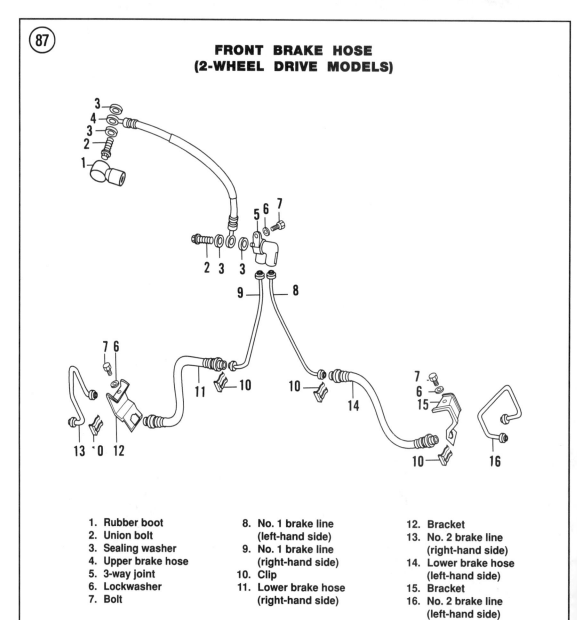

**FRONT BRAKE HOSE
(2-WHEEL DRIVE MODELS)**

1. Rubber boot
2. Union bolt
3. Sealing washer
4. Upper brake hose
5. 3-way joint
6. Lockwasher
7. Bolt
8. No. 1 brake line
(left-hand side)
9. No. 1 brake line
(right-hand side)
10. Clip
11. Lower brake hose
(right-hand side)
12. Bracket
13. No. 2 brake line
(right-hand side)
14. Lower brake hose
(left-hand side)
15. Bracket
16. No. 2 brake line
(left-hand side)

3. Push the piston assembly into the bore and hold it in place. Install the circlip (**Figure 85**) and make sure it seats correctly in the master cylinder body groove (**Figure 71**).

4. Install the rubber boot and push it all the way down until it stops.

5. Install the brake lever (B, **Figure 69**) onto the master cylinder body, then install the bolt and nut (A, **Figure 69**). Tighten the bolt and nut securely.

6. Install the diaphragm (**Figure 68**) and cover (**Figure 67**) and screws (**Figure 86**). Do not tighten the cover screws at this time as fluid will have to be added later.

7. Install the master cylinder as described in this chapter.

FRONT BRAKE HOSE REPLACEMENT

Suzuki recommends replacing the brake hoses every four years or when they show signs of cracking, deterioration or damage.

Removal/Installation

Refer to the following illustrations for this procedure:

    a. **Figure 87**: 2-wheel drive models.
    b. **Figure 88**: 4-wheel drive models.

CAUTION
Cover the surrounding area with a
heavy cloth or plastic tarp to protect

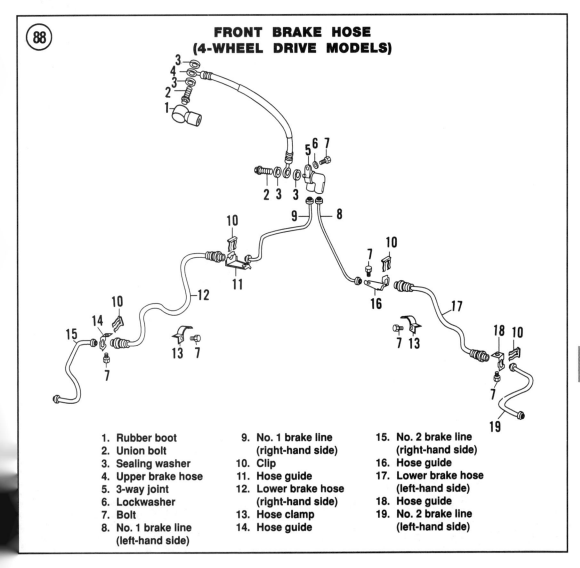

88

FRONT BRAKE HOSE
(4-WHEEL DRIVE MODELS)

1. Rubber boot
2. Union bolt
3. Sealing washer
4. Upper brake hose
5. 3-way joint
6. Lockwasher
7. Bolt
8. No. 1 brake line (left-hand side)
9. No. 1 brake line (right-hand side)
10. Clip
11. Hose guide
12. Lower brake hose (right-hand side)
13. Hose clamp
14. Hose guide
15. No. 2 brake line (right-hand side)
16. Hose guide
17. Lower brake hose (left-hand side)
18. Hose guide
19. No. 2 brake line (left-hand side)

13

*from accidental brake fluid spills. Wash
brake fluid off any painted or plastic
surfaces immediately, as it will destroy
the finish. Use soapy water and rinse
completely.*

1. Place the ATV on level ground and set the parking brake. Block the rear wheels so the vehicle will not roll in either direction.

2. Remove the seat and front fender as described in Chapter Fourteen.

3. Remove the cap from the bleed screw on both front wheel cylinders.

4. Attach a piece of hose to each bleed screw (**Figure 89**) and place the loose end in a container.

5. Open both bleed screws and operate the master cylinder lever to pump the brake fluid out of the master cylinder, the brake lines, hoses and the wheel cylinders. Operate the lever until the system is clear of brake fluid.

6. Clean the top of the master cylinder of all dirt and foreign matter.

7. Remove the screws securing the cover (**Figure 90**). Remove the cover and the diaphragm.

*WARNING
If a cooking baster is used for this purpose, DO NOT reuse it for cooking purposes due to any residual brake fluid within it.*

8. If you have a shop syringe or a cooking baster, draw all of any residual brake fluid from the master cylinder reservoir.

9. Unscrew the union bolt (A, **Figure 91**) securing the upper brake hose to the master cylinder. Don't

lose the sealing washer on each side of the hose fitting.

NOTE
Bleed valve removal is necessary in order to fit an open-end wrench correctly on the fitting in Step 12.

10. Unscrew the bleed valve (**Figure 89**) from the back of the wheel cylinder.

11. Use an open-end wrench, loosen then disconnect the hydraulic brake line fitting (A, **Figure 92**)

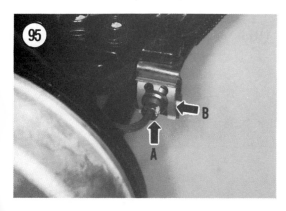

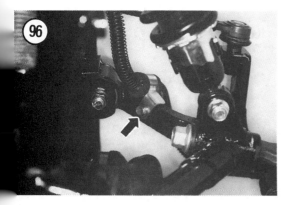

from the backside of the wheel cylinder on the brake panel.

12. Remove each brake line (B, **Figure 92**) and let and the residual brake fluid drain out into the container used in Step 4. Dispose of this brake fluid—never reuse brake fluid.

13. Remove the union bolt and sealing washers securing the upper hose (A, **Figure 93**) to the 3-way connector (B, **Figure 93**).

14. Remove the upper brake hose (B, **Figure 91**). Pull the upper hose (A, **Figure 94**) through the frame loop (B, **Figure 94**) and remove it from the frame.

NOTE
The following steps are shown removing the brake components from the left-hand side of the vehicle. Repeat Steps 15-22 for components on the right-hand side of the vehicle.

15. Use an open-end wrench, loosen then disconnect the No. 2 brake line fitting (A, **Figure 95**) from the lower brake hose. Remove the No. 2 brake line.

16. Remove the clip (B, **Figure 95**) securing the lower brake hose to the steering knuckle.

17. Remove the bolt and clamp (**Figure 96**) securing the lower brake hose to the upper suspension arm.

18. Use an open-end wrench, loosen then disconnect the No. 1 brake line fitting (A, **Figure 97**) from the lower brake hose.

19. Remove the clip (B, **Figure 97**) securing the lower brake hose to the frame bracket.

20. Remove the lower brake hose (C, **Figure 97**) from the frame.

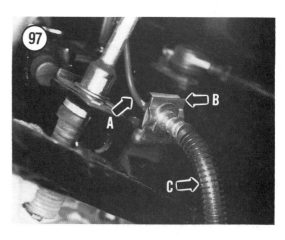

13

21. Using an open-end wrench, loosen then disconnect the No. 1 brake line fitting (A, **Figure 98**) from the 3-way joint.

22. Remove the No. 1 brake line (B, **Figure 98**) from the frame.

23. If necessary, remove the bolt securing the 3-way joint (B, **Figure 93**) to the frame bracket and remove the 3-way joint.

24. Refer to **Figure 87** and **Figure 88** and install new lines, hoses, sealing washers and union bolts in the reverse order of removal while noting the following:

  a. Be sure to install new sealing washers (**Figure 99**) in their correct positions on each side of the brake hose fittings.

  b. Tighten the union bolts to the torque specification listed in **Table 1**.

  c. Tighten the brake line fittings to the torque specification listed in **Table 1**.

  d. Install the bleed valve into the back of the wheel cylinder and tighten securely.

  e. Bleed the brake as described under *Bleeding the System* in this chapter.

BLEEDING THE SYSTEM

This procedure is not necessary unless the brakes feel spongy, there has been a leak in the system, a component has been replaced or the brake fluid has been replaced.

If only one side of the brake system was removed for component replacement, start out by bleeding that side first, then, if necessary, bleed the other side.

If the entire system is completely dry after the replacement of the brake hose(s) and/or line(s) both sides must be bled.

Bleeding One Side Only

1. Place the ATV on level ground and set the parking brake. Block the rear wheels so the vehicle will not roll in either direction.

2. Remove the front wheel, for the side to be serviced, as described under *Front Wheel Removal/Installation* in Chapter Ten.

3. Remove the dust cap from the bleed valve on the wheel cylinder assembly.

4. Connect a piece of clear tubing to the bleed valve (**Figure 100**) on the wheel cylinder.

5. Place the other end of the tube into a clean container.

6. Fill the container with enough fresh brake fluid to keep the end submerged.

CAUTION
Cover the wheel with a heavy cloth or plastic tarp to protect it from the accidental spilling of brake fluid. Wash any brake fluid off of any plastic, painted or plated surface immediately; as it will

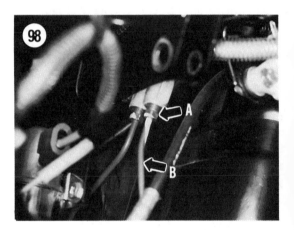

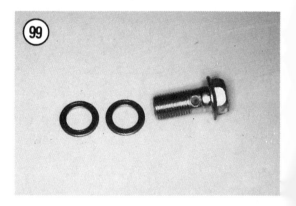

destroy the finish. Use soapy water and rinse completely.

7. Clean the top cover or cap of the master cylinder of all dirt and foreign matter.

8. Remove the screws securing the cover (**Figure 101**). Remove the cover and the diaphragm.

WARNING
Use brake fluid from a sealed container marked DOT 3 or DOT 4 only (specified for disc brakes). Other types may vapor-

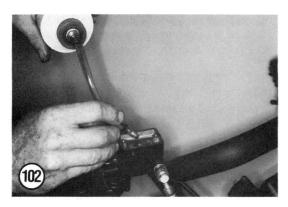

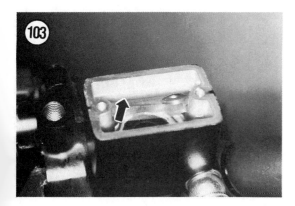

ize and cause brake failure. Do not intermix different brands or types as they may not be compatible. Do not intermix a silicone based (DOT 5) brake fluid as it can cause brake component damage leading to brake system failure.

9. Fill the reservoir with fresh brake fluid (**Figure 102**) almost to the top lip (**Figure 103**); insert the diaphragm and the cover loosely. Leave the cover, in place during this procedure to prevent the entry of dirt.

NOTE
During this procedure, it is very important to check the fluid level in the brake master cylinder reservoir often. If the reservoir runs dry, you'll introduce more air into the system which will require starting the bleeding procedure all over.

10. Apply the brake lever several times as follows:
   a. Pump the brake lever several times, then pull the lever in and hold it in the applied position.
   b. Open the bleed valve on the wheel cylinder about one-half turn. Allow the lever to travel to its limit.
   c. When this limit is reached, tighten the bleed valve.
   d. Release the brake lever.

11. As the fluid enters the system, the fluid level will drop in the reservoir. Maintain the level to just about the top of the reservoir to prevent air from being drawn into the system.

12. Continue to pump the lever, refer to Step 10, and fill the reservoir until the fluid emerging from the hose is completely free of bubbles.

13. Maintain the fluid level to just about the top of the reservoir to prevent air from being drawn into the system.

NOTE
Do not allow the reservoir to empty during the bleeding operation or more air will enter the system. If this occurs, the entire procedure must be repeated.

NOTE
If you are having trouble getting all of the bubbles out of the system, refer to **Reverse Flow Bleeding** *at the end of this section.*

13

14. Hold the lever in, tighten the bleed valve, re-move the bleed tube and install the bleed valve dust cap.

15. If necessary, add fluid to correct the level in the reservoir.

16. When the air has been removed from the system, the lever should travel less than one-half the total distance, be firm and travel no farther.

17. Repeat this procedure for the other side of the vehicle if necessary.

18. Install the diaphragm and the cover (**Figure 101**) onto the front master cylinder. Tighten the screws securely.

19. Test the feel of the brake lever. It should be firm and should offer the same resistance each time it's operated. If it feels spongy, it is likely that there is still air in the system, and it must be bled again. When all air has been bled from the system, and the fluid level is correct in the reservoir, double-check for leaks and tighten all fittings and connections.

WARNING
Before riding the vehicle, make certain that the brakes are operating correctly.

20. Test ride the ATV slowly at first to make sure that the brakes are operating properly.

Bleeding Entire System After Replacement of Brake Lines and Hoses

Since the entire system is almost free of brake fluid and therefore full of air, the entire system must be first filled with brake fluid and then each side bled and then bled again to remove all trapped air.

Start with either side of the vehicle since the brake lines and hoses in the system are of almost equal length. This procedure starts with the left-hand side.

1. Place the ATV on level ground and set the parking brake. Block the rear wheels so the vehicle will not roll in either direction.

2. If not already removed, remove both front wheels as described under *Front Wheel Removal/Installation* in Chapter Ten.

3. Make sure the bleed valve on the right-hand wheel cylinder is closed completely.

4. Remove the dust cap from the bleed valve on the left-hand wheel cylinder assembly.

5. Connect a piece of clear tubing to the bleed valve (**Figure 100**) on the left-hand wheel cylinder.

6. Place the other end of the tube into a clean container (A, **Figure 104**).

WARNING
Use brake fluid from a sealed container marked DOT 3 or DOT 4 only (specified for disc brakes). Other types may vaporize and cause brake failure. Do not intermix different brands or types as they may not be compatible. Do not intermix a silicone based (DOT 5) brake fluid as it can cause brake component damage leading to brake system failure.

7. Fill the container with enough fresh brake fluid and keep the end submerged in the brake fluid.

8. Clean the top cover or cap of the master cylinder of all dirt and foreign matter.

9. Remove the screws securing the cover (**Figure 101**). Remove the cover and the diaphragm.

WARNING
Use brake fluid from a sealed container marked DOT 3 or DOT 4 only (specified for disc brakes). Other types may vaporize and cause brake failure. Do not intermix different brands or types as they may not be compatible. Do not intermix a silicone based (DOT 5) brake fluid as it can cause brake component damage leading to brake system failure.

10. Fill the reservoir with fresh brake fluid (**Figure 102**) almost to the top lip (**Figure 103**); insert the diaphragm and the cover loosely. Leave the cover, in place during this procedure to prevent the entry of dirt.

NOTE
During this procedure, it is very important to check the fluid level in the brake

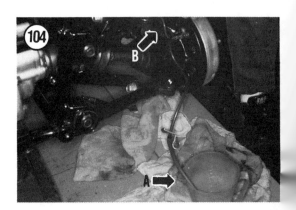

master cylinder reservoir often. If the reservoir runs dry, more air will be introduced into the system which will require starting over.

11. Slowly apply the brake lever several times as follows:

a. Pull the lever in and hold it in the applied position.

b. Open the bleed valve on the left-hand wheel cylinder (B, **Figure 104**) about one-half turn. Allow the lever to travel to its limit.

c. When this limit is reached, tighten the bleed valve.

d. Release the brake lever.

12. As the fluid enters the system, the level will drop in the reservoir. Maintain the level to just about the top of the reservoir to prevent air from being drawn into the system.

13. Continue to pump the lever, refer to Step 11, and fill the reservoir until the fluid emerging from the hose is completely free of bubbles.

14. Do not remove the clear tubing from the left-hand wheel cylinder at this time.

15. Remove the dust cap from the bleed valve on the right-hand wheel cylinder.

16. Connect another piece of clear tubing to the bleed valve on the right-hand wheel cylinder.

17. Place the other end of the tube into another clean container.

18. Fill the container with enough fresh brake fluid and keep the end submerged in the brake fluid.

19. Slowly apply the brake lever several times as follows:

a. Pull the lever in and hold it in the applied position.

b. Open the bleed valve on the right-hand wheel cylinder about one-half turn. Allow the lever to travel to its limit.

c. When this limit is reached, tighten the bleed valve.

d. Release the brake lever.

20. As the fluid enters the system, the level will drop in the reservoir. Maintain the level to just about the top of the reservoir to prevent air from being drawn into the system.

21. Continue to pump the lever and fill the reservoir until the fluid emerging from the hose is partially free of bubbles. At this point there will still be air in the system. Tighten the bleed valve.

NOTE
Do not allow the reservoir to empty during the bleeding operation or more air will enter the system. If this occurs, the entire procedure must be repeated.

NOTE
At this point the entire system is filled with brake fluid and some remaining air bubbles. The system is now ready for the final bleeding procedure.

22. Repeat Steps 11-13 for the left-hand wheel cylinder and Steps 19-21 for the right-hand cylinder. However, this time continue to pump the lever and fill the reservoir until the fluid emerging from the hose is *completely* free of bubbles. At this point there should be no air in the system. Tighten both bleed valves.

NOTE
*If you are having trouble getting all of the bubbles out of the system, refer to the **Reverse Flow Bleeding** at the end of this section.*

23. Remove the bleed tubes from each wheel cylinder and install the bleed valve dust caps.

24. If necessary, add fluid to correct the level in the reservoir.

25. Install the diaphragm and the cover onto the front master cylinder. Tighten the screws securely.

26. Test the feel of the brake lever. It should be firm and should offer the same resistance each time it's operated. If it feels spongy, it is likely that there is still air in the system and it must be bled again. When all air has been bled from the system and the fluid level is correct in the reservoir, double-check for leaks and tighten all fittings and connections.

WARNING
Before riding the vehicle, make certain that the brakes are operating correctly.

27. Test ride the ATV slowly at first to make sure that the brakes are operating properly.

Reverse Flow Bleeding

This bleeding procedure can be used if you are having a difficult time freeing the system of all bubbles.

13

Using this procedure, the brake fluid will be forced into the system in a reverse direction, pushing the air bubbles up and out of the top of the system. The fluid will enter the wheel cylinders, flow through the brake hose and lines and into the master cylinder reservoir. If the system is already filled with brake fluid, the existing fluid will be flushed out of the top of the master cylinder by the new brake fluid being forced into the caliper. Siphon the fluid from the reservoir, then hold a shop cloth under the master cylinder reservoir to catch any additional fluid that will be forced out.

A special reverse flow tool called the EZE Bleeder is available or a home made tool can be fabricated for this procedure.

To make this home made tool, perform the following:

NOTE
The brake fluid container must be plastic—not metal. Use vinyl tubing of the correct inner diameter to ensure a tight fit on the caliper bleed valve.

a. Purchase a 12 oz. (345 ml) *plastic* bottle of DOT 3 or DOT 4 brake fluid (**Figure 105**).
b. Remove the cap, drill an appropriate size hole and adapt a vinyl hose fitting onto the cap (**Figure 106**).
c. Attach a section of vinyl hose to the hose fitting on the cap and secure it with a hose clamp. This joint must be a tight fit as the plastic brake fluid bottle will be squeezed to force the brake fluid out of the bottle, past this fitting and through the hose.
d. Remove the moisture seal from the plastic bottle of brake fluid and screw the cap and hose assembly onto the bottle.

NOTE
Perform this procedure for the side of the vehicle where you are having a problem removing all air bubbles.

1. Remove the dust cap from the bleed valve on the wheel cylinder.
2. Clean the top cover of the master cylinder of all dirt and foreign matter.
3. Remove the screws securing the cover (**Figure 101**). Remove the cover and the diaphragm.
4. Attach the vinyl hose to the bleed valve. Make sure the hose is tight on the bleed valve.

5. Open the bleed valve and squeeze the plastic bottle forcing this brake fluid into the system.

NOTE
If necessary, siphon brake fluid from the master cylinder reservoir to avoid overflow of fluid.

6. Observe the brake fluid entering the master cylinder reservoir. Continue to apply pressure from the tool, or bottle, until the fluid entering the reservoir is free of all air bubbles.
7. Close the bleed valve and disconnect the bleeder or hose from the bleed valve.
8. Install the dust cap onto the bleed valve.
9. Repeat Steps 1-8 for the other wheel cylinder assembly.
10. At this time the system should be free of bubbles. Apply the brake lever and check for proper brake operation. If the system still feels spongy, perform the typical bleeding procedure in the beginning of this section.
11. Install the diaphragm and the cover onto the front master cylinder. Tighten the screws securely.

Table 1 DRUM BRAKE SPECIFICATIONS

Model	New	Service limit
Front brake drum I.D.	—	165.7 mm (6.52 in.)
Rear brake drum I.D.	—	165.7 mm (6.52 in.)
Brake shoe lining		
Front and rear	—	1.5 mm (0.06 in.)
Front master cylinder		
Cylinder bore I.D.	12.700-12.743 mm (0.5000-0.5017 in.)	—
Piston O.D.	12.657-12.684 mm (0.4983-0.4994 in.)	—

Table 2 BRAKE TIGHTENING TORQUES

Item	N·m	ft.-lb.
Brake panel bolts	18-28	13-20
Brake line fitting-to-wheel cylinder	13-18	9.5-13
Wheel cylinder-to-brake panel bolt	10-13	7-9.5
Rear brake arm clamping bolt	8-12	6-8.5
Master cylinder clamp bolt	6-9	4.3-6.5
Master cylinder union bolt	20-25	14.5-18
Brake line fittings	13-18	9.5-13

13

CHAPTER FOURTEEN

BODY

This chapter contains removal and installation procedures for the front and rear fender assemblies and their carry racks.

SEAT

Removal/Installation

1. Place the ATV on level ground and set the parking brake. Block the rear wheels so the vehicle will not roll in either direction.

2. On the left-hand side of the seat, move the lever forward and release the seat locking mechanism.

3. Raise the front of the seat (**Figure 1**) and slide the seat forward to release the locking tabs at the rear.

4. Remove the seat assembly.

5. Install by reversing these removal steps while noting the following:

    a. Make sure the locking tabs at the rear of seat are correctly locked into the metal seat brackets on the frame.

> *WARNING*
> *After the seat is installed, pull up on it firmly to make sure it is securely locked in place. If the seat is not correctly locked in place, it may slide to one side or the other when riding the ATV. This could lead to loss of control and a possible accident.*

    b. Push firmly down until the seat latch "snaps" in the locked position.

REAR RACK

1. Rear rack
   (1987-1988)
2. Bolt
3. Nut
4. Rear rack
   (1989-on)
5. Spacer

REAR FENDER AND REAR RACK

Removal/Installation

Refer to the following illustrations for this procedure:

a. **Figure 2**: Rear rack.

b. **Figure 3**: Rear fender.

1. Place the ATV on level ground and set the parking brake. Block the front wheels so the vehicle will not roll in either direction.

2. Remove the seat as described in this chapter.

3. To remove the rear rack, perform the following:

a. Remove the rear bolts (**Figure 4**) and nuts.

b. Working under the rear fender, remove the 2 bolts securing the front (A, **Figure 5**) portion of the rack to the frame. On 1989-on models, don't lose the spacer on the front bolts.

c. Remove the rear rack (B, **Figure 5**) from the fender.

4. Remove the mounting brackets (**Figure 6**) securing the fender mud guards to the footrest assembly.

5. Remove the front bolts, lockwashers and washers (**Figure 7**) securing the front of the rear fender to the frame.

6. Remove the rear bolts, lockwashers and washers (**Figure 8**) securing the rear of the rear fender to the frame.

7. Pull the front fender toward the rear to release the side locking tab on each side, then pull straight up and off the frame.

8. To remove the rear storage box, perform the following:

a. Disconnect the taillight electrical connector (**Figure 9**).

b. Remove the bolt and washer (A, **Figure 10**) on each side securing the box to the frame.

c. Pull the rear storage box (B, **Figure 10**) and taillight assembly (C, **Figure 10**) from the frame.

d. If necessary, remove the bolts and washer securing the heat shield (**Figure 11**) to the frame and remove it. Don't lose the rubber cushion at each mounting hole on the heat shield.

9. On models equipped with the optional rear mudguard assembly, remove the bolts and nuts securing the assembly to the frame. Remove the rear mudguard assembly.

10. If necessary, remove the fasteners securing the mudguards to the front and side of the rear fender. Install and tighten the fasteners securely.

14

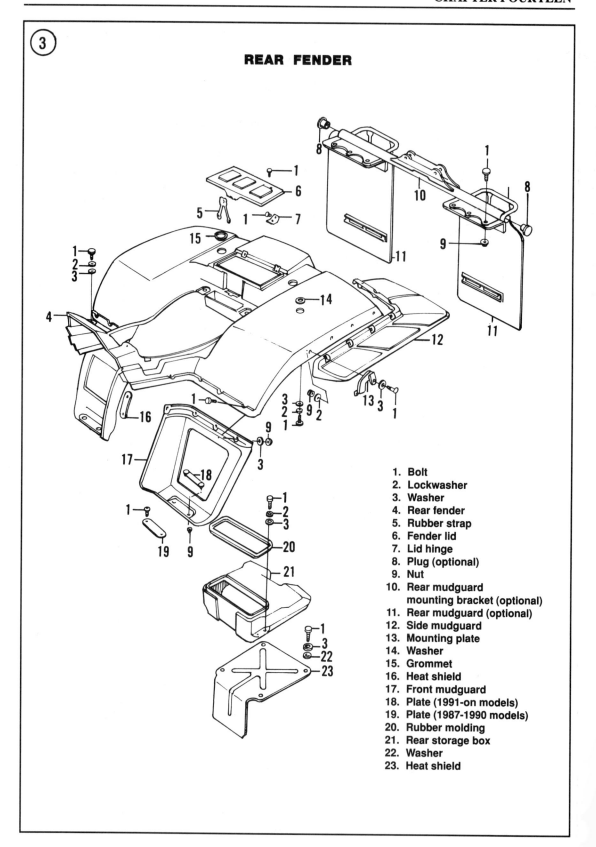

REAR FENDER

1. Bolt
2. Lockwasher
3. Washer
4. Rear fender
5. Rubber strap
6. Fender lid
7. Lid hinge
8. Plug (optional)
9. Nut
10. Rear mudguard
    mounting bracket (optional)
11. Rear mudguard (optional)
12. Side mudguard
13. Mounting plate
14. Washer
15. Grommet
16. Heat shield
17. Front mudguard
18. Plate (1991-on models)
19. Plate (1987-1990 models)
20. Rubber molding
21. Rear storage box
22. Washer
23. Heat shield

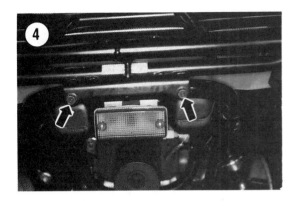

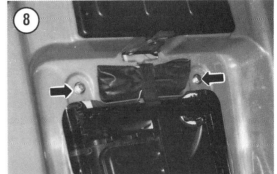

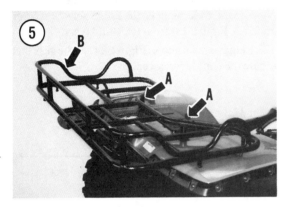

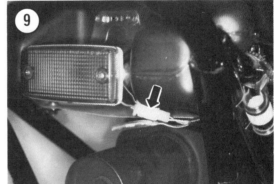

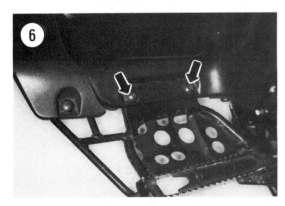

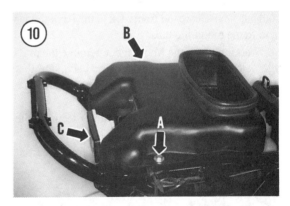

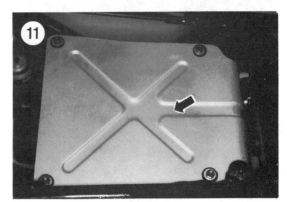

14

11. Install by reversing these removal steps while noting the following:

   a. Insert the rear fender front side locking tab (A, **Figure 12**) into the slot (B, **Figure 12**) in the front fender on each side. Push the rear fender forward until it stops.

   b. Tighten all fender mounting bolts securely, but do not overtighten as the plastic fender may fracture in the mounting area.

FRONT FENDER, FRONT RACK AND FRONT GRIP

Removal/Installation

Refer to the following illustrations for this procedure:

   a. **Figure 13**: Front rack.

   b. **Figure 14**: Front fender.

1. Place the ATV on level ground and set the parking brake. Block the rear wheels so the vehicle will not roll in either direction.

2. Remove the seat, rear fender and rear rack as described in this chapter.

3. Remove the rear bolts (**Figure 15**), lockwashers and nuts that secure the front rack to the front fender and frame mounting tabs.

4. Working under the front fender, remove the middle bolt and washer (**Figure 16**) on each side that secure the front rack to the front fender and frame mounting tabs.

5. Remove the front bolts (**Figure 17**) securing the front rack to the front grip.

6. Remove the front rack (**Figure 18**) from the front fender.

7. Remove the bolts that secure the front skid plate and remove the skid plate.

8. Remove the front bolts (**Figure 19**) and the side bolts (**Figure 20**) that secure the front grip. Remove the front grip (**Figure 21**) from the frame.

9. Remove the battery as described under *Battery Removal/Installation and Electrolyte Check* in Chapter Three.

10. Remove the set screw (**Figure 22**) that secures each shift knob.

11. Remove the sub-transmission shift knob (A, **Figure 23**), the reverse shift knob (B, **Figure 23**) and on 4-wheel drive models, the range selection lever knob (C, **Figure 23**) from the shift levers.

12. Remove the screws (**Figure 24**) at the rear that secure the shift lever cover.

NOTE
Move the handlebar from full lock side-to-side to expose the front screws.

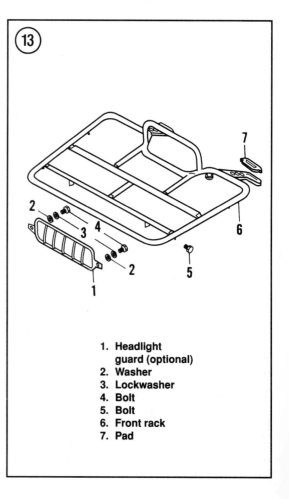

1. Headlight guard (optional)
2. Washer
3. Lockwasher
4. Bolt
5. Bolt
6. Front rack
7. Pad

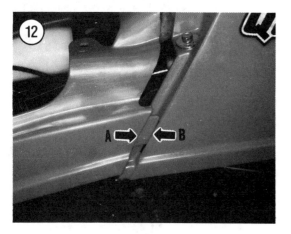

FRONT FENDER

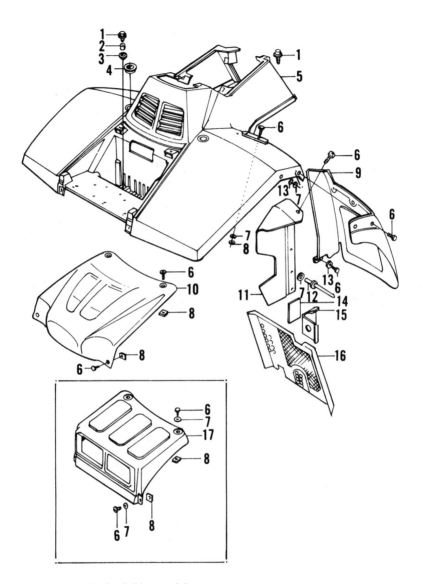

4-wheel drive models

14

1. Bolt
2. Collar
3. Rubber cushion
4. Grommet
5. Front fender
6. Screw
7. Washer

8. Nut
9. Outer mudguard
10. Front cover
    (2-wheel drive models)
11. Inner mudguard
12. Rivet

13. Washer
14. Cushion
15. Bracket
16. Exhaust system guard
17. Front cover
    (4-wheel drive models)

13. Remove the screws at the front that secure the shift lever cover. Refer to **Figure 25** and A, **Figure 26**.

14. Unscrew the fuel filler cap (B, **Figure 26**).

15A. On 2-wheel drive models, partially lift the front of the cover. Disconnect the odometer cable from the odometer unit and disconnect the electrical connector for the odometer illumination light.

15B. On 4-wheel drive models, remove the shift lever cover.

16. Reinstall the fuel filler cap and tighten securely.

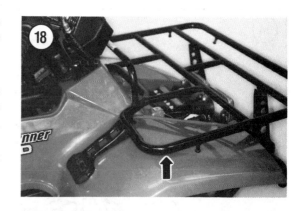

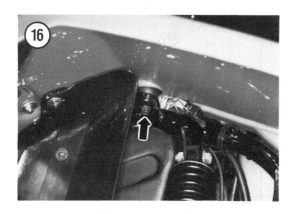

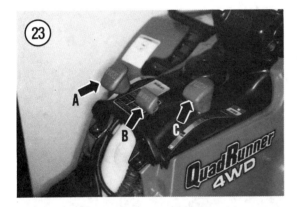

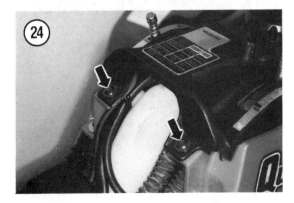

17. Remove the screw and collar (**Figure 27**), on each side, that secure the mudguard to the frame.

18. Within the battery compartment, disconnect the electrical connectors from all electrical components.

19. Remove the bolts, washers and collars (**Figure 28**) that secure the front portion of the front fender to the frame.

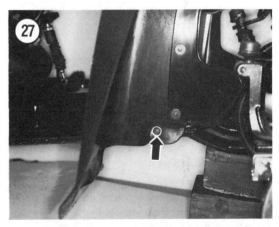

14

20. Remove the bolts, lockwashers and washers (**Figure 29**) that secure the rear portion of the front fender to the frame.

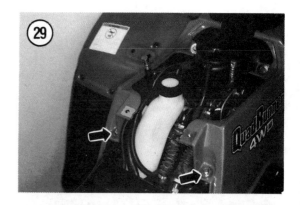

NOTE
The following steps require the aid of an assistant. The front fender is not heavy, but it is bulky and the electrical harnesses must be guided through the openings in the battery compartment.

21. Carefully pull the front fender up. Have an assistant guide the electrical harnesses through the openings (**Figure 30**) in the battery compartment. Remove the front fender from the frame.

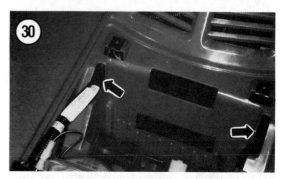

22. If necessary, remove the fasteners securing the mudguards to the side of the front fender. Install and tighten the fasteners securely.

23. Install by reversing these removal steps while noting the following:

a. Be sure to install the spacers and rubber cushions on the bolts where used. If not used, the plastic fender may fracture in the area of the bolt hole.

b. Tighten all screws and bolts securely. Do not overtighten as the plastic fender may fracture.

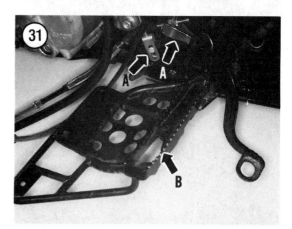

FOOTREST ASSEMBLY

Removal/Installation

1. Place the ATV on level ground and set the parking brake. Block the front wheels so the vehicle will not roll in either direction.

2. Remove the seat, rear fender and rear rack as described in this chapter.

3. On 4-wheel drive models, remove the drive shaft assembly as described under *Drive Shaft Removal/Installation* in Chapter Eleven.

4. Disconnect the rear brake cables (A, **Figure 31**) from the rear foot pedal as described under *Rear Brake Pedal Removal/Installation* in Chapter Thirteen.

5. Remove the bolts from each side securing the footrest assembly (B, **Figure 31**) to the frame and remove the footrest from the frame.

TRAILER HITCH PLATE

Removal/Installation

NOTE
Figure 32 *shows only 3 of the 4 bolts, be sure to remove all 4 bolts.*

1. Remove the 4 bolts (**Figure 32**) securing the trailer hitch plate to the rear of the frame.
2. Remove the hitch plate.
3. Examine for wear damage or mounting hole elongation. Replace the hitch plate if necessary.
4. Apply red Loctite (No. 271) to the bolt threads prior to installation. Tighten the bolts securely.

14

INDEX

15

1988, 1989 LT-250
(U.S., U.K. AND CANADA)

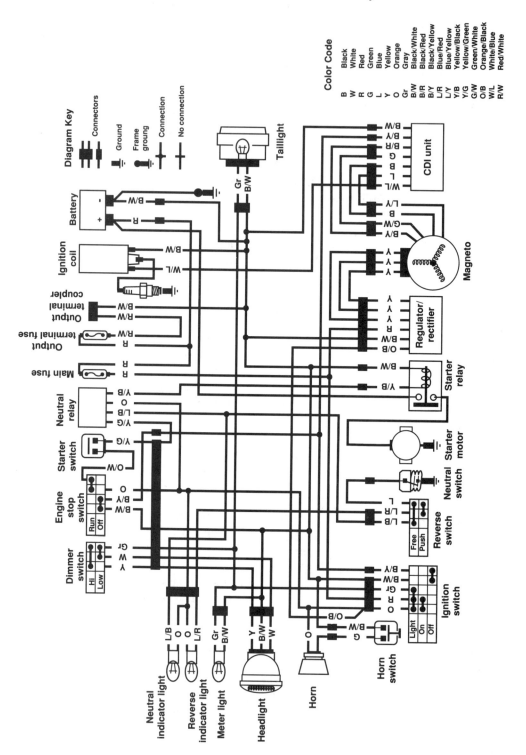

1990-1995 LT-250
(U.S., U.K. AND CANADA)

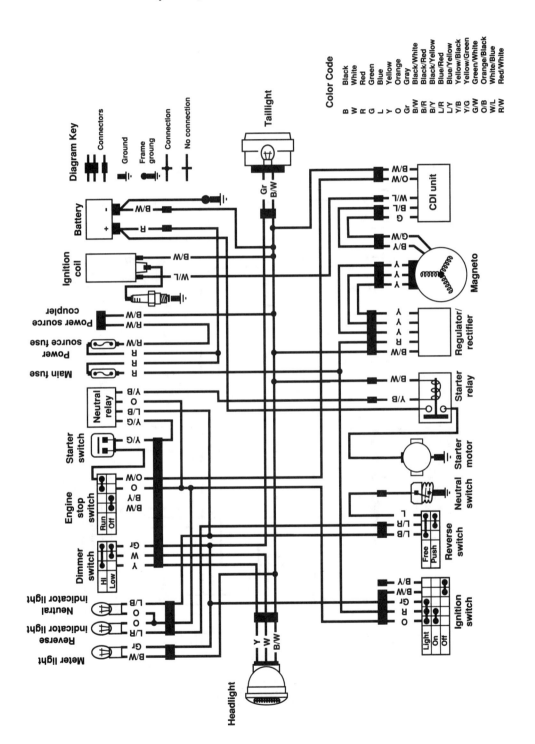

16

1990 LT-250
(AUSTRALIA)

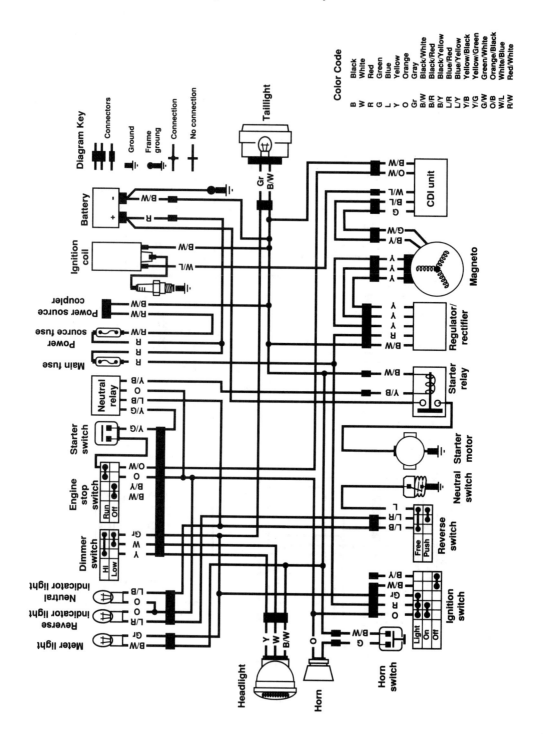

1991-1993 LT-250
(AUSTRALIA)

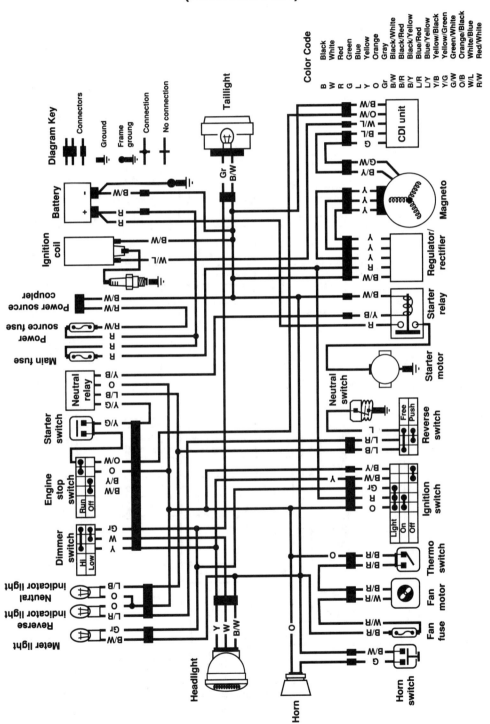

1994-1995 LT-250
(AUSTRALIA)

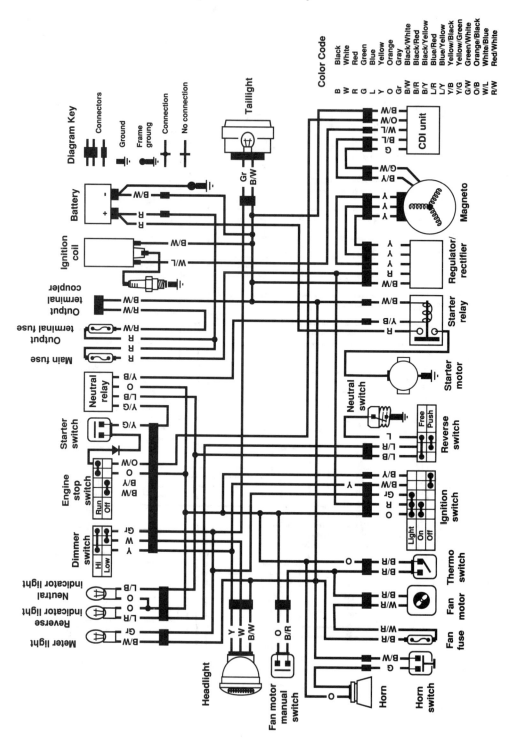

1987 LT-F4WD
(U.S., U.K. AND CANADA)

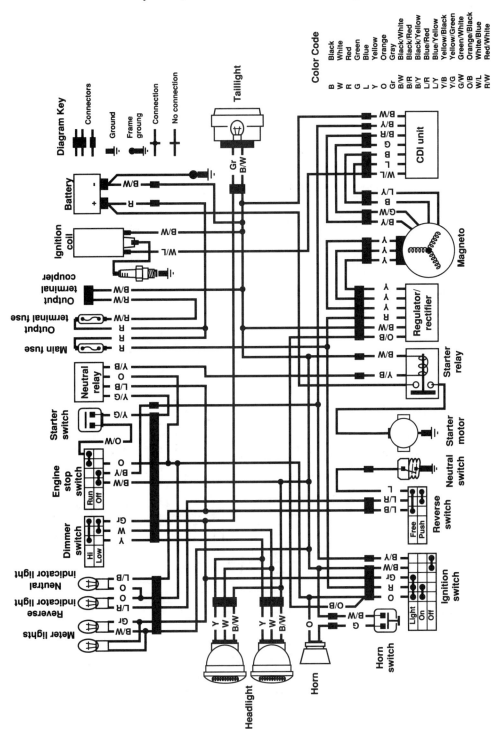

Color Code

B	Black
W	White
R	Red
G	Green
L	Blue
Y	Yellow
O	Orange
Gr	Gray
B/W	Black/White
B/R	Black/Red
B/Y	Black/Yellow
L/R	Blue/Red
L/Y	Blue/Yellow
Y/B	Yellow/Black
Y/G	Yellow/Green
G/W	Green/White
O/B	Orange/Black
W/L	White/Blue
R/W	Red/White

16

1988 LT-F4WD
(U.S., U.K. AND CANADA)

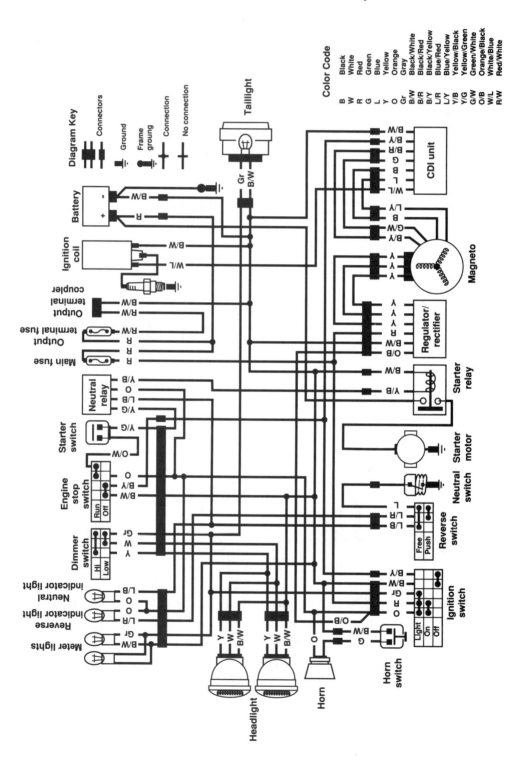

1989 LT-F4WD
(U.S., U.K. AND CANADA)

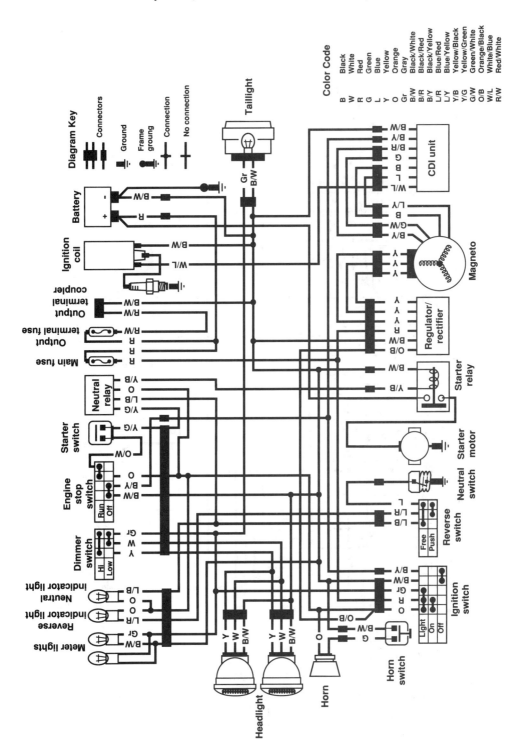

1990 LT-F4WD
(U.S., U.K. AND CANADA)

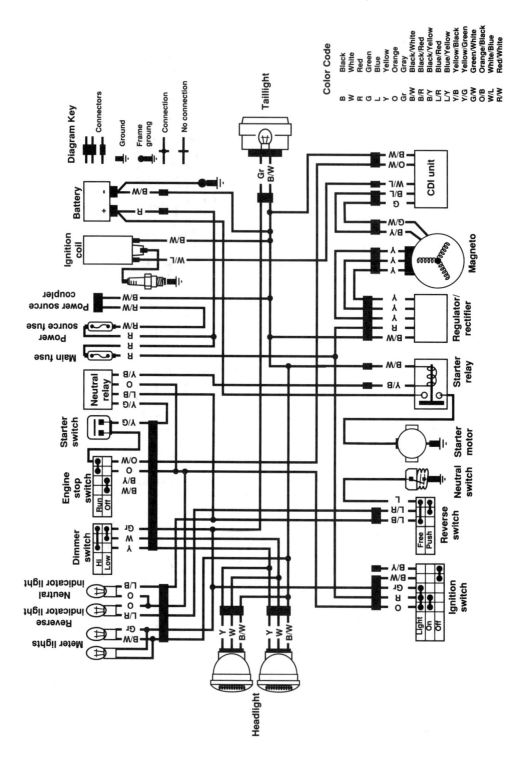

1990 LT-F4WD
(AUSTRALIA)

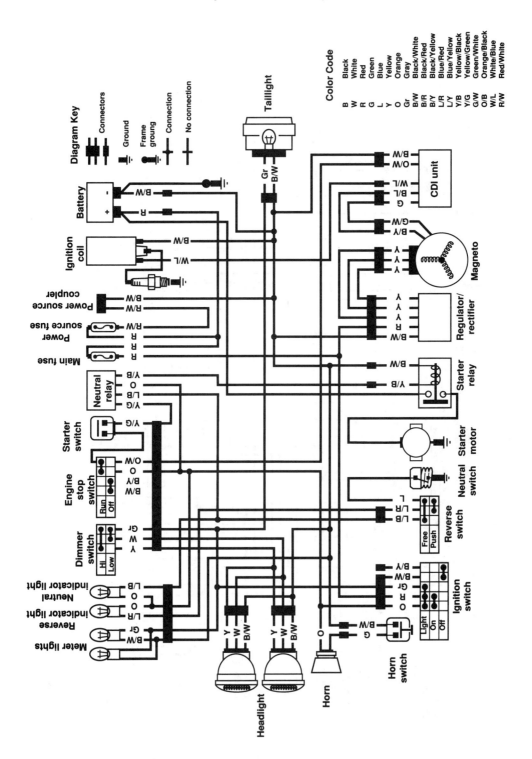

1990 LT-F4WD
(SWEDEN)

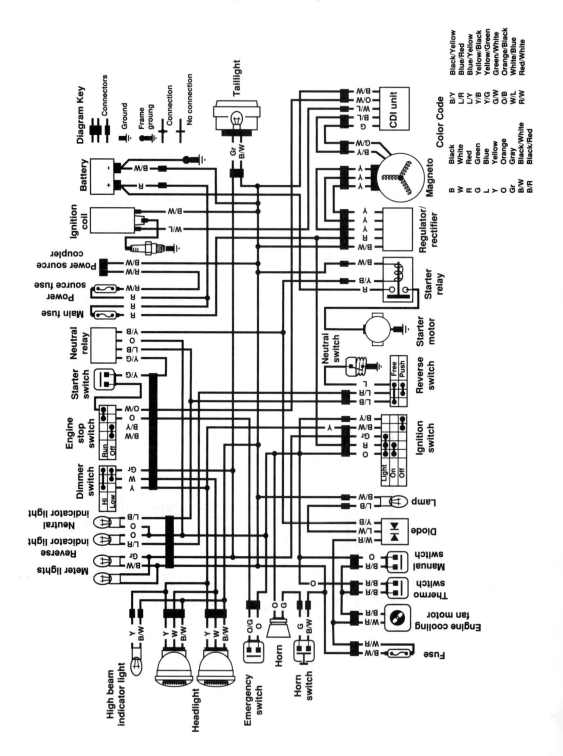

1991-1995 LT-F4WD
(U.S., U.K. AND CANADA)

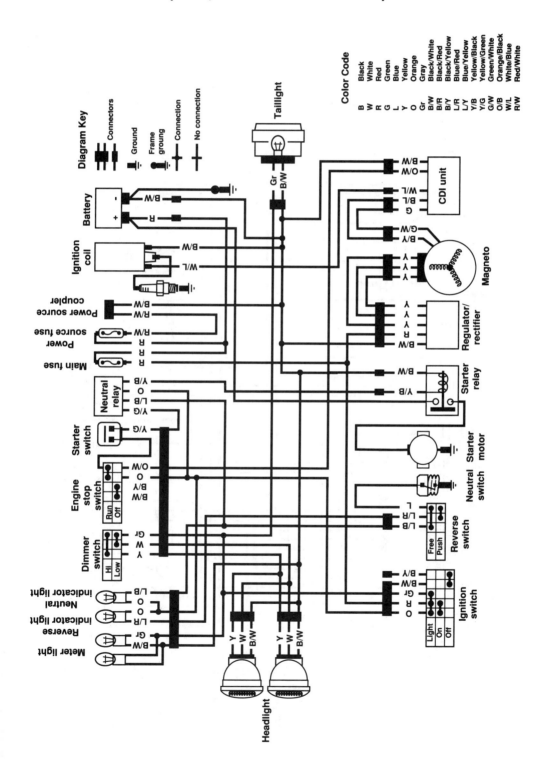

1991-1995 LT-F4WD
(AUSTRALIA)

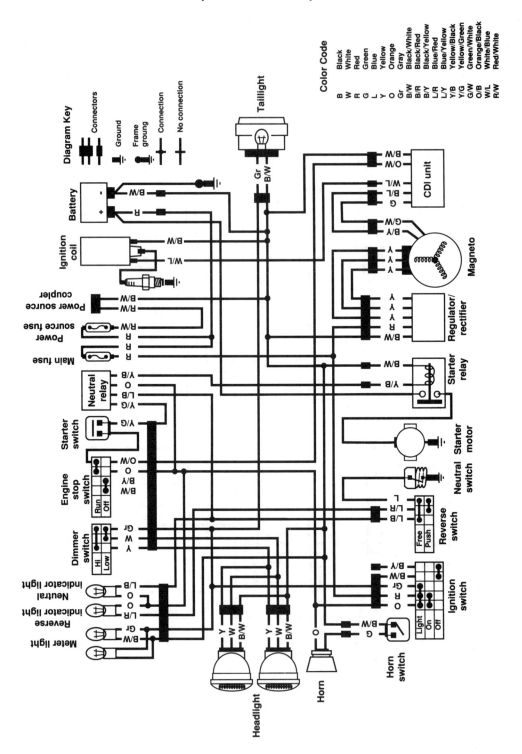

1991-1995 LT-F4WD
(SWEDEN)

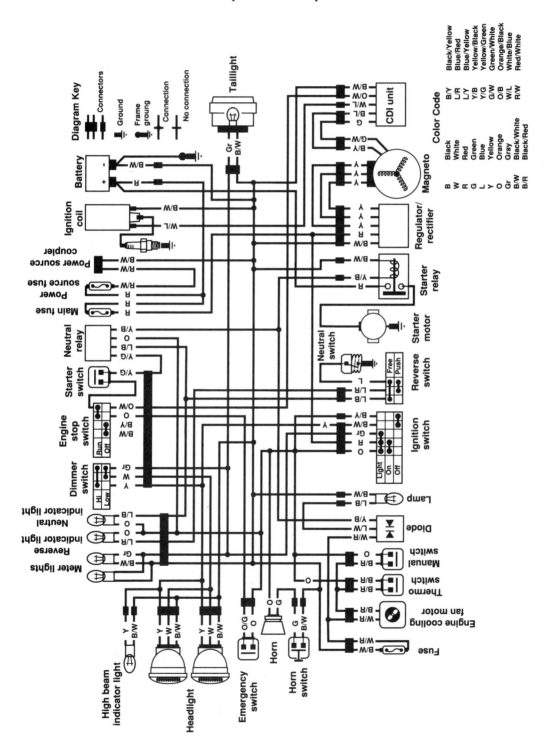

1991-1995 LT-F4WDX
(U.S., U.K. AND CANADA)

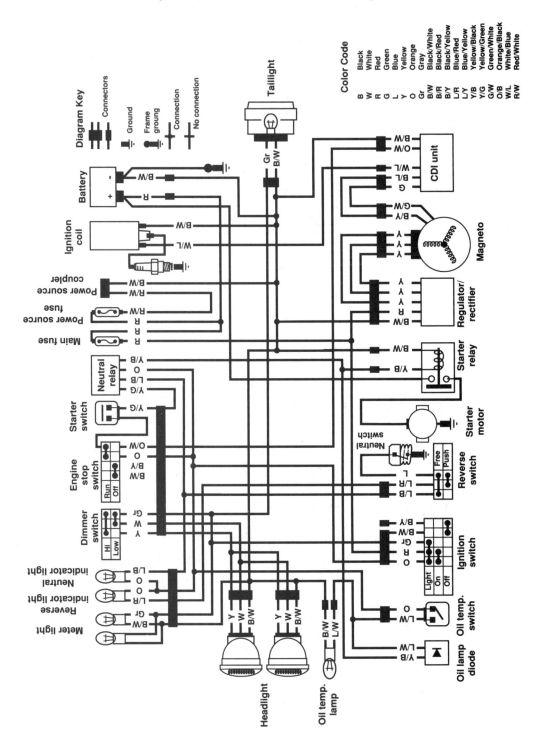

1991-1995 LT-F4WDX
(AUSTRALIA)

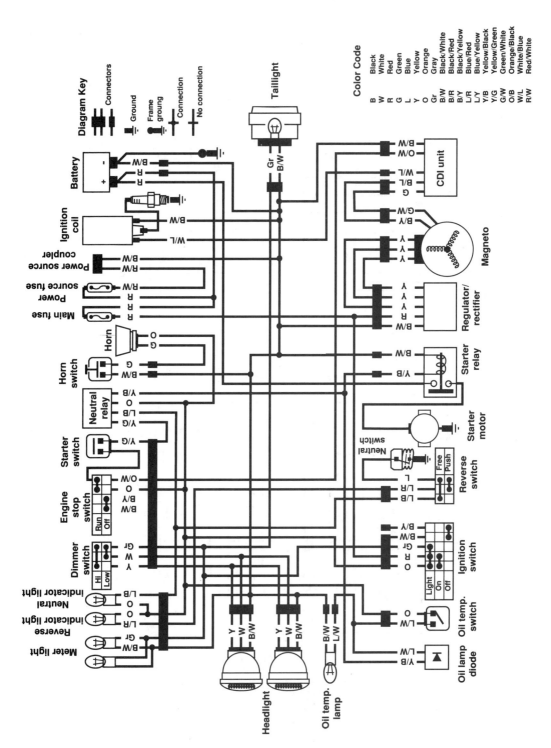

1991-1995 LT-F4WDX
(SWEDEN)

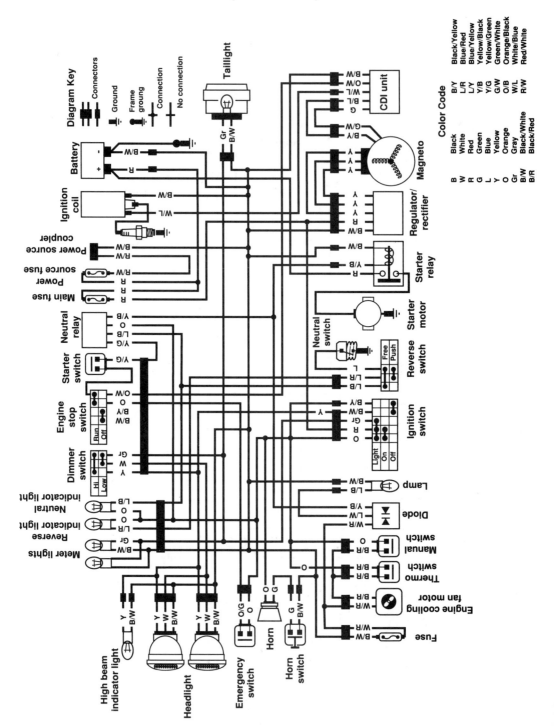

NOTES

MAINTENANCE LOG

Date	Miles	Type of Service